Jan 4, 2022

"Ther⸍ ⸍⸍ ⸍d *gospel*, that are commonly thought to be understood but which, upon closer analysis, are shaped too much by a lack of study. Enter *glory*. Enter Haley Jacob's examination of glory, and we inherit a study filled with careful analysis, theological sophistication, and practical insights. What is meant by 'conformed to the image of Christ' is now clarified and ready for pastoral and ecclesial exploration. I found this study judicious and insightful at every turn."

Scot McKnight, Julius R. Mantey Professor of New Testament at Northern Seminary

"What is conformity to Christ? Is it participation in him or glorification with him? Haley Jacob contends that Romans 8 presents a functional understanding of glorification as believers' sharing in Christ's benevolent messianic rule and thus in God's care for creation. Resolutely argued and consistently provocative, this significant book will challenge readers of Romans to look afresh at one of its most theologically important themes—and its implications for the life of the church."

Michael J. Gorman, Raymond E. Brown Professor of Biblical Studies and Theology at St. Mary's Seminary & University, Baltimore

"Haley Jacob has taken a text that everyone thought they understood (in one way or another) and has given it the treatment that it deserves. With her help we can see much more clearly how Romans 8:28-29 relates to Paul's larger argument in Romans (and elsewhere). And the result is revolutionary! The destiny Paul has in mind is not merely that of finding ourselves in a luminous splendor, but of the privilege of participating in and extending Christ's rule over all of creation. Jacob's argument should reshape the conversation about the goal of salvation as Paul understood it, and it has the power to reshape the way Christians live out their understanding of salvation in practical ways. Here we find a model of careful scholarship carried out in the service of the church."

Roy E. Ciampa, Armstrong Professor of Religion at Samford University

"Haley Jacob presents a powerful and convincing argument that Paul portrays believers as participating in the Son's messianic rule over creation as adopted sons and daughters. What God intended for Adam has now been brought to completion in the Davidic Messiah's glorious reign over creation—an exalted and glorious reign in which Christ the King's people share. This is another noteworthy contribution to the recovery of Jewish messianism as a critical context for Paul's Christology and participatory soteriology!"

Joshua Jipp, associate professor of New Testament at Trinity Evangelical Divinity School

CONFORMED TO THE IMAGE OF HIS SON

RECONSIDERING PAUL'S THEOLOGY OF GLORY IN ROMANS

Haley Goranson Jacob

IVP Academic

An imprint of InterVarsity Press
Downers Grove, Illinois

InterVarsity Press
P.O. Box 1400, Downers Grove, IL 60515-1426
ivpress.com
email@ivpress.com

InterVarsity Press® is the book-publishing division of InterVarsity Christian Fellowship/USA®, a movement of students and faculty active on campus at hundreds of universities, colleges, and schools of nursing in the United States of America, and a member movement of the International Fellowship of Evangelical Students. For information about local and regional activities, visit intervarsity.org.

All Scripture quotations, unless otherwise indicated, are the author's translation.

Cover design: David Fassett
Interior design: Jeanna Wiggins
Images: crown: illustration by David Fassett
  Jesus Christ: © sedmak / iStock / Getty Images Plus

ISBN 978-0-8308-5210-9 (print)
ISBN 978-0-8308-8577-0 (digital)

Printed in the United States of America ♾

InterVarsity Press is committed to ecological stewardship and to the conservation of natural resources in all our operations. This book was printed using sustainably sourced paper.

Library of Congress Cataloging-in-Publication Data
Names: Goranson Jacob, Haley, 1983- author.
Title: Conformed to the image of His Son : reconsidering Paul's theology of
  glory in Romans / Haley Goranson Jacob.
Description: Downers Grove : InterVarsity Press, 2018. | Includes
  bibliographical references and index.
Identifiers: LCCN 2018012250 (print) | LCCN 2018016438 (ebook) | ISBN
  9780830885770 (eBook) | ISBN 9780830852109 (pbk. : alk. paper)
Subjects: LCSH: Glory of God—Biblical teaching. | Bible. Romans—Criticism,
  interpretation, etc. | Glory. | Jesus Christ. | Conformity.
Classification: LCC BS2665.6.G55 (ebook) | LCC BS2665.6.G55 G67 2018 (print)
  | DDC 227/.106—dc23
LC record available at https://lccn.loc.gov/2018012250

P   25   24   23   22   21   20   19   18   17   16   15   14   13   12   11   10   9   8   7   6   5   4   3   2   1

Y   37   36   35   34   33   32   31   30   29   28   27   26   25   24   23   22   21   20   19   18

To my parents, Leroy and Nancy

CONTENTS

FOREWORD

N. T. Wright

The letters of Paul are notoriously complex. However exciting and stimulating the subject matter, there always seems to be more going on than meets the eye of the casual reader, even of the Christian reader used to hearing sermons and other expositions of well-known texts. It is therefore always worthwhile investigating even the most familiar passages to be sure they have yielded up their secrets. This is what Haley Goranson Jacob has done in this remarkable work, and the results are striking. If she is right—and I am convinced that she is—then the standard assumptions about a central Pauline passage will need to be revised.

You can hardly get a more central Pauline passage than Romans 8, and it is a measure of the author's courage that she has dived into the heart of this astonishing chapter, full as it is of converging and interlocking themes, biblical allusions and echoes, powerful rhetoric, and complex literary structure. The rich arguments of Romans 1–8—and, with them, some of the major themes in all of Paul—come to their astonishing climax here, and many generations of preachers and teachers have thrilled their hearers with Paul's triumphant conclusion: those whom God justified he also glorified (Rom 8:30).

But wait a minute, asks Dr. Jacob: What does "glorified" actually mean here? And what, in particular, does Paul mean in the previous verse when he says that God had always planned that believers would be "conformed to the image of his son, so that he might be the firstborn among many brothers and sisters"? It turns out that almost all exegetes (including the present writer) have taken for granted that "glorification" is more or less a synonym for "salvation," with most (though not including the present writer) seeing salvation itself in terms of "going to heaven when we die," with the "glory" in question being the status, and perhaps the radiance, that believers will possess in that new location. (The past tense in "glorified," in verse 30, is then normally read in terms of "assurance": because God has promised it, it is as good as done.) Being "conformed to the image of the son" would then be a matter of sharing Jesus' resurrection life, and/or his holiness, and/or the radiance of his divine glory.

But is that what Paul meant by "glorification"? And what else might "conformed to the image of the son" be getting at? There are several clues to the fresh answer, but perhaps the most important is found in Paul's echoing of Psalm 8, which in turn brings into play his sense of *the vocation of Adam*, and hence of the human race. The human vocation, focused on the "image" in Genesis 1 and spelled out in Psalm 8, was that we should be set in authority over the created order. The psalm speaks of humans as being "crowned with glory and honor," with all things "put in subjection" under their feet. Other passages in Paul, notably 1 Corinthians 15 and Philippians 3, indicate that Paul can use this line of thought in cognate passages. Does it make sense here?

It does indeed, but it requires quite a different focus from that normally envisaged, and Dr. Jacob does not shrink from arguing for this significant adjustment in our reading of the whole passage. The ultimate aim, she insists, is not a statement of "salvation" in the sense of humans being rescued from the world, but a statement of *vocation*, in which humans, redeemed from their sinful state, are now to resume the task envisaged in Romans 5:17. There the "reign of death" is replaced, not (as one might have expected) with the "reign of life," but rather with the "reign" (in life) of *those who receive God's gracious gift*. Exactly as in Revelation 5, where the victory of the Lamb results in redeemed humans receiving back the genuinely human vocation (to be the "royal priesthood"), so in Romans, we begin to see, the point of the whole argument is not to rescue humans *from* the world but to rescue them *for* the world. The aim of it all is that, through rescued and renewed humans, the Creator God will restore creation itself, as in Romans 8:18-26.

This breathtaking revision of an extremely familiar and much worked-over passage comes at a cost, namely the patient sifting through, and cleaning up, of all the moving parts of the argument. Here the author demonstrates a calm determination, leading us step by step through areas in themselves complex and controversial: the key technical terms and the semiotic challenges they present; the vexed question of "participation" in the Messiah; the meaning of "divine sonship" as applied first to Jesus and then to believers. She then proceeds to assemble these elements back into the single whole of Paul's train of thought, focusing on 8:29: What then *does* it mean to be "conformed to the image of the son"? Among the many striking results are that the passages about suffering and prayer in Romans 8 take their proper place as part of the means of the *present* glorification. They are not asides or separate topics; they are part of the way in which God is working *through* the Messiah's people to accomplish his purposes in and for creation. And this opens up a dramatically revised possibility for reading that famous verse, Romans 8:28. . . .

It might spoil the effect if I revealed much more at this point. Suffice it to say that, after a lifetime of study and teaching on Romans, I was not expecting to be confronted at my age with a fresh understanding of its central chapter, requiring a radical rethink of many familiar landmarks both exegetical and theological. But that is what Dr. Jacob has achieved. Not everyone will agree with all segments of her argument. But both in its parts and as a whole it has, to my mind, compelling force. I urge all students of Paul and of Romans to work carefully through the step-by-step presentation of the case.

For preachers and teachers who simply want to know "the results": well, you could always just read chapters 6 and 7. But since you will then want to know whether these striking conclusions are warranted, I suspect you will need to read the first five chapters as well. In doing so, you will enjoy a refresher course in the fascinating if complex world of current Pauline studies. This is a classic example of theological exegesis both careful and creative, faithful and fruitful. I congratulate the author on this book and commend it warmly to both the church and the academy.

PREFACE

In my senior year of college, the Bible became alive to me. The literary and theological artistry that makes it the greatest story ever told unfolded before me in an unexpected place: a course on Paul's letter to the Galatians. It is not a stretch to say that studying in depth the significance of the covenant promises, the arrival of the law 430 years later, and the seed of Abraham changed the course of my life. That semester the Bible became for me for the first time not a collection of stories or the place to find guidance for life and salvation. Suddenly the New Testament made no sense apart from the Old Testament, and the Bible as a whole became the one single story of God redeeming his people through the long-awaited Messiah, Jesus. From that semester until now, the overarching story of how God redeemed the world has shaped my research, my career, and my faith.

This book is not about Galatians. It is, however, the first tangible result of that undergraduate Galatians course that set me on this path of interest in biblical theology—a path that has now continued through my PhD, the product of which is this book. The letter that occupies my attention in this book is Romans. Perhaps the thought of this will prompt my reader to question whether the pages that follow will contain anything truly new. On one level, the Teacher is correct: there is nothing new under the sun. And yet, imagine his response to the scene before him if he were transported from his place in history into Times Square today. His teaching would require a caveat—perhaps only a small one, but a highly significant one nonetheless. Such is the case with the pages that follow.

When I started my PhD at St. Andrews, my stipulation for my research was that it would focus on something pertinent to the theology of the church and the average person within the church. What can be more pertinent than thinking afresh through the goal of salvation? For nearly two millennia Paul's words about being conformed to the image of God's Son in Romans 8:29 and believers' glorification in Romans 8:30 have encouraged the church and offered insight into what, together, are commonly understood as the goal of salvation. But if five different Christians are asked what such conformity to Christ means, or what glorification actually entails, five different answers will probably ensue. And none of them will likely take into consideration the literary or theological context of Romans in which they are found, let alone the larger biblical narrative that undergirds Paul's message in the letter. I cannot claim to answer these questions with any sense of completion in this book. But my hope is that the pages that follow will challenge readers to consider again how the church reconstructs Paul's theology of believers' glory and conformity to Christ. Put another way, my hope is that it will challenge readers to consider again the goal of salvation, the reason for God's redeeming work in the life of the believer. How one understands these theological themes determines how one understands, at least in part, the goal of salvation. It is a topic pertinent to the professor, the minister, and the layperson alike; this book is written for each person. A basic knowledge of Greek will serve the reader well, but my hope is that the arguments throughout the chapters can be gleaned even without the basic language skills.

A few debts of gratitude need to be offered. The first and greatest thanks I owe is to Tom Wright, whose supervision through this PhD process has consistently exceeded every expectation. Above all, I am grateful for the way in which he modeled for me how one's academic, pastoral, and personal life of worship can be integrated into a singular vocation. Additionally, I am grateful for my PhD examiners, Grant Macaskill and Matthew Novenson, whose feedback and helpful criticisms assisted me not only in solidifying my arguments throughout the chapters but also in readying the thesis for publication. One of the greatest blessings of my time in St. Andrews was

Judith Graham, who welcomed me into her Scottish home, her family, and her circle of Ladies Who Lunch. Though I was but a lodger in her home, she embraced me as a friend and even as a daughter. Words cannot express my gratitude for her. I am also deeply indebted to my family at Mount Republic Chapel of Peace in Cooke City, Montana. Their love, prayers, constant communication, and generous financial support throughout my time in Scotland made the completion of the PhD, and ultimately this book, possible. A note of thanks goes also to the Whitworth University Theology Department, whose abundant source of support and cheer during my first two years at Whitworth have made for a brilliant first two years of teaching. A special thanks also goes to Dan Reid and IVP Academic, who agreed to publish the work and thus to encourage the church to reconsider such topics.

I am grateful to my husband, Alan, whose patience during these months of editing has been unending. And, last but not least, I am grateful for the constant love and support of my parents, Leroy and Nancy. My educational, international, and pastoral pursuits have not always coalesced with the rural Minnesota context in which I was raised, and have often left them scratching their heads. But more than anyone else, my parents taught me the priceless value of hard work and the importance of being faithful to my roots and to the person I have become because of those roots. Of all my years of study, those lessons will remain two of the most formative and cherished. I dedicate this book to them.

Haley Goranson Jacob
Whitworth University
June 2016

ABBREVIATIONS

1 En.	1 Enoch
1 Esd	1 Esdras
1 Macc	1 Maccabees
1QH^a	Hodayot^a *or* Thanksgiving Hymns^a
1QM	Milḥamah *or* War Scroll
1QpHab	Pesher Habakkuk
1QS	Serek Hayaḥad *or* Rule of the Community
2 Bar.	2 Baruch
2 Macc	2 Maccabees
3 Bar.	3 Baruch
3 Macc	3 Maccabees
4 Macc	4 Maccabees
4Q285	Sefer ha-Milhamah
4Q504	DibHam^a
4Q174	Florilegium
4Q252	Commentary on Genesis A
4Q161	Pesher Isaiah^a
Apoc. Mos.	Apocalypse of Moses
Bar	Baruch
CD	Cairo Genizah copy of the Damascus Document
Gen. Rab.	Genesis Rabbah
Jub.	Jubilees
LAE	Life of Adam and Eve
OG	Old Greek
Pss. Sol.	Psalms of Solomon
Sir	Sirach/Ecclesiasticus
T. Mos.	Testament of Moses
Tg. Isa.	Targum of Isaiah
TH	Theodotion
Wis	Wisdom of Solomon

1

INTRODUCTION

1.1. GETTING TO THIS POINT

"The inner sanctuary within the cathedral of Christian faith; the tree of life in the midst of the Garden of Eden; the highest peak in a range of mountains—such are some of the metaphors used by interpreters who extol [Romans] chap. 8 as the greatest passage within what so many consider to be the greatest book in Scripture."[1] As the pinnacle of Paul's letter to Rome, Romans 8 is laden with gold nuggets of encouragement and assurance: "There is therefore now no condemnation for those who are in Christ Jesus" (Rom 8:1); "We know that in everything God works for good for those who love him" (Rom 8:28); "He who did not spare his own Son but gave him up for us all, will he not also give us all things with him?" (Rom 8:32); "[Nothing] will be able to separate us from the love of God in Christ Jesus our Lord" (Rom 8:39). Among those verses most cherished is Romans 8:29: "For those whom he foreknew he also predestined to be conformed to the image of his Son, in order that he might be the firstborn within a large family." Like much of Romans 8, Romans 8:29 and particularly Romans 8:29b—"conformed to the image of his Son"—has encouraged, assured, and strengthened Christians throughout the centuries. To some it expresses the goal of salvation.[2]

---

[1]Moo 1996: 468. For a note on the frequent use of Rom 8 throughout Christendom, see Wright 2002: 573-74.

[2]E.g., Hendriksen (1980: 283): "[The] goal is not just 'to enter heaven at last' but 'to be conformed to the image of God's Son.'"

But a problem seems to exist, one that confronted me in the early days of my research into what was then a larger examination of the themes of Genesis 1–3 in Paul's letters. I began to notice a wide swath of interpretations of the phrase and no solidly substantiating arguments for any of them. Within both popular Christianity and academic New Testament studies, there is little agreement as to what Paul *means* by the arcane or, at a minimum, ambiguous phrase. This lack of agreement is due in part to the fact that Romans 8:29b is often obscured by Paul's use of *foreknew* and *predestined* in Romans 8:29a. More often, though, "conformed to the Son's image" is used as support for a presupposed theological or eschatological ideal—again, with little to no substantiation for the interpretation. Perhaps it is surprising that, to date, the meaning of the phrase συμμόρφους τῆς εἰκόνος τοῦ υἱοῦ αὐτοῦ has received exegetical treatment in only four articles and no monographs.[3] Despite the lack of any sustained treatments of the phrase, various interpretations are nonetheless assumed by commentators and authors alike, none of which are upheld by solid literary or theological evidence. And yet many use the phrase to capture what is considered the end goal of the Christian life: conformity to Christ. How can this phrase be used so often within both popular and scholarly conversations, and yet have so few in agreement over its basic meaning? In this book I have one ultimate objective: to examine Romans 8:29b within its own literary and theological context so as to discover what this oft-used but rarely substantiated phrase means within Romans. Due to the multifarious uses of the phrase by practical theologians, biblical theologians, and laity alike, the phrase cries out for some attention.

But not this alone. As we progress through this examination of Romans 8:29, it will quickly become obvious that an interpretation of "conformed to the image of his Son" must be informed by several other theological motifs that are equally as ambiguous and/or assumed. If Romans 8:29 is at center stage, then occupying the front left and front right of the stage will be Paul's use of *glory* and *glorify*, terms that have for centuries been used within Christian theology and jargon basically without question. It is one thing for God to receive glory or be glorified; it is another thing entirely for humanity to do so. Yet this is the heart of Romans 8—a motif that determines how one reads the "goal of salvation" in Romans 8:29. At

---

[3]Fahy 1956; Kürzinger 1958; Leaney 1964; Hasitschka 2010.

the rear of the stage, then, is the Pauline motif of union with Christ. More specifically, it is the dual motifs of *union* and *participation* with or in Christ, the relationship between the two terms, and what, if any, role they play in deciphering "conformed to the image of [God's] Son."

The majority of this book will propose an interpretation of Romans 8:29b that can be substantiated on both literary and theological grounds—one that differs from nearly all interpretations of the phrase thus far offered. Such interpretations are found primarily in commentaries but also in particular monographs and articles. Writers who refer to Romans 8:29b in their work usually fall into one of six common categories, those who offer or propose

1. no attempt at an explanation of the meaning of "conformity to the Son," content to say that it refers to being made "like Christ";

2. a variety of explanations, often a combination of those listed below;

3. a physical conformity, i.e., receiving the same "form" as Christ's resurrected body;

4. a spiritual or moral conformity, i.e., the process of sanctification;

5. a conformity to the Son's eschatological glory, with *glory* understood as radiance;

6. a sacrificial conformity, wherein the believer becomes "like Christ" as she suffers with Christ.

An awareness of these six proposals will be important in recognizing how this comprehensive treatment is both necessary and unique.

Those who offer no meaning and those who suggest a variety of meanings behind Romans 8:29b arrive at the same result: ambiguity. We can treat them together for this reason. Leon Morris provides a typically ambiguous description of the phrase, saying,

> We are to become *like Christ*. . . . It is God's plan that his people become *like his Son*, not that they should muddle along in a modest respectability. . . . We have been admitted to the heavenly family. . . . We are accordingly to live as members of the family, and that means being made *like our elder brother*. . . . [God] predestined us . . . in order that we might become *like his Son*.[4]

---

[4]Morris 1988: 333; emphasis mine. Morris does state that "becoming like Christ," "as Hendriksen points out, means sanctification," but he fails to qualify this statement as he progresses.

"This is wonderful news!" one wants to exclaim. But what does it *mean* to be "like Christ"? Likewise, with three times the theology and complexity, C. E. B. Cranfield yet manages to offer the same amount of ambiguity:

> Behind the συμμόρφους τῆς εἰκόνος τοῦ υἱοῦ αὐτου there is probably the thought of man's creation κατ᾽ εἰκόνα θεου (Gen. 1:27) and also the thought of Christ's being eternally the very εἰκὼν τοῦ θεοῦ (not, be it noted, just κατ᾽ εἰκόνα θεου). The believers' final glorification is their full conformity to the εἰκὼν of Christ glorified; but it is probable that Paul is here thinking not only of their final glorification but also of their growing conformity to Christ here and now in suffering and in obedience—that is, that συμμόρφους, κ.τ.λ. is meant to embrace sanctification as well as final glory, the former being thought of as a progressive conformity to Christ, who is the εἰκὼν of God, and so as a progressive renewal of the believer into that likeness of God which is God's original purpose for man.[5]

When Romans 8:29b is approached in this way, it is often the natural result of gathering all the other verses in which these same themes appear throughout the Pauline corpus (1 Cor 15:49; 2 Cor 3:18; Phil 3:10, 21; Col 1:15, 18)[6] and packing them tightly into a very stretchy but durable bag, as if Paul intended the phrase συμμόρφους τῆς εἰκόνος τοῦ υἱοῦ αὐτου to include every theme at once. Of course, it is possible that more than one referent exists behind Paul's phrase, and unarguably several of the preferred categories are related to one another, that is, glory and vocation; sanctification and suffering; suffering and glory; glory and body. But it is rarely wise to assume that in six Greek words Paul is packing a ForceFlex trash bag that just keeps stretching.

The four other common interpretations are more narrow in focus. The first is a shared physical conformity to that of the Son. A notable example is Ben Witherington's translation, "to share the likeness of the form of his Son," and explanation: "The end or destiny of believers is to become fully Christ-like, even in their bodily form. Paul has just said that the believer's hope is the redemption of his or her body, and here he explains how God will be working to get the believer to that

---

[5]Cranfield 1975: 432; emphasis mine. Also, Harvey (1992: 335), who relies on Cranfield, and Hasitschka 2010: 353.
[6]The relationship between these texts and Rom 8:29b will be discussed at various points.

goal."[7] His explanation comes on the basis of two primary factors: that Paul refers to the physical resurrected body in Romans 8:23 and that, with Paul's use of εἰκών in Romans 8:29, Adam is most likely in view, which therefore entails a return to Adam's prefall physical state. I will leave any critique of these suggestions for when I more fully survey the larger literary and theological context.

A second, more focused explanation of conformity is that of spiritual or moral conformity, that is, sanctification. This is perhaps the most commonly assumed interpretation of σύμμορφος, particularly within popular church settings. The general assumption is that to be "made like Christ" is to be "holy like Christ." What Morris voices in his ambiguous treatment of the phrase noted above is, when fleshed out, an interpretation of Romans 8:29b as moral or spiritual conformity—a present, spiritual conformity rather than a future, physical conformity. William Hendriksen takes this approach in his commentary, writing there: "If gradual renewal into the image of Christ is not what Paul had in mind, are we not forced to conclude that one very important link in the chain of salvation, namely the link of *sanctification*, is missing? The answer given by some that justification includes sanctification does not satisfy."[8]

Hendriksen and Morris are not alone in their interpretation. F. F. Bruce agrees, and, though he offers little by way of explanation of σύμμορφος itself, he does suggest, like Hendriksen, that the reader must note Paul's lack of mention of sanctification in the "golden chain" of Romans 8:30. Why does Paul choose not to include *sanctified* between *justified* and *glorified*? Bruce suggests that it is because

> The coming glory has been in the forefront of his mind; but even more because the difference between sanctification and glory is one of degree only, not one of kind. Sanctification is progressive conformity to the mind or image of Christ here and now (cf. 2 Cor. 3:18; Col. 3:10); glory is perfect

---

[7]Witherington with Hyatt 2004: 221, 229. See also Witherington 1994: 101. Witherington (1994: 173) also writes of "*the process of* being conformed to the image of the son *in this life*" (emphasis mine) but fails to state what that process is. He later writes (1994: 230): "conformity to the image of the son . . . likely means gaining a resurrection body like Christ's, though progressive sanctification might also be implied": see also p. 330 and Witherington with Hyatt 2004: 220-35. James Dunn (1988a: 483-84) also emphasizes the end result of the Christian life as well as that Paul is referring to the risen Son and not the incarnate Son.
[8]Hendriksen 1980: 284.

conformity to the image of Christ there and then. Sanctification is glory begun; glory is sanctification consummated.[9]

For Bruce, Paul understands the coming glory as a future instantiation of a Christian's status. Nevertheless, he primarily views the conformity of Romans 8:29b as a present, spiritual conformity. This spiritual conformity is, more specifically, one of sanctification—becoming holy like Christ.[10]

This approach is also the most recognizable in popular Christian theology and writing. In fact, a number of popular works even bear the phrase in their titles. Two commonly known examples are Oswald Chambers's *Conformed to His Image* and Kenneth Boa's *Conformed to the Image of His Son*. Both titles use Romans 8:29b as a shorthand phrase for spiritual formation, but unfortunately neither book offers exegetical attention to the phrase. Rather, the books seek to challenge believers in their spiritual formation and use Romans 8:29b as the text that—the authors assume—encourages that formation. Neither of these will assist us in this more comprehensive investigation of Romans 8:29b; I mention them only for the purpose of demonstrating the prominence of understanding "conformed to the image of his Son" as spiritual formation or conformity within popular Christianity.

Present conformity to Christ's suffering and death is also a common reading of *conformity*.[11] Ernst Käsemann suggests that

---

[9]Bruce 2003: 168. Bruce exemplifies the typical scholar who freely combines the potential categories of present and future conformity. This dual-temporal understanding of σύμμορφος is not difficult to sustain, as I will demonstrate in chapter six. What is difficult to sustain, however, is a dual-temporal meaning that includes one form of conformity in the present and another form of conformity in the future.

[10]Also included in this section is A. R. C. Leaney's 1964 article "Conformed to the Image of His Son (Rom. 8:29)." Leaney explores one "of the strands which may have contributed to the pattern of Paul's thinking about conformity to Christ," namely Jewish ceremonial law (p. 470). He writes, "We are released from all ceremonial demands in the Law; our salvation does not lie in our conformity even to the laws of the universe but in God's conforming us not to his creation, not even to a restored and flawless creation, but to himself in his Son" (p. 479). Unfortunately, this is the most specific statement about Rom 8:29b that Leaney makes in the entire article, and, regrettably, it comes as the very last line. Nearly the entire article is dedicated to examining the role of ceremonial law in ancient and early Judaism, the basis of which is not connected to Rom 8:29b until the final paragraph.

[11]See Barth 1933: 323; Calvin 1960: 181; Käsemann 1980: 244; Wilckens 1980: 164; Barrett 1991: 170; Peterson 2001: 120; Keesmaat 1999: 89, 124, 141; Gorman 2001; Wright 2002: 602; Burke 2006: 148; Gorman 2009; Wright 2013a: 440.

passages like 1 Cor. 15:49; 2 Cor. 3:18; Col. 1:18; Phil. 3:10f. have *seduced* some
to think in terms of the risen Christ and participation in his resurrection
body as in Phil 3:21. . . . Against that it is to be objected that in the text Paul
consistently establishes the present salvation by use of the aorist and he does
not speak merely of the exalted Christ. . . . We are made like him in the
birth of which Gal. 4:19 speaks in baptismal language and which leads to
participation in his death according to Phil. 3:10. The final clause states
unmistakably that this takes place already in our earthly existence.[12]

He goes on to write,

In baptism the divine image which was lost according to 3:23 is restored by
conformation to the Son. Although this statement seems to be in contradiction with his eschatological caution, Paul adopts it here, as in 2 Corinthians
3:18; 4:6, in order that in the context of vv. 19-27 he may paradoxically set
forth the link between suffering with Christ and the glory of divine sonship.[13]

Käsemann argues that Romans 8:28-30 returns to Romans 8:18 and the
reality that "the sufferings of the present time cannot be denied." Käsemann's
argument against a present-future paradox in Romans 8:29b is contradicted
by his own argument that conformity is baptismal language and that at
baptism this paradox of death and life, suffering and glory begins
(see Rom 6:1-11).[14]

Within this category, Käsemann is unique among those who suggest
suffering as conformity. Whereas Käsemann limits conformity to suffering,[15]
most who suggest that Romans 8:29b refers to suffering suggest that it is
part one of a two-part process: part one being suffering and part two being
resurrection.[16] C. K. Barrett offers: "At present we are conformed
(συμμορφιζόμενοι) to his *death* (Phil. 3:10); we shall be conformed (σύμμορφοι)
. . . to the *body of his glory* (Phil. 3:21)."[17] And Ulrich Wilckens writes:

Die Formulierung in Röm 8,29b is so allgemein gehalten, daß man am besten
einen dementsprechend umfassenden Sinn heraushört. . . . In der Taufe
haben Christen an Tod und Auferstehung Christi teilgewonnen, so daß sie

---

[12]Käsemann 1980: 244; emphasis mine.
[13]Käsemann 1980: 245.
[14]Käsemann 1980: 244, 255.
[15]As does Calvin (1960: 181-82).
[16]E.g., Wilckens 1980; Barrett 1991; Gorman 2001; Wright 2002.
[17]Barrett 1991: 170.

in ihrem gegenwärtigen Leiden und den Leiden Christi teilhaben und in ihrer künftigen Auferstehung an der Auferstehung Christi teilhaben werden.[18]

Not unlike Barrett's and Wilckens's treatment of Romans 8:29b, Michael Gorman says that "conformity, for Paul, is narrative in character, a two-part drama of suffering/death followed by resurrection/exaltation. . . . Conformity to Christ—'to the image of [God's] Son'—in resurrection is the logical and guaranteed sequel to a life of death to self and of suffering for the gospel that corresponds to the narrative of Christ's dying and rising."[19] For Gorman, conformity is certainly a "two-part drama," but one gets the sense that it is on the first part that Paul is focused with his use of σύμμορφος. Sylvia Keesmaat also argues for a two-part process: "The glory of Adam, the image of God, is revealed in the one who came into this same suffering creation and saved it. The pattern of Jesus is the pattern of the rest of believers; his way of exercising his dominion over creation was to stretch out his arms and die for it. *This image of suffering is the image to which believers are conformed.*"[20] Here, again, suffering takes precedence.

Most scholars who suggest suffering with Christ or sharing in Christ's sufferings as an explanation for σύμμορφος are primarily dependent on Romans 8:17, where suffering with Christ (συμπάσχω) is deemed a prerequisite for being glorified with Christ (συνδοξάζω). The connection is rightly drawn between Romans 8:17 and Romans 8:29bc,[21] as we will see, but the problem with this interpretation of Romans 8:29b will be revealed to be multifold.

Meanwhile, conformity to Christ's glory is perhaps the most common interpretation of the verse within the New Testament guild.[22] This is primarily

---

[18]Wilckens 1980: 164. "The phrasing in Romans 8:29 is so general that it is best to keep with a correspondingly comprehensive meaning. . . . In baptism, Christians have gained participation in the death and resurrection of Christ, so that in their present suffering they are participating in the sufferings of Christ and will participate in the resurrection of Christ in their future resurrection."

[19]Gorman 2001: 327. Cruciformity as a whole is an exposition of this two-part process.

[20]Keesmaat 1999: 124; emphasis mine; see also 141.

[21]See esp. Wilckens 1980: 164.

[22]See Dodd 1932: 141-42; Black 1981: 125; Cranfield 1975: 432; Wanamaker 1987: 187; Dunn 1988a: 483-84; Ziesler 1989: 227; Scott 1992: 245-47; Moo 1996: 534-35; Gorman 2001: 35; Witherington 2004: 230; Gorman 2009: 169. Included here is also Fahy's 1956 article on Rom 8:29. Fahy (p. 411) writes: "There can be no doubt that συμμόρφους denotes glorification." His primary purpose in the extremely brief article, however, is to contrast the Greek text (συμμόρφους) and its proper translation, "conformed (as they were)" (according to Fahy), with the Vulgate

because it is also the category of understanding "conformity," which is most commonly combined with others: glory and the resurrection body[23] and, as noted above, present suffering and future glory. In fact, as with suffering, the meaning behind "conformed to the image of his Son" is rarely understood as glory alone. Douglas Moo offers an excellent example:

> Paul may think of the believer as destined from his conversion onward to "conform" to Christ's pattern of *suffering followed by glory*. . . . But the closest parallels, Phil. 3:21 and 1 Cor. 15:49, are both eschatological; and eschatology is Paul's focus in this paragraph. . . . It is as Christians have their *bodies resurrected* and transformed that they *join Christ in his glory* and that the purpose of God, to make Christ the "firstborn" of many to follow, is accomplished.[24]

So also does Kürzinger's 1958 treatment of the verse: "Ob dabei nur an die Herrlichkeit des erhöhten Herrn oder ob nicht eher—ganz im Sinn der übrigen Aussage des Römerbriefes—an das Teilnehmen am ganzen Erlösungsgeschehen (Tod—Begrabenwerden—Auferstehen) gedacht ist, mag offen bleiben."[25] Nearly every scholar suggests that final glorification has some role to play in understanding Romans 8:29b, even if it is joined by sanctification, suffering, or physical renewal.

Support for Romans 8:29 as eschatological conformity to Christ's glory is, like that of suffering, found in the connection between Romans 8:17, in which Paul says the children of God will be "coglorified" (συνδοξασθῶμεν) with the Son, and Romans 8:30 (see also Rom 5:2), in which glorification is the final result of the process of conformity in Romans 8:29.[26] The believer is "conformed to the image of the Son," usually understood as

---

translation of *conformes fieri*, which he says is provided "as if the reading were συμμόρφους εἶναι, 'to be conformed,' the infinitive expressing 'purpose'" (p. 411). In so doing he argues that the Latin translation presents God as predesting Christians to glory apart from "any extrinsic consideration" (p. 411), and the Greek, he suggests, presents God as predestining Christians to glory on the basis of their foreknown merits. The article is more accurately about the nature of προέγνω, καὶ προώρισεν in Rom 8:29a and, like Leaney's article mentioned above, will therefore have little bearing on this investigation.

[23]Hunter 1955: 85; Siber 1971: 155; Dunn 1988a: 483-84; Wright 2002: 601; Witherington 2004: 230.

[24]Moo 1996: 534-35; emphasis mine.

[25]Kürzinger 1958: 298. "It remains to be determined if only the glory of the ascended Lord is here in view, or if rather – in line with the meaning of the rest of the statements in the letter to the Romans – participation in the entire salvation process (death – burial – resurrection)."

[26]This semantic link will be examined in detail in §6.2.3.

taking place at the resurrection, at which point the believer is glorified
with Christ.

These thematic and textual connections with coglorification in Romans
8:17 are indeed the keys to understanding Paul's intentions behind
συμμόρφους τῆς εἰκόνος τοῦ υἱοῦ αὐτου. This being said, however, there
is one primary weakness in these suggestions. When scholars suggest that
Romans 8:29b refers to believers' glorification, they often fail to define
glory or *glorification*. And it seems to me that if being conformed means
being glorified, then one ought to say what glorification *is*. Paul's use of
δόξα and δοξάζω has received little treatment within Pauline scholarship
and, when scholars do attempt to define *glory*, they denote it as an eschatological splendor, radiance, or brilliance—words that are sometimes used
to connote the manifest presence of God.[27] But these definitions of glory
are inadequate for their occurrences in Romans. I will argue anon that
Romans 8:29b refers to believers' eschatological glory only if *glory* is understood as something *other than* splendor/radiance or the visible, manifest
presence of God.

A final suggestion is also proposed, though not widely adopted. James
Dunn, Robert Jewett, Tom Schreiner,[28] Brendan Byrne, N. T. Wright[29]—five
scholars from diverse traditions and perspectives—have all suggested that
conformity in Romans 8:29 refers to a functional conformity;[30] that is,
when believers are conformed to the image of the Son, they are conformed
to his status and function as the Son of God who rules over creation. Each
scholar argues his case from a different perspective, but all share the
common focus on conformity as function or vocation. I will argue that

---

[27]Interestingly, if one does a Google Images search for "glory," the primary visual image is of
sun rays bursting through clouds, sunsets, and sunrises. The popular understanding of glory
and the default scholarly understanding of glory are not too different. Both need some helpful caveats.

[28]Schreiner 1998. This interpretation does not come through, however, in his *Paul, Apostle of
God's Glory in Christ* (2001).

[29]I previously included Wright with those who suggest that Rom 8:29b implies a sacrificial
conformity. With others, he holds to a two-part conformity, i.e., suffering now and glory later.
However, unlike most who hold to a two-part conformity, Wright not only emphasizes glory
over suffering, but he primarily interprets *glory*, like *conformed*, as a functional motif. That is,
unlike most scholars who hold to a two-part conformity, Wright understands the second of
the two parts differently from most (i.e., glory is not splendor but status/function).

[30]Also Scott 1992 and Worthington 2011 hint at functional interpretations, though only in dialogue with one or more of the other common suggestions.

this suggestion, made almost in passing, is at the heart of Paul's meaning behind "conformed to the image of his Son" in Romans 8:29b. Nevertheless, though these scholars pose this alternative reading of the phrase, they each do so very briefly and without the substantive support necessary to make their case. I will adapt, expand, and most importantly substantiate this functional reading of Romans 8:29b hinted at by these scholars.

1.2. A FEW NOTES ON METHODOLOGY

Before proceeding, let me first note a few methodological considerations. First, anyone who has ever dabbled in Pauline studies is aware of the seemingly endless list of scholars, monographs, and articles dedicated to the exploration of Paul's letters and theology. In an effort to gain both continuity and breadth, I have selected eight primary interlocutors of various perspectives, including Joseph Fitzmyer, Brendan Byrne, C. E. B. Cranfield, Thomas Schreiner, Douglas Moo, James Dunn, N. T. Wright, Ernst Käsemann, and Robert Jewett. With the exception of Cranfield and Käsemann, these selected commentators have one significant feature in common: all are influenced to some degree by the "Sanders revolution" of the late 1970s and the New Perspective on Paul that resulted from it. The New Perspective on Paul has shaped the course of Pauline studies over the last three decades to the degree that consulting a wealth of Romans scholarship prior to Ed Sanders's 1977 work, *Paul and Palestinian Judaism*, would do little to carry forward the discussion of Romans 8:29b. Other scholars will of course be consulted as their work becomes relevant.[31]

Second, the primary path to discovering the meaning of Romans 8:29b will be—first and foremost—through the literary and theological context of Romans in general and Romans 8 in particular. Romans 8:29b is most often addressed in discussions pertaining to Paul's transmorphic language and use of εἰκών in other Pauline texts. These texts will arise naturally at numerous points throughout the discussion but are not the primary means of discovering the meaning that lies behind Romans 8:29b. Rather, it will be discovered on the basis of its position as the climax of the semantic and theological structure of Romans 5–8 and its

---

[31]Those of most significance will include Carey Newman (1992), Stanley Stowers (1994), Philip Esler (2003), Caroline Johnson Hodge (2007), and George van Kooten (2008a).

relationship to the underlying narrative of glory threaded through the fabric of Romans 1–8.

A third and critical methodological element of this investigation is that, at times, it will rely on the recognition of intertextual allusions within Paul's argument. For my purposes here, I have appropriated the criteria for the detection of allusions offered by both Richard Hays and William Tooman. In Hays's 1989 work, *Echoes of Scripture in the Letters of Paul*, he offers seven tests for determining the presence of intertextual echoes in Paul's letters: availability, volume, recurrence, thematic coherence, historical plausibility, history of interpretation, and satisfaction.[32] Though a number of scholars have critiqued Hays's work, none have provided a set of criteria that has proven to be more useful.[33]

---

[32]Hays 1989: 29-32.

[33]A number of scholars have critiqued Hays's suggestions, though, interestingly, few have offered criticisms of the seven tests, instead taking up his larger, more fundamental presuppositions. In *Paul and the Scriptures of Israel*, Craig Evans, James Sanders, William Scott Green, and J. C. Beker offer their praises and critiques of Hays's work. Of the four, Beker alone suggests that Hays's seven tests are insufficient; even his criticism, though, is primarily expressed not by engagement with Hays's arguments but rather by praise of the work of others, most notably that of Michael Fishbane (Evans and Sanders 1993: 64-65). Hays says in response that not only are his tests more constraining, due not least to the fact that he offers seven when Fishbane offers just two, but that Beker, in misreading the text, has chosen as his example for why the tests are inadequate the very example Hays offers to demonstrate the tests identifying a *lack* of echo (Evans and Sanders 1993: 85-86)! Beker's critique of Hays's proposed seven tests is ultimately rather weak. See also Porter and Stanley 2008: 36-39 for a critique of Hays's criteria. Porter, however, offers no alternative criteria for determining the presence of an echo, despite his criticisms of Hays's. Moreover, Porter's definition of allusion—a "figure of speech that makes indirect extra-textual references" (p. 30)—can, by definition, include Hays's understanding of echo. Their criteria and terminology may differ, but their understandings of Paul's intertextual use of Scripture are not very far apart. Richard Longenecker (1999) also suggests Hays's seven tests are insufficient, and, like Beker, his evidence of their insufficiency rests entirely on his examination of the sufficiency of Fishbane's. Longenecker says only this about Hays's suggestions (p. xvl): "Richard Hays, on the other hand, tends to treat biblical quotations as merely louder echoes of Scripture, and he uses them principally as springboards for the discovery of much more significant resonances in the allusive biblical materials that appear in Paul's letters. In the hands of an able and articulate practitioner, such a method produces some rather exciting results. What it lacks, however, are the necessary controls and constraints of careful research, thereby allowing the inclusion of data that can be questioned as being primary." From this, the reader is forced to decide between two conclusions: either Hays is the only "able and articulate practitioner" to utilize the tests appropriately, or the tests—which Longenecker does not analyze—are insufficient even for one who is an "able and articulate practitioner" such as Richard Hays. Moreover, Longenecker ultimately critiques Hays for his lack of emphasis on explicit citations, compared to that of Fishbane—an unjustified critique due to the simple fact that Hays's goal in *Echoes* was to present a case for reading the *echoes* of Scripture in Paul, rather than present an overarching method of analysis of all levels of innerbiblical exegesis.

Like Hays, though approaching the topic of the reuse of Scripture within the Hebrew Bible, William Tooman has also offered a set of what he calls "preliminary" criteria for determining reuse.[34] In his 2011 work, *Gog and Magog: Reuse of Scripture and Compositional Technique in Ezekiel 38–39*, Tooman distinguishes between quotation, allusion, echo, and influence, using *allusion* in much the same way as Hays uses "allusive echo" or, more typically, just *echo*. For Tooman, the fundamental difference between allusion and echo is that allusions function as "semantically transformative," while echoes do not.[35] Tooman's criteria for determining innerbiblical reuse include uniqueness, distinctiveness, multiplicity, thematic correspondence, and inversion.[36] Tooman's criteria have not received scrutiny like those of Hays but do have some significant elements of overlap.

I will appropriate a combination of the proposed methods for determining innerbiblical allusion. Given that Hays's first criterion, availability, is generally not an issue for Paul's use of Israel's Scriptures, it will not be included. Likewise, because I find Hays's final three criteria (historical plausibility, history of interpretation, and satisfaction) too subjective for determining reuse, these also will not be considered as criteria. And Tooman's final criterion, inversion, is applicable primarily to issues of scriptural reuse in the Hebrew Bible, so it too will not be included. Therefore, the criteria used in this investigation will be a combination of Hays's and Tooman's most valuable suggestions: uniqueness (Tooman); volume (Hays), which includes elements of distinctiveness (Tooman) and multiplicity (Tooman); recurrence (Hays), and thematic correspondence (Tooman/Hays).

It is important to note, too, what Hays says about his own treatment of intertextual echoes: "To run explicitly through this series of criteria for each of the texts that I treat would be wearisome. I trust the reader's competence to employ these criteria and to apply appropriate discounts to the interpretive proposals that I offer throughout."[37] I echo this sentiment, though I will offer a note on the "shades of certainty" of those intertextual allusions that bear significant weight on my proposed argument.

---

[34]Tooman 2011: 24.
[35]Tooman 2011: 8.
[36]Tooman 2011: 27-32.
[37]Hays 1989: 32.

Finally, the breadth of literature and theological emphases currently driving interest in Pauline theology is vast. Without question all who proceed through this particular contribution will look for discussions on the particularities of those emphases that interest them, especially as they relate to the theological themes contained in Romans 8 in particular and to Romans scholarship and Pauline theology in general. It goes without saying that I will not address a number of such topics, at least not directly or fully; to do so would take us too far afield. Such topics include (1) the meaning or function of προγινώσκω and προορίζω in Romans 8:29a as theological terms either within Paul's biblical theology or within contemporary discussions of systematic theology; (2) the *ordo salutis* of Romans 8:29-30 as a systematic and logical rendering of the stages of salvation; (3) the manifold discussions of δικαιόω currently flooding Pauline studies; (4) issues of apocalyptic discourse and Paul as an apocalyptic theologian; (5) Paul's engagement with empire, the imperial cult, and Caesar; (6) pneumatology and (7) eschatology as discussions in themselves; and (8) a full treatment of environmental ethics. Lengthy discussions of any of these would no doubt add to the discussion surrounding Romans 8:29b; they must nevertheless be reserved for subsequent projects.[38]

My purpose here is solely to address the meaning of "conformed to the image of his Son" in Romans 8:29b as a phrase that arises out of Paul's biblical theology—no mean feat even by itself. Romans 8:29b is composed of six Greek words that allegedly comprise the goal of salvation, are determined by motifs that are themselves not easily deciphered, are used in countless side arguments, and yet boast no single, shared interpretation, even within Pauline scholarship.

1.3. OUTLINE AND AGENDA FOR EACH SECTION

My argument in this book will expand and substantiate the functional reading of Romans 8:29b noted above. The book is divided into two halves, with the first half addressing Pauline and biblical, semantic, and theological concerns, and the second half addressing the interpretation of Romans 8:29b

---

[38]For a recent treatment of current discussions on these and other topics within Pauline theology, see Wright 2015.

within the context of Romans 8 and on the basis of the conclusions drawn in the first half.

Because believers' conformity in Romans 8:29b is linked to believers' glorification (δοξάζω) in Romans 8:30, as well as their coglorification (συνδοξάζω) in Romans 8:17 and δόξα in Romans 8:18, 21, it is necessary to examine Paul's use of these terms. Chapters two and three will serve this end. Chapter two will offer a brief description of semiotic theory before investigating the semantic use of δόξα and δοξάζω throughout the LXX, and briefly in the apocalyptic texts of Daniel and 1 Enoch. The terms will be analyzed according to their denotative and connotative functions throughout the text, with a particular view to how they function, in particular, in relation to God and to humanity. We will discover that δόξα and δοξάζω are used in ways more variegated than are often recognized.

On the basis of the conclusions drawn in chapter two, chapter three will investigate the meaning of δόξα and δοξάζω in Romans, particularly as the terms are used in Romans 1:23; 2:7, 10; 3:23; 5:2; 8:17, 18, 21, 30; 9:4. After assessing current interpretations of the terms and their inadequacies, I will address a number of considerations that must be made in such discussions, considerations that include the presence and role of Adam in Romans and the significance of Psalm 8 for Paul's new-Adam Christology. The heart of the chapter will be an examination of what I will call Paul's "narrative of glory"—the theological storyboard for Romans 1–8 and the context in which "conformed to the image of his Son" in Romans 8:29b will be interpreted.

Chapter four focuses on the Pauline motifs of union and participation. I suggest that throughout Paul's letters he articulates a motif of what I will call "vocational participation" with Christ, which is believers' active share in the resurrection life and glory of Christ as redeemed humans in him. I then examine this motif of vocational participation in Philippians 3:21, where the only other New Testament occurrence of σύμμορφος is found. I also examine it in 1 Corinthians 15:49 and Colossians 3:10, where εἰκών is also used within a context of vocational participation. The chapter will conclude with an examination of 2 Corinthians 3:18; 4:4

and a discussion of their usefulness in determining the meaning of
Romans 8:29b.

In the second half of the book, I will turn the attention to Romans 8:29
itself. Chapter five will address the identity of the Son within the context
of the phrase "image of his Son." I will suggest that, on the basis of Paul's
references to Jesus as the "Firstborn" and the significance of Psalms 89; 110
for Paul's identification of the Son elsewhere, in Romans 8:29 the Son
should be understood as the long-awaited Davidic king, Israel's Messiah.
Additionally, I will argue that Paul's εἰκών-language elsewhere, particularly
in contexts of his new-Adam Christology, and his use of πρωτότοκος
designate the Son as the new Adam in Romans 8:29, an identity that picks
up Paul's Adam-Christ typology of Romans 5:12-21. As he is both Messiah
and new Adam, I will argue that he reigns over creation as the highest of
the kings of the earth and that he stands as the representative of a new
family of God and a redeemed humanity.

Chapter six will serve as the heart of the investigation. Here I will draw
together the conclusions of the previous five chapters into an examination
of Paul's vocational participatory motif latent in Romans 8:17, 29, 30. I will
address the theological significance of adoption and sonship in Romans 8
and its relationship to Romans 8:29bc. The chapter will then suggest that
Paul's references to being "co-inheritors" and "coglorified" in Romans 8:17
and "glorified" in Romans 8:30 all refer to believers' participation with the
Son in his unique role as sovereign over creation. Because of the semantic
link between Romans 8:17, 29, and 30, I will argue that, in being conformed
to the Son, believers participate with the Son in his rule over creation as
people renewed in the image of God.

Chapter seven will examine the structural and theological relationship
that exists within Romans 8:28-30. There I will propose that, despite
its importance, Romans 8:29b does not constitute Paul's main point.
Rather, Paul's point in Romans 8:28-30 is in Romans 8:28b, where Paul
articulates that God's children are called with a purpose. This purpose
is their glorification—a future reality, no doubt, but also a present
reality. I will argue that this motif of present glorification, if only in
part, is implied in the preceding verses: in the prayers of the believers
and the Spirit in Romans 8:26-27, and in God's working all things

toward good in Romans 8:28. God's children are called to function as vicegerents of God, not only in the eschaton but, however paradoxically, also in the present.

With our path laid out, let us now take the first steps. We begin by entering into the world of semiotics and glory.

PART
1

THE HOPE
OF GLORY IN
ROMANS 5–8

2

GLORY AND GLORIFICATION
IN JEWISH LITERATURE

The use of δόξα and δοξάζω in Jewish literature may seem like an odd place to begin. But in order to make sense of Romans 8:29b, one must first make sense of the syntactical connections it shares with δόξα and δοξάζω in the surrounding context. Most immediately, Romans 8:29b is connected to ἐδόξασεν ("[those] he glorified") in the final clause of Romans 8:30—the climax of Romans up to that point.[1] Moreover, Romans 8:29-30 draws together the strands of the argument that began in Romans 8:17 with references to the "glorification" of believers "with the Messiah." And, on a larger scale, Romans 5–8 as a unit is framed by believers' "hope of glory" in Romans 5:2 and "glorification" in Romans 8:30, making believers' hope of glory and/or glorification with Christ—the telos of the redeemed life—a key, perhaps even the key, to interpreting Romans 8:29b. So that is where we must begin.

The meanings of δόξα and δοξάζω directly affect the meaning of Romans 8:29b. But the problem, as mentioned in the introduction, is that little work has been done on what the glory or glorification of believers actually means. A common assumption is that it refers to a believer's eschatological radiance, which exudes from the resurrected body when in the presence of the radiance of God. For some, there is an added component of transformation

---

[1]I will examine this connection in detail in §7.1.1.

in holiness. I will suggest in chapter three that the common interpretation of humanity's δόξα and δοξάζω—that is, (receiving) an eschatological splendor or radiance associated with one's transformation in the presence of God—needs rethinking, particularly in terms of their function within Romans. But this suggestion will not be without reason—one located in the scriptural roots of Paul's notion of glory.

This first chapter will provide that necessary background investigation into the ways in which δόξα and δοξάζω function within the LXX and in some apocalyptic texts. What is their primary meaning? Do those primary meanings differ when used vis-à-vis humanity from when used vis-à-vis God? And what role does the function of language have in understanding how terms such as δόξα, δοξάζω, and their cognates are understood in the narratives? These are the questions this chapter seeks to ask, each of which bears significance for understanding Paul's use of the terms, not least in Romans 8 when used in reference to the eschatological glory and glorification of humanity.[2]

2.1. A DISCUSSION OF SEMIOTICS

Before turning to the Jewish literature, a brief introduction to the issues of linguistic semiotics relevant to our investigation is in order. For assistance, I turn to another potentially odd place: the classic discussion of the word *glory* between Humpty-Dumpty and Alice in Lewis Carroll's *Through the Looking Glass*. Their discussion is relevant to this chapter not only because it highlights the meaning of *glory* but because their discussion is on issues that pertain to semiotics, albeit implicitly so.[3] You may remember the narrative:

"There's glory for you!"
"I don't know what you mean by 'glory,'" Alice said.
Humpty Dumpty smiled contemptuously. "Of course you don't—till I tell you. I meant 'there's a nice knock-down argument for you!'"
"But 'glory' doesn't mean 'a nice knock-down argument,'" Alice objected.

---

[2]All references to the Old Testament in this chapter will be LXX versification.
[3]Ironically, most academic references to Humpty-Dumpty's use of *glory* are for the purpose of placing it within larger discussions of semiotics and semantics (see, e.g., Hancher 1981). I wish to note his use of *glory* for that reason, but only as an introduction to an investigation of what the term actually *can* mean, at least within ancient Jewish literature.

"When I use a word," Humpty Dumpty said, in rather a scornful tone, "it means just what I choose it to mean—neither more nor less."

"The question is," said Alice, "whether you **can** make words mean so many different things."

"The question is," said Humpty Dumpty, "which is to be master—that's all."

. . .

"When I make a word do a lot of work like that," said Humpty Dumpty, "I always pay it extra."

"Oh!" said Alice. She was too much puzzled to make any other remark.

"Ah, you should see 'em come 'round me of a Saturday night," Humpty Dumpty went on, wagging his head gravely from side to side, "for to get their wages, you know."

Humpty-Dumpty and Alice approach the word *glory* in different ways; they also approach the philosophy of language, that is, semiotics, in different ways. I will note their differing approaches anon, but first I think a brief introduction to the field of semiotics will serve us well.

The study of semiotics was established by Swiss linguist Ferdinand de Saussure (1857–1913) and American philosopher Charles Sanders Peirce (1839–1914), whose models of semiotics, or sign-systems, continue to undergird discussions today.[4] According to George Aichele, semiotics is "the study of signs, or of language considered in its broadest possible sense," with *sign* (or *symbol*) referring to "any phenomenal object that may be taken to signify something."[5] Daniel Chandler lists possible "phenomenal objects" as "words, images, sounds, gestures, and objects."[6] In particular, what form the basis of linguistic semiotics today are Saussure's distinction between signifier (the symbol/sign itself) and signified (the mental concept generated by the sign),[7] and Peirce's triadic model, which includes a sign/representamen, an object (that which is represented by the sign), and an

---

[4]See Chandler 2007: 1-11 and Cobley and Jansz 2010 for an overview and development of the study of semiotics from Saussure until today.

[5]Aichele 1997: 9. A distinction is often made between *sign* as the signifier and *sign* as that which includes a signifier and signified (and the interpretant, the "sense" made of the sign, in Peirce's tri-part model); see Chandler 2007: 29-30. Here I use *sign* as synonymous with *signifier* and *symbol* to refer to a sign that "relates to its object by means of convention alone, e.g. a word, a flag" (opposed to an icon: a sign that shares resemblance with its object, e.g., photograph); Cobley and Jansz 2010: 33.

[6]Chandler 2007: 2.

[7]Silva 1994: 35; Cobley and Jansz 2010: 8-17.

interpretant (the "sense" made of the sign by the interpreter, or the result of the sign).[8] Peirce's three-part model has led to what is called "unlimited semiosis," where a signifier points to a signified, wherein the signified becomes a new signifier pointing to another signified, and so on.[9] This three-part path to meaning prohibits reducing meaning to an oversimplified "word-thing/concept" approach often associated with lexicons.[10]

Peirce's triangle ultimately recognizes the role of how signs *function* within syntagma, that is, as both literal and figurative signs that exist in unlimited semiosis.[11] "Literality is easier to illustrate than to define," notes George Caird, who goes on to suggest that "words are used literally when they are meant to be understood in their primary, matter-of-fact sense."[12] In contrast, words, or signs in general, are used figuratively or symbolically when used as one of numerous possible tropes or motifs, with the four "master tropes," according to Chandler,[13] being metaphor,[14] metonym, synecdoche, and irony. Figurative language, while found on every street corner, is most commonly associated with poetry.

Metaphor and metonymy are the most important forms of figurative language for our purposes here. Metaphor involves an implicit comparison between the signifier and signified,[15] or "a literary device in which the description of one reality expresses another."[16] Chandler suggests three forms of metaphor: orientational ("metaphors primarily relating to spatial organization," e.g., up/down, near/far); ontological ("metaphors which associate activities, emotions, and ideas with entities and substances [most obviously,

---

[8]See Chandler 2007: 32-36 and Cobley and Jansz 2010: 21-26. Also notable is Ogden and Richards's (1945: 11) influential linguistic semiotic triangle, consisting of symbol (the written word), thought (the mental content generated by the symbol), and referent (the extralinguistic thing in reality to which the symbol points), similar to Peirce's tri-part model; see Silva 1994: 102.

[9]See Chandler 2007: 33 and Cobley and Jansz 2010: 25.

[10]The critique of this approach began with James Barr's 1961 criticism of "word-thing/concept" approaches to hermeneutics, otherwise commonly known as "word studies" (and, in Barr's time, the hermeneutical approach particularly represented by the *Theological Dictionary of the New Testament*). See Newman 1992: 8; Silva 1994: 101-8.

[11]Chandler 2007: 123.

[12]Caird 1980: 133.

[13]Chandler 2007: 126-37.

[14]Caird (1980: 129-200) suggests *metaphor* as the overarching term for all other forms of figurative language; see also Chandler 2007: 126. Ricoeur's 1975 *La métaphore vive* remains the classic study on the use of metaphor.

[15]Caird 1980: 144.

[16]Patella 2005: 328; see Chandler 2007: 127.

metaphors involving personification]"); and structural (overarching metaphors "which allow us to structure one concept in terms of another [e.g. rational argument is war or time is a resource])."[17] On the level of words, metaphors (and metonyms) can be a single word or a phrase (e.g., "pain in the neck")[18] and can be both visual and verbal.[19] Additionally, some metaphors are living metaphors, and some are dead. Caird writes that "through constant use [a metaphor] then becomes a faded or worn metaphor, and finally a dead one," at which point speakers "treat the word as a new literalism."[20] That is to say that, when a metaphor is living, it is commonly recognized as figurative language; when it is dead, it is assumed to be literal language.[21]

Metonymy is "the evocation of the whole by a connection. It consists in using the name of a thing or a relationship, an attribute, a suggested sense, or something closely related."[22] Put more simply, metonymy is "calling a thing by the name of something typically associated with it."[23] Metonymy includes various subforms, including the substitution of *part* for the *whole* or *object* for *user* ("the Crown" for the monarchy).[24]

These literal and figurative forms can also be expressed in terms of denotation and connotation—the basis of Peirce's unlimited semiosis. Generally speaking, denotation represents the literal form, the form exhibited in a dictionary, and connotation represents the figurative, that which is characterized by metaphor, metonymy, and so on. Chandler notes that "connotation and denotation are often described in terms of levels of representation or levels of meaning—what Louis Hjelmslev first called 'orders

---

[17]Chandler 2007: 129. Caird (1980: 145-49) suggests four forms of metaphor: perceptual (appealing to any of the five senses), synesthetic (when two senses overlap, e.g., thick darkness), affective (a feeling of one thing is compared to another), and pragmatic (the activity of one thing is compared to another).

[18]Silva 1994: 103.

[19]Chandler 2007: 131.

[20]E.g., the eye of a needle; Caird 1980: 152; see also 131-32, 191, where he notes how the "body of Christ" has come to be treated by some as a dead metaphor, in that some have come to take *body* "to *mean* 'the visible, organized form which an entity assumes.' They could then argue that, since the church is the outward, organic form of Christ's presence in the world, it is literally the body of Christ."

[21]Caird 1980: 185. He writes (p. 185): "If there is any correlation between literalism and the evolution of language, the biblical evidence would suggest that literalism came quite late on the scene, the product of that semi-sophistication which is the parent of pedantry."

[22]Chandler 2007: 130, quoting Wilden 1987: 198.

[23]Caird 1980: 136.

[24]Chandler 2007: 130.

of significance." For purposes of exactness and clarity here, it will be helpful
to quote Chandler in full:

> The *first order* of signification is that of denotation: at this level there is a
> sign consisting of a signifier and a signified. Connotation is a *second order*
> of signification which uses the denotative sign (signifier and signified) as
> its signifier and attaches to it an additional signified. In this framework,
> connotation is a sign which derives from the signifier of a denotative sign
> (so denotation leads to a chain of connotations). A signified on one level
> can become a signifier on another level. This is the mechanism by which
> signs may seem to signify one thing but are loaded with multiple meanings.
> Indeed, this framing of the Saussurean model of the sign is analogous to
> the "infinite semiosis" of the Peircean sign in which the interpretant can
> become the representamen of another sign.[25]

This relationship between denotation and connotation, like that of literal
and figurative signs/symbols, will bear significantly on our discussion of
semiotics in the Old Testament.

Returning our attention to Humpty-Dumpty's use of *glory* with this
introduction to semiotics in mind, it becomes clear that *both* Alice and
Humpty-Dumpty were using the word correctly. While Alice wished to
emphasize the word's denotation,[26] Humpty-Dumpty recognized that, like
any word in a living language, the word *glory* has the practically limitless
ability to function figuratively.[27] Alice and Humpty-Dumpty's differing uses
of glory illustrate the difference between what Saussure called *langue* and
parole, or language and speech. "*Langue* refers to the system of rules and
conventions which is independent of, and pre-exists, individual users;
parole refers to its use in particular instances."[28] The question that follows

---

[25]Chandler 2007: 140; emphasis original.

[26]With any language, though, etymological definitions do not always remain in common use:
e.g., *nice* in English today means "pleasant" but is derived from the Latin *nescius*, which means
"ignorant" (Caird 1980: 44).

[27]In any particular context a word can be made to do "extra work," as Humpty-Dumpty does
with *glory*, simply by allowing their denotations to function as signs of something else: connotations. Humpty-Dumpty uses *glory* to function anthropomorphically as words made to do
more "work," and which he thus "pays" extra when they "come 'round [him] of a Saturday
night . . . for to get their wages." In this example, then, not only does *glory* function as more
than its denotation, but so also do *work* and *pay*.

[28]Chandler 2007: 12; emphasis original; Cobley and Jansz (2010: 15) describe the system by
saying: "*Langue* can be thought of as a communal cupboard, housing all the possible different

is whether *parole* is limited to *langue* or whether it has the capacity to transform *langue*. The importance of this question will be recognizable in our examination of the Old Testament below.

Before approaching the Jewish Scriptures, however, one further point of significance is necessary to note: whether a sign is literal or figurative has no bearing on its ontological reality. With Caird, I caution that "just as words are not identical with their referents, so linguistic statements (i.e. statements about words) are not to be confused with metaphysical statements (i.e. statements about reality)."[29] If in referring to my Harley-Davidson I say that I gave my hog a good run, I am clearly speaking metaphorically; it is not actually a hog, and it did not literally run. Nevertheless, that does not rule out my motorcycle's ontological existence or movement. Or, if I suggest that Garrison Keillor is the voice of Minnesota, Minnesota is clearly a metonym not only for the people of Minnesota but (here begins a "chain of connotations") a particular culture with which the people of Minnesota identify—a culture that is represented by the literal but also metaphorical "voice" of Keillor. It is not an ontological statement about the political state of Minnesota or the literal sound produced when Keillor speaks.

2.1.1. Semiotics and the Old Testament. With this introduction to semiotics, I turn our attention to its application to the Old Testament, particularly in recognition of the role of figurative language.[30] Understanding semiotics is crucial to interpreting the Old Testament, not least because the Old Testament is largely composed of poetic/figurative—specifically, analogous and symbolic—language.[31] For the biblical writers, as for anyone, "reality is framed within systems of analogy,"[32] and biblical analogy (or poetry in general), according to Stephen Prickett, appeals "not just to the

---

signs which might be pulled out and utilized in the construction of an instance of *parole*" (emphasis original).

[29]Caird 1980: 193-94; see also 132-33.

[30]A number of recent studies exist on semiotics/language and imagery in the Old Testament or Bible: e.g., Caird 1980; Prickett 1986; Silva 1994; Aichele 1997; Gibson 1998; Grelot 2006.

[31]This fact is only recently recognized. Prickett (1986: 214) suggests, "With the emergence of the idea of the 'poetic' in the eighteenth century we find also a rehabilitation of the classical notion of metaphor as its appropriate centre of activity."

[32]Chandler 2007: 125. Grelot (2006: 19-24) suggests four categories of symbol/metaphor in the Bible: analogical (pp. 25-66), mythical (pp. 67-102), figurative (pp. 103-48), relational (pp. 149-98).

intellect, but also to the imagination."[33] The importance of this fact cannot
be overstated.

More important yet is the fact that all language about God is necessarily
analogous language. According to Gibson,

> All God-talk, all theology, even ours, is metaphorical, describing God in
> terms that properly belong to the human sphere. It cannot be otherwise,
> as human words, like human thought, belong this side of creation, and
> cannot begin to describe its other side, God as he is in his own interior
> life. Such knowledge as we have of God is not of God as he is, but as he
> shows himself towards human beings. . . . When we say that God saves,
> redeems, pities us, is our Father, our shepherd, our King, we are using
> metaphors or images drawn from human life and experience. In other
> words, we are using anthropomorphisms, ascribing to God human actions
> and human feelings.[34]

When this limitation of language is forgotten in the pursuit of theology
understood through the lens of the biblical text, not only must once-living
metaphors be declared dead, but the interpreter's understanding of God
will necessarily be obscured by figurative language read literally.

Various metaphors are used to describe God, but, according to Gibson,
"the leading image of God in the Old Testament is undoubtedly of him
as king, and king of the whole universe rather than merely of Israel."[35]
One need only turn to the enthronement psalms to see this, as well as
to any number of other texts with royal imagery.[36] This fact will become
important in our analysis of δόξα in its associations with God in the
Old Testament.

---

[33]Prickett 1986: 217-18.

[34]Gibson 1998: 22. Caird (1980: 144) concludes something similar: "[Metaphor] comprises a
large part of our daily speech and almost all the language of theology. God speaks to man in
similitudes, and man has no language but analogy for speaking about God, however inadequate
it may be." See also Carey 2005: 12.

[35]Gibson 1998: 121. For a recent study on the kingship of God in the Old Testament, see Flynn
2014; see also Gray's 1979 classic treatment of the theme of God's kingship, kingdom, and
reign throughout the biblical narrative.

[36]Enthronement psalms of God: Ps 47; 93; 95–99; God identified as king: e.g., Ps 5:2, 4; 29:3,
10; 74:12, 14; 95:3-5; 96:10; 103:19-22; Is 6:5; Zech 14:6-9; texts with royal imagery in Isaiah
alone: God sits on a throne (Is 6:1; see Is 66:1); the earth is his footstool (Is 66:1); God reigns
(Is 52:7). This figurative language of God is picked up in the New Testament: e.g., Mt 5:35;
Acts 7:49; Rev 19:6. Gibson (1998: 123-28) suggests that images of God as divine warrior, judge,
and the living God are connected with the imagery of God as king.

Much more could be said about the application of the study of semiotics to the Old Testament. With this introduction, however, we are able to apply it to the various uses of δόξα and δοξάζω in the LXX and offer a cursory introduction to the meaning of glory and glorification in Jewish apocalyptic literature.

2.2. GLORY AND GLORIFICATION IN THE LXX

2.2.1. Lexical overview. 2.2.1.1. Establishing the terms: כבוד. Given that my interest is ultimately in the New Testament use of δόξα and δοξάζω, this study will focus specifically on the semantic range of δόξα and δοξάζω in the LXX. In doing so, it will rely on the two most recent studies of the terms: Millard Berquist's 1941 PhD dissertation and George Caird's 1944 DPhil dissertation, both unpublished.[37] Had one or both of the dissertations been published in its time, the suggestion I am making in this chapter might now be commonplace. Before tracing an overview of δόξα and δοξάζω, a brief word on כבוד and its verbal cognates is necessary.[38]

In its most fundamental form, כבוד means something that is literally "weighty."[39] The majority of its uses, however, are figurative or symbolic. As I will do with δόξα and δοξάζω anon, כבוד must be categorized according to its meaning vis-à-vis both God and man. Berquist and Caird each do so and arrive at similar conclusions.

According to Berquist, when associated with mankind and objects, כבוד is used to connote "the honor, repute, respect, or esteem in which a man is held by reason of the 'heaviness' or abundance of his earthly possession, or because of the 'weight' or importance of his achievements, or by virtue of the qualities of his character" (Gen 45:13; Job 19:9; Ps 49:16-17).[40] In its

---

[37]I am unable to find any evidence that suggests that Caird was aware of Berquist's work, completed three years previously.

[38]The כבוד-δόξα relationship between the Hebrew Bible and the LXX is extensive and need not detain us here. The question of why δόξα was chosen to translate כבוד, given the terms' lexical differences, has yet to find a straightforward answer. In his survey Newman (1992: 150-52) proposes that δόξα was used to translate כבוד because both terms (1) overlap in their meaning of "honor," (2) can function subjectively or objectively, and (3) were used in literature that included ascents and dream visions. See also Forster 1930; Kittel 1934: 34-47; Berquist 1941: 17-50; Caird 1944: 122-41; Brockington 1955; Kittel 1964: 233-37, 242-45; 253; Caird 1969: 267-68, 273-77; Newman 1992: 134-53.

[39]Kittel 1964: 238; Holladay 1971; Koehler and Baumgartner 2001: 455-58; see also Berquist 1941: 17-18; Davies 1962: 401.

[40]Berquist 1941: 18; see Caird 1944: 52.

association with God, Berquist suggests that כבוד carries three overarching connotations:[41] (1) כבוד is "a summary term for the self-manifestation of God as he reveals himself to Israel in various phases and characteristics of his divine nature" (Ex 33:18; Ps 25:7; 29:19, 20; 31:19; 97:21; esp. Ps 104:23; Hos 3:5).[42] (2) כבוד is "a more sensuous manifestation of Jehovah, represented by natural phenomena such as fire, smoke, radiance, brilliance, or splendor" (Ex 16:7-10, 27-34). Berquist points out that this use is limited to the Pentateuch and Ezekiel, and even here a difference exists between them. In the Pentateuch, the phenomena are not equated with the כבוד, but they are the symbols in which or through which God's "might and power and wisdom and judgment and providential care are made known to Israel and to her enemies."[43] Ezekiel, however, departs from the Pentateuch in that the כבוד becomes not just a symbol but "a definite physical manifestation, anthropomorphic, and radiant, and the light and fire elements are constituent parts of the כבוד, not merely accompaniments" (Ezek 9:3; 10:14, 45; 11:22-23, 46).[44] (3) כבוד is "God's self-manifestation as deliverer or savior" (Ex 16:10; Num 14:10, 20-22; Ps 84:11; 85:9; Is 40:5; 42:8; 48:11; 60:1-2).[45] Found in the Pentateuch, Psalms, Prophets, and especially Isaiah 40–66, this is the most extensive use of the term in the Hebrew Bible. Moreover, Berquist suggests, it is the meaning that informed Paul's use of δόξα in the New Testament. Unlike in the Ezekiel texts, "it is not the mere fact of his presence that is significant, but that he is present as a redeemer-deliverer."[46] These three connotations will prove significant for our lexical assessment of δόξα in the following paragraphs.

Caird is more nuanced in his categorization of כבוד in its association with mankind and objects. He suggests four categories. First is riches or material

---

[41]Koehler (1995: 457-58) suggests: (1) giving glory to Yahweh; (2) Yahweh's glory, which etymologically means "power, authority and honour of God; however it is often connected with manifestations of light"; (3) manifestation of Yahweh; (4) "essence and power in a broader sense, reserved only for God." See also Brown, Driver, and Briggs 1972: 457-59; Jenni and Westermann 1997: 595-602.

[42]Berquist 1941: 21-22.

[43]Berquist 1941: 31-32.

[44]Berquist 1941: 38-39.

[45]Berquist 1941: 39. On those texts such as Is 60:1-2 that combine glory with light imagery, Berquist suggests that the light imagery symbolizes the "impending deliverance, salvation, and restoration of Israel, by the hand of Jehovah God" (1941: 48).

[46]Berquist 1941: 42.

possessions (Gen 31:1; Esther 5:11; 2 Chron 32:27; Is 61:6; 66:11-12; Hag 2:3, 7-9). Second is honor; Caird states that "the last meaning of kabod is closely associated with honour, and the one meaning merges into the other so that it is often hard to say under which head a passage should be placed" (1 Kings 3:13; 1 Chron 19:12; 29:28; 2 Chron 1:11; 32:33; Prov 3:16; 8:18; 11:21; 15:33; Jer 48:18).[47] A man or object's status of honor can be symbolized by "any outward display of magnificence" (Gen 44:13; Job 19:9; Dan 11:39) or in association with a crown (Ps 8:5) or throne/chief seat (1 Sam 2:8; Is 22:23).[48] Third is manpower (Is 8:7; 16:14; 21:16; Hos 9:11). Fourth is self or soul (Ps 7:6; 16:9; 30:12; 108:1). The first and second categories are the most extensive.

In association with God, the terms carry three connotations for Caird. First is honor, by analogy (Jer 14:21; 17:12; Mal 1:6) or in general (1 Chron 16:24; Ps 19:1; 72:19; 104:31; Is 6:3; 42:8; 43:6-7), and particularly in the use of the *piel* (Judg 13:17; Is 43:23; Dan 11:38; Ps 22:23; 86:9, 12; Is 24:15). Caird concludes this category by saying:

> Like the kings of the earth, God requires honour to be paid to Him; but His honour, that which commands the respect and adoration of His creatures, is not as the honour of men. The honour, the rank and authority of men is symbolized by wealth and magnificence, by the throne and the crown. The honour of God is that which exalts Him high above all creatures; it is symbolized by His dealings with men in nature and in providence, by the stars in their courses and by the earth with its fullness. It has much in common with His holiness and His righteousness.[49]

Second is "a title for God; He is the kabod of His people Israel" (1 Sam 4:21-22; Jer 2:11; Ps 3:1-3; 106:19-22). "God is the kabod of Israel because He profits them, because He saves them and does wondrous works on their behalf, in short, because He is the source of their honour."[50] Third is "an outward quasi-physical manifestation of the presence or activity of God, usually in the form of light or fire, and sometimes with a surrounding envelope of cloud" (Ex 33:18-22; Lev 9:6; 10:3; Ezek 1:27).[51] After assessing the relationship

---

[47]Caird 1944: 60.
[48]Caird 1944: 62; also here: "To show respect or to do honour to a man is to recognise that he has this status."
[49]Caird 1944: 76.
[50]Caird 1944: 76.
[51]Caird 1944: 78.

between this quasi-physical manifestation in relation to the other uses of
כבוד, Caird concludes: "Just as the honour of the king was the material
splendor or show of power by which his worth could be recognised, and
which constituted a claim upon the respect of men, so too the Glory . . .
was a manifestation of the honour of God, of His greatness, majesty, power,
kingliness, of all that makes Him honourable in the eyes of men."[52]

Berquist's and Caird's categories do not align exactly, but the overlap is
obvious. In association with mankind and objects, the noun כבוד means
riches, material greatness, and honor. The term functions the same when
applied to God, with the addition that, in the Priestly and Ezekiel accounts,
God's honor *as a result of his status, power, or character* is symbolized by
his self-manifestation in theophany.[53]

A number of points are significant to note at this stage. Berquist and
Caird conclude that:

(1) כבוד associated with mankind refers to a person's status or honor;[54]
(2) the most extensive use of כבוד associated with God *does not mean*
    a theophanic revelation; and
(3) the theophanic revelations which do occur symbolise God's status,
    power, or character.

That Berquist and Caird draw these conclusions *independently of each other*
should caution us against too easily assigning δόξα such theophanic weight
in the New Testament, particularly when it is used in association with
humanity. I will return to this cautionary note at the end of this section.
But first we must categorize our primary concerns, δόξα and δοξάζω, into
their respective denotations and connotations.

---

[52]Caird 1944: 83, 86-87; see also 123-41.
[53]See also von Rad 1964: 238-42 in Kittel 1964. From here it is not difficult to see how δόξα
went from referring to the visible manifestation of God in splendor to refer to the beauty of
objects. On this, Harrison (1982: 478-79) writes: "Since *doxa* could be used legitimately to
translate *kābôd* in the areas of reputation and honor, only a slight step was required to make
it a blanket term for rendering other meanings of *kābôd* that had not belonged to *dóxa* in its
classical Greek setting. Once *dóxa* had become established as a translation for *kābôd* in the
sense of majesty or splendour, which was something of a departure from native Greek usage,
apparently this was sufficient precedent to go further and employ *dóxa* to render a whole
group of Hebrew words involving the notion of beauty or adornment." Harrison confirms
what Berquist and Caird demonstrate at length: δόξα primarily means honor/status, which
then came to be symbolized by visible splendor, which then was extended to connote adornment or beauty.
[54]As is supported by Brown, Driver, and Briggs 1972: 458-59.

Δόξα and δοξάζω. It is widely acknowledged that δόξα in nonbiblical Greek means "opinion" or "reputation"[55] and that in the LXX it assumes the most basic and connotative meanings of כבוד: status, honor, character, splendor.[56] Takamitsu Muraoka lists four categories of meaning for δόξα in the LXX: (1) "status of honour and distinction"; (2) "external splendor, magnificent appearance"; (3) "an opinion which appears to be or commonly held to be right"; and (4) "partiality; favouritism." He also lists three categories for δοξάζω: (1) "to bring or accord honour to"; (2) "to accord splendor to"; and (3) "to express oneself with reverence over."[57]

An obvious overlap exists between Muraoka's categories for δόξα and those of Berquist and Caird for כבוד, something not unexpected given the relationship between the two terms. But one significant difference does exist. Whereas Berquist distinguishes between כבוד as the external manifestation of God's character/power/status and כבוד as theophanic splendor, and Caird does so through nuancing the external manifestations as *symbolic* of God's character/power/status, Muraoka's generalized categories distort such distinctions. This is particularly the case in his second category: "external splendor/ magnificent appearance." It is precisely this kind of generalization, one that compounds the imbalanced emphasis on glory in the Bible as splendor associated with theophany, that is present in biblical scholarship today.[58] I will return to assess further Muraoka's second category below.

---

[55]Kittel 1964: 233-34.

[56]Berquist suggests it maintains its nonbiblical Greek denotation in Jewish literature only in 4 Macc 5:17 (1941: 49).

[57]Muraoka 2009: 176; see also Owen 1932; Newman 1992: 149.

[58]Compared to Berquist's (pp. 49-50) nuanced categorizations for δόξα associated *with man*: (1) "material possessions, or moral or spiritual qualities that cause an individual to be held in esteem"; (2) "the inner being or essential nature of impersonal objects or bodies being personified"; (3) "man's inner being or soul, the seat of human character"; and *with God*: (1) "theologically, a summary term for the self-revelation of Jehovah's nature in its various elements by actual or figurative manifestation"; (2) "term of ascription by which affirmation is given to such nature"; (3) "Jehovah himself, being used as a designation for the Divine Being"; (4) "Brilliance, splendor, brightness, glowing fire, etc., of divine origin and significance, and even divine representation"; (5) "Specifically, God's manifestation of himself among men as savior and redeemer." And though Caird does not categorize δόξα as he did with כבוד or as Berquist does with δόξα, he no less traces δόξα and δοξάζω throughout what he calls the "canonical books of the LXX" (pp. 42, 122-41) and the Apocrypha (pp. 142-55). Caird concludes that, among the distinct functions and meanings of δόξα in the LXX, δόξα was used "with the meaning honour, either because this was the meaning of the corresponding word in the Hebrew text, or because it seemed an adequate paraphrase. In particular, it was used for kabod because the basic meaning of kabod was honour" (p. 140) and that "like kabod, doxa in the LXX must be regarded as a single, many-sided term" (p. 141).

At this stage, I wish only to offer a lexical overview of δόξα and δοξάζω in the LXX and, in conjunction with the work of Berquist, Caird, and Muraoka, to offer a basic presentation of the lexical categories into which the terms best fit. While the work of Berquist, Caird, and Muraoka stands in the background, the categories I suggest are primarily a result of understanding the meaning of δόξα and δοξάζω in the LXX through the application of linguistic semiotic theory.

2.2.1.2. Linguistic semiotics and δόξα. As we saw earlier, one of the chief weaknesses of lexical entries is their presentation of signs/referents as word-thing/word-concept; they overlook the fact that signs also perform functions within syntagmas and often participate in "connotation chains."[59] For this reason, among others, Muraoka's 2009 lexical entry on δόξα presents a less than complete depiction of the terms.[60] As noted above, the issue is primarily with the overly generalized second category, which combines "external splendor" and "magnificent appearance," though other issues exist as well. The works of Berquist and Caird both independently demonstrate that δόξα should be distinguished between meaning (a) a status of honor/ distinction, which is *sometimes* represented or symbolized by (a.1) a magnificent appearance or (a.2) a visible splendor; and (b) an external, visible splendor associated with theophany. Δόξα in the LXX simply does not have the same meaning when applied to an object of beauty as it does when understood as the glory of the Lord filling the temple. It has both literal and figurative nuances—a fact that must be recognized and that is not necessarily recognized through the use of a lexicon alone.

Muraoka's entry condenses to this:

- Category 1: "status of honour and distinction": Hosea 4:7; Sirach 5:13; Habakkuk 2:16; Wisdom 8:10; Hosea 10:5; Malachi 1:6; Hosea 9:11; Malachi 2:2; Habakkuk 2:14; Micah 5:4; Genesis 31:1, 16; Jeremiah 13:18; 14:21; Sirach 1:11; Proverbs 3:16; 8:18; *referring to God*: Esther 4:16; Tobit 12:12; 3:16; 12:15; Psalm 105:20

---

[59]See Silva 1994: 101-8. For an overview of critiques made about theological lexicography, particularly since James Barr's critique of Kittel's *Theological Dictionary of the New Testament*, see Silva 1994: 17-32. Silva (1994: 137) also notes that lexicons fall subject to the "hermeneutical circle," noting in particular our semidependence on BDAG, which is dependent on prior exegesis and, I add, exegesis common to the accepted hermeneutical methods of the time.

[60]This is particularly the case if one tries to build an understanding of the New Testament use of δόξα on his depiction of the LXX use of δόξα.

- Category 2: "external splendor, magnificent appearance": Exodus 16:7, 10; 24:16; 28:2; 33:5; Numbers 12:8; Isaiah 35:2; Jubilees 37:22; Haggai 2:3, 9; Sirach 6:29; 24:16; 24:17; 27:8; 43:9; Isaiah 52:14; 53:2; 2 Chronicles 18:1; Isaiah 2:7; 3:18; *magnificent-looking object*: 1 Maccabees 14:9; Isaiah 8:7; *not visible*: Sirach 17:13

- Category 3: "an opinion which appears to be or commonly held to be right": Isaiah 11:3; Sirach 8:14; *reputation*: 4 Maccabees 5:18[61]

- Category 4: "partiality; favouritism": Sirach 32:15[62]

Unfortunately, Muraoka misdescribes the key category (the second) in the following ways, ultimately giving it far more weight than it deserves. First, Exodus 16:7 is clearly a reference *not* to theophany but to the manna that God makes appear for the sustenance of the Israelites (a sign of his power/salvation). Second, the glory of God that the people will see in Isaiah 35:2 is most likely a reference to the redemptive works of God listed in Isaiah 35:4-9. Third, the priestly garments of honor and glory in Exodus 28:2 have a magnificent appearance symbolic of honor/status, but in no way does this mean they are splendid (i.e., radiant). The same can be said of the temple in Haggai 2:3, 9 and the garments/accessories in Exodus 33:5; Isaiah 3:18; Sirach 6:29; 27:8. Fourth, not only are these garments and accessories probably not luminous, but they should be categorized under "magnificent-looking object." Fifth, here also, the glory of Assyria in Isaiah 8:7 in no way qualifies as a "magnificent-looking object" and should be classified under category number one. Sixth, Jehoshaphat, with his πλοῦτος καὶ δόξα πολλή in 2 Chronicles 18:1, should clearly be listed under category number one as a "status of honour and distinction" rather than under "external splendor/magnificent appearance." Seventh, to top it off, Isaiah 2:7 is a typographical error; it should read Haggai 2:7 (and Sir 32:15 in category four should read Sir 35:12/15). These observations alone warrant a strong word of caution to anyone looking to a lexicon on the LXX use of δόξα in order to understand the word's meaning in the New Testament. That

---

[61]Is 11:3 and Sir 8:14 are more probably references to the honor/status/power of the person being judged rather than the opinion of the judge (the Messiah) himself.

[62]Muraoka 2009: 175. The first three categories denote the majority of occurrences; the fourth is listed specifically for Sir 32:15. See also Forster 1930: 312-14; Owen 1932; Caird 1944: 122-41 (Old Testament); 142-55 (Apocrypha); 156-47 (later translations); Brockington 1955; Kittel 1964: 242-45; Newman 1992: 149-50.

Berquist and Caird's conclusions could be so different from Muraoka's lexical entry is due to the fact that Berquist and Caird both recognized the diverse semiotic *functions* of δόξα throughout various contexts of the LXX, the derivation between δόξα's denotation and connotations, and how δόξα's connotations expanded over time.

In the following pages I include my own lexical and concordance entries. The purpose behind doing so is twofold: First, most simply, a comparison of the lexical and concordance entries demonstrates that, in terms of number of occurrences, a lexicon can be a misleading or inaccurate depiction of reality. Texts selected for inclusion in a lexical entry are a reflection of a particular lexicographer's perspective. Second, unlike a lexicon, a concordance presents a visual breakdown of how lexemes function within the text(s). For this reason, the reader's primary attention should be directed at the concordance, where the relationship between the denotation and connotations of δόξα in the LXX is tabulated on the basis of applied basic linguistic semiotic theory. The reader will see that δόξα exists in three denotative forms, one of which is associated with various symbolic connotation chains. These connotation chains (b, d, e below) are associated with metaphors and metonymy—symbolic language often associated with phenomenal imagery. When such symbolic imagery is utilized in poetic language, as in many of the texts below, the reader must ask, What exactly does this imagery symbolize? As will be clear in the concordance entry, the phenomenal images are signs that connote the honor or exalted status of the object they signify.

2.2.1.3. Lexical entry.

δόξα

1. δόξα as honor or status associated with character, power, or wealth
   a. ascription given to God or that God receives: Josh 7:19; 1 Chron 16:28-29; Ps 28:1-2, 9
   b. *God's* honor or status associated with his character or power: 1 Chron 16:27; Prov 25:2; *manifested or demonstrated in (symbolized by) redemptive or saving activity:* Ps 101:16, 17; Sir 17:13; Bar 4:24, 37; *manifested in (symbolized by) splendor/theophany:* Ex 16:10; 24:16, 17; 33:18, 19, 22; 40:34, 35; Lev 9:6, 23; Num 12:8; 14:10; 16:19; 17:7; 20:6; Deut 5:24; 1 Kings 8:11; 2 Chron 2:5; 5:13-14; 7:1-3; Is 4:5; 6:1; Ezek 1:28; 3:12,

23; 8:4; 9:3; 10:4, 18, 19, 22; 11:22, 23; 43:2, 4, 5; 44:4; Zech 2:9; Sir 36:13; 45:3; 49:8; 2 Macc 2:8; Pss. Sol. 11:6

c. a *person's* honor or status associated with his character, power, or wealth: 1 Kings 3:13; Ps 3:4; 1 Esd 8:4; Sir 8:14

d. a *nation's* honor or status associated with its character, power, or wealth: Is 8:7; Jer 31:18; Ezek 27:10; *symbolized by radiant beauty or splendor:* Prov 18:11; Pss. Sol. 2:5

e. an *object or place's* honor, status, authority, character, power, or wealth, *often symbolized by beauty or magnificent appearance:* Ex 28:2; Is 3:18, 20; Hag 2:3, 7, 9; Sir 6:29, 31; 1 Macc 2:9; 2 Macc 5:16, 20

2. δόξα as God himself, as a title for God: 1 Sam 4:22; Ps 3:4; Is 64:10

3. δόξα as splendor or beauty (not symbolizing honor/status): Ezek 27:7, 10; Sir 24:16, 17; 43:1, 9, 12; 50:7

δοξάζω (+ ἐνδοξάζομαι)

1. δοξάζω and ἐνδοξάζομαι as according a status of honor, power, or authority:

a. God: 1 Sam 2:30; Ps 49:15; *symbolized by visible splendor:* Ezek 28:22; 38:23; 39:13[63]

b. Individuals: Ps 14:4; 1 Macc 2:18, 64; Sir 49:16; *symbolized by visible splendor:* Sir 50:5

c. Israel/Jews: Wis 18:8; Sir 24:12; 1 Macc 11:42, 51; 14:29; 15:9

d. Objects/Places: Is 10:15; Lam 1:8; 1 Macc 14:15; *symbolized by visible splendor:* Pss. Sol. 17:31[64]

2. δοξάζω and ἐνδοξάζομαι as making radiant/splendid or beautiful:

a. Individuals: Ex 34:29-30, 35[65]

b. Objects/Places: Pss. Sol. 17:31[66]

2.2.1.4. Concordance entry. A categorized and tabulated concordance entry is a more accurate depiction of the meanings of δόξα and δοξάζω and their frequency of occurrence in the LXX.

---

[63]Given its closeness to Ezek 28:22 and Ezek 38:23, it is probably God revealing his status as God/King through his wrath on the nations.

[64]Dependent on how the glory of God is taken in the same verse.

[65]No indication exists that Moses' face was splendid due to his own status of honor, power, or authority.

[66]Again, this is questionable, depending on the rest of the verse.

Table 2.1

		δόξα as Honor, Status, Power, Character				Glory as splendor or beauty (not symbolizing honor/status)
	A title for God	Given to God in ascription	Possessed by God	Manifested in signs/symbols (e.g. light/actions usually associated with salvation/redemption or judgment)	Manifested in theophany	Symbolized by splendor or radiant beauty
God δόξα κυρίου texts are represented by *	1 Sam 4:22; Ps 3:4; Is 64:10; Tob 3:16 (GII only); 12:12 (GII only); 15	Josh 7:19; 1 Sam 6:5; 1 Chron 16:28-29; 2 Chron 30:8; Ps 28:1-2, 9; 65:2; 67:35; 70:8; 71:19; 95:3, 7, 8; 113:9; Is 42:12; 66:19; Jer 13:16; Dan 3:43, 52; 4:34 (TH); Mal 1:6; 2:2; 1 Esd 9:8; 1 Macc 14:29; Sir 47:8; 51:17; Bar 2:17, 18; Pss. Sol. 17:6; 4 Macc 1:12; 18:24	1 Chron 16:27; 29:12; Ps 23:7-10; 28:3; 78:9; 103:31*; 105:20; 137:5*; 144:11, 12; Prov 25:2; Is 24:14, 15*; 40:26; 42:8; 43:7; 45:24; 48:11; 59:19; 63:12, 14, 15; Jer 23:9; Dan 3:53 (TH); Hab 2:14*; Mic 5:3; Zech 2:12; Sir 42:16, 17; 1 Esd 4:59; 5:58; 2 Macc 2:9, 14; Pss. Sol. 5:19*; 11:8; 3 Macc 2:9, 14, 16	Ex 15:7, 11; 16:7*; Num 14:21*, 22; 1 Chron 16:24; Ps 16:15; 18:1; 56:6, 12; 62:3; 84:10; 96:6; 101:16, 17; 107:6; 112:4; 144:5; Is 2:10, 19, 21; 4:2; 26:10; 30: 27, 30; 35:2*; 40:5*; 58:8*; 60:1* 2; 66:18, 19; Ezek 39:21; Sir 17:13; Tob 13:16; Bar 4:24, 37; 5:1, 2, 7, 9 — Sir 17:31 [?]	Ex 16:10*; 24:16* 17*; 29:43; 33:18, 19, 22; 40:34, 35; Lev 9:6*; Num 12:8*; 14:10*; 16:19*; 17:7*; 20:6*; Deut 5:24; 1 Kings 8:11*; 2 Chron 2:5; 5:13, 14*; 7:1-3*; Is 4:5; 6:1, 3; 60:19; Ezek 1:28*; 3:12*; 23*; 8:4*; 9:3; 10:4* 18* 19, 22; 11:22, 23*; 43:2, 4* 5*; 44:4*; Zech 2:9; Sir 36:13; 45:3; 49:8; 2 Macc 2:8; Pss. Sol. 11:6 — Sir 17:31 [?]	

	δόξα as Honor, Status, Character, or Wealth/Possessions		Glory as splendor or beauty (not symbolizing honor/status)
	Given to or Possessed by (often symbolized by magnificent appearance or general beauty)	Symbolized by splendor or radiant beauty	
People	Abraham (Sir 44:19); Jacob (Gen 31:1, 16); Joseph (Gen 45:13); Moses (Sir 45:2); Aaron (Sir 45:20); Phinehas (Sir 45:23); sons of Aaron (Sir 50:13); Balaam (Num 24:11); Joshua (Num 27:20); the needy (1 Sam 2:8); Solomon (1 Kings 3:13; 1 Chron 29:25; 2 Chron 1:11, 12; Sir 47:20); David/David the king (1 Chron 29:28; Ps 7:6; 20:6; 29:13; 56:9; 61:8; 72:24 [?]; Sir 47:6, 11); Jehoshaphat (2 Chron 17:5; 18:1); Uzziah (2 Chron 26:18); Hezekiah (2 Chron 32:27, 33); Josiah (1 Esd 1:31); kings of Israel/Judah (Sir 49:5); the son of man (Ps 8:6); those who fear the Lord (Ps 111:3, 9; Sir 1:11, 19; 40:27); general person (Ps 83:12; 107:1; Prov 18:12; 20:3, 29; 28:12; Eccles 6:2; 10:1; Is 11:3; 40:6; Mal 1:6; Sir 1:11*; 5:13; 33:23; 1 Esd 4:17); king's daughter (Ps 44:14); the fool and stupid (Ps 48:15, 17, 18; Prov 26:8); the devout (Ps 149:5, 9); Job (Job 19:9; 29:20); Wisdom (Prov 3:16; 8:18; Wis 7:25; 8:10; 9:11; Sir 14:27 [?]; 24:16-17); the wise (Prov 3:35; Sir 4:13); king in general (Prov 14:28); the righteous (Prov 21:21; 22:4; 28:12); the humble (Prov 29:23); king of Assyria (Is 8:7); Eliakim (Is 22:[22], 23, 25); Solomon as king has glory because of wisdom (Wis 8:10); king (Is 33:17; Jer 13:18, 20); the servant (Is 52:14; 53:2); kings (Prov 14:28; Jer 13:18); Artaxerxes (Esther 1:4); Haman (Esther 6:3; 10:2); Nebuchadnezzar (Dan 2:37; 4:31, 32, 36 [OG]; Dan 4:30; 5:18 [TH]); One Like a Son of Man (Dan 7:14); king (Dan 11:20, 21, 39 [OG, TH]); Daniel (Dan 10:8 [TH]); Ezra (1 Esd 8:4); Mattathias's sons (1 Macc 2:51); one who makes idols (Wis 15:9); ancestors (Wis 18:24; Sir 44:2, 13); sinners (1 Macc 2:62; Sir 9:11); Ptolemy and Alexander as kings (1 Macc 10:58); Jonathan Maccabeus (1 Macc 10:60, 64; 11:6, 42); Simon Maccabeus (1 Macc 14:4, 5, 10, 21, 35, 39; 15:9, 32, 36); Alcimus (ancestral glory: 2 Macc 14:7); "Jeremias" (2 Macc 15:13; gray hair); Jews (Sir 45:26); judges (Sir 10:5); lenders (Sir 29:6); scribes (Sir 8:14); the king, the son of David [Pss. Sol. 17:31]; general persons [Pss. Sol. 1:4]; Jews [3 Macc 7:21; 4 Macc 5:18]) (Solomon [Pss. Sol. 2:31];		

	δοξάζω and ἐνδοξάζομαι as giving, showing/demonstrating, or receiving honor, an exalted status, or wealth/possessions	Symbolized by having visible splendor or theophany	δοξάζω and ἐνδοξάζομαι as having/reflecting splendor or "shining" (not symbolizing honor/status)
Nations	Ephraim (Hos 9:11; flower/Ephraim: Is 28:1, 4); Moab (Is 16:14; Jer 31:18); Kedar (Is 21:16); Babylon (Is 13:19 [ἔνδοξος]; 14:11); Lebanon (Is 35:2; 60:13); Assyria (Is 8:7; 10:12, 16); Egypt (Is 20:5); nations in general (Is 66:12) Israel: 1 Sam 4:22 [?]; Is 3:8; 10: 3; 12:2; 17:3-4; 30:18; 43:7; 46:13 [δόξασομαι]; 60:21; 61:3; 62:2 [?]; Jer 2:11*; 13:11; Hos 4:7; Mic 1:15; Hab 2:16; Bar 4:3 (could also be title for God); 5:4, 6		Sor/Tyre (Ezek 27:7, 10; beauty) Israel: Lam 2:1 (δόξασμα)
Objects and Places	Garments (Ex 28:2, 40; 33:5; Is 3:18, 20; 61:3; 1 Macc 14:9; Sir 6:29, 31; 27:8; 45:7; 50:11; Pss. Sol. 2:21; 11:7); unicorn (Num 23:22; 24:8; see MGB version); temple (1 Chron 22:5; Hag 2:3, 7, 9; 2 Macc 5:16, 20; Sir 49:12); building operations (1 Esd 6:9); Jerusalem (Is 52:1; 66:11); vessels (1 Macc 2:9); sabbath day (2 Macc 6:11; 15:2; Sir 11:4); idol (Hos 10:5); flower/Ephraim (Is 28:1, 4; see above); kingdom (Dan 11:20, 21 [TH]); human affairs (3 Macc 6:28) **Throne of Glory:** 1 Sam 2:8; Prov 11:16; Is 22:23; Jer 14:21; 17:12; Sir 7:4; 47:11; Wis 9:10 [?]; Pss. Sol. 2:19 **Crown of Glory:** Ps 8:5; Is 22:18 (esp. with Is 22:19); Jer 13:18; Lam 2:15; Sir 47:6 (διάδημα)	City (Prov 18:11); sanctuary (Pss. Sol. 2:5)	Sun (Sir 43:1); stars (Sir 43:9); rainbows (Sir 43:12); clouds (Sir 50:7); Wisdom's branches and flowers (Sir 24:16, 17)

	δοξάζω and ἐνδοξάζομαι as giving, showing/demonstrating, or receiving honor, an exalted status, or wealth/possessions	Symbolized by having visible splendor or theophany	δοξάζω and ἐνδοξάζομαι as having/reflecting splendor or "shining" (not symbolizing honor/status)
God	Ex 14:4, 17, 18 (each is ἐνδοξάζομαι); 15:1, 2, 6, 11, 21; Lev 10:3; Judg 9:9 (B); 1 Sam 2:30; Ps 21:24; 49:15; 50:23; 85:9, 12; 86:3; 88:8 (ἐνδοξάζομαι); Is 5:16; 24:23 (reign); 25:1; 33:10; 42:10; 43:23; 44:23; 49:3; 66:5; Ezek 28:22 (ἐνδοξάζομαι); 38:23 (ἐνδοξάζομαι); 39:13; Dan 3:26, 51, 56; 5:23; Dan 3:55 (OG); Dan 4:34/37 (TH); 5:23; Hag 1:8 (ἐνδοξάζομαι); Mal 1:11; Jer 3:20; 36:5; 43:28, 30; Pss. Sol. 10:7; 17:5, 30	Ezek 28:22; 38:23; 39:13 (all possible but more likely "show honor")	
People	Moses (Ex 33:16: ἐνδοξάζομαι; Sir 45:3); Joseph (Deut 33:16); Abimelech (olive tree; Judg 9:9 [A]); angel of the Lord (Judg 13:17); Eli's sons (1 Sam 2:29, 30); Saul (1 Sam 15:30); David (2 Sam 6:20, 22; 1 Chron 17:18; Sir 47:6); Elijah and those raised by Elijah (Sir 48:4, 6); Naas, father of Hannon (2 Sam 10:3; 2 Chron 19:3); Amaziah (2 Kings 14:10; ἐνδοξάζομαι); those who fear the Lord (Ps 14:4); enemies of the Lord in times of trouble (Ps 90:15); the one who convicts (Prov 13:18); elders (Lam 5:12); Haman (Esther 6:6, 7, 9, 11; 10:3); father (Mal 1:6); Mordecai (Esther 3:1); Wisdom's "noble birth" (Wis 8:3); Esdras's family (1 Esd 8:25); Judith (Judith 12:13); oneself over a father (Sir 3:10); oneself (Sir 10:26, 27, 28, 29); poor/rich (Sir 10:30, 31); father (Sir 3:2; 7:27); mother (Sir 3:4); priest (Sir 7:31); sinner (Sir 10:23); nobleman, judge, and ruler (Sir 10:24); general persons (Sir 25:5); pharmacists (Sir 38:6; ἐνδοξάζομαι); Shem and Seth (Sir 49:16); Israel's ancestors (Sir 44:7); Joshua (Sir 46:2); buried judges (Sir 46:12); Mattathias and his sons (1 Macc 2:18; 2:64); Seron, commander of Syrian army (1 Macc 3:14); Judas and his brothers (1 Macc 10:65, 88); Simon (1 Macc 14:39); king of Phoenicia (2 Macc 4:24); Daniel (4 Macc 18:13)	Simon high priest (Sir 50:5)	Moses' face (Ex 34:29-30, 35)
Israel and Jews	Ex 33:16 (ἐνδοξάζομαι); Deut 26:19 (δοξαστός); Is 4:2; 43:4; 45:25 (ἐνδοξάζομαι); 49:5; 52:13; 55:5; 1 Esd 8:64; 9:52; Sir 24:12; 1 Macc 11:42, 51; 14:29; 15:9; Wis 18:8; 19:22		
Objects and Places	Axe (Is 10:15); temple (Is 60:7, 13; 1 Esd 8:64, 78; 2 Macc 3:2); holy places (1 Macc 14:15); Jerusalem (Lam 1:8; Pss. Sol. 17:31 [?]; see right)		Jerusalem (Pss. Sol. 17:31 [?]; dependent on how "glory of the Lord" is taken in same verse; see above)

2.2.2. Lexical analysis. *2.2.2.1. δόξα, δοξάζω, and God.* Understanding the meaning of δόξα in association with God is often difficult because a number of occurrences of δόξα fit equally into multiple categories, and the division of categories seems almost limitless. Δόξα seems to defy classification. Because of this fact, it is here, if anywhere, that *the categorization of the term is relative to the reader's presuppositions and the contextual ambiguities of its location in the text.*[67] Nevertheless, a number of conclusions can be drawn. I begin with the most important for our purposes here.

1. *Δόξα does not primarily mean splendor.* For God, δόξα functions as symbolic, anthropomorphic imagery just as frequently as it functions denotatively as honor or status. Glory is often used as metonymy for God's unsurpassable identity, which necessarily includes his unequaled honor, status, power, or character. When it is applied to God as a title, God is identified as the one who is unequaled in these things. When glory is something God possesses, it can be either a metonym for any of these unsurpassed characteristics, or it can refer more literally to one denotative element (e.g., God's power). Δόξα is often used figuratively as light or as a metonym for the activity of God, both of which are often associated with the salvation, redemption, or judgment of God. What does it mean for the heavens to declare the glory of God in Psalm 18:1? Carey Newman writes that "looking at creation allows one to perceive the presence of God, for the heavens declare the כבוד אל."[68] I suggest, rather, that "the heavens declare the glory of God" is itself figurative language (personification), and the "glory of God" that "the heavens" (metonymy for everything in created existence) "declare" is the unsurpassed power and artistry of the Creator God manifested in his created works.[69]

Similarly, what is intended in Psalm 107:6 when the psalmist declares ὑψώθητι ἐπὶ τοὺς οὐρανούς ὁ θεός καὶ ἐπὶ πᾶσαν τὴν γῆν ἡ δόξα σου?[70]

---

[67]In chapter three I will highlight the work of Carey Newman, whose interpretation of "the glory of God" is remarkably different from those of Berquist and Caird. I note here that it is this issue of contextual ambiguity and relativity that allows for such stark differences of interpretation.

[68]Newman 1992: 22.

[69]As Harrison (1982: 479) comments: "In nature God presents in tangible form a demonstration of His own power, beauty, and order," as can be seen "in connection with God's raising the dead (Jn. 11:40; Rom. 6:4)."

[70]This is one of many verses that associate glory and God without any reference to light imagery or theophany that Newman does not include in his study (which I will examine in

Is the reader meant to envision something like the sun's rays being cast from heaven and down onto the earth? I suggest not. In the same way that God's "mercy is above the heavens" and God's "truth is unto the clouds" in Psalm 107:5, God's glory (i.e., God's redemption) is recognized among the nations. This is made clear by the verses that follow, beginning with Psalm 107:7: "That your loved ones might be rescued; save by your right hand and listen to me." Likewise, in Isaiah 2:7, 10, 21 people do not hide in rocks to escape the radiant splendor of God, nor even the more general presence of the Lord, but the "power of his strength" manifested when he "rises to break the earth into pieces" (i.e., when he judges and redeems).

When God's glory is personified as dwelling in the temple, it symbolizes the visible presence of the one who is glory—the one who is unequaled, unsurpassed, and unrivaled in every respect; *that* God is the God who is present. Or, similarly, when God's glory is symbolized in terms of phenomenal imagery (e.g., fire), the imagery is not symbolizing itself. In Deuteronomy 5:24, for example, the fire symbolizes the unsurpassed power and greatness of God—concepts identified as δόξα by the LXX translators. I will mention this theophanic depiction of God's glory more below.

I have not emphasized the role metaphor plays here because the glory of God, when used figuratively, is used as metonymy more than metaphor. The latter does occur on occasion, however. One example is Isaiah 60:1: φωτίζου φωτίζου Ιερουσαλημ ἥκει γάρ σου τὸ φῶς καὶ ἡ δόξα κυρίου ἐπὶ σὲ ἀνατέταλκεν. The glory of the Lord is aligned with light imagery, which then raises the question: Is the light visible in real time and space? As in most poetic language, the light is a poetic symbol; we are not meant to think that Jerusalem is literally bathed in light. Rather, the light is a symbol for the glory of God—*the redemption of God that has established Jerusalem and her people in exaltation*: a glorified (symbolized in splendor) city and people. Though assumed at the start of the chapter in the poetic language, it becomes obvious by Isaiah 60:14:

> The sons of those who afflicted you shall come bending low to you, and all
> who despised you shall bow down at your feet; they shall call you the City

---

chapter three). Others include: Josh 7:19; 1 Chron 29:12; 2 Chron 30:8; Ps 70:8; 78:9; 95:7, 8; 144:5; Is 42:12; 45:24; 66:19; Jer 13:16; Dan 3:43, 52, 53; 4:34 (TH); Zech 2:12; Mal 1:6; 2:2; 1 Esd 4:59; 5:58; 9:8; 1 Macc 14:29; 2 Macc 2:9, 14; 4 Macc 1:12; 18:24; Sir 36:13; 47:8; 51:17; Bar 2:17, 18; 4:37; 5:2; Pss. Sol. 17:6; Tob 12:12.

of the LORD, the Zion of the Holy One of Israel. Whereas you have been forsaken and hated, with no one passing through, I will make you majestic forever, a joy from age to age. You shall suck the milk of nations; you shall nurse at the breast of kings; and you shall know that I, the LORD, am your Savior and your Redeemer, the Mighty One of Jacob. (ESV)

Before addressing the second conclusion, a cautionary word on the interpretation of light imagery is in order. Light imagery, when used symbolically such as it is above and elsewhere throughout the Old Testament, should not be assumed to exist in time and space. Light is one of the most common metaphors used in the Bible, and one need only turn to the Gospel of John to realize that it does not always imply a material substance that exists concretely in reality.[71] As Prickett helpfully notes, "The metaphor that Christ is the 'light of the world' changes not merely the way in which we are to understand Christ, but also the way we understand *light*. The condition is not unexpected: this language of signs is essentially that of 'poetry.'"[72] Light imagery, in the Old Testament as much as in the New Testament, is symbolic; it represents something beyond itself, a point that will become more evident and important as we turn briefly to apocalyptic writings.

These serve as a few examples of how δόξα, when associated with God, is used as both literal and figurative language, and that, when used as metonymy, metaphor, or general symbolic imagery, the images used often symbolize the unsurpassed power, character, or redemption of God. When we read δόξα in association with God in the LXX, we should not in the first instance translate it as "splendor." And when it does clearly indicate splendor, the reader should recognize it as symbolic language ultimately pointing to the unsurpassed God.

2. *God's glory is commonly associated with his status or his identity as king.* Harrison writes that "to recognize God's glory is thus to acknowledge Him as the supreme moral ruler."[73] A few examples will suffice here:

---

[71]See John 1:4, 5, 7, 8, 9; 3:19, 20, 21; 5:35; 8:12; 9:5; 11:9, 10; 12:35, 36, 46.

[72]Prickett 1986: 217; emphasis original. Chandler (2007: 126) notes that Derrida too highlighted this point: "Derrida shows how philosophers have traditionally referred to the mind and the intellect in terms of tropes based on the presence or absence of light (Derrida 1974); everyday language is rich in examples of the association of thinking with visual metaphors (bright, brilliant, dull, enlightening, illuminating, vision, clarity, reflection, etc.)."

[73]Harrison 1982: 478.

- The Chronicler makes this obvious in 1 Chronicles 16:23-31. In 1 Chronicles 16:27 he writes: δόξα καὶ ἔπαινος κατὰ πρόσωπον αὐτοῦ ἰσχὺς καὶ καύχημα ἐν τόπῳ αὐτοῦ. The glory that God possesses and is declared among the nations is the glory of the King in 1 Chronicles 16:31: εὐφρανθήτω ὁ οὐρανός καὶ ἀγαλλιάσθω ἡ γῆ καὶ εἰπάτωσαν ἐν τοῖς ἔθνεσιν κύριος βασιλεύων.[74]

- Psalm 23:7-10: ἄρατε πύλας οἱ ἄρχοντες ὑμῶν καὶ ἐπάρθητε πύλαι αἰώνιοι καὶ εἰσελεύσεται ὁ βασιλεὺς τῆς δόξης τίς ἐστιν οὗτος ὁ βασιλεὺς τῆς δόξης κύριος κραταιὸς καὶ δυνατός κύριος δυνατὸς ἐν πολέμῳ ἄρατε πύλας οἱ ἄρχοντες ὑμῶν καὶ ἐπάρθητε πύλαι αἰώνιοι καὶ εἰσελεύσεται ὁ βασιλεὺς τῆς δόξης τίς ἐστιν οὗτος ὁ βασιλεὺς τῆς δόξης κύριος τῶν δυνάμεων αὐτός ἐστιν ὁ βασιλεὺς τῆς δόξης (see also Ps 95:1-13).[75]

- Psalm 144:1: ὑψώσω σε ὁ θεός μου ὁ βασιλεύς μου,[76] followed by Psalm 144:10-13: ἐξομολογησάσθωσάν σοι κύριε πάντα τὰ ἔργα σου καὶ οἱ ὅσιοί σου εὐλογησάτωσάν σε δόξαν τῆς βασιλείας σου ἐροῦσιν καὶ τὴν δυναστείαν σου λαλήσουσιν τοῦ γνωρίσαι τοῖς υἱοῖς τῶν ἀνθρώπων τὴν δυναστείαν σου καὶ τὴν δόξαν τῆς μεγαλοπρεπείας τῆς βασιλείας σου ἡ βασιλεία σου βασιλεία πάντων τῶν αἰώνων καὶ ἡ δεσποτεία σου ἐν πάσῃ γενεᾷ καὶ γενεᾷ.[77]

- God has a throne of glory in Jeremiah 14:21: κόπασον διὰ τὸ ὄνομά σου μὴ ἀπολέσῃς θρόνον δόξης σου μνήσθητι μὴ διασκεδάσῃς τὴν διαθήκην σου τὴν μεθ᾽ ἡμῶν.[78]

---

[74]"Glory and commendation are before him, strength and boasting in his place" (NETS). "Let the sky be glad and the earth rejoice, and let them say among the nations that the Lord is king" (NETS).

[75]"Raise the gates, O rulers of yours! And be raised up, O perpetual gates! And the King of glory shall enter. Who is this King of glory? The Lord, strong and powerful, the Lord, powerful in battle. Raise the gates, O rulers of yours! And be raised up, O perpetual gates! And the King of glory shall enter. Who is this King of glory? The Lord of hosts, he is the King of glory" (NETS).

[76]"I will exalt you, my God, my King" (NETS).

[77]"Let all your works acknowledge you, O Lord, and let all your devout bless you. Your kingdom's glory they shall relate, and of your dominance they shall speak, to make known to the sons of men your dominance and the glory of the magnificence of your kingdom. Your kingdom is a kingdom of all the ages, and your dominion is in every generation and generation" (NETS).

[78]"Stop for your name's sake; do not destroy the throne of your glory; remember, do not scatter your covenant with us" (NETS).

- Psalms of Solomon 5:19: εὐλογημένη ἡ δόξα κυρίου ὅτι αὐτὸς βασιλεὺς ἡμῶν.[79]

3. *The "glory of the Lord"*[80] *does not always refer to God's theophanic manifestation.* Or, put another way, when כבוד יהוה/δόξα κυρίου appears in the Old Testament, the reader should not assume that it refers to the manifest presence of God in visible splendor.[81] As William Holladay notes on כבוד יהוה, it is a "fixed phrase" for the "power, authority, honor of God, but also connected with manifestations of light."[82] On occasion it is associated with God's manifestation in visible splendor, particularly in Ezekiel,[83] but δόξα κυρίου often makes more sense as metonymy for God's unsurpassed honor/power or for God's works of creation/redemption evident in the cosmos. This is the case even when the glory of the Lord is "seen" (Is 35:2) or is presented with light imagery (Is 58:8; 60:1). Other examples include Exodus 16:7; Numbers 14:21-22; Psalms 103:31; 137:5; Habakkuk 2:14.

4. *When the glory of God does indicate the visible, manifest presence of God, that presence must be recognized as only part of the equation.*[84] The δόξα κυρίου does connote the presence of God, but not *just* "God." By the time δόξα is used in Ezekiel and the Priestly traditions, its meaning has expanded from honor or status to include beauty, light, and God's theophanic presence. Nevertheless, one should not therefore assume that the foundational meaning has disappeared. As elsewhere where δόξα is

---

[79]"Blessed is the glory of the Lord, for he is our king" (NETS). Pss. Sol. 5:19 is the one יהוה כבוד/δόξα κυρίου text Newman does not include in his study.

[80]Represented by an asterisk in the concordance above.

[81]This will be a point of contention when I turn to Carey Newman's work in the next chapter.

[82]Holladay 1971: 151.

[83]Even in Ezekiel, however, the reader's interpretation of the "glory of the Lord" should not be limited to a visible splendor but should recognize it as imagery symbolic of God's unsurpassed honor and greatness. Caird (1944: 97), too, emphasizes this point. He writes on the vision in Ezek 1: "[Ezekiel] may also have regarded his vision as the symbol of the divine activity, which outside his visions he calls the holiness or the glory of God. Such a conception would be made easier by the parallel notion of human glory. If a man's worth or greatness can be symbolized by the outward show of his magnificence, then the worth or greatness of God, which in history is manifested in His righteous government and in His faithfulness to the covenant, might in a vision be symbolized by a brightness round about Him. The honour of God, the glory of the vision, was enthroned in the temple."

[84]This is what I will identity as perhaps the greatest weakness of Newman's important work on יהוה כבוד as a technical term signifying "the visible and mobile presence of Yahweh": Newman 1992: 24, 20-24.

light imagery symbolizing God's unsurpassed greatness, so also when that light imagery expresses the presence of God: *the visible glory of the God who is present is the visible manifestation of his unsurpassed greatness, his absolute power, his status as King and his dominion over creation.*[85] It is *this* God that is present—the God of glory. Not the God of presence, but the God of glory, the King of glory—He Who Is Unsurpassed In Every Way. He is the one who is present and who dwells in the temple; he is the one on whom Moses and Aaron and the people were allowed to gaze. His glory signifies that the God who is present is the God who rules over Israel, the nations, and over creation. What other idol/god has such power? God's glory in visible, phenomenal imagery identifies him as the God who creates, who rules, who judges, who redeems, and who, as such, exists as Israel's God dwelling in the temple on his royal throne—his throne of glory.

5. Related theologically to analysis number four above, it is important to note that, while it is possible to distinguish between the glory of God as that which represents God's ontological existence,[86] that is, the presence of God or who the God is who is present, and that which represents God's functional existence, that is, what God does, such metaphysical categories tend to obscure more than they clarify. This is the case for two reasons. The first is that, theologically, the "who" and the "what" of God are indivisible; his ontological and functional existence are mutually coalescent and thus inseparable.[87] Put another way, according to the presentation of the identity of God by the translators of the LXX, the identity of God is irreducible to his presence. God is presented as a God who reigns *because*

---

[85] "Δόξα seems therefore to connote to the translators the external manifestation of male and female power and position whether it appears in money or clothes or appearance": Forster 1930: 314; see also Kittel 1964: 243.

[86] Here and throughout this book I do not use *ontology* (or *ontological*) in its classic definition of referring to the existence of a thing, i.e., God; see Craig 1998. I take it for granted that the writers of the Hebrew Scriptures assumed God's existence. Rather, I use the term here to refer to the essence or characterization of that thing that exists: who God is in his existence. God exists and is present, but what is the essence or identity of that God that exists and is present, and how is that identity distinct from his function/activity?

[87] The logical and ontological relationship between God's being and act, particularly as it is presented in Karl Barth's *Church Dogmatics* but also beyond Barth's work, is taken up by George Hunsinger and Bruce McCormack. McCormack argues that the possibility of understanding an "ontological priority" of God's essence over his actions in relation to humanity (beginning in but not limited to the act of election), according to Barth and in McCormack's own perspective, is impossible (2010: 207). See Hunsinger 2008 and McCormack 2010.

he is omnipotent and, as an omnipotent God who ranks above all idols and other gods, he *therefore* reigns as king. As the Chronicler says in 1 Chronicles 16:31: εὐφρανθήτω ὁ οὐρανός καὶ ἀγαλλιάσθω ἡ γῆ καὶ εἰπάτωσαν ἐν τοῖς ἔθνεσιν κύριος βασιλεύων. The Lord reigns because of who he is.

In "God Crucified,"[88] Richard Bauckham argues something similar, albeit under the auspices of different terms and with further regard to the identity of Jesus. Bauckham argues that Jews of the Second Temple period identified the God of Israel by *who* God is (his activities, character, etc.) rather than by *what* God is (metaphysical attributes, e.g., immutability).[89] Bauckham writes,

> That God is eternal, for example—a claim essential to all Jewish thinking about God—is not so much a statement about what divine nature is, more an element in the unique divine identity, along with claims that God alone created all things and rules all things, that God is gracious and merciful and just, that God brought Israel out of Egypt and made Israel his own people and gave Israel his law at Sinai and so on. If we wish to know in what Second Temple Judaism considered the uniqueness of the one God to consist, what distinguished God as unique from all other reality, including beings worshipped as gods by Gentiles, we must look not for a definition of divine nature but for ways of characterizing the unique divine identity.[90]

This is to say that the "divine identity" of God, as understood by Second Temple Jews, was *who* God is: that is, *both* who he is in his person (his character/personality) *and* what he does as that person. According to Bauckham, God's unique identity, as it is known in all reality, is that "he is Creator of all things and sovereign Ruler of all things."[91]

The second reason that attempting to distinguish between ontological and functional categories for the identity of God typically leads to obfuscation rather than elucidation is that the various uses of δόξα and its cognates fall more naturally into semantic categories rather than theological categories. As indicated in the concordance entries and analysis above, the various uses

---

[88]See Bauckham's 2008 *Jesus and the God of Israel* (1-59).
[89]Bauckham 2008: 7.
[90]Bauckham 2008: 7.
[91]Bauckham 2008: 8.

of δόξα in relationship to God are either denotative or connotative, and these categories are not synonymous with those of ontology and function. God's visible splendor is not synonymous with an ontological description of God. His visible splendor is *figurative* imagery that *connotes* his power or character or status. Put another way, the visible splendor of God does not connote the presence of God but the presence of a particular God with particular attributes and who acts in the world in particular ways (aka the Ruler rules). Whether functioning literally or symbolically, the glory of God identifies who God is, and who God is includes both his person (ontology) and his activity (function).

    2.2.2.2. δόξα, δοξάζω, and humanity. 1. Most notable here is the unmistakable fact that the answer to Humpty-Dumpty's question regarding which meaning is *master* is that, at least in the LXX and when used in association with humanity, *glory* as splendor or radiance is certainly *not* master. Rather, glory (and its cognates) *primarily bears its denotative meaning of status/honor associated with power, authority, character, or riches.* Only once is there clear indication that a *human* possesses glory as splendor or is glorified such that they are made to shine: Moses is glorified and thus reflects the visible glory of God on his face in Exodus 34:29-30, 35. The only other person possibly to be glorified in this way is Simon in Sirach 50:5-11: on leaving the inner sanctuary, Simon is said to be "glorified" (ἐδοξάσθη) like the morning star, full moon, shining sun, rainbow on clouds of glory, roses, lilies, green shoots, fire and incense, jeweled vessels, and olive and cypress trees, before putting on his "robe of glory" or "glorious robe" (στολὴν δόξης). Even here, however, glory as splendor is contestable. Caird writes:

> That this wealth of imagery should be used in a single description is a further indication that the glory of sun, moon, stars, and rainbow was akin to the glory of the flowers and trees, to the glory of gold, of jewels, and of the priestly robe; that all could be symbols of the same honour, and that the mind of a Hebrew could move freely from one image to another.[92]

Additionally, Israel possibly has glory as splendor in Lamentations 2:1 (though this is ambiguous), and Tyre has glory in Ezekiel 27:7, 10

---

[92]Caird 1944: 146.

(though here it is clearly beauty rather than splendor). *In nearly every instance of δόξα and δοξάζω in association with humanity in the LXX, it is a reference to the exalted status or honor the person possesses or in which they exist rather than a visible splendor after the likeness of God's theophanic splendor.*[93]

2. More precisely, *humanity's glory and glorification as exalted status or possessed honor is often associated with the person's status as king, ruler, or person of authority.* A selection of obvious examples includes:

δόξα:

- Joseph: ἀπαγγείλατε οὖν τῷ πατρί μου πᾶσαν τὴν δόξαν μου τὴν ἐν Αἰγύπτῳ (Gen 45:13)[94]

- David: κύριος ἀφεῖλεν τὰς ἁμαρτίας αὐτοῦ καὶ ἀνύψωσεν εἰς αἰῶνα τὸ κέρας αὐτοῦ καὶ ἔδωκεν αὐτῷ διαθήκην βασιλέων καὶ θρόνον δόξης ἐν τῷ Ισραηλ (Sir 47:11; see also Ps 20:6; Sir 47:6)[95]

- Solomon: καὶ ἐμεγάλυνεν κύριος τὸν Σαλωμων ἐπάνωθεν ἐναντίον παντὸς Ισραηλ καὶ ἔδωκεν αὐτῷ δόξαν βασιλέως ὃ οὐκ ἐγένετο ἐπὶ παντὸς βασιλέως ἔμπροσθεν αὐτοῦ (1 Chron 29:25; see also 1 Kings 3:13; 2 Chron 1:11, 12; Wis 8:10)[96]

- Son of man: ἠλάττωσας αὐτὸν βραχύ τι παρ' ἀγγέλους δόξῃ καὶ τιμῇ ἐστεφάνωσας αὐτόν (Ps 8:6)[97]

- Haman: καὶ ὑπέδειξεν αὐτοῖς τὸν πλοῦτον αὐτοῦ καὶ τὴν δόξαν ἣν ὁ βασιλεὺς αὐτῷ περιέθηκεν καὶ ὡς ἐποίησεν αὐτὸν πρωτεύειν καὶ ἡγεῖσθαι τῆς βασιλείας (Esther 5:11)[98]

---

[93]Harrison (1982: 478) writes that "when glory was used of persons, it reflected noteworthy elements such as dignity of character, position (cf. Gen. 45:13), wealth (Gen. 31:1; Ps. 49:16 [MT 17]), or power. Thus the king's glory consisted in the multitude of his people (Prov. 14:28), but by contrast the glory and pomp of the rebellious people would receive its reward by being banished to Sheol (Isa. 5:14)."

[94]"So report to my father all my glory in Egypt" (NETS).

[95]"The Lord took away his sins, and he exalted his horn forever, and he gave him a covenant of kings and a throne of glory in Israel" (NETS).

[96]"And the Lord magnified Salomon over and above before all Israel and gave him royal majesty the like of which had never happened to any king before him" (NETS).

[97]"You diminished him a little in comparison with angels; with glory and honor you crowned him" (NETS).

[98]"And he announced to them his riches and the glory that the king had bestowed on him and how he had made him to be first and to be leader of the kingdom" (NETS).

- Nebuchadnezzar: σύ βασιλεῦ βασιλεὺς βασιλέων καὶ σοὶ ὁ κύριος τοῦ οὐρανοῦ τὴν ἀρχὴν καὶ τὴν βασιλείαν καὶ τὴν ἰσχὺν καὶ τὴν τιμὴν καὶ τὴν δόξαν ἔδωκεν (Dan 2:37)[99]

- One Like a Son of Man: καὶ ἐδόθη αὐτῷ ἐξουσία καὶ πάντα τὰ ἔθνη τῆς γῆς κατὰ γένη καὶ πᾶσα δόξα αὐτῷ λατρεύουσα καὶ ἡ ἐξουσία αὐτοῦ ἐξουσία αἰώνιος ἥτις οὐ μὴ ἀρθῇ καὶ ἡ βασιλεία αὐτοῦ ἥτις οὐ μὴ φθαρῇ (Dan 7:14)[100]

- Other clear examples include Numbers 27:20;[101] 1 Samuel 2:8; 2 Chronicles 17:5; 18:1; Proverbs 14:28; Isaiah 8:7; 13:19; 14:11; 16:14; 21:16; 22:22, 23, 25; 33:17; 35:2; Jeremiah 13:18, 20; 31:18; Esther 1:4; 6:3; 10:2; Daniel 4:30; 11:20, 21, 39 (OG, TH); Dan 5:18 (TH; see Dan 5:20 [TH]); Daniel 4:31, 32, 36; 12:13; Hosea 9:11; Malachi 1:6; 1 Maccabees 10:64; 14:4, 5, 10, 21, 35, 39; 15:9, 32, 36; Sirach 49:5

δοξάζω:

- Daniel and other wise men: καὶ ἐν παντὶ λόγῳ καὶ συνέσει καὶ παιδείᾳ ὅσα ἐζήτησε παρ᾽ αὐτῶν ὁ βασιλεύς κατέλαβεν αὐτοὺς σοφωτέρους δεκαπλασίως ὑπὲρ τοὺς σοφιστὰς καὶ τοὺς φιλοσόφους τοὺς ἐν πάσῃ τῇ βασιλείᾳ αὐτοῦ καὶ ἐδόξασεν αὐτοὺς ὁ βασιλεὺς καὶ κατέστησεν αὐτοὺς ἄρχοντας καὶ ἀνέδειξεν αὐτοὺς σοφοὺς παρὰ πάντας τοὺς αὐτοῦ ἐν πράγμασιν ἐν πάσῃ τῇ γῇ αὐτοῦ καὶ ἐν τῇ βασιλείᾳ αὐτοῦ (Dan 1:20)[102]

- Haman: μετὰ δὲ ταῦτα ἐδόξασεν ὁ βασιλεὺς Ἀρταξέρξης Αμαν Αμαδάθου Βουγαῖον καὶ ὕψωσεν αὐτόν καὶ ἐπρωτοβάθρει πάντων τῶν φίλων αὐτοῦ (Esther 3:1)[103]

---

[99]"You, O king, are king of kings, and to you the Lord of heaven has given the kingdom and power and honor and glory" (NETS).

[100]"And royal authority was given to him, and all the nations of the earth according to posterity, and all honor was serving him. And his authority is an everlasting authority, which shall never be removed—and his kingship, which will never perish" (NETS).

[101]On Num 27:20, Harrison (1982: 479) notes that "divine appointment to a position of leadership and responsibility bestows the glory of authority."

[102]"And in every topic and understanding and education, which the king inquired of them, he took them to be ten times wiser, surpassing the savants and scholars that were in the whole kingdom. And the king glorified them and appointed them in affairs in his whole kingdom" (NETS).

[103]"After these things King Artaxerxes honored Haman son of Hamadathos, a Bougean, and exalted him and set him above all his Friends" (NETS).

- Jonathan Maccabeus: καὶ ἐδόξασεν αὐτὸν ὁ βασιλεὺς καὶ ἔγραψεν αὐτὸν τῶν πρώτων φίλων καὶ ἔθετο αὐτὸν στρατηγὸν καὶ μεριδάρχην (1 Macc 10:65)[104]

- Israel: ἔθνη ἃ οὐκ ᾔδεισάν σε ἐπικαλέσονταί σε καὶ λαοί οἳ οὐκ ἐπίστανταί σε ἐπὶ σὲ καταφεύξονται ἕνεκεν τοῦ θεοῦ σου τοῦ ἁγίου Ισραηλ ὅτι ἐδόξασέν σε (Is 55:5)[105]

- Father: ὁ γὰρ κύριος ἐδόξασεν πατέρα ἐπὶ τέκνοις (Sir 3:2)[106]

Two points of significance are notable here. First, in each of the examples for δοξάζω above, the aorist active indicative third-person singular form is used—the same form used in Romans 8:30 for God's glorification of humanity. Second, in nearly every instance of humanity's glorification in the LXX (the exceptions being Ex 34:29-30, 35; Sir 50:5), δοξάζω refers primarily to a status or position of honor, authority, or rule and *not* to being radiant or brought into the presence of God. I will return to and develop both points in chapter three.

3. The topic of human glorification as transformation will be taken up in chapter four in discussion of believers' union and participation with Christ. It is important to note here the clear distinction between what we have seen in this chapter and traditional understandings of human glorification. Traditionally, glorification is understood as synonymous with sanctification, where a person is made holy or morally righteous or pure, as God is, often though not always as a result of being in God's presence. It is a process of ontological transformation from being a person with less Godlikeness to a person with greater Godlikeness. However, *at least in the LXX, zero indication exists to suggest that a person's glorification is ever about transformation of one's sanctity. In being glorified, humanity is never made "like God," other than the fact that humans are honored or exalted to a status of power or rule.* Their glorification neither makes them more pure or holy, nor does it transform their bodies into bodies of visible splendor because of God's theophanic

---

[104]"And the king honored him and listed him among his First Friends and made him general and provincial governor" (NETS).

[105]"Nations that did not know you shall call upon you, and peoples that do not understand you shall flee to you for refuge, for the sake of your God, the Holy One of Israel, because he has glorified you" (NETS).

[106]"For the Lord has glorified father over children" (NETS).

presence. Undoubtedly, Moses' face reflected the splendor of God, but in no way does that imply that Moses was sanctified or that the glorification of God's people is either eschatological sanctification or physical transformation into radiant beings. If this were the case, then believers should expect no more than radiant faces, since even Moses experienced only a radiant face. What changes, rather, is their status or the honor associated with their status.

I make these statements only in regard to the use of glory and glorification language for humans in the LXX. In the LXX, there is no tangible difference between the ontological identity of a person and that person's glory; it simply is not a focus of the Hebrew/Greek narratives. Undoubtedly, this is not the case in apocalyptic Jewish literature of the Second Temple period, particularly in visions of throne ascents where a stronger emphasis is placed on the ontology of the heavenly mediators or human worshipers. Even there, however, the imagery of glory and ontological transformation should be read with an abiding awareness of the function of symbolism, on which see below. When we turn to Paul's understanding of human glorification,[107] I will address this issue in terms of union and participation with Christ, what I consider the only theologically sound way of understanding any distinction between believers' ontology and function, particularly with regard to their possession of or participation in Christ's glory.

2.2.2.3. Crowns and thrones of glory. Before turning our attention to the use of δόξα and δοξάζω in Jewish apocalyptic literature, a brief word on the metaphoric thrones and crowns of glory is necessary. On several occasions δόξα modifies θρόνος and στέφανος, and on one occasion διάδημα.[108] And, similar to glory language elsewhere, these metaphors are also commonly held captive by the assumption that glory language generally implies radiance. But is the reader expected to envision a crown on a figure's head bathing him in light, or a throne emanating what looks like sun rays? Because of the range of meaning that δόξα can have, including radiant light, this certainly is possible. But it is also possible that it means beauty, *without* implying *radiant* beauty. Or that δόξα exists in

---

[107]See §§3.1; 3.3; 6.2; 6.3.
[108]See the table above.

its denotative form, meaning honor or admiration associated with a status of exaltation and authority.

Which option is best is dependent on the literary context, its syntagmatic relation.[109] It may be that a throne of glory is primarily intended as a throne of beauty, such as in Psalms of Solomon 2:19, where κάλλος is used as a related sign: ὠνείδισαν γὰρ ἔθνη Ιερουσαλημ ἐν καταπατήσει κατεσπάσθη τὸ κάλλος αὐτῆς ἀπὸ θρόνου δόξης. In several texts the metaphors exist within clearly royal contexts: Isaiah 22:18-19; Jeremiah 13:18; 14:21; Sirach 7:4; 47:6, 11.[110] In these contexts, the metaphors are royal metaphors, with the throne/crown by definition implying kingly functions: that is, dominion and rule. In Psalm 8, for example, when the psalmist writes that the son of man is "crowned with glory and honor," he is not implying that the son of man is given a pretty hat to wear; he is explicitly stating that the son of man is given the status and thereby function of a king.[111] That this is the intended meaning of δόξα is confirmed by the inclusion of its related signifier: τιμή. Furthermore, the syntagma δόξῃ καὶ τιμῇ ἐστεφάνωσας exists in synonymous parallelism with κατέστησας αὐτὸν ἐπὶ τὰ ἔργα τῶν χειρῶν σου, which is also parallel with πάντα ὑπέταξας ὑποκάτω τῶν ποδῶν αὐτου. The semantic structure of Psalm 8 demands that δόξα means a status of honor that is associated with dominion or rule.

In the case of Psalm 8, then, the whole metaphor "crowned with glory and honor" means that the son of man is established as a royal figure with an exalted status of rule and authority. And, as noted above, because the status of one who has glory or who is glorified has a status of rulership, the implicit message is that that person of glory *rules*. If they have a kingly status, they function as a king: they reign. If they have glory in association with their governance, in their glory they *govern* (see Is 22:18, 19).

---

[109]See Silva 1994: 143. Silva uses the example of Lk 15:25 to indicate that ὁ πρεσβύτερος means "older son" rather than "religious elder" because of its "'syntagmatic relation' with all the preceding words in the story, particularly ὁ νεώτερος in verse 11."

[110]Newman notes that the metaphors in the apocalyptic literature, particularly in Sir 47:11, are reused from the glory tradition of the monarchic period, when the tradition was associated with the Davidic promises; see Newman 1992: 119-20; also 44-52.

[111]See Gibson 1998: 141. I will return to Ps 8 in chapter three.

2.3. GLORY AND GLORIFICATION IN APOCALYPTIC LITERATURE

Continuing from the above discussion of δόξα and δοξάζω in the LXX, here my aim is to provide an abbreviated overview of how the term *glory* functions in apocalyptic texts.[112] Given the vastness of apocalyptic literature and of the discussions currently surrounding it, the following overview will seem exceptionally brief. It will seem particularly brief in comparison with the discussion of δόξα and δοξάζω in the LXX above. Because Paul's primary sources, at least those texts from which he quotes, consist in what is now the Septuagint, the following discussion of how glory functions in apocalyptic texts will receive less focused treatment. Space here allows me to highlight only three topics relevant to Jewish apocalyptic literature: the nature of apocalyptic symbolism in relation to its literary function, the occurrences of the relevant uses of *glory* and its verbal forms in Daniel (which serves as a link between the LXX and apocalyptic literature more specifically) and 1 Enoch, and the conclusions one can safely draw from those occurrences.

2.3.1. Apocalyptic symbolism and literary function. The discussion of literary semiotics above is applicable to apocalyptic literature as much as it is to the Old Testament. Any reading of apocalyptic texts must begin with the recognition of the distinction between literal and figurative language and their overlapping use throughout the texts. According to Greg Carey, "apocalyptic discourse inhabits the realms of imagination, of comparison, symbol, and vision."[113] He goes on to say that "apocalyptic discourse employs the sort of dense language typical of poetic art," where "evocative symbols, images, and allusions animate the apocalyptic visions."[114] John J. Collins, too, emphasizes the symbolic reading: "The apocalyptic literature provides a rather clear example of language that is expressive rather than referential, symbolic rather than factual."[115] Much like

---

[112]I take as apocalyptic those included in Charlesworth's 1983a collection, as well as Daniel in the LXX and portions of Jubilees and the Dead Sea Scrolls. These qualify as apocalyptic under the definition proposed in *Semeia* 14 (1979): "a genre of revelatory literature with a narrative framework, in which a revelation is mediated by an otherworldly being to a human recipient, disclosing a transcendent reality which is both temporal, insofar as it envisages eschatological salvation, and spatial insofar as it involves another supernatural world."

[113]Carey 2005: 12.

[114]Carey 2005: 13; e.g., "Astral powers fall from the sky; holy people walk golden streets; and beasts embody the features of several animals at once." This is the basis of Collins's *Apocalyptic Imagination.*

[115]Collins 1998: 17. He also notes that "biblical scholarship in general has suffered from a preoccupation with the referential aspects of language and with the factual information that can be extracted from a text. Such an attitude is especially detrimental to the study of poetic and

the poetic and prophetic texts of the Old Testament, caution should be taken against any reading of apocalyptic literature that interprets symbolic language literally.

Part of the task of interpreting apocalyptic literature and symbolism is recognizing the text's historical context. Establishing the nature of that historical context, however, is not easy, and no consensus currently exists as to what inferences can be made. Scholars acknowledge that many apocalyptic texts arise out of some form of distress or, if not distress, some problematic issue.[116] According to Anathea Portier-Young, apocalypse as a literary genre is one of "resistant counter-discourse."[117] She writes:

> Apocalypse answered the empire. The writers of the apocalypses countered hegemonic cosmologies, imperial spectacle, and false claims to power by articulating and promulgating an alternative vision of the world. They turned the symbols and values of the empire upside down and asserted truth in the place of falsehood. They also countered domination and repression with a call to resistance.[118]

Carey goes so far as to state that "although the early ancient Jewish and Christian apocalyptic texts seem to reflect diverse social contexts, *all* of them share one common feature: a radical dissatisfaction concerning some dimension of public life."[119] There is the sense that "the world has gone horribly wrong and that God must intervene to change things."[120] For this reason, David Hellholm suggested that the definition of apocalyptic proposed by *Semeia* 14 should include "intended for a group in crisis with the purpose of exhortation and/or consolation by means of divine authority."[121] At the risk of undue speculation, it is perhaps enough to recognize, cautiously, that apocalyptic texts arose out of some form of historical problem, without assigning unknown details or speculations as to the extent of such problems.

---

mythological material, which is expressive language, articulating feelings and attitudes rather than describing reality in an objective way."

[116]Collins 1998: 41.

[117]Portier-Young 2011: xxii.

[118]Portier-Young 2011: 217.

[119]Carey 2005: 15; emphasis original; also 7-8. See also Horsley 2000: 304-9.

[120]Carey 2005: 15; see also Collins 2000: 158-59.

[121]Hellholm 1986: 27; see also 27n27 for others in support of such a reading and Yarbro Collins's addendum to the definition in *Semeia* 36: 7.

Collins notes that the development of apocalyptic texts progressed through three historical phases: the postexilic era;[122] the Hellenistic period, climaxing in 168–164 BCE with the persecution under Antiocus IV Epiphanes and the Maccabean revolt; and during the rise of Christianity.[123] My focus here is on those composed in the Hellenistic era and, in particular, Daniel and 1 Enoch. While a full treatment of the use of *glory* throughout all apocalyptic literature, and even all apocalyptic literature that arose in the Hellenistic era, is ideal, space simply does not permit such an investigation here. Daniel and 1 Enoch are by no means representative of the whole genre but are acknowledged as two of the earliest and more influential pieces of apocalyptic literature. As such, they will serve as representative *examples* of the meaning of glory in apocalyptic texts perhaps influential in the first century CE.[124]

What must be remembered in reading Daniel and 1 Enoch is that the figurative language is often, though not always, symbolic of and in direct correlation with literal historical realities. And, as with figurative language elsewhere, a sign's metaphorical existence is neither precluded by nor assumed by its syntagmatic function as symbol, metaphor, or metonym in apocalyptic literature. Moreover, as with the glory of God and humanity in the LXX, the writers of apocalyptic literature make no distinction between the ontological and functional identities of the one who has glory or is glorified.

2.3.2. Daniel. 2.3.2.1. Concordance. The Daniel texts are included in the tabulated concordance of δόξα and δοξάζω in the LXX above. Given Daniel's importance for apocalyptic literature during the Hellenistic period, and potentially thereafter,[125] it is important to see clearly how δόξα and δοξάζω are used in Daniel as an apocalyptic text that is distinct from the majority of LXX literature.

---

[122]E.g., Ezek 40–48; Is 6; 24–27; 56–66; Zech 9–14.

[123]Collins 2000: 129-61.

[124]Moreover, these two texts bear similarities to Paul's letters, purely in terms of their historical situation: they are written by (and perhaps read by) religious minorities under the dominion of (and possibly oppressed by) Hellenistic rulers and culture: Horsley 2000: 306. Paul, like the authors of Daniel and 1 Enoch, wrote his letter to Rome with the purpose of exhortation and consolation. Nothing definitive can be said beyond this without making false or, at best, speculative generalizations. See Collins 2000: 147 on the function of Daniel and 1 Enoch as texts that serve to exhort and console because of a "cultural crisis precipitated by Hellenism and aggravated by the persecution of Antiochus Epiphanes."

[125]See Carey 2005: 38.

Table 2.2

	A title for God	δόξα as Honor, Status, Power, Character		Manifested in signs/symbols (e.g., light/actions usually associated with salvation/redemption or judgment	δόξα as splendor or beauty (not symbolizing honor/status) — Manifested in theophany
		Given to God in ascription	Possessed by God		Manifested in theophany
God		Dan 3:43; 3:52 (OG, TH)	Dan 3:53 [?] (OG, TH)		Dan 3:53 [?] (OG, TH)

δόξα as Honor, Status, Character, or Wealth/Possessions

	Given to or possessed by (often symbolized by magnificent appearance or general beauty)	δόξα as splendor or beauty (not symbolizing honor/status) — Symbolized by splendor or radiant beauty
People	Nebuchadnezzar: Dan 2:37; 4:31, 32, 36 (OG); Dan 4:18 (TH); Dan 4:30 (OG, TH); One Like a Son of Man: Dan 7:14 (OG); king: Dan 11:20, 21, 39 (OG, TH); Daniel: Dan 12:13 [?] (OG); Dan 10:8 (TH)	Daniel: Dan 12:13 [?] (OG)
Nations		
Objects and Places		

δοξάζω and ἐνδοξάζομαι as giving/demonstrating, or receiving honor, an exalted status, or wealth/possessions

	δοξάζω and ἐνδοξάζομαι as giving, showing/demonstrating, or receiving honor, an exalted status, or wealth/possessions	δοξάζω and ἐνδοξάζομαι as having/reflecting splendor or "shining" (not symbolizing honor/status) — Symbolized by having visible splendor or theophany
God	Dan 3:55 (OG); Dan 3:26, 51, 56 (OG, TH); 4:34, 37; 5:23 (TH)	
People	Daniel and company: Dan 1:20 (OG); Chaldeans: Dan 2:6 (OG)	
Other Gods	Maozin: Dan 11:38 [2x] (TH)	

2.3.2.2. Analysis. The most obvious conclusion is that nearly every occurrence of δόξα in Daniel unequivocally means honor, power, or an exalted
status associated with some form of rule or governance that is possessed
by God or people. There are two exceptions: God's glory in Daniel 3:53
(OG/TH) and the glory of those who will rise in Daniel 12:13. I leave Daniel
3:53 ambiguous and note the use of δόξα in Daniel 12:13c: καὶ ἀναστήσῃ
ἐπὶ τὴν δόξαν σου εἰς συντέλειαν ἡμερῶν. It is purely assumption to suggest
that the glory to which the righteous will rise is one of visible splendor.
Based on how δόξα is used elsewhere in Daniel, particularly for the One
Like a Son of Man in Daniel 7:14, the reader should not assume the glory
to which one rises is anything but an exalted status associated with rule
and dominion. The reason for the assumption stems from Daniel 12:3,
where the wise shall φανοῦσιν ὡς φωστῆρες τοῦ οὐρανου (OG); ἐκλάμψουσιν
ὡς ἡ λαμπρότης τοῦ στερεώματος (TH). Here, however, several key points
need to be kept in mind. First, the wise will shine like the stars, not like
God. Second, though not obvious here, the brilliance of the luminaries is
associated with their rule, as will be seen in the analysis of 1 Enoch below.
Third, similarly, it is kings who are spoken of as luminaries elsewhere (e.g.,
Num 24:17).[126] Fourth, the shining of the wise is directly correlated with
their exaltation, a fact made obvious by the progression of thought from
Daniel 12:1 to Daniel 12:3. Daniel 12:1 (OG) says that, after the time of
tribulation, those whose names are written in the book of life are exalted:
καὶ ἐν ἐκείνῃ τῇ ἡμέρᾳ ὑψωθήσεται πᾶς ὁ λαός ὃς ἂν εὑρεθῇ ἐγγεγραμμένος
ἐν τῷ βιβλίῳ.[127] In Daniel 12:2 (OG) the reader is told that, at the resurrection, some will rise to eternal life while others rise to shame (i.e., the
opposite of honor/glory): οἱ μὲν εἰς ζωὴν αἰώνιον οἱ δὲ εἰς ὀνειδισμόν οἱ
δὲ εἰς διασπορὰν καὶ αἰσχύνην αἰώνιον. Eternal life is contrasted with shame,
implying that the life to which the dead will rise is one of honor, a reading
validated by the resurrection exaltation in Daniel 12:1. In Daniel 12:1-2, then,

---

[126]See Wright 2003: 112.

[127]Here one should keep in mind the historical setting of Daniel. As Carey (2005: 41) notes:
"Daniel's primary *historical setting*, however, clearly relates to the Maccabean Revolt, 167–164
B.C.E. No doubt, some of the material in Daniel 1–6, and perhaps even its complete form,
may have developed quite a bit earlier. Parts of Daniel 7–12 may be older than others, but
Daniel as a whole surfaced during this period of crisis"; emphasis original. It is not difficult
to imagine the desire for the reversal of authority and power and for Jewish exaltation to
rightful rule over their own people and land.

the dead rise to a life of exaltation and honor, and in Daniel 12:3 they are said to shine like the stars in the heavens. I suggest that this "shining like the stars" is metaphorical language to describe the exalted status/life of the dead who rise to eternal life.[128] Finally, moreover, when Daniel 12:13 in the Old Greek is compared to Theodotion's Daniel 12:13, δόξα in the former aligns with κλῆρόν in the latter—what contemporary translations identify as "allotted place" (ESV, RSV), "allotted inheritance" (NIV), or "reward" (NRSV). As elsewhere in Daniel, then, δόξα in Daniel 12:13 most closely indicates one's honor or status of exaltation.

Additionally, every occurrence of δοξάζω, in both the Old Greek and Theodotion versions, means giving, showing, or receiving honor as an exalted status associated with some form of rule or governance. In reference to God, every occurrence means giving or being given praise or adoration, as it does in Daniel 11:38 (TH) with the god Moazin. In Daniel 2:6 (TH), the Chaldeans' glorification probably means their receiving of riches or another form of physical honor. This leaves only the glorification of Daniel and his friends in Daniel 1:20: καὶ ἐδόξασεν αὐτοὺς ὁ βασιλεὺς καὶ κατέστησεν αὐτοὺς ἄρχοντας καὶ ἀνέδειξεν αὐτοὺς σοφοὺς παρὰ πάντας τοὺς αὐτοῦ ἐν πράγμασιν ἐν πάσῃ τῇ γῇ αὐτοῦ καὶ ἐν τῇ βασιλείᾳ αὐτοῦ. Glorification here unequivocally means one thing: exaltation to a status of power and authority in which the person rules or governs. And if the meaning of ἐδόξασεν here is not in synonymous parallelism with the status of rule, then it remains undeniable that the two are very closely associated with one another.

The One Like a Son of Man in Daniel 7:14 clearly is given glory understood as power, authority, honor associated with a status of rule: καὶ ἐδόθη αὐτῷ ἐξουσία καὶ πάντα τὰ ἔθνη τῆς γῆς κατὰ γένη καὶ πᾶσα δόξα αὐτῷ λατρεύουσα καὶ ἡ ἐξουσία αὐτοῦ ἐξουσία αἰώνιος ἥτις οὐ μὴ ἀρθῇ καὶ ἡ βασιλεία αὐτοῦ ἥτις οὐ μὴ φθαρῇ. No indication exists that δόξα should be understood as God's theophanic presence or light symbolism of any kind in Daniel 7:14.

2.3.3. 1 Enoch. *2.3.3.1. Concordance.*[129]

---

[128]Cf. Wright 2003: 112–13.

[129]I am using Charlesworth's 1983 translation of 1 Enoch and Nickelsburg's 2001 and Nickelsburg/ VanderKam's 2012 commentary translations.

Table 2.3

	Adoration	Splendor	Honor, Power, or Status of Rule	Name	Glorified	Glorious	Throne/Seat of Glory
God	1 En. 47:2; 48:6; 61:7, 9, 12; 63:2, 4, 5, 7; 69:25, 27; 90:41	1 En. 39:12 [?]; 40:2 [?]; 41:7; 50:4; 63:6 [?]; 104:1 [?]	1 En. 27:2, 5, 63:3 [?]; 91:13; 103:1; 104:1 [?]	Great Glory: 1 En. 14:20; 102:3; Glorious One: 1 En. 14:20; Lord of Glory: 1 En. 22:14; 23:5; 27:5; 36:4; 40:4; 63:2; 83:8; God of Glory: 1 En. 25:7; God of Eternal Glory: 1 En. 75:3; King of Glory: 1 En. 81:3		1 En. 9:4; 45:3	1 En. 9:4; 34:1; 47:3; 60:3; 62:2, 3; 71:8
Son of Man; Elect One	1 En. 46:5; 62:6		1 En. 49:1, 3		1 En. 51:4		1 En. 45:3; 51:3; 55:4; 61:8; 62:6; 69:29
Righteous/Elect		Noah: 1 En. 106:6	1 En. 50:1; 62:16 [?]; 65:12			1 En. 58:2	1 En. 108:13
Unrighteous	1 En. 99:1		1 En. 98:3; 99:15; 103:6				
Angels			Fallen angel: 1 En. 56:4; Kasbe'el: 1 En. 69:14 [?]				
Objects/Places		Garments of glory: 1 En. 62:16 [?]; sheep (metaphor of king): 1 En. 89:46	1 En. 14:6			Stones: 1 En. 24:2; trees: 1 En. 32:3; mist: 1 En. 60:19; land: 1 En. 89:40	
Other			1 En. 93:7				

2.3.3.2. Analysis. First, the lexical range of *glory* is found throughout
1 Enoch, and, unlike in Daniel, the occurrences of each meaning are relatively balanced. Second, *glory* used in association with God means the
honor or exalted status possessed by God *and* God's theophanic splendor.
Third, glory as splendor is used primarily in the Similitudes, whereas glory
as honor/exalted status is found throughout the text. Fourth, the two most
frequently recurring uses of glory are in the name of God, which is often
closely associated with his identity as King (e.g., 1 En. 14:20; 22:14; 25:3, 7;
27:5; 63:2; 81:3),[130] and in the genitival relationship with *throne* or *seat*.[131]
As with the crown of glory in Psalm 8 noted above, the throne of glory
in 1 Enoch is consistently associated with kingly functions: for example,
1 Enoch 9:4: "They said to the Lord of the potentates, 'For he is the Lord
of lords, and the God of gods, and the King of kings, and the seat of his
glory (stands) throughout all the generations of the world. . . . You have
made everything and with you is the authority for everything.'"

Fifth, only once does a person have a radiant glory: the infant Noah in
1 Enoch 106:6: "He is not like an (ordinary) human being, but he looks
like the children of the angels of heaven to me; his form is different, and
he is not like us. His eyes are like the rays of the sun, and his face glorious."
In 1 Enoch 106:2 it is said that "when he opened [his eyes], the whole
house glowed like the sun." Here *glorious* undoubtedly indicates splendor
or radiance in 1 Enoch. Nevertheless, it must be kept in mind that, unlike
Moses in Exodus 34, the infant Noah was not reflecting the splendor of
God. Furthermore, it was not his whole body that was splendid but, like
Moses, only his face.[132]

---

[130]For God as King, see 1 En. 12:4; 25:3, 5, 7; 84:1-6. Nickelsburg (2001: 43) notes: "1 Enoch's
principal metaphor for God is King, and transcendent holiness, glory, greatness, power, and
justice dominate the authors' descriptions of God and statements about him. . . . By depicting
God as king, the Enochic authors provide their readers or audience with a familiar point of
reference; they lived in a world that was ruled by earthly kings. At the same time, the terminology made it possible to assert God's status as the *unique* king. On the heavenly level,
among the holy ones, he was the Great Holy One, the God of gods, and the Lord of spirits.
On earth kings are subject to the heavenly King (9:4; 46:4-8), who is the ultimate sovereign,
the King of kings and Lord of lords."

[131]For other throne of God imagery, see 1 En. 18:8; 24:4; 25:3.

[132]More can and must be said on this point, but here I suggest only one point: the understanding that believers' heavenly glory will be to have splendid bodies is primarily based on the
example of Moses in Ex 34 and 2 Cor 3. If, however, believers' heavenly bodies, having been

Sixth, only once is someone "glorified"—the Elect One in 1 Enoch 51:4—
and there it is clearly in reference to his exaltation to a status of rule/dominion:
"In those days, (the Elect One) shall sit on my throne, and from the conscience
of his mouth shall come out all the secrets of wisdom, for the Lord of the
Spirits has given them to him and glorified him" (1 En. 51:3-4). Seventh, only
twice is glory used in association with angels: fallen angels in 1 Enoch 56:4
and Kasb'el in 1 Enoch 69:13. In both cases, glory probably refers to their
former status. Kasb'el's "dwelling in the highest in glory" may also refer to
the place that is characterized by splendor/light, though the light of heaven
is often described as something that will occur in the future (e.g., 1 En. 45:4:
"On that day, I shall cause my Elect One to dwell among them, I shall
transform heaven and make it a blessing of light forever").

Eighth, when heavenly mediators[133] or humans have glory it is primarily
a reference to honor/power/status associated with rule, as is made clear by,
for example, the glory of the Elect One in 1 Enoch 49:3: "The Elect One
stands before the lord of the Spirits; his glory is forever and ever and his
power is unto all generations"; or the righteous in 1 Enoch 65:12: "He has
preserved your righteous seed for kingship and great glory";[134] or the glory
of the fallen angels in 1 Enoch 56:4: "Then the valley shall be filled with
their elect and beloved ones; and the epoch of their lives, the era of their
glory, and the age of their leading (others) astray shall come to an end."
Ninth, the term is as versatile and symbolic in apocalyptic literature as it
is in the LXX: in 1 Enoch 60:19 even mist, or the "wind of the mist," is
glorious: "The wind of the mist is not mingled with [the winds of the sea,
frost, and snow (1 En. 60:16-18)] in their storehouses, but has a special
storehouse, because its course is glorious,[135] both in light and in darkness,
and in winter and in summer and in its storehouse is an angel."

---

in the presence of God as Moses was, thus reflect that glorious presence, then it is only the
face of believers that should be understood to have a splendid glory. It was not the case that
Moses' entire body shone for the world to see, nor should it be assumed to be the case for
resurrected believers.

[133]For a taxonomy of heavenly mediators in apocalyptic literature, see Davila (1999: 4-5), who
suggests five kinds of mediatorial figures: personified divine attributes (Philo's *Logos*), exalted
patriarchs (and matriarchs; e.g., Enoch, Moses), principal agents (e.g., Metatron in 3 Enoch),
charismatic prophets and royal aspirants (e.g., Theudas in Josephus's *Antiquitates judaicae*
20:28), and ideal figures (e.g., Davidic king, Mosaic prophet, Aaronid high priest).

[134]See also 1 En. 96:1, though *glory* is not used.

[135]Literally "in glory"; see Nickelsburg and VanderKam 2012: 232.

And two other pieces of analysis are worthy of mentioning, though they are not included in the concordance on *glory*. Tenth, light imagery is not always God's splendor/theophanic glory, for example, 1 Enoch 58:2: "The righteous ones shall be in the light of the sun and the elect ones in the light of eternal life which has no end." Eleventh, light imagery occurs frequently but is rarely used in association with the word *glory*. This does not mean there is no lexical association, but it is worth keeping in mind. Moreover, as indicated in the analysis of δόξα in Daniel above, the light imagery can be used in association with language of rule and authority, for example, 1 Enoch 96:1, 3: "You shall be given authority upon [the sinners], such (authority) as you may wish (to have) . . . a bright light shall enlighten you." Similarly, the sun, moon, and stars shine and cast light, but they also rule; for example, 1 Enoch 75:3: "In order that they—the sun, the moon, the stars, and all the created objects which circulate in all the chariots of heaven—should rule in the face of the sky and be seen on the earth to be guides for the day and the night."[136] This follows the pattern set already in Psalm 135:8-9 LXX: the sun has authority over the day and the moon authority over the night. Light imagery is used symbolically as visual imagery that connotes a status of honor/rule/power.

2.4. CONCLUSION

This analysis of the use of δόξα and δοξάζω in the LXX and some of the earliest pieces of apocalyptic literature is unquestionably brief. Yet its length is enough to indicate that, when used vis-à-vis humanity in the LXX and Daniel and 1 Enoch, δόξα and δοξάζω primarily refer to or are associated with the concepts of honor, power, wealth, and/or authority that come with an exalted status. Other than Moses' face reflecting the splendor of God, at no point is it unequivocally the case that a human is given glory or glorified such that the human's body is made to shine due to being in the presence of God. Rather, it is almost entirely the case that the glory given to a person (or a person's glorification) either constitutes or is closely related

---

[136]See also 1 En. 83:16; 108:11, 12, where the righteous are brought "out into the bright light" and will be "resplendent for ages that cannot be numbered," but where they are also seated "one by one upon the throne of his honor." These are each perfect examples of how an object's/person's ontology cannot be removed from its function. The sun has the greatest rule because its light is the brightest; it *does* what it *is*.

to the honor, power, wealth, or authority associated with an exalted status of rule. The case is similar for the use of δόξα and δοξάζω vis-à-vis God, though the terms are more nuanced when applied to God and refer to the splendor or radiance of God in approximately half of their occurrences. However, when understood in terms of semiotics—how individual signs form a language and function within it—I suggest that, when used as light imagery or in reference to phenomenological events, the terms are used *figuratively*, usually as metonymy for the unsurpassed greatness (and thus power, authority, etc.) of Israel's God. This is the lexical background for understanding not only the use of δόξα and δοξάζω in Jewish literature but also how δόξα and δοξάζω are used vis-à-vis God and humanity in Pauline literature. In particular, it is the background to Paul's use of the terms in Romans, to which we can now turn our attention.

3

HUMANITY'S GLORY AND
GLORIFICATION IN ROMANS

Paul's use of δόξα and δοξάζω are not topics at the forefront of current Romans scholarship. But they should be. The motif reveals to a greater degree than is normally recognized Paul's theological indebtedness to his Jewish heritage, the significance of Adam for Paul's anthropology and Adam-Christ typology, and his view of the relationship between humanity and creation. Moreover, the motif of glory should be a discussion point because, as hinted at in the previous chapter, in scholarly and lay circles alike, Paul's references to Christians' glory and glorification are too often understood either on the basis of preconceived cultural notions of glory as splendor or radiance or on the basis of assumed lexical definitions of glory as the presence of God manifested in light phenomena. Unfortunately, this notion of glory has affected the message of redemption in Romans and thereby also the meaning of "conformed to the image of [God's] Son" in Romans 8:29b. Romans 8:29b can be understood only when the motif of glory in its surrounding context (especially Rom 5:2; 8:17, 18, 21, 30) is properly understood within the larger context of Romans and within the parameters of its use in Jewish literature set in the previous chapter.

This is a large order to fill for one chapter—but not an impossible order. The chapter will include three sections. We will first look at how δόξα and δοξάζω are commonly defined in Romans and how, at times, such definitions are inadequate. Once this assessment is laid out, I will briefly note five considerations that must be kept in mind as we examine Paul's use of the terms in Romans. We will be in a position then to systematically analyze the texts in Romans in which Paul refers to the glory or glorification of humanity (Rom 1:23; 2:7, 10; 3:23; 5:2) and Israel (Rom 1:23; 9:4, 23). The exception at this point will be a close analysis of those in Romans 8 (Rom 8:17, 18, 21, 30), which will be more closely examined at a later point. I will offer what I refer to as Paul's "narrative of glory"—an underlying narrative of eschatological renewal, of humanity, Israel, and creation—implicit in Romans. This narrative of glory will serve as the primary context in which to discuss Romans 8:29.

3.1. HUMANITY'S GLORY AND GLORIFICATION IN ROMANS: CURRENT APPROACHES

In the last half-century alone, three works have shared the title (*In*) *Hope of (God's) Glory*.[1] Yet in few such books whose titles include the term do the authors provide a clearly articulated definition of *glory*—a striking fact considering its frequency of occurrences within the Pauline corpus and the emphasis placed on glory or glorification as a Christian's hope or purpose.[2] *Glory* and its cognates are words used often in Pauline scholarship but, at least in proportion to their usage, rarely investigated.[3]

Within Pauline studies *glory* is typically either defined as or assumed to be a visible splendor, radiance, or brilliance that often, though not always, connotes the manifest presence of God and is derived from δόξα, the

---

[1]Loane 1968; Giblin 1970; Wilson 1997.

[2]Within the Pauline canon, δόξα has sixty-one occurrences, with frequent appearances in Romans (Rom 1:23; 2:7, 10; 3:7, 23; 4:20; 5:2; 6:4; 8:18, 21; 9:4, 23 [2x]; 11:36; 15:7; 16:27); 1 Corinthians (1 Cor 2:7, 8; 10:31; 11:7 [2x], 15; 15:40, 41 [4x], 43); 2 Corinthians (2 Cor 1:20; 3:7 [2x], 8, 9 [2x], 10, 11 [2x], 18 [3x]; 4:4, 6, 15, 17; 6:8; 8:19, 23), and, relatively speaking, in Ephesians (Eph 1:6, 12, 14, 17, 18; 3:13, 16, 21) and Philippians (Phil 1:11; 2:11; 3:19, 21; 4:19, 20). This frequency reduces when the verb form is used, with only five references in Romans (Rom 1:21; 8:30; 11:13; 15:6, 9); two in 1 Corinthians (1 Cor 6:20; 12:26); three in 2 Corinthians (2 Cor 3:10 [2x]; 9:13); one in Galatians (Gal 1:24); and one in 2 Thessalonians (2 Thess 3:1).

[3]Neither the *Dictionary for Theological Interpretation of the Bible* (2005) nor the six-volume *Anchor Bible Dictionary* (1992) includes any reference to glory. Gaffin, in the *Dictionary of Paul and His Letters* (1993: 348-50), spends 2.5 pages discussing Paul's use of δόξα and never once provides a proper definition of the term as it is understood and used by Paul. *Harper's Bible Dictionary* (1985: 349) includes not one single reference to glory in Romans in its explanation of the term.

Septuagintal gloss for כבוד.[4] Precedents do exist for this traditional interpretation: for example, the Damascus Christophany (Acts 9:3); Paul's clear
use of δόξα as visible splendor (2 Cor 3); later Jewish traditions of Adam
losing his garment of glory (Gen. Rab. 12.6) and/or the light of God with
which he was at first clothed (Apoc. Mos. 21);[5] and, as seen in the previous
chapter, the Septuagintal and early apocalyptic occurrences where δόξα,
δοξάζω, glory, or glorification are associated with light imagery and theophany.

The most discussion these words receive is in dictionaries or focused
studies.[6] Perhaps most helpful, if even on a cursory level, is L. H. Brockington's 1955 essay "The New Testament Use of δόξα." Brockington suggests
that "there are four ways in which δόξα is used in the New Testament
which may be said to be directly due to corresponding usage in the LXX:
(1) the conception of brightness; (2) the power and wonder-working activity
of God; (3) the saving power of God; (4) the conception of God-likeness."[7]
Brockington argues that the New Testament use of δόξα is primarily dependent on Old Testament theophanic traditions, but his emphasis on the
differing ways in which the tradition was rendered throughout the New
Testament is helpful.[8]

James Harrison's more recent approach to understanding Paul's use of
δόξα also deserves mention. In *Paul and the Imperial Authorities at Thessalonica and Rome* (2011), Harrison aligns himself with the growing emphasis
on the sociopolitical context confronting the churches in Rome. In doing

---

[4]BDAG (2000: 256-58) provides four meanings of δόξα: (1) "the condition of being bright or
shining, *brightness, splendor, radiance*"; (2) "a state of being magnificent, *greatness, splendor*";
(3) "honor as enhancement or recognition of status or performance, *fame, recognition, renown,
honor, prestige*"; (4) "a transcendent being deserving of honor, *majestic being*"; emphasis original. BDAG (2000: 258) also lists two meanings of δοξάζω: (1) "to influence one's opinion about
another so as to enhance the latter's reputation, *praise, honor, extol*"; (2) "to cause to have
splendid greatness, *clothe in splendor, glorify*"; emphasis original. Louw and Nida (1989) suggest
nine glosses for δόξα: *splendor, brightness, amazing might, praise, honor, greatness, glorious being,
heaven*, and *pride*; and three for δοξάζω: *praise, honor, glorify*.
[5]See 3 Bar. 4:16.
[6]Owen 1932: 265-79; Berquist 1941; Brockington 1950: 172-76; 1955: 1-8; Jervell 1960: 180-96,
324-31; Davies 1962: 401-3; Carrez 1964; Kittel 1964: 233-37, 242-45, 253; Caird 1969: 265-77;
Aalen 1976: 44-52; Harrison 1982: 477-83; BDAG 2000: 256-58. Though George Caird's 1944
DPhil dissertation is titled "The New Testament Conception of Doxa," it purely addresses the
Old Testament backgrounds to the term. See also Ben Blackwell's "Immortal Glory and the
Problem of Death in Romans 3:23," where he traces Paul's use of *glory* throughout the letter.
[7]Brockington 1955: 3.
[8]Brockington's distinctions are less obvious, however, in his 1950 treatment of "Glory," located
under "Presence" in *A Theological Word Book of the Bible*.

so he emphasizes the Roman imperial notion of *gloria* and suggests that Paul and his readers would primarily have associated glory with the quests of Roman nobles for *gloria ancestra* ("glory of the ancestors"),[9] which defined their social status within the empire. Harrison writes,

> For Paul in Romans, glory was a gift of divine grace dispensed to his dependants [*sic*] through the dishonour of the crucified Christ who had become their *hilasterion*. . . . It challenged the anthropocentric boasting of the Roman *nobiles,* as much as it challenged the cosmic and ancestral myths of the imperial ruler. Paul's radical inversion of the traditional understanding of *Gloria* ultimately changed the face of Western civilization by enshrining humility as the distinguishing sign of a truly great and successful man.[10]

Paul's glory is not derived from what Harrison describes as "reserves" of ancestral glory[11] (i.e., glory gained through service to the state[12]) but from the God of Israel. For Paul, Harrison argues, the glory of Israel's God is the only status shaper of any eternal significance. Harrison provides a rigorous and comprehensive treatment of philosophical, political, benefactor, and virtue-based notions of glory in imperial Roman culture. His treatment of δόξα in Romans in light of such imperial uses was both long overdue and insightful to all who wish to read the text against the backdrop of its first-century political and social context. I will return to his treatment of δόξα throughout my investigation.

Along with Harrison, Robert Jewett's treatment of the term in his Romans commentary is notable.[13] Unlike Harrison, Jewett emphasizes not the ancestral traditions but the paradigm of honor and shame that permeated the social strata of the empire. Together, both scholars have helpfully highlighted Paul's use of the term from an increasingly important socio-historical perspective.

With Harrison's treatment of δόξα noted above, another highly significant study for our purposes here is the influential work of Carey Newman. He examines Paul's use of δόξα in *Paul's Glory-Christology* (1992), where he

---

[9]Harrison 2011: 205.
[10]Harrison 2011: 269.
[11]Harrison 2011: 214.
[12]Harrison 2011: 206.
[13]Jewett and Kotansky 2007.

investigates "how and why Paul came to identify Jesus as glory."[14] Newman argues that Paul interpreted the Christophany as the appearance of God's eschatological glory in the resurrected Christ. Newman begins by tracing the development of כבד יהוה as a "technical term to refer to God's visible, mobile divine presence" throughout the Old Testament,[15] and examines its development as a technical term through four traditio-historical strands: Sinai, theophanic, royal and prophetic.[16] These four strands, Newman suggests, coalesce in Paul's interpretation of the Christophany. He writes:

> In Paul's convictional interpretation of the Christophany, the various strands
> of the Glory tradition coalesce. Paul echoed the Glory tradition in his in-
> terpretation of the Christophany as a (i) theophany of δόξα, (ii) a Sinai-like
> revelation כבד יהוה, (iii) as the Davidic Messiah's exaltation to Glory, (iv)
> as a fulfilment of the prophetic promise that God would inaugurate the
> new age with a revelation of his כבד, (v) as a prophetic call in which he
> was confronted by the Glory of God, and (vi) as an apocalyptic throne
> vision in which he saw the principal agent of God, the manlike כבד יהוה
> of Ezekiel 1:28. Paul's identification of Christ as δόξα centers upon the
> convergence of multiple construals of the Glory tradition in his interpretation
> of the Christophany.[17]

For Paul, Newman says, "the Christophany is a revelation of the end-of-time, resurrection presence of God—his δόξα."[18] The glory of God—the visible, manifest presence of God—rests in Christ, thus "proleptically in-augurating the eschatological age of blessing."[19] Though Paul never says so explicitly, "Christ = δόξα,"[20] and Newman argues a case for this on the basis of 1 Corinthians 9:1-2; 15:1-11, where Christophany points to resur-rection, and therefore end-time glory; Galatians 1:11-17, where Paul indicates that the Christophany was a throne vision where he "encountered the special agent, Jesus, who is to be equated with the Glory of God";[21] and Philippians 3:2-21, where the Christophany is the model for the Christian

---

[14]Newman 1992: 164.
[15]Newman 1992: 190.
[16]Newman 1992: 25-75.
[17]Newman 1992: 246.
[18]Newman 1992: 186.
[19]Newman 1992: 192.
[20]Newman 1992: 211.
[21]Newman 1992: 211.

life—a life that begins and ends in eschatological glory.[22] Newman further suggests that glory functions in Paul's rhetoric as a "sociomorphic portrayal of transference" and as "physiomorphic description of Christian progress,"[23] and that, at least in two places, we see Paul "self-consciously [echoing] the [glory] tradition" in a reinterpretation of his narratival and symbolic world now interpreted through his Christophany: 2 Corinthians 3:4–4:6 and 1 Corinthians 2:8.

3.1.1. Inadequacies of Carey Newman's glory Christology. No publication has yet been produced on Paul's use of δόξα that surpasses Newman's investigatory depth or breadth, and much of his work is to be highly praised.[24] In particular, I fully support his conclusions that in his Christophany, Paul understood Christ as the "visible, manifest presence of God"; that Paul reinterpreted his narratival and symbolic world in terms of his Christophany; and that Paul employed his Christophany to serve to validate his apostolic authority, message, and suffering in 2 Corinthians 3:4–4:6. Nevertheless, I suggest that his conclusions are not prescriptive for how δόξα should be interpreted when used to refer to the glory or glorification of believers or when δόξα is used more generally in Paul's letters, and particularly in Romans.

The most pressing issue is that, while Newman traces the lexical use of the כבד-δόξα word group through the Old Testament, his study deals almost exclusively with its use in relation to God. He acknowledges outright that "the כבד word group possesses a fluid semantic range. This study, however, focuses upon just a small slice of the כבד's meaning: namely, those places where כבוד (both denotatively and connotatively) is used as a symbol of 'divine presence.'"[25] More specifically, Newman focuses on כבוד יהוה, which he argues is a technical term signifying "the visible and mobile presence of Yahweh."[26] He does not examine how either δόξα or δοξάζω function for humanity in the LXX, and, while he acknowledges the nontechnical uses of *glory* in the Old Testament, he does not elaborate

---

[22]Newman 1992: 211.

[23]Newman 1992: 240.

[24]As are the insights of Harrison and Jewett, who are correct to emphasize the notion of honor or praise, usually as a result of a status (in Romans). I will return to these insights in a closer examination of δόξα in Romans in the second half of the book.

[25]Newman 1992: 18.

[26]Newman 1992: 24, 20-24.

on them. The trajectory of development of what Newman titles the "Glory tradition" is exclusively a development of how the כבוד יהוה was interpreted and utilized throughout the passages of Israelite and Jewish history.

The logical result of this is that, when Newman turns to Paul's use of δόξα and Paul's reinterpretation of the glory tradition in terms of his Christophany, the primary "Glory tradition" Newman uses is that of the development of the כבוד יהוה.[27] First, *this* glory tradition is labeled "the Glory tradition" and not just "a glory tradition" because it is *the* glory tradition from which Newman primarily draws his conclusions. Second, in Newman's final statements in the work he concludes: "In Paul's interpretation of the Christophany, God's glory appeared in the once crucified, but now resurrected person of Jesus."[28] In this Newman's case is strong. However, his final sentence betrays him: "I submit this thesis best explains Paul's use of δόξα." No doubt this definition has its place, particularly in Paul's interpretation of his Christophany experience, but this does not demand that every use of δόξα denotes the eschatological presence of God. Basing Paul's use of δόξα on this definition/tradition does no justice either to the multifarious uses of δόξα throughout the LXX or to the clearly linear use of δοξάζω when used in reference to humanity in the LXX.[29]

Further, Newman argues that δόξα and δοξάζω function as sociomorphic and physiomorphic transfer signifiers, but his evidence for such a reading is scant at best. Humanity's exchange of the glory of God in Romans 1:23 and falling short of the glory of God in Romans 3:23, Newman argues, are references to a "ruptured relationship" with God, a relationship that is restored in their "glorification" in Romans 8:30.[30] He suggests that the

---

[27]I say "primary" here because Newman does trace the semantic range of δόξα throughout Paul's letters on pp. 157-63. At the end of this chapter on semantic range, however, he lists forty-two occurrences of δόξα that he says are "left for consideration," many of which are never again discussed (160n22).

[28]Newman 1992: 247.

[29]I wish to be clear: I am not suggesting that Newman emphasizes an "ontological" interpretation of glory, whether applied to that of God, Christ, or humanity, at the expense of a "functional" interpretation of glory. As noted in chapter two, such categories are less than helpful here. Rather, Newman is giving one semantic use of the term precedence over numerous others. In his conclusion that the glory of God is the visible manifestation of God, whether vis-à-vis God or humanity's relationship to that visible manifestation, Newman neglects the numerous other semantic uses of the term that have no relationship to the visible splendor of God (i.e., the majority of occurrences of δόξα and δοξάζω vis-à-vis humans in the LXX) and the ways in which they may contribute to Paul's use of the term (see note above).

[30]Newman 1992: 225-27.

passive συνδοξάζω in Romans 8:17 and the aorist δοξάζω in Romans 8:30 both refer to a "metaphorphosis into Glory and therefore [relate] the verb to a paradigmatic field of words and constructions for spiritual transformation."[31] Justification for the suggestions that, first, they refer to "spiritual transformation" and, second, they refer to transformation into "Glory," that is, divine presence, is nonexistent, however, other than to say that it is a result of "incorporation into Jesus,"[32] which itself is a loaded statement left entirely unpacked. No discussion is provided for why the verbal forms should be understood as such. And, more importantly, no justification is given for why the verb forms in Romans 8:17, 30 are not categorized with those instances where, according to Newman himself, the "verb is used to mean 'honor' or 'magnify'" (e.g., Rom 11:13; 1 Cor 12:26).[33] This is particularly significant given that δοξάζω is never once used in the LXX to refer to humanity's "spiritual transformation."

Other than the short and relatively unsubstantiated mentions of δόξα or δοξάζω in the Romans texts noted above, Newman's conclusions on Paul's use of δόξα rest almost exclusively on Paul's references to δόξα outside Romans. Most explicit references to any key δόξα or δοξάζω texts in Romans primarily appear in his chapter on the word's semantic range but bear little weight otherwise. Similarly, he acknowledges that δόξα can denote "social status" or "honour"[34] but does not suggest that the use of δόξα in either Romans 2:7 or Romans 2:10 belongs here, despite their associations with τιμή in the same verses. He suggests, rather, that they belong with forty-two other occurrences of δόξα that are "left for consideration."[35] Neither verse, however, is ever mentioned again.

Additionally, Newman's study rests heavily on the function of δόξα in 2 Corinthians 3, as it should; 2 Corinthians 3 has more occurrences of δόξα than any other New Testament passage, and here Paul explicitly mentions the reflection of God's visible splendor on Moses' face in Exodus 34:29-35. In 2 Corinthians 3:7-11, Paul draws a contrast between the glory associated with the ministry of the law, presented as a visible manifestation

---

[31]Newman 1992: 158.
[32]Newman 1992: 245.
[33]Newman 1992: 158.
[34]Newman 1992: 158.
[35]Newman 1992: 160.

of God's glory on Moses' face, and the glory associated with the ministry of the Spirit:

> Now if the ministry of death, chiseled in letters on stone tablets, came in glory [δόξα] so that the people of Israel could not gaze at Moses' face because of the glory [δόξα] of his face, a glory [δόξα] now set aside, how much more will the ministry of the Spirit come in glory [δόξα]? For if there was glory [δόξα] in the ministry of condemnation, much more does the ministry of justification abound in glory [δόξα]! Indeed, what once had glory [δόξα] has lost its glory [δόξα] because of the greater glory [δόξα]; for if what was set aside came through glory [δόξα], much more has the permanent come in glory [δόξα]!

Newman is correct to suggest that Paul "contrasts the Sinaitic revelation to Moses with his Christophany" in order to argue for a "superior role and message based upon a superior revelation."[36] By doing so, Newman says, Paul legitimizes his apostolic authority, preaching, and suffering on the basis of the revelation of δόξα in Christ: "The Christophany as a revelation of final, eschatological δόξα appropriates to Paul the legitimizing power inherent in the Sinaitic Glory construal in order to defend his apostleship."[37] Paul's invocation of the Exodus narrative as a basis for his own Christophanic revelation is at the heart of Newman's thesis. There, in Christ, is the visible, radiant, manifest presence of the one true God.

That being said, however, two points are worthy of note. First, while δόξα in 2 Corinthians 3 does clearly refer to God's visible splendor as it was revealed on Moses' face, Paul's point is not to emphasize God's presence. Paul uses it as background context to describe the authority of the Spirit's ministry as superior to that of the law. Thrall suggests that *glory* in 2 Corinthians 3:7-18 refers to a "manifestation of (divine) power," "divine presence," or "divine nature."[38] Here in 2 Corinthians 3:7-11, "divine power" is most fitting. The old covenant (παλαιά διαθήκη, 2 Cor 3:14) is abolished in Christ (ἐν Χριστῷ καταργεῖται, 2 Cor 3:14); the glory (i.e., the authority) of the law is replaced with that of the Spirit's glory and not the Spirit's visible presence but the superiority of the Spirit's ministry (or power) in the world.

---

[36]Newman 1992: 235.

[37]Newman 1992: 235.

[38]Thrall 1994: 246. Thrall is one of the few commentators to question the underlying meaning of δόξα in 2 Cor 3:7-11.

The glory is presented in the context of the Sinaitic glory tradition, where Moses reflects the δόξα of God as God's *visible splendor,* symbolic of his *presence,* but the point is to describe the glory of the law as that which held less *authority/power* than the glory of the Spirit's ministry. This is to say that, even in 2 Corinthians 3:4–4:6, Paul uses various denotations of δόξα.[39]

Second, given the terms' variegated uses throughout the LXX and Newman's own admission that they are used in various ways throughout Pauline literature, one cannot justifiably interpret the theology of glory or glorification in Romans on the basis of Paul's reflections on the Christophany in 2 Corinthians 3—a different passage in a different letter with an altogether different purpose, message, and background.[40] How *glory* and *glorification* function in Romans must be determined first and foremost on the basis of their purpose and function within the message and context of Romans.

These inadequacies are substantial enough to warrant a rereading of how δόξα and δοξάζω function in Romans. I do not wish to minimize Newman's study but rather applaud his work on this overlooked but significant topic for Pauline studies. Though I suggest that Newman's glory Christology is not applicable to most occurrences of δόξα and δοξάζω in Romans, it is applicable elsewhere, and it goes a long way in understanding Paul's interpretation of his Christophany.

3.2. HUMANITY'S GLORY AND GLORIFICATION IN ROMANS: CONSIDERATIONS

If we are to understand Paul's use of δόξα and δοξάζω in Romans, then we need to understand the terms against the background of the letter's sociopolitical environment and literary context. We need to consider (1) the importance and denotation of glory/honor within the first-century Roman imperial environment, (2) the significance of Psalm 8 in understanding human glory in Romans, (3) Adam in Paul's image and morphic language, (4) the presence of echoes of Adam in Romans 1; 3, and (5) Adam's paradigmatic function in Romans. Considerations two through five all *relate to the fact that the image and glory of Adam, or of humanity in Adam, is a key interpretative piece of Paul's Christology and*

---

[39]See also §4.2.2.3.

[40]This is more a critique of those who seek to apply Newman's conclusions on Paul's glory language vis-à-vis the Christophany to Paul's use of δόξα elsewhere, i.e., Rom 8.

anthropology in Romans. The second and fourth considerations will require extended treatments.

3.2.1. Glory in Romans and glory/honor within the first-century Roman imperial environment.

Jewett argues that "competition for honor was visible in every city of the Roman Empire in which members of the elite competed for civic power through sponsoring games and celebrations, financing public buildings, endowing food distributions, and so on. The public life in the Roman Empire was centered in the quest for honor."[41] Paul's letter to Rome, Jewett further states, "employs honor categories from beginning to end."[42] Harrison similarly interprets δόξα in Romans through a socio-political lens, recognizing the importance of ancestral glory traditions familiar to every Roman household. He writes, "Paul addressed [the issue of glory] especially for the benefit of Roman believers living in the capital in the late 50's and integrated his presentation with the eschatological traditions of glory that he inherited from the Septuagint and from Second Temple Judaism. *Thus Paul's understanding of glory, while being profoundly theological, was also political in its polemic.*"[43] Glory for believers, according to Harrison, was rooted only in Israel's God, the "truthful Judge" and the "grace of the crucified Benefactor," and it was received only through humility and boasting in tribulations—a starkly different understanding of glory from that of Roman nobility.[44] In Romans, "we see Paul *retelling* the story of Israel and its fulfilment in Christ . . . as a powerful counterpoint to the ancestral stories of glory that framed the Roman understanding of history, republican and imperial."[45] Given this, we should not be surprised to

---

[41]Jewett and Kotansky 2007: 50.

[42]Jewett and Kotansky 2007: 49.

[43]Harrison 2011: 263; emphasis mine.

[44]Harrison 2011: 264-65.

[45]Harrison 2011: 267; emphasis original. Harrison's work is supremely helpful in establishing the foundation of Paul's use of glory in Romans in light of the imperial Roman environment. One particular weakness of his discussion, however, is the denotative ambiguity of Paul's use of δόξα at various points in Romans. Harrison follows Newman and Raurell (1979) in suggesting that Paul's LXX-based, Jewish "glory-tradition" is a tradition based almost exclusively on theophanic examples of glory in the LXX. How Harrison views Paul bridging the gap between the theophanic traditions of glory in the LXX with Roman nobiles' quest for ancestral glory, i.e., honor, power, is never addressed, particularly given that Raurell is specifically arguing against glory as honor in the book of Wisdom. Humans are created to share in God's glory, Harrison argues, but whether that glory is assumed to be God's presence (à la Newman) or God's supreme honor/power/character (as it would stand in contrast to Caesar's glory or Roman nobiles' glory) is left unaddressed.

discover that Paul's references to glory in Romans imply references to one's honor or status.

3.2.2. Psalm 8 and the glory of humanity in Romans. In chapter two I demonstrated that the motif of glory, when applied to humanity in the LXX, is consistently applied in terms of honor/power/authority/character and is not a visible manifestation of the presence of God. Within this motif, Psalm 8 functions as a particularly important and representative example. Its significance is based both on its semantic use of δόξα for humanity in the LXX and on its christological application by Paul and other early church writers. In particular, I suggest that Psalm 8 is a key text that stands behind Paul's use of δόξα and its cognates in Romans. Psalm 8 as a unit and the vocational use of δόξα within it underscore both Paul's use of the term in Romans and the unfolding narrative of anthropological redemption presented therein. These claims are significant and thus warrant further defense.

Psalm 8:5-7 (LXX) reads: τί ἐστιν ἄνθρωπος ὅτι μιμνήσκῃ αὐτοῦ ἢ υἱὸς ἀνθρώπου ὅτι ἐπισκέπτῃ αὐτόν ἠλάττωσας αὐτὸν βραχύ τι παρ᾽ ἀγγέλους δόξῃ καὶ τιμῇ ἐστεφάνωσας αὐτόν καὶ κατέστησας αὐτὸν ἐπὶ τὰ ἔργα τῶν χειρῶν σου πάντα ὑπέταξας ὑποκάτω τῶν ποδῶν αὐτοῦ.[46] Most notable is that the psalmist's use of δόξα falls into the semantic domain of honor/praise as a result of a status of kingly rule and not a visible splendor or radiance. Psalm 8 is a psalm of praise that extols YHWH for the way in which he ordered creation and placed humanity in a position of sovereignty over every created thing. The psalmist reflects in Psalm 8:3-4 on the enigmatic thoughtfulness of YHWH toward humanity, which presumably is as weak and powerless and equally as mortal as the rest of creation. The outworking of this thoughtfulness is then expressed in Psalm 8:5-8 as the constitution of humanity as a sovereign who rules over the creation in the name of the Creator.[47] The psalmist paints a picture of YHWH as the majestic Creator-King, a King reigning within his kingdom as sovereign over all that is, yet a King who does not rule unmediatedly. YHWH has created humanity in order that humans might reign as vicegerents over his creation, maintaining via their dominion the goodness and beauty of which the cosmos inherently consists (Gen 1:4, 9, 12, 18, 21, 25, 31). As

---

[46]No variants exist that might change the reading provided by Ralfs.
[47]See Limburg 2000: 25-26.

Gerald Wilson notes, YHWH has allowed "his power to be displayed through those creatures he has graciously chosen to extend his authority into the world."[48] As those with the unique image-bearing vocation, humans share in the glory of God as they rule over his good creation.[49]

The appearance of Psalm 8 in early Jewish literature is limited at best. For this reason, Mark Kinzer, who has provided one of only two treatments of the text in Second Temple and rabbinic literature, suggests that the limited presence of Psalm 8 in early Jewish texts has led to an assumption that "the key to understanding the early Christian interpretation of Psalm 8 is found exclusively in internal developments within the Christian community."[50] But Kinzer, along with Wenceslaus Urassa, suggests otherwise.[51]

Both scholars suggest that echoes of Psalm 8:5-8 LXX are found in 1 Enoch, particularly with regard to the identity of the Son of Man figure and his enthronement on the "throne of glory" (1 En. 61:8).[52] Urassa concludes that "the son of man in *I Enoch* has much to do with ADAM in relation to both ethical and anthropological reinterpretations of the dominion text in Genesis."[53] Likewise, Kinzer suggests that Psalm 8 lies in the background of 2 Enoch 58:3 (recensions J and A);[54] 1 Enoch 71:14; and 3 Enoch at several points.[55] Psalm 8:5-8 LXX is also echoed in 4 Ezra, particularly at 4 Ezra 6:45-46, 53-59, where Ezra alludes to Adam's, and thus Israel's, right to rule over creation. From here Urassa notes that Philo, in *De Opificio Mundi*, "midrashically paraphrased Ps. 8 to interpret Gn. 1:26f," and that, though he never mentions Psalm 8, Josephus's "literary style and interpretation of the creation account could shed some light on its later

---

[48]Wilson 2002: 207.

[49]See Schmidt 1969: 1-15, cited in Goldingay 2006: 159; Wilson 2002: 206-9, 213-20.

[50]Kinzer 1995: 6.

[51]Urassa 1998.

[52]See Kinzer 1995: 122-25, where he argues that—along with the commonly accepted texts of Dan 7; the Servant of YHWH in Is 40–53; the Davidic Messiah in Is 11; Ps 2; 110; and the enthroned glory in Ezek 1:26-28—Ps 8 forms the identity of the "Son of Man" in 1 En. 37–71.

[53]Urassa 1998: 91; capitals original.

[54]Kinzer 1995: 127. In 2 En., Ps 8 is not applied to a heavenly figure but to a particular human, Enoch.

[55]In 3 En. the Son of Man figure of 1 En. is Metatron, the one "who sits on 'a throne like the throne of glory' (3 En. 10:1), is clothed in 'a glorious cloak in which brightness, brilliance, splendor, and luster of every kind were fixed' (3 En. 12:2), and is crowned with 'a glorious crown' (3 En. 14:5) which is inscribed with the name of God (12:4; 13:1-2)": Kinzer 1995: 133-34.

interpretations in the NT."[56] In addition to these, Kinzer suggests that Psalm 8 is echoed in Qumran's references to the "glory of Adam"[57] and that an echo of Psalm 8 exists in the Apocalypse of Moses 10:1, 3; 11:1. Urassa notes the presence of the psalm in the Midrash Tehillim,[58] but Kinzer spends an entire chapter making his way through the diverse rabbinic literature and its echoes of the psalm.[59] Both scholars demonstrate the broad use of Psalm 8 in Jewish literature outside the New Testament.

From his survey of the literature, Kinzer draws two conclusions. First, though the son of man in the psalm is applied to Adam, Enoch, Abraham, and Moses throughout Jewish literature, "those individuals were usually presented as in some way fulfilling the vocation of Adam."[60] Second, Kinzer notes, "Gen 1 and Ps 8 were not read as descriptions of the present human position before God and the created order. . . . *They were read protologically and eschatologically.* Ps 8 was thus seen to promise heavenly wisdom, glory, and immortality for those who were cleansed from the polluting sin of Adam and his descendants."[61] These two conclusions will be significant for reading the echoes of Psalm 8 in Paul, to which I now turn.

The psalmist's use of δόξα in Psalm 8 falls indisputably within the semantic domain of honor/rule in the LXX. Paul's use of δόξα in Romans, then, I contend stems directly from his reading of Psalm 8 in the light of a new understanding of Israel's plight. The question of plight (and solution) was initially prompted by Ed Sanders and was recently readdressed by N. T. Wright.[62] Wright contends that on the road to Damascus,

> Saul of Tarsus was there confronted with the fact of the risen Jesus, and with the immediate conclusion that *he* was therefore the Messiah, that *he* had been exalted to the place of glory and authority at God's right hand—and that monotheism itself had therefore to be reconfigured around a man of recent memory who had not delivered Israel from the pagans, had not intensified Israel's own Law-observance, had not cleansed and rebuilt the

---

[56]Urassa 1998: 99, 108.

[57]Kinzer 1995: 105n17.

[58]Urassa 1998: 108-12; see Kinzer 1995: 94.

[59]Kinzer 1995: 40-78.

[60]Kinzer 1995: 215.

[61]Kinzer 1995: 110; emphasis mine.

[62]See Sanders 1977: 442-43, 474-74. For an extensive discussion of the debate, see Wright 2013a: 747-71.

temple, and had not brought justice and peace to the world after the manner of Isaiah's dream. This was, in its way, as cataclysmic a reversal of expectations for Saul of Tarsus as the fall of Jerusalem would be for the next generation. It compelled, as did that shocking event, a radical rethink, all the way back to Adam.[63]

Israel's real problem, Saul realized, was sin and death—a problem that started at the beginning of Israel's history, was recorded for the generations in Genesis 3, and had affected Israel just as it did the Gentiles. This revelation led Paul to rethink and reread his own Scriptures, and in so doing Genesis 1–3 began to tell a new story. Psalm 8 told a new story as well. When read in the light of Genesis 1–3, it told a story of intentions and failures; yet when read in the light of the Messiah's resurrection, it told a story of hope and redemption. If this is the case, then, according to Kinzer's conclusion above that the psalm was read either protologically or eschatologically, Paul's reading of the psalm followed the patterns of the day.

The following pages are dedicated to Paul's retelling of these stories in Romans. But first we must establish, as much as is possible, that Psalm 8 has any place in Romans at all. Since this is a matter of detecting scriptural echoes/allusions rather than direct quotations, it is of course impossible to attain complete certainty. Nevertheless, the joint criteria of Hays and Tooman,[64] which I established in chapter one, can bring us a long way in establishing the presence of Psalm 8 in Paul's letters.

Four factors lend weight to the possibility that Psalm 8 stands behind Paul's use of δόξα in Romans: (1) Paul uses Psalm 8 in 1 Corinthians 15:27, a verse thematically similar to the key δόξα passages in Romans; (2) Paul's post-Damascus understanding of redemptive history is dependent, at least in part, on the role of Adam in Genesis 1–3; (3) the thematic and linguistic relationship between Genesis 1:26-28 and Psalm 8:5-8 LXX, particularly the link between the glory of mankind in Psalm 8 and the image of mankind in Genesis 1, both of which are set within the context of

---

[63]Wright 2013a: 751. For an argument against this view, see Eisenbaum (2009: 142-43), who argues that Paul's "mystical encounter with the risen Jesus cannot be used as the key to understanding Paul." She also argues that Paul's theology is fundamentally not christocentric but theocentric (2009: 173).

[64]Namely: uniqueness; volume, which includes elements of distinctiveness and multiplicity; recurrence; and thematic correspondence.

humanity's rule over creation; and (4) the noncoincidental overlap of δόξα and εἰκών in Romans and other Pauline texts.[65] These four factors establish at least the possibility that Psalm 8 stands behind Paul's use of δόξα within Romans. Their significance for my larger argument encourages us to examine them further.

The first indication that Paul echoed Psalm 8 in Romans is that he demonstrates his awareness of the psalm and its significance for the same narrative of redemption in 1 Corinthians 15:27—a verse in a thematically similar context to the key δόξα passages in Romans.[66] As Keesmaat suggests: "Given . . . Paul's use of Psalm 8 in 1 Cor. 15:27, it is quite possible that Paul linked the glory of humanity with humanity's rule over creation. As Romans 8 progresses we discover that this is indeed the case."[67] In 1 Corinthians, Psalm 8 is evidence of the restoration of God's intended order of rule within his kingdom by the resurrection of his Son. The presence of death in 1 Corinthians 15:21 (δι' ἀνθρώπου θάνατος), which came through Adam in 1 Corinthians 15:22 (ἐν τῷ Ἀδὰμ πάντες ἀποθνήσκουσιν), is counteracted by the resurrection of the Son. In his resurrection from the dead, the Messiah subjected all enemies, including death, under his feet (1 Cor 15:24b-27), thereby restoring the kingdom of God to his Father (1 Cor 15:24a). Paul interprets Psalm 8 christologically, yet he makes clear that the kingdom of God, and presumably the "subjection of all things under his feet," is not the inheritance of the Son only. Dominion will be for all those whose bodies will be "raised in glory" (1 Cor 15:43) with the Son and who will thus "bear the image of the man of heaven" (1 Cor 15:49).[68] If this is an accurate reading, then Psalm 8, even if implicit, is a viable background for Paul's similar texts in Romans.

Second, it is undeniable that Paul relies on the figure of Adam in Genesis 1–3 for the formation of his understanding of YHWH's redemption of his people. This dependence is seen in Paul's Adam Christology. New Testament scholarship has produced a wealth of discussion on this topic—

---

[65]1 Cor 11:7-15; 15:40-49; Col 3:4, 10; esp. Rom 1:23 and 2 Cor 3:18; 4:4; see Van Kooten 2008a: 69-91.

[66]Paul also alludes to Ps 8 in Phil 3:21 and Eph 1:22. The writer of Hebrews also placed great weight on the psalm in demonstrating the Son's dominion in Heb 2:5-9. This fulfills Hays's criteria of recurrence and both Hays's and Tooman's criteria of thematic correspondence.

[67]Keesmaat 1999: 85.

[68]See Ciampa and Rosner 2007: 745-46.

a wheel not needing reinvention here.[69] Within Romans, Adamic echoes potentially exist in Romans 1:23; 3:23; 7:7-11; 8:29,[70] while Romans 5 includes the only explicit mention of Adam. For the sake of this study I draw attention to the role of Adam in Romans 5 as the one through whom sin and death came into the world (Rom 5:12, 17) and as the man with whom Paul contrasts the Messiah (Rom 5:17-21; see 1 Cor 15). Here Paul depends on the role of Adam in the creation narratives of Genesis as *a*, if not *the*, foundation for his anthropology, hamartiology, and soteriology in Romans.[71]

Third, Craigie notes that the thematic and possible textual relationship[72] between the creation poetry of Psalm 8:5-8 LXX and the creation poetry/narrative of Genesis 1:26-28 is identified by numerous authors and commentators on the texts.[73] Several elements of overlap are prominent: (1) Both pieces are set in the context of kingship with ties to ancient Near Eastern kingship narratives.[74] (2) In both poems, mankind has dominion over creation. (3) In both texts it is Adam or mankind (ἄνθρωπος) in focus. Schaefer remarks that "literally the

---

[69]E.g., Davies 1980; Jervell 1960; Barrett 1962; Brandenburger 1962; Scroggs 1966; Dunn 1989; Hooker 1990; Dunn 1998b. In the last decade, surprisingly few publications focus specifically on Paul's Adam-Christ typology. This is perhaps due to Levison's (1988) warnings against scholars' too-easy tendency to declare particular early Jewish Adamic texts as normative among first-century Jews. Levison successfully demonstrated that a variety of "portraits" of Adam existed in early Jewish literature, and to suggest that any one was normative, usually on the basis of its suggested relationship to Paul's theology, is to do an injustice to the varied readings and perspectives on Adam.

[70]For discussions of Paul's use of Adam in these texts, see Hooker 1959–1960: 297-306; Scroggs 1966; Dunn 1989: 98-125; Dunn 1998b: 79-101; Hooker 1990; Wright 1991: 18-40; Schreiner 2001: 146-50. Cf. Stowers (1994: 86-89), who argues that Adam is not in view. I will return to the question of echoes of Adam in Romans in detail in the second half of this chapter.

[71]See Thielman 1995: 169-95.

[72]**Table 3.1**

τῶν ἰχθύων τῆς θαλάσσης (Gen 1:26) τῶν ἰχθύων τῆς θαλάσσης (Gen 1:28)	τοὺς ἰχθύας τῆς θαλάσσης (Ps 8:9 LXX) τοὺς ἰχθύας τῆς θαλάσσης (Ps 8:9 LXX) τὰ διαπορευόμενα τρίβους θαλασσῶν (Ps 8:9 LXX)
τῶν πετεινῶν τοῦ οὐρανοῦ (Gen 1:26) τῶν πετεινῶν τοῦ οὐρανου (Gen 1:28)	τὰ πετεινὰ τοῦ οὐρανοῦ (Ps 8:9 LXX)
τῶν κτηνῶν (Gen 1:26) τῶν κτηνῶν (Gen 1:28)	τὰ κτήνη τοῦ πεδίου (Ps 8:8 LXX)
πάσης τῆς γῆς (Gen 1:26)	πάντα ὑπέταξας (Ps 8:7 LXX)

[73]See Craigie 1983: 106; Urassa 1998: 72.

[74]See Beale 2004: 66-121; Middleton 2005: 26-29; Beale 2008: 127-35.

second query in [Ps 8] v. 4 could be translated '[what are] the children of Adam that you care for them,' evoking not Abraham or Israel, but everyone tainted by sin."[75] (4) Most importantly for this study, in both poems Adam/humanity is given authority to rule over this inclusive creation: ἀρχέτωσαν (Gen 1:26 LXX); κατακυριεύσατε αὐτῆς (Gen 1:28 LXX); ἄρχετε (Gen 1:28 LXX); κατέστησας αὐτὸν ἐπὶ (Ps 8:7 LXX), serving in both texts as the depiction of his being "made in the image of God"[76] or "crowned with glory" by God.

Given these similarities between the two poems, it is possible that the forming of Adam "in the image of God" in Genesis 1:27 and the crowning of Adam "with glory and honor" in Psalm 8:6 LXX are different but coterminous metaphors.[77] Both suggest the bestowal of God's authority on Adam/humanity to rule over the creation within God's kingdom and on God's behalf. The metaphorical synonymy is not negated by the facts that δόξα is not found in Genesis 1:26-28 and εἰκών is not found in Psalm 8:5-8 LXX. Whether the psalm is textually based on Genesis 1 or vice versa presently remains unclear,[78] but the thematic and linguistic evidence warrants the strong possibility of either textual relationship.[79] It is certainly possible that a first-century Jewish writer such as Paul would have seen the connection between the two poems, both of which he utilized in his letters.[80]

---

[75]Schaefer 2001: 24. Though the Greek is ambiguous, the writer of the psalm in the MT most likely did not have Adam in mind in Ps 8:5, as the Hebrew term used was not אדם but אנוש.

[76]The "image of God" is, of course, an ongoing topic of debate. For extended discussions on the history of interpretations of the phrase and on understanding the "image of God" as a functional image and/or royal image, see Clines 1968; Bird 1981; Hall 1986; Jónsson 1988; Hughes 2001; Middleton 2005; Beale 2008; McDowell 2015. After noting the five main solutions suggested for understanding what the "image" or "likeness" refers to, Wenham (1987: 31-32) states that "the strongest case has been made for the view that the divine image makes man God's vice-regent on earth." He writes: "The image makes man God's representative on earth. That man is made in the divine image and is thus God's representative on earth was a common oriental view of the king. . . . Man is here bidden to rule and subdue the rest of creation, an obviously royal task (cf. 1 Kgs. 5:4 [4:24], etc.) and Ps. 8 speaks of man as having been created a little lower than the angels, *crowned* with glory and made to *rule* the works of God's hands. The allusions to the functions of royalty are quite clear in Ps. 8": 1987: 30; emphasis original.

[77]See 4Q504 frag. 8, where the image and glory of God are conflated: "Thou hast fashioned [Adam], our [f]ather in the likeness of [Thy] glory."

[78]Craigie 1983: 106.

[79]See 2 Bar. 14:17-19.

[80]Not faced with today's text-critical conversations, Paul presumably understood Gen 1 to be written significantly earlier than Ps 8.

Fourth, it is no coincidence that in certain key passages where Paul uses δόξα in Romans it is in close proximity to his use of εἰκών (Rom 1:23-25; 8:29-30; see 1 Cor 11:7; 15:40-49; 2 Cor 2:7–4:6; Col 1:11, 15, 27; 3:4-10) or, more generally, to texts that already are listed as possible echoes of Adam (Rom 3:23).[81] Romans 1:23; 3:23; 8:29-30, based on both Genesis 1:26-28 and Psalm 8:6-9 LXX, establish Paul's story line of redemption within Romans, telling his readers what Adam/humanity was meant to do, what Adam/humanity did wrong (informed by his rereading of Gen 3:1-19), and, because of what the Son has done, what those who share in the Son's inheritance do now in part and will do in the future in full (Rom 8:17, 29). I shall argue this more completely below.

These four reasons will not convince everyone. Grant Macaskill, for example, has argued in *Union with Christ* that scholars should recognize less readily the presence of Adam and specifically the glory of Adam in Pauline texts. He dedicates a chapter to examining the Adamic backgrounds to union with Christ, from which he draws three conclusions: (1) the lack of Adamic glory in Second Temple texts should make New Testament interpreters hesitate to assign Adamic glory to New Testament texts that are not clearly based on solid evidence; (2) the diversity of Adam traditions within Jewish literature should challenge Paul's readers to allow for the same level of diversity; and (3) the Adamic glory traditions within Jewish texts are never the primary motifs but are integrated into the larger narrative of Israel's history, a fact that should lend itself to Paul's use of Adam in the same manner.[82]

Macaskill rightly critiques those who want to collapse the diverse traditions of Adam that exist in Jewish literature into Paul's reading of Adam. As I will make clear in my argument, I do not believe that Paul reappropriates in the person of Christ a tradition that speaks of Adam's loss of an innate splendor in the fall. That being said, Paul does bring together Adam, image, glory, Christ, and morphic language (noted below), which must be reckoned with. A more defensible position, I suggest, particularly with regard to the glory of Adam or humanity in Psalm 8 but also elsewhere,

---

[81]In this, Tooman's criteria of distinctiveness and multiplicity are both present. The δόξα trope can, no doubt, stem from a number of antecedent texts, but its relationship to εἰκών makes it quite distinct to Ps 8, particularly in those texts where εἰκών is used nearby.

[82]Macaskill 2013: 133-43.

is recognizing the possibility that the glory can be understood in terms other than splendor. As I made clear in the previous chapter, within the LXX the glory or glorification of humans is rarely presented as splendor. Rather, it is almost exclusively presented as man's honor or exalted status and is very often associated with a position of authority or rule.[83] When Adam's glory is understood as honor that is associated with a status of rule and is viewed coterminously with his vocational rule as bearer of the image of God, then Psalm 8 and its significance for Pauline Christology and anthropology become unmistakable.

One further note: Macaskill also warns against "assigning Adamic connotations to Psalm 8 in the mind of a Jewish reader." He does so on the basis of the rabbinic use of Psalm 8 in Pesiqta Rabbati 25:4, in which the glory is not ascribed to humanity or Adam but to the Torah given to Israel. Based on this, Macaskill concludes that the psalm's "christological significance was not primarily seen as Adamic."[84] In the context of Pesiqta Rabbati 25:4, this conclusion is correct. Yet as Kinzer concluded above, though the son of man in the psalm is applied to Adam, Enoch, Abraham, Moses, and the Torah (the connotation Macaskill picks up on) throughout the literature, "those individuals were usually presented as in some way fulfilling the vocation of Adam."[85] Moreover, the textual similarities alone, which I noted above, warrant assigning the *primary* connotations of Psalm 8 to those of Adam.

These four factors—Psalm 8 in 1 Corinthians 15:27; Paul's rereading of Genesis 1-3; the relationship between Genesis 1:26-28 and Psalm 8:5-8 LXX; and the overlap of δόξα and εἰκών in Paul—by no means confirm Paul's use of Psalm 8 within Romans. Nevertheless, they solidify the *possibility* that when Paul used δόξα in Romans, especially in the texts in proximity to εἰκών but not necessarily limited to them, Psalm 8 and the crowning of Adam with glory and honor was a possible textual backdrop. *Within Romans, therefore, it is—at a minimum—possible that humanity's*

---

[83]I note again that the distinction between reading glory as splendor versus honor/exalted status/power is not one of ontology versus function. The distinction, rather, is semantic. Both are ontological qualities, both are qualities that are gifted by God and experienced only in relation to God, and both have their place in Paul's language of glory. See further the discussion of glorification as an ontological transformation in union with Christ in §4.1.2.

[84]Macaskill 2013: 142.

[85]Kinzer 1995: 215.

hope for glory (Rom 2:7, 10; 5:2; 8:18, 21; 9:23) and glorification (Rom 8:17, 30) means humanity's hope to share in the exalted status with Christ in his rule over creation, having received the crown of glory originally given to Adam in their coglorification with Christ, the new Adam. This is confirmed by two things: the inadequacy of understanding δόξα as a visible light associated with the manifest presence of God or imperial notions of glory, and the plausibility of the presence of Psalm 8 in Romans.

3.2.3. Adam in Paul's image and morphic language. Adam is mentioned explicitly only seven times in Paul's letters: in the contexts of Romans 5:12-21; 1 Corinthians 15:21-28, 45-47; and 1 Timothy 2:12-15. From this only two conclusions are typically drawn: (1) Adam is not as important to Paul's theology as he is often made out to be; he is hardly mentioned; and (2) Adam is critical to Paul's theology; he is mentioned explicitly in Romans and 1 Corinthians in passages that are central to and/or climactic in and/ or theologically significant to Paul's letters. I suggest the latter expression is more accurate, not least because the figure of Adam is arguably present in intertextual echoes elsewhere in Paul's letters, most importantly for our purposes in Romans 1:23; 3:23; 8:29, which I will discuss below.

Those familiar with the question of the presence of Adam naturally and rightly think of the work of James Dunn. But in more recent years, the mantle has been taken up by George van Kooten in his 2008 *Paul's Anthropology in Context*, where he traces Paul's "image" and morphic language in contrast with "image of god" and morphic language of both Jewish and Greco-Roman literature.[86] Van Kooten concludes, in part, that *image* and *form* are fundamentally connected in both sets of sources, and that Paul's use of *image* and *form* (or morphic language) are similarly connected. Furthermore, and perhaps more importantly here, van Kooten suggests that Paul's image and morphic language are part and parcel of Paul's Adam Christology. Van Kooten suggests:

> The extent of the semantic and conceptual field of the divine image is larger than might be assumed at first glance; the scope of Paul's Adam Christology

---

[86]Van Kooten (2008a: 70) writes: "I agree with [Dunn] that 'Adam plays a larger role in Paul's theology than is usually realized,' that 'Adam is a key figure in Paul's attempt to express his understanding both of Christ and of man,' and that 'it is necessary to trace the extent of the Adam motif in Paul if we are to appreciate the force of his Adam Christology,'" quoting Dunn from his 1989 *Christology in the Making*: 101.

is extensive. The extent of this field is so large, and especially its inclusion of morphic language so important that, without much exaggeration, one could characterize Paul's Christology and anthropology as "morphic." This semantic taxonomy of only a part of Paul's Adam Christology shows that this type of Christology is indeed very dominant in Paul.[87]

In his hearty agreement with Dunn's emphasis on Paul's Adam Christology but in recognition that even Dunn has overlooked this image-form taxonomy, van Kooten writes:

> I wish to contribute to this search by focusing on the semantic field of the image of God, which is part of Paul's Adam Christology. It seems that the semantic-conceptual field of the notion of the image of God is larger and more coherent than is often realized. I shall argue that the notion of the image of God not only comprises the terminology of "image" (εἰκών) but also that of μορφή ("form") and its cognate terms μορφόομαι ("take on form, be formed"), σύμμορφος ("having the same form, similar in form"), συμμορφίζομαι ("be conformed to, take on the same form as"), and, last but not least, μεταμορφόομαι ("be transformed, be changed into the same form").[88]

For van Kooten, Adam lurks behind the surface of numerous texts that are often not recognized as Adamic, namely those in which Paul's image-form taxonomy occurs (e.g., Rom 1:23; 8:29; Phil 3:21, among others). I will take up van Kooten's argument at various places throughout the chapters in this book.

3.2.4. Echoes of Adam in Romans 1 and 3. I will discuss briefly the evidence for viewing Romans 1:23; 3:23 as implicit allusions to Adam on the basis of Tooman's and Hays's criteria, leaving that of Romans 8:29 to chapter five, where a more comprehensive treatment will be given.[89] Despite its reception since antiquity and its continued wide acceptance in modern

---

[87]Van Kooten 2008a: 71; see 75, 91, 340-92.

[88]Van Kooten 2008a: 70.

[89]I note a critical point: *even if* the argument is not persuasive that Rom 1:23; 3:23 allude to the figure of Adam, Paul's explicit use of Adam in Rom 5:12-21 as a partial basis to his Christology—a Christology at the heart of his eschatological anthropology in Rom 5–8—is warrant enough to read the "hope of glory" texts in Rom 8 as references to the glory that will be *given by God* to a *humanity redeemed in the new Adam*, who is not ruled by sin and death but who rules over sin and death. Put another way: understanding humanity's glory as a renewed Adamic glory in Rom 8 is not dependent on the presence of allusions to Adam in Rom 1:23; 3:23. The presence of Adam in these texts simply makes it all the more likely in Rom 8:29.

scholarship, many now reject the Edenic fall narrative as the backdrop of Romans 1:18-32 and specifically of Romans 1:23. Those who reject an allusion to Genesis 3 in Romans 1:23 do so on the basis that neither Adam nor the fall is mentioned in Romans 1:18-32. Some thus opt for a middle ground: Paul is not describing Adam's fall as it is recorded in Genesis 3, but he would no doubt see the correlation between it and the fall of humanity more generally. Moo writes, "That Paul may view the 'fall' of individual human beings as analogous *in some ways* to the Fall of the first human pair is likely, but the text does not warrant the conclusion that he is specifically describing the latter."[90]

Stanley Stowers raises a serious objection to the implicit reference to a fall narrative in *A Rereading of Romans*.[91] What is described in Romans 1:18-32, Stowers suggests, is neither the fall of humanity nor specifically of the primal pair but the "sinful degradation into which the non-Jewish peoples have declined owing to their worship of many gods and idols."[92] "Since they have refused to acknowledge him," Stowers continues, "the true God has punished these idol worshipers by allowing their enslavement to the passions (*pathē*) and the desires (*epithumiai*) of their bodies. Thus they live in societies characterized by evil and vice."[93] Romans 1:18-32 is about the "human degeneration into the non-Jewish peoples,"[94] and not the primal pair's fall into sin, nor that of humanity at large. Three critiques must be made at this point.

First, Stowers finds partial support for his rejection of the Adamic fall narrative in John Levison's *Portraits of Adam in Early Judaism*. With Levison, he argues that Adam is not echoed in Romans 1:23 because it was not until post-70 CE when Jewish writers such as those of 4 Ezra and 2 Baruch began assessing anew the consequences of Adam's transgression. The new assessment, Stowers writes, "stems from a profound pessimism generated

---

[90]Moo 1996: 110n85; emphasis original. In the same place, Moo argues that, because "Rom. 1 focuses on human neglect of 'natural revelation,' whereas Rom. 5:13-14 shows that Paul linked Adam with Israel in being responsible for 'special revelation,' Adam is not in view in 1:23. Moreover, this is the case because no clear allusions to Gen. 3 exist in the text." For views against the echo of Adam in Rom 1:23, see also Scroggs 1966: 75-79; Fitzmyer 1993: 283; Stowers 1994: 83-125; Esler 2003: 148-50.

[91]Stowers 1994: 83-125.

[92]Stowers 1994: 36-37; see also 83-125.

[93]Stowers 1994: 37.

[94]Stowers 1994: 107.

by the catastrophe to Judaism caused by the destruction of Jerusalem. Paul lived on the other side of this divide. The Judaism of 4 Ezra and Baruch would have been unimaginable to the apostle."[95]

This assumption, however, raises a number of questions. (1) If Jews began to reconsider the consequences of Adam's sin after the destruction of Jerusalem in 70 CE, what prevented the same conclusion in 586 BCE? (2) Stowers and Levison both rightly acknowledge the variety of Jewish interpretations of Genesis 1–3, none of which are deemed dependent on the others. Why, then, is Paul's interpretation of Genesis 1–3 expected to align with a previously held Jewish interpretation? Why is Paul's Damascus Road experience not enough of a *Tendenz* particular to Paul as a zealous Pharisee who now understands that Jesus is the anticipated Messiah—a Messiah who has not only died by crucifixion but also resurrected from the dead? (3) Would a personal encounter with a resurrected human not challenge a person's preconceptions of reality equally as much as (if not more so than) the relatively anticipated military defeat and thus redestruction of holy places? (4) Is the argument for what "would have been unimaginable to the apostle" dependent on extant sources, as both Levison and Stowers assume it to be? (5) Can one assume that the writers of 4 Ezra and 2 Baruch were wholly unfamiliar with Paul's writings on Adam, sin, and death? Space does not permit discussion of these questions, but they are important to note nonetheless. Both Stowers and Levison are correct to point out the variety of Jewish interpretations of Genesis 1–3 but are mistaken in the argument that Paul's interpretation must therefore align with one of the preexisting interpretations.

Van Kooten also finds fault with Levison's treatment of the various occurrences of Adam in Jewish literature, describing it as showing "traces of reductionism where he emphasizes, again and again, that all views on the 'image of God' are wholly incorporated into the *Tendenzen* of a particular author, so that the notion almost ceases to have any substance of its own."[96] Van Kooten finds unity in the midst of diversity in the various "image of God" texts in three motifs: (1) a shared "antithesis between the image of

---

[95]Stowers 1994: 88.
[96]Van Kooten 2008a: 44.

God and other images," (2) a "divine anthropology," and (3) "a physical understanding of God's image."[97]

Second, Stowers's rereading of Romans 1:18-32 fits within his larger rereading of Romans, in which he concludes that the "encoded readers" of Romans are not a combination of Jewish and Gentile believers, as traditionally understood, but Gentile believers alone.[98] The purpose of Romans, according to Stowers, is to inform Gentile followers of Christ that their attempts at self-mastery through obedience to the Jewish law will not profit. Righteousness (or "self-mastery") comes through the one perfect law-keeper, Jesus Christ.[99] But this reading of the audience has not gone uncritiqued. Several reviewers have found it provocative and insightful but ultimately unpersuasive.[100] On the basis of the reviews of Hays and Barclay in particular, I am unpersuaded that the "encoded readers" are entirely Gentile, a crucial argument in Stowers's overall argument.[101] Hays systematically critiques Stowers's examination or lack of examination of key Romans texts[102] as evidence of Jews forming some part (even if minor) of the encoded audience.[103] Stowers's argument is shared by Mark Nanos, who published just after Stowers and also argued that Paul's "implied audience" was "primarily, if not exclusively, Christian gentiles."[104] Because Nanos's provocative work on Romans will not affect my argument at large, I will not elaborate at this point, other than to suggest that many of Hays's critiques of Stowers apply equally to Nanos's argument as well.

---

[97]Van Kooten 2008a: 45-48.

[98]Stowers 1994: 21.

[99]Stowers 1994: 36.

[100]Barclay 1995: 646-51; Bassler 1996; Hays 1996; Peterson 1997.

[101]See also Esler 2003 for what is perhaps the most recent thorough treatment of Romans as a letter to both Jews (Judeans) and Gentiles, as well as Longenecker's (2011: 55-91) helpful summary of the issues and arguments surrounding the question of Paul's addressees in Romans.

[102]Rom 1:16; 2:17; 3:22-23; 4:1; 5:1-11; 7:1; 15:7-13; 16:1-27.

[103]Hays 1996: 36-39.

[104]Nanos 1996: 84. Nanos argues that "while [Paul's] concerns in Romans involve Jews, they are not directed toward Jews, or Jewish exclusivism, except paradigmatically to clarify the problems inherent in the misguided views that were gaining ground among the *gentile* believers in Rome toward Jews, though perhaps springing from resentment because of the response of some Jews who may have been questioning their faith claims in Christ. . . . The mystery of Romans is revealed when we realize that the Paul we meet in this letter is engaged in confronting the initial development of just such a misunderstanding of God's intentions in Rome manifest in Christian-*gentile* exclusivism"; 1996: 10; emphasis original.

Additionally, Stowers's argument was picked up by Caroline Johnson Hodge, whose work will be noted throughout this book and especially when I turn to Romans 8 in particular. I am critical of a number of her arguments, many of which are reliant on Stowers's rereading of Romans as a letter to an exclusively Gentile audience. Issues that are in the first instance potential weaknesses in her work are made explicit flaws by her almost entire lack of any significant response to the critiques presented against Stowers, particularly Hays's critiques of an exclusively Gentile audience in Romans. She briefly highlights the conversation,[105] and on the partial Jewish audience in Romans, in particular, she writes only that the arguments put forth in favor of a mixed audience "have been unconvincing."[106] Due to her self-acknowledged recognition that the nature of the audience is the "pivotal issue for determining one's reading of Paul"[107] and forms the fundamental basis for her entire argument, her lack of response to critics simply will not do.

Third, and more important for our purposes here, Stowers's reading of Romans 1:23 as a description of humanity's degradation into non-Jewish idolaters does not necessitate a rejection of an implicit echo of Adam. Stowers may be correct that this is Paul's intended description in the passage. Nevertheless, nothing warrants the impossibility of using the Genesis narrative as an illustrative primal text for humanity's degradation into Gentile idolaters. In fact, van Kooten does just this:

> In Romans 1, Paul criticizes those who have degenerated into idol-worshippers. . . . Whereas exchanging the glory of God for images of idols is a sign of mankind's decline, its restoration takes place when man is conformed to God's image [Rom 8:29]. The antagonism between the image of God and idols seems already to be part of the Old Testament background to the notion of the image of God. . . . It is not unlikely that the assertion that man is created "in God's image" (Gen 1.26-27) could bear anti-idolatrous overtones, as the term "image" is one of the words used to refer to idols.[108]

Van Kooten recognizes that Paul can make his point about Gentile idolatry *on the basis of* the primal text. Joseph Fitzmyer, too, acknowledges that

---

[105]Johnson Hodge 2007: 9-11.
[106]Johnson Hodge 2007: 10.
[107]Johnson Hodge 2007: 9.
[108]Van Kooten 2008a: 73-74.

Paul is using the Hebrew Scriptures to characterize pagan idolatry. Referring to Paul's allusions to Psalm 106:20 and Jeremiah 2:11, allusions whose presence in the text he does not reject, Fitzmyer writes, "[Paul] is simply extrapolating from such incidents in the history of the chosen people and applying the ideas to the pagan world."[109] With Fitzmyer, and in reference not to Genesis 1–3 but to the possible echoes of Jeremiah and Psalm 105 (LXX), Philip Esler also notes that "there was nothing to stop Paul applying to non-Israelites derogatory descriptions previously used of Israelites, especially when the language in question concerned idolatrous activities by Israelites."[110] Fitzmyer and Esler ultimately reject an echo of Genesis 3 in Romans 1:18-32, but their recognition that Paul writes to Gentiles and that he uses ancient Israelite texts as his basis demonstrates the weakness of Stowers's argument. Against Stowers, reading Romans 1:23 as the Gentiles' degradation into idolatry does not thereby bar an echo of Genesis 1–3 from the verse.

Scholars traditionally reject arguments for the implicit Genesis narrative in Romans 1:23 because the evidence of a fall narrative from Genesis 3 is lacking,[111] and *rightly so*; the embrace of idolatry, whether by humanity as a whole or Gentiles in particular, is not labeled in Genesis 3 as it is in Romans 1. But this does not mean that the Genesis narrative is therefore nonexistent in Romans 1:23; nor does it mean that because what is described in Romans 1:23 as idolatry does not in some way reflect or bear witness to any Genesis narrative. In fact, it is precisely in the *creation* narrative of Genesis 1:26-28 rather than the fall narrative of Genesis 3 that the echo of "Adam," aka "humanity" in Romans 1:23, exists (see esp. Gen 5:2 LXX: καὶ ἐπωνόμασεν τὸ ὄνομα αὐτῶν Αδαμ; אָדָם in Gen 1:26, without distinction of male and female). Here, both textually and theologically, I suggest Paul's point has been overlooked.[112]

---

[109]Fitzmyer 1993: 271.The same can be said for the implicit background of Wisdom of Solomon, especially at Wis 13:10–15:19. As rightly noted by most scholars, the Jewish polemic against idolatry is unmistakable in the text. But, as with Ps 105:20 LXX and Jer 2:11 (see below), it does not overshadow the clear reuse of Gen 1:26-28.

[110]Esler 2003: 148-49.

[111]For arguments for the implicit echo, see, e.g., Davies 1980; Hooker 1959–1960; Jervell 1960; Barrett 1962; Brandenburger 1962; Scroggs 1966; Dunn 1989; Hooker 1990; Dunn 1998b.

[112]This is not to suggest that scholarship has failed to see the textual echo of Gen 1:26-28 in Rom 1:23. Niels Hyldahl wrote an article in 1956 describing the textual relationship between the two passages, a point that numerous scholars have followed. Even Fitzmyer (1993: 274),

Textually, the allusion to Adam as humanity in Genesis 1:26-28 is difficult to miss, at least on the grounds for determining intertextuality laid out by Richard Hays and William Tooman:

1. Volume. With its associated elements of distinctiveness and multiplicity, volume is represented by the threefold reference to the animal world in both Romans 1:23 and Genesis 1:26, 28. Πετεινόν and ἑρπετόν occur in both Romans 1:23 and Genesis 1:26, 28, and while Paul uses τετράπους in Romans 1:23 rather than κτῆνος, which is found in Genesis 1:26, 28, τετράπους is found immediately before it, in Genesis 1:24. Moreover, lexical correspondence is demonstrable in three other words: εἰκών and ἄνθρωπος in Romans 1:23 and Genesis 1:26, 27, and at least a strong possibility of correspondence between ὁμοίωσις in Genesis 1:26 and ὁμοίωμα in Romans 1:23. The volume of shared lexemes, then, between Romans 1:23 and Genesis 1:26-28 is weighty: five words correspond between Romans 1:23 and Genesis 1:26-28, with an additional word (τετράπους) bearing extremely close proximity.[113]

2. Thematic correspondence. Genesis 1 implies no wickedness in humanity, in contrast to Paul's description of humanity's sinful state in Romans 1. Nevertheless, the two texts share the same theme of a creation context: "since the creation of the world [κτίσεως κόσμου]," Paul writes in Romans 1:20. Given the lexical overlap noted above, it is difficult to assign this contextual/thematic correspondence to coincidence.

3. Recurrence. Paul later refers to the "first man," Adam, explicitly in Romans 5:12, 17. Moreover, he refers in Romans 8:19-22 to the impact on creation of humanity's rejection of its created purpose, thus picking up (albeit implicitly) the theme of the curse placed on the ground in Genesis 3:17 as a result of the sin of the "first man" and, theologically, as a result

---

who rejects the idea that Paul is referring to Adam in Rom 1:23, acknowledges that any allusions that do exist regard Gen 1. For this reason, Esler's (2003: 149) comment that "it is far-fetched to introduce Adam into the picture" is perhaps itself too farfetched, or at least overstated. Esler himself acknowledges the possibility of Deut 4:16-18 as the source from which Paul "derived" the "paraphernalia of idol worship mentioned in Rom. 1:23" (2003: 147) but does not acknowledge the lexical similarities between Rom 1:23 and Gen 1:26-28 recognized by Fitzmyer. Esler goes on to suggest that the Sodom tradition stands behind Rom 1:18-32 (2003: 149-50), an insight that may offer another valid reading. But this does not explain away the linguistic link between Rom 1:23 and Gen 1:26-27.

[113]See Hooker 1959–1960; Dunn 1989: 101-2; Dunn 1988a: 60-61; Beale 2008: 203. Also in agreement are Byrne 2007: 68; Wright 2002: 432; Harrison 2011: 257; Levison 2004: 523-25.

of his rejection of his created purpose: to be the image (Gen 1) and glory (Ps 8) of God.

If Hays's and especially Tooman's criteria—with Tooman's having received little to no criticism—for determining intertextual echoes/allusions are demonstrably fulfilled, which they are, then the textual burden of proof for objecting to an allusion to Adam in Romans 1:23 lies on those who object to its possibility. Käsemann recognizes the correspondences without elaborating on them but rejects the idea that Paul could here be alluding to Genesis 1:26-28 on the basis of the fact that Paul applies the term εἰκών to the animals as well. Käsemann nevertheless acknowledges that "the association certainly may be derived from the creation story."[114] Yet, as van Kooten persuasively demonstrates, there is an antagonism between the image of God and the images and/or forms of idols throughout the Old Testament as well as in other Jewish literature.[115] This lack of distinction is illustrated by Sibylline Oracles 3.8: "Men, who have the form which God molded in his image" (ἄνθρωποι θεόπλαστον ἔχοντες ἐν εἰκόνι μορφήν).[116] The strict metaphysical distinction Käsemann wants to keep between the image of God and those of idols is not a distinction held within early Judaism. With Harrison, "Jewish auditors familiar with the Genesis narrative would have spotted Paul's *clear allusion* to the subjugation of the created order (Gen 1:26b: birds, livestock, creeping things) that mankind, as the image of God (Gen 1:26a), was commanded to undertake."[117] Stowers, in all his argumentation against the presence of Genesis 1–2, fails to mention the textual correspondences between Genesis 1:26-28 and Romans 1:23.[118] He writes only that "the commonly cited Jewish parallels ought to be viewed as peculiar versions of the larger phenomenon of ancient primitivism," or what he calls "decline narratives."[119]

The textual evidence for an allusion to Genesis 1:26-28 in Romans 1:23 is unmistakable, however. Moreover, once the textual link is identified, the

---

[114]Käsemann 1964: 45.
[115]Van Kooten 2008a: 69-91.
[116]See van Kooten 2008a: 89, where he quotes this text in response to Fee, saying, "Fee's distinction between 'form' and 'image' runs contrary to the way in which (the combination) of these terms would have been commonly understood in Antiquity." The same argument can be made against Käsemann on Rom 1:23.
[117]Harrison 2011: 257.
[118]See Bassler 1996: 367, who critiques Stowers's lack of emphasis on the Jewish narratives.
[119]Stowers 1994: 85.

theological link between Romans 1:23 and Genesis 1:26-28 is also made clear. As noted above, the traditionally suggested allusion is to an implied fall narrative of the primal pair—a narrative rooted in Genesis 3 and a narrative that, in agreement with Stowers, Esler, and Fitzmyer, does not exist in Romans 1. Paul's point in each of the texts is *not* to emphasize the fall of humanity (though humanity's sin is nonetheless implied, as is made clear in Rom 3:23) but rather to emphasize the fact that, in its rejection of God, *humanity failed to be the image of God in its created purpose as those who are meant to rule over the created order.* Byrne rightly recognizes the heart of the verse:

> Behind the line of argument here would seem to be the biblical tradition, stemming from Gen 1:26-28, where human beings, created in the image and likeness of God, are given dominion over the rest of creation (fish, birds, animals, reptiles), a motif given more poetic expression in Psalm 8 (esp. vv 5-8). Idolatry represents the summit of "futility" (v 21) in that it has human beings submitting themselves in worship to the creatures over which they were meant to rule. This perverts the whole *raison-d'être* of the non-human created world, subjecting it to "futility" (8:30).[120]

The point of Romans 1:23 is not the fall into sin of the primal pair from Genesis 3, particularly through idolatry, which thus affected either Gentiles specifically or humanity more generally, but humanity's (אדם) "exchange of the glory of the immortal God" in terms of its failure to fulfill its created purpose or identity as creatures made in the image of God, having dominion over creation as vicegerents of the Creator God—*hence Paul's obvious allusion to Genesis 1:26-28 and not Genesis 3:6.* Dane Ortlund rightly argues that Paul's reference here is not to God's own glory, which then implies an "exchange of worship," but that "it is probably human glory (the divine image) that is in view."[121] Humanity's rejection of its created purpose throughout history took the form of idolatry—a form found in both Gentile and Jewish history—and resulted in a humanity that existed in their actions and desires as shadows of their created selves (Rom 1:24-32). Though the fall narrative of Genesis 2–3 is not implicit in Romans 1:23, Genesis 1:26-28 certainly is. Moreover, though the name "Adam" is not

---

mentioned in Romans 1, the created purpose or identity of corporate humanity ("adam"; אָדָם) in Genesis 1:26-28 is undoubtedly of central importance in Romans 1:23.

An Adamic (i.e., all humanity in Adam) echo also exists in Romans 3:23: πάντες γὰρ ἥμαρτον καὶ ὑστεροῦνται τῆς δόξης τοῦ θεοῦ.[122] When this echo is recognized, scholars generally assume a link exists between the δόξα in Romans 3:23 and Jewish traditions of Adam losing his garment of glory (Gen. Rab. 12.6) and/or the light of God with which he was at first clothed (Apoc. Mos. 21).[123] That Paul was even aware of these Adam traditions, however, is dubious, especially given that the date of writing of Genesis Rabbah was significantly past the mid-first century and that the existence of a Hebrew *Vorlage* for Apocalypse of Moses is based entirely on speculation. The texts were possibly written as late as 400 CE.[124] If Paul referred to Adam's "fall from glory" narrated in the two nonbiblical texts, he relied on either an oral or nonextant written tradition on which these two nonbiblical texts were also based. This is not to say that all scholars who hear an echo of Adam assume a connection to the Jewish texts. As noted above, Newman and Harrison correctly suggest that the glory of humanity in Romans 3:23 is not a reference to these later accounts of Adam's loss of glory but to a "ruptured relationship" between God and humanity;[125] but in this assessment, they stand quite alone.

I do not, however, suggest that the figure of Adam is thus absent in Romans 3:23. If the textual echo of Genesis 1:26-28 were lacking from Romans 1:23, such a conclusion would be warranted. But Genesis 1:26-28 is present in Romans 1:23, and Romans 3:23 is a restatement of Romans 1:23 in summarized form: πάντες γὰρ ἥμαρτον καὶ ὑστεροῦνται τῆς δόξης τοῦ θεοῦ.[126] The thematic connection between Romans 1:23 and Romans

---

[122]Contra Stowers (1994: 190), who argues that Paul here refers "only to gentiles or perhaps to extremely wicked and unrepentant Jews," the grammatical dependence of Rom 3:23 on Rom 3:22 requires that both Jews and Gentiles be in view. As Hays (1996: 38) directly and appropriately critiques Stowers at this point: "This simply will not wash." See also Barclay 1995: 649.

[123]See 3 Bar. 4:16. See Hooker 1960; Barrett 1962; Scroggs 1966: 26-27, 54-56; Käsemann 1980: 95; Dunn 1988a: 168; Schreiner 1998: 187; Seifrid 2007: 618; Byrskog 2008: 9-10, to name just a few.

[124]Charlesworth 1983b: 251-52.

[125]Newman 1992: 225-27; Harrison, following Newman, in 2011: 264-65.

[126]See Harrison 2011: 263, 265.

3:23 is unmistakable, with the only differences being that in Romans 3:23 Paul replaces ἀλλάσσω with ὑστερέω and the reference to humanity's rejection of its created purpose as "sin." As in Romans 1:23, Paul does not mention Adam specifically, but the textual and thematic correspondences between the two verses warrant reading them as referring to the same rejection of humanity's created identity: God's glory. Moreover, given the previously demonstrated correlation between image and glory in Genesis 1:26-28 and Psalm 8:6-9 LXX, and the thematic relationship between humanity being crowned with glory in Psalm 8:6 and "lacking" the glory of God in Romans 3:23, it is also within the scope of possibility that not only is humanity in Adam from Genesis 1:26-28 behind the text but so also is the humanity crowned with glory and honor from Psalm 8. The glory that humanity lacks (because of their sin) is the glory of God. It is the glory that forms the identity and purpose of humanity—to have all things under their feet (Ps 8:7 LXX). The links between the motif of human glory in the LXX, as illustrated in Psalm 8, and image, as in Genesis 1:26-28, warrant the strong possibility that here in Romans 3:23 it is the Adamic glory (honor associated with their status as vicegerents over creation) that humanity now lacks. I will return to the nature of this glory in the final section of this chapter.

3.2.5. Adam's identity as paradigmatic. Here in Romans 1:23 and Romans 3:23, the image and glory of Adam is presented as the paradigmatic image and glory ascribed to all humanity in Genesis 1:26-27 and Psalm 8:6-9 LXX. Paul describes Adam's (humanity's) created identity and vocation negatively by describing humanity's rejection of that image in Romans 1:23 and lack of that glory in Romans 3:23. As noted above, this is the function of the echo of Adam in both texts: humanity in Adam was created to be and to act as God's royal representatives on earth—an identity that humanity rejected.

The function of the Adamic echo shifts slightly in Romans 5:12-21, where the echo is first presented in an Adam-Christ typology and where the fall narrative of Genesis 3 is first presented.[127] Here Paul's focus turns from the image and glory of humanity in Adam from Genesis 1:26-28/Psalm

---

[127]Again, this proposed reading is in opposition to traditional readings that attempt to establish echoes of Gen 3:6 in Rom 1:23; 3:23.

8:6-9 LXX to the sin and death that resulted from the one man, Adam (Gen 2–3). Romans 5:12 reads: "sin entered the world through [δι'] one man," which indicates, according to Douglas Moo, that "Paul's focus is on [Adam's] role as the instrument through whom sin and death were unleashed in the world."[128] Paul continues in Romans 5:12 by saying that "death came to all people because [ἐφ' ᾧ] all sinned." Esler notes that when this final phrase (ἐφ' ᾧ) is taken as a causal conjunction (rather than as an introduction of a relative clause[129]), as most modern scholars see it,[130] then "Paul's idea seems to be that while Adam's sin unleashed death, so that he was the ultimate cause ('many died through one's person's wrong-doing,' Rom 5:15), nevertheless all other human beings still needed to subject themselves to it, and did so."[131] In this way, then, Adam's sin was paradigmatic as well.

The sin, death, and condemnation that resulted from the sin of one man, Adam, Paul then sets in direct contrast with the grace, life, and righteousness that resulted from the obedience of the one man, Christ (Rom 5:15-19). In this way, the one man, Adam, is "a type of the one to come," Christ (Rom 5:14). Again, Esler helpfully notes: "Here τύπος carries the meaning of 'type' in the sense of a person from the primordial time who provides a pattern for a phenomenon in the New Testament period, an example or rule, an 'advance presentation' intimating end-time events."[132] And yet, more seems to be involved in Paul's Adam-Christ typology here than recognition of the two individuals as mere patterns. In Romans 5:19 the relationships between Adam and Christ and those associated with each "one man" become more obviously corporate: "For just as by the one man's disobedience the *many were made sinners*, so by the one man's obedience the many will be made righteous." Humanity's sin, which was individual in nature in Romans 5:12, has now become corporate in nature: "Adam's disobedience placed the mass of humanity in a condition of sin and estrangement from God; the text does not imply that they became sinners merely by imitating

---

[128]Moo 1996: 321.
[129]See Fitzmyer 1993: 413.
[130]See again Moo 1996: 322 for a breakdown of the various translations offered of the conjunction. Fitzmyer 1993: 413-17 also has a helpful, extended discussion of the various renderings of this final conjunction.
[131]Esler 2003: 200.
[132]Esler 2003: 200-201.

Adam's transgression; rather, they were constituted sinners by him and his act of disobedience."[133] This corporate relationship that Paul hints at in Romans 5:19 will become foundational in his description of baptism into Christ in Romans 6 and the incorporation of believers in Christ as the Son in Romans 8.

But the relationship between humanity's personal responsibility for its sin in Romans 5:12 and the corporate relationship that seems to stand behind Adam and humanity in Romans 5:19 should not be pressed further than the text allows. All humanity in Adam was created to serve as God's representatives; the image and glory invested in the first Adam are the same image and glory with which all humanity was invested. Adam represents what humanity was intended to be and what they, through sin, elected to be.

3.2.6. Conclusion. Based on these considerations and by way of introduction to the final section of this chapter, I suggest that Paul utilized the Greek Scriptures to tell the story of God's faithfulness to Israel, and he did so in a way that directly corresponded with the culture in which his readers lived. The denotation of δόξα and δοξάζω in Romans, both in reference to God and to humanity, was intelligible in first-century Rome to both Jewish and Gentile Christians because it shared the same denotative function in reference to both God and humanity as was used throughout the LXX and in first-century sociopolitical Roman parlance. In reference to God, δόξα and δοξάζω in Romans primarily denote the honor, esteem, power, or governing status of God as a result of his identity as Creator and King.[134] And in reference to humanity, δόξα and δοξάζω primarily denote the honor, esteem, power, and governing status of people as a result of their identity as renewed humans in the new Adam. This argument will be fleshed out on multiple levels over the course of this chapter and those that follow. Here I offer only an observation-deck analysis of δόξα and δοξάζω in Romans. In subsequent chapters the analysis will be done on ground level.

Following a similar categorization scheme as the one in the previous chapter, here is what is clearly visible in Romans, even from a distance:

---

[133]Fitzmyer 1993: 421.
[134]See §2.2.2.1.

Table 3.2

		Honor, Praise Given/ Received in Ascription	Honor, Status, Power, Character Possessed by	Visible Splendor (as Theophany, Presence of God, etc.)
δόξα	God	Rom 3:7; 4:20; 11:36; 15:7; 16:27	Rom 6:4	
	Humanity		Rom 2:7, 10	
δοξάζω	God	Rom 1:21		
	Humanity			

Left to be determined, then, are the denotations of δόξα and δοξάζω with reference to God in Romans 1:23; 3:23; 5:2; 9:23a and to humanity/believers in Romans 8:17 (συνδοξάζω), and Romans 8:18, 21, 30; 9:4, 23b.

3.3. PAUL'S ANTHROPOLOGICAL "NARRATIVE OF GLORY" IN ROMANS

I have argued that Paul uses δόξα and δοξάζω to refer to the glory of humanity in Psalm 8 in relationship to Genesis 1; 3. I now turn our attention to Paul's specific use of the terms throughout Romans. I will argue here that throughout the letter there is an implied narrative of glory, a narrative that begins with humanity forsaking the glory of God, that is, humanity's purposed identity and vocation (Rom 1:23; 3:23) and God's people receiving again the glory of God (Rom 2:7, 10; 5:2; 8:17, 21, 30; 9:23). This narrative of glory forms the heart of the meaning behind Paul's dense phrase "conformed to the image of [God's] Son."

Samuel Byrskog also attempts this narrative construction of glory in Romans in his 2008 article "Christology and Identity in an Intertextual Perspective: The Glory of Adam in the Narrative Substructure of Paul's Letter to the Romans." Byrskog traces Adam's fall from glory in Romans 1–3 to humanity's redemption to glory in conformity to Christ in Romans 8:18-30. He does so with the purpose of "asking about the existence of a narrative substructure that holds together the allusions and the explicit references to Adam in Romans and opens up avenues to a more dynamic thinking about Christology and identity."[135] Byrskog concludes that Christian

---

[135]Byrskog 2008: 2. See also Blackwell 2010: 285-308 for a similar study.

identity and Christology find their link in Paul's Adam Christology, a conclusion that I too will share.[136]

Why then is this examination of humanity's glory and glorification in Romans necessary? While Byrskog explores the same intertextual links between Romans and Genesis 1–3, and rightly suggests that the echoes in Romans 8:18-30 refer to the renewed glory that was lost in Romans 1:23; 3:23,[137] he makes one major assumption: that the source material for Paul's references to Adam's glory is the Greek Life of Adam and Eve. Because of this, he presupposes that humanity's original glory is the splendor or radiance with which Adam was clothed in Life of Adam and Eve 21.6. Moreover, Byrskog links *image* and *glory* but never articulates what it means to be "made in the image of God." Though I appreciate a vast amount of Byrskog's essay on the narrative substructure of glory in Romans, it should not be assumed that Paul drew from the same tradition as the writer of Life of Adam and Eve 21.6, and thus further work is required.

This narrative substructure of glory in Romans that Byrskog rightly notes will quickly become clear. Throughout the letter δόξα is used fifteen times: Romans 1:23; 2:7, 10; 3:7, 23; 4:20; 5:2; 6:4; 8:18, 21; 9:4, 23; 11:36; 15:7; 16:27. Δοξάζω is used six times: Romans 1:21; 8:30; 11:13; 15:6, 9 (and συνδοξάζω in Rom 8:17). I suggest that the "glory of God" in Romans 1:23; 3:23; 5:2; 9:23 refers not only to the glory possessed by God but also to the glory possessed by humanity via their participation in the glory of God,[138] in much the same way that δόξα in Romans 2:7, 10; 8:18, 21, and perhaps Romans 9:4 refers to a glory possessed by humans. And, with the exception of Romans 8:17, 30, which we must defer for the moment, δοξάζω always refers to the giving of honor or praise on the basis of a status, presumably that of dominion/sovereignty. This case will be made for Romans 8:17, 30 as well. Similarly, nearly every instance of δόξα can be understood likewise.[139] When we read δόξα in Romans through the lens of a

---

[136]Byrskog 2008: 14-18.

[137]Byrskog 2008: 10-14.

[138]The term *participation* will be examined and defined in §4.1.2.

[139]Rom 6:4 is less explicit, but no indication exists that it is a reference to God's radiance or manifest presence. In fact, one would expect Paul to say "power" here instead. See Dunn 1988a: 315; Schreiner 1998: 311. Byrne (2007: 196n4) writes: "The translation takes the preposition *dia* instrumentally, so that *doxa* is virtually equivalent to the power of God, a sense which it frequently has in the LXX."

post-Damascus rereading of Psalm 8 (and its relationship to Gen 1; 3),[140] the texts begin to tell a remarkable story—a story of the enthronement, abdication, and reenthronement of God's people as God's representatives within his kingdom. God's people do have a hope of glory—not just to reflect the glorious presence of God but to be the fullest expression of true humanity in their vicegerency with the Son of God. This narrative substructure of glory will become clear on examination of the critical δόξα texts in Romans, to which we now turn.

3.3.1. Adam/humanity forsake the glory of God. What, then, is the glory of God that humanity exchanged and thus lacked? For most scholars it is, without question, the visible manifestation of the presence of God. Moo describes τὴν δόξαν τοῦ ἀφθάρτου θεοῦ in Romans 1:23 as the *"splendor and majesty that belong intrinsically to the one true God"*[141] and τῆς δόξης τοῦ θεου in Romans 3:23 as the "magnificent presence of the Lord."[142] Dunn maintains his understanding of glory from Romans 1:23 to Romans 3:23, having defined δόξα in Romans 1:23 as "the *awesome radiance* of deity which becomes the visible manifestation of God in theophany and vision."[143] Käsemann describes this glory as *"the radiance . . . which awaits the justified in heaven"*;[144] according to Fitzmyer, it is *"the radiant* external manifestation of his presence."[145] Richard Gaffin, who shares this view, writes, "Having so drastically defaced the divine image, they have, without exception, forfeited the privilege of *reflecting his glory*."[146] The list could go on. This is not to suggest that these are not viable options. Indeed, they make good sense, given the Damascus Christophany and the clear use of *glory* as visible splendor in 2 Corinthians 3, a text to which I will turn anon.

Two cautionary points must be made here. First, given the multiple denotative variations of δόξα as it pertains to God and the entire lack of denotative variations of δόξα when applied to humanity in the LXX, as demonstrated in chapter two, one should not assume that the glory of God in Romans, and especially in Romans 1:23 and Romans 3:23, refers to the

---

[140]See Wright's discussion of "Plight and Solution" in 2013a: 747-71.
[141]Moo 1996: 108; emphasis mine.
[142]Moo 1996: 226.
[143]Dunn 1988a: 168, 59; emphasis mine.
[144]Käsemann 1980: 94; emphasis mine.
[145]Fitzmyer 1993: 283; emphasis mine.
[146]Gaffin 1993: 348.

visible, manifest presence of God with which humanity was originally endowed and thus lost. Second, given the dubiousness of Paul articulating the motif of the loss of an Adamic glory only found in later Jewish texts, as argued above, the rationale for understanding "the glory of God" in Romans 3:23 as Adam's prefall visible splendor is thus entirely speculative.[147] Though the paradigmatic representative of male and female (אדם in Gen 1:26) stands behind πάντες in Romans 3:23, as it did the third-person plural of ἀλλάσσω in Romans 1:23, Adam's loss of an outer garment of glory does not. Humanity in Adam abdicated their throne and the glory with which they were crowned, the glory of God in which they shared.[148] "Falling short of" or "lacking"[149] the glory of God meant for the apostle exceedingly more than Adam losing his luster. It was Adam/humanity losing his/their crown.

Rather than these two commonly held assumptions, I suggest this: because Genesis 1:26-28 is echoed in Romans 1:23, and because Genesis 1:26-28 is textually and thematically parallel to Psalm 8:5-9 LXX, and because Romans 1:23 and Romans 3:23 refer to the same event, all of which I have demonstrated above, we can *therefore* argue that Genesis 1:26-28 and Psalm 8:5-9 LXX together form the textual and thematic backdrop to the narrative echoed in Romans 1:23 and Romans 3:23: the creation of humanity in God's image and with the endowment of God's glory as God's representatives within his kingly realm. Romans 1:23 and Romans 3:23 both describe humanity's *intended* identity and purpose as God's vicegerents by describing its exchange of and thus loss of God's glory—the glory that the son of man in Psalm 8 is intended to possess.

Romans 1:23 fits within the larger discourse framed by Romans 1:18-25.[150] Here Paul sets the stage for humanity's rebellion against God and rejection

---

[147]This is not to suggest that there is not overlap between the presentation of Adam in Paul (esp. Rom 5:12-21; 1 Cor 15:21-28) and in Apocalypse of Moses/Life of Adam and Eve. Most significantly, both accounts associate the *imago dei* with dominion; see Apoc. Mos. 10–12; 39; Levison 1988: 164-67, 185; Levison 2004: 519-34.

[148]See Byrne 2007: 125.

[149]The majority of contemporary versions translate ὑστεροῦνται as "fall short of," given the genitive following the verb. The KJV and WEB have "come short of," and only the NJB has "lack"—the gloss used in nearly every other New Testament use of the verb. "Lack" is most appropriate here as well, despite the verb-genitive construction, as "fall short of" merely obfuscates Paul's dense phraseology and theology. "Fall short of" is not used as a gloss for ὑστερέω at any other place in any translations of either the LXX or GNT.

[150]Rom 1:18-25 is a text questioned most recently and notably by Douglas Campbell, who suggests that Paul was using the rhetorical device of "speech in character." Rather than

of its created purpose and consequently the need for the redemptive work of death and resurrection on the part of the Messiah.[151] Romans 1:18-25 is the part of the story in which mankind rejects its created purpose, namely to worship and serve the Creator, by instead worshiping and serving the creation (Rom 1:25). Man "exchanged the glory of the immortal God for the likeness of the image of mortal man and animals and reptiles" in Romans 1:23, thereby abdicating the throne of dominion originally established for him at the time of creation (Gen 1:26-28; Ps 8:7 LXX).[152] As Ortlund writes, "We stopped resembling the Creator and started resembling the creation. We became sub-human."[153] From creation onwards, every person could know God and honor him as such (Rom 1:19-21) but chose instead to disregard their created duty and gave glory where the least glory was due (Rom 1:21-25).[154]

This abdication of the throne is again expressed in Romans 3:23, in which the "they" of Romans 1 is explicitly "all (humanity)" (and "all humanity" will be viewed as "in Adam" in Rom 5). Everyone sinned (πάντες γὰρ ἥμαρτον), which is to say that everyone "exchanged the glory of the immortal God for images of corruptible animals" (Rom 1:23), and everyone

---

espousing the content of Rom 1:18-25 (Rom 1:18–3:20), Paul was establishing it as a misguided understanding—an understanding he would then go on to refute; see Campbell 2009: 519-41. On the basis of the criticisms put forth by Macaskill (2011), I also am unpersuaded by Campbell's suggestion.

[151]Ἁμαρτία does not appear until Rom 3:9 but is nevertheless the focus of Rom 1:18-32; see Wright 2002: 430, 457.

[152]Wolter (2015: 388-92) makes an interesting though ultimately unpersuasive assessment of God's glory here. He begins in Rom 4:20 by suggesting that the phrase "[Abraham] gave glory to God" is synonymous with "[Abraham] believed God was God"; "Abraham believes in the promise, because he believes that God is God" (389). Wolter then works backwards to Rom 1:23 and suggests that, on the basis of Abraham giving "glory to God" (aka "believing God is God"), the Gentiles in Rom 1:23 make the same mistake: they fail to believe that God is God. Though Abraham undoubtedly did believe that "God is God," such belief is not necessarily synonymous with "giving glory to God," aka praising, exalting, or honoring God on the basis of the fact that he is God. Moreover, the exchange of God's glory in Rom 1:23 is irreducible to a lack of belief that God is God. Lack of belief is certainly fundamental to the exchange of glory, but it is not synonymous with the exchange of glory.

[153]Ortlund 2014: 117. I will return to Ortlund's work on Rom 8:30 at length in §§6.3 and 7.2.

[154]Schreiner (1998: 88) is one of only a few commentators who properly define sin as the lack of giving God glory, stating: "Failing to glorify God is the root sin. Indeed, glorifying God is virtually equivalent with rendering him proper worship since Paul describes (v. 25) the same reality as surrendering the truth of God for worship of the creature.... Sin does consist first and foremost in acts that transgress God's law.... These particular acts are all rooted in a rejection of God as God, a failure to give him honor and glory."

now bears the consequences of this sin by lacking the glory of God (καὶ ὑστεροῦνται τῆς δόξης τοῦ θεοῦ).

The narrative substructure of glory, and particularly Adam/humanity's rejection of glory, which Paul begins in Romans 1:23 and continues in Romans 3:23, resurfaces again in Romans 5:12-21. Δόξα and δοξάζω are both absent from Romans 5:12-21, but that Adam's disobedience was his abdication of his throne is not. Rather than δόξα and δοξάζω, Paul uses βασιλεύω (Rom 5:14, 17 [2x], 21 [2x]; also Rom 6:12), a word with implicit significance here due to the fact that it occurs only here in Romans and occurs in this passage with notable frequency. Roy Ciampa notes that few scholars have acknowledged the importance of this fact.[155] In this text, Paul uses βασιλεύω to describe death's dominion, which existed in place of Adam's (and all humanity in Adam's) intended dominion over creation.[156] In Romans 5:12-21 it is not Adam who reigns but ὁ θάνατος (Rom 5:14, 17), οἱ τὴν περισσείαν τῆς χάριτος καὶ τῆς δωρεᾶς τῆς δικαιοσύνης λαμβάνοντες (Rom 5:17), ἡ ἁμαρτία (Rom 5:21), and ἡ χάρις (Rom 5:21). Nevertheless, Adam's intended reign is implied in Romans 5:12 by the link between the presence of sin to Adam and the presence of death to sin. Had humanity in Adam not "exchanged the glory of the immortal God" (Rom 1:23) and come to "lack the glory of God" (Rom 3:23), humanity would reign, and sin and death would be nonexistent.

Though the subjects of the narrative are identified rather cryptically as "they" in Romans 1:23 and "all [humanity]" in Romans 3:23, in Romans 5:12 those subjects become explicit: "all who sinned," that is, all humanity in Adam. It was no longer merely "man" (ἄνθρωπος) in Psalm 8:5 LXX who was crowned with glory and honor and given dominion over creation, but the Adam (ἄνθρωπος) of Genesis 1:26. And it was under Adam's feet that God had put all things (πάντα ὑπέταξας ὑποκάτω τῶν ποδῶν αὐτοῦ) in Psalm 8:7 LXX. In Romans 1:23 and Romans 3:23 we see that, though this was the case at creation, Adam/humankind grievously rebelled. By exchanging the glory of God for that of the created world, Adam/humankind ultimately abdicated his God-given throne and invited sin and death to

---

[155]Ciampa 2013: 107.

[156]Here a shift occurs in the use of the Adamic figure. Whereas in Rom 1:23; 3:23 Adam's creation in the image and glory of God was paradigmatic for that of all humanity, in Rom 5:12-21 Adam's rejection of that image and glory was etiological for humanity.

reign in his stead (explicit in Rom 5:12, 17, 21). He rejected his created role as God's vicegerent over creation.

What then does this say about Paul's use of *glory* in Romans 1:23; 3:23? First, it is not a visible shining light that Adam loses in Romans 3:23, or "the awesome radiance of deity which becomes the visible manifestation of God in theophany and vision," as Dunn describes it.[157] Second, rather, it is the glory with which mankind is crowned—the glory man has as mediator between God and his creation, as God's keeper of creation, as his vicegerent on his royal throne. This is the glory, the honor, that man rejects and forsakes for another (Rom 1:23, 25), and the glory of God in which all humans were created to participate but have chosen instead to forsake by rejecting their created purpose.

3.3.2. *The glory of Israel.* Israel, too, has a leading role in Paul's narrative of glory in Romans. Paul mentions Israel's glory in Romans 9:4, Israel's rejection of that glory in Romans 1:23, and Israel's redemption to glory in Romans 9:23. Because Paul reveals more about the nature of Israel's glory in Romans 1:23, I begin there with Israel's rejection of glory before examining their original possession of glory in Romans 9:4 and restoration of glory in Romans 9:23.

In Romans 1:23 Paul alludes also to the golden calf episode of ancient Israelite history, as it is recorded in Psalm 105:20 LXX and Jeremiah 2:11. As noted above, not all agree that Paul implicates Israel in Romans 1, which then raises the question of why Paul alludes to this Israelite narrative. According to Fitzmyer, Paul alludes to these texts in order to apply the ideas to the pagan world.[158] And, as I noted above, Stowers and Eisenbaum, among others, reject the idea that Paul is implicating Israel in this section. But as Jewett notes, "Since every culture displays evidence of suppressing the truth by the adoration of perishable images, demonstrating that the perverse will to 'change the glory of the imperishable God' is a universal problem, the gospel elaborated in this letter has an inclusive bearing."[159] His assessment is preceded by Käsemann's similar conclusion: "Precisely the point of the verse is that Paul extends to the whole human race what

---

[157]Dunn 1988a: 59.
[158]Fitzmyer 1993: 271.
[159]Jewett and Kotansky 2007: 162; see also Cranfield 1975: 105.

Jer 2:11 restricted to the people of God."[160] No strong evidence supports the idea that only the pagan world should be read in these verses.

Like Adam, Israel possessed God's glory but also rejected that God-given glory. Paul implies that Israel rejected their God-given glory by "exchanging the glory of the immortal God."[161] Whereas Adam's rejection of his created purpose is echoed in textual links to Genesis 1, Israel's rejection of their purpose is echoed in textual links to Psalm 105:20 LXX and Jeremiah 2:11, which refer to Israel's creation of the golden calf in Exodus 32. In each of these texts, the nature of the glory that Israel exchanged is revealed: it was a glory possessed by Israel, and it was a glory associated with rule/dominion. Let us quickly examine these texts.

In both Psalm 105:20 LXX and Jeremiah 2:11, Israel is described as exchanging their glory for that of idols. Psalm 105:20 LXX reads ἠλλάξαντο τὴν δόξαν αὐτῶν ἐν ὁμοιώματι μόσχου ἔσθοντος χόρτον, and Jeremiah 2:11b says ὁ δὲ λαός μου ἠλλάξατο τὴν δόξαν αὐτοῦ ἐξ ἧς οὐκ ὠφεληθήσονται.[162] The glory in question here is possessed by Israel: in Psalm 105:20 LXX it is clearly "*their* glory" (τὴν δόξαν αὐτῶν), and in Jeremiah 2:11: "[*my people's*] glory" (τὴν δόξαν αὐτοῦ).[163] William Holladay notes that this is a *tiqqun sopherim* in the Hebrew manuscripts of both Psalm 106:20 and Jeremiah 2:11, indicating that the glory in both texts was possibly originally followed by a first-person suffix. He argues, however, that an original third-person suffix may be valid, given the example of Psalm 3:4 and the surrounding context of the passages.[164] LXX manuscripts

---

[160]Käsemann 1980: 46.

[161]Genesis Rabbah provides precedence for regarding the exchange of glory in Rom 1:23 as that of *both* Israel and Adam. Morris (1992: 124) notes that this overlap occurs in two places: (1) "It is written 'But they like Adam (men) have transgressed the covenant' (Hos. 6:7). They are like men, in particular, the first man. 'I brought the first man to the Garden of Eden (Gen. 2:15), I commanded him (2:16) but he broke my commandment (3:11). I sentenced him to be . . . driven out (3:23), but I grieved for him, saying "How . . ."'" (Gen. Rab. 3:9); and (2) "The same is for his descendants. I brought them to the Land of Israel (Jer. 2:7), I commanded them (Lev. 24:2), but they broke my commandment (Dan. 9:11). I sentenced them to be . . . driven out (Jer. 15:1), but I grieved for them, saying 'How . . .' (Lam. 1:1)" (Gen. Rab. 19:9).

[162]See Hos 4:7; also Wis 11–15; Deut 4:16-18. See Jewett and Kotansky's (2007: 160-61) treatment of ἀλλάσσω in Rom 1:23. Dunn (1988a: 61), Moo (1996: 109), and Beale (2008: 205-6) say Ps 105 LXX and Jer 2 might be in the background but do not discuss it further. See also Hyldahl 1956: 285-88.

[163]The MT also has כבוד as a third-person plural in both texts. The ESV, RSV, NRSV obscure this by translating it as "the glory of God." The NASB, NIV, and NJB all have "their glory."

[164]Holladay 1986: 50.

witness this possible alteration.[165] It is possible that the psalmist and Jeremiah both describe Israel's worship of idols as an exchange of their glory for that of the idols.

Following this, Morna Hooker suggests that the glory in Romans 1:23 is Israel's, as it is in the background texts. She writes, "δόξα may here . . . refer not only to the glory which God possesses in himself, but to that same glory in so far as it was originally possessed also by man."[166] And further, "Paul . . . does not say that man ever lost the image of God. . . . The things which man *did* lose were the glory of God and the dominion over Nature which were associated with that image."[167] In Romans 1:23, τὴν δόξαν τοῦ ἀφθάρτου θεοῦ refers to a glory that comes from the immortal God and is possessed by Israel.

Moreover, in each text Israel is described as becoming subject to the nations (Jer 2:14-16; Ps 105:41-42, 46 LXX) *because of* their "exchange of glory" (i.e., worship of idols). The reader can assume on this basis that Israel's glory was their honorable position as rulers over the land they were to possess (Lev 20:24; Num 33:53; Deut 5:31-33; see esp. Deut 28:63-64; 30:5, 16-18; Josh 23:5).[168] Israel forsook that created purpose by submitting themselves to idols and thus to other nations (see Sir 49:5). As with that of all humanity in Adam in Romans 1:23, the nature of Israel's glory was their honorable status associated with dominion and authority.

Paul includes Israel's rejection of glory in Romans 1:23 (and implies it in Rom 3:23) but writes positively about Israel's possession of glory in Romans 9:4, 23. In these texts we see the diversity of the semantic functions of δόξα at play, even in Paul's theology. Beginning in Romans 9:4, it is unclear how Paul intends ἡ δόξα to function. He writes: οἵτινές εἰσιν Ἰσραηλῖται, ὧν ἡ υἱοθεσία καὶ ἡ δόξα καὶ αἱ διαθῆκαι καὶ ἡ νομοθεσία καὶ ἡ λατρεία καὶ αἱ ἐπαγγελίαι. Unlike Romans 1:23, ἡ δόξα in Romans 9:4

---

[165]The Göttingen editors of Ps 105:20 chose αὐτῶν, evidenced in B', Sa, Sy, 55, *suam*, La, Ga = Mas in rejection of αὐτοῦ in R, *L*, A', and τοῦ θεοῦ in *L^{pau}*.

[166]Hooker 1959–1960: 305. Schreiner says Hooker's assessment is "valid as long as we see that human beings lose glory when they fail to give God glory" (1998: 87). Contra Fitzmyer 1993: 283.

[167]Hooker 1959–1960: 305; see also Ortlund 2014: 117.

[168]Also noteworthy is the texts' shared response of YHWH to Israel's subjection of itself to idols and, hence, nations, in forsaking him. YHWH is depicted as having "detested his inheritance" (ἐβδελύξατο τὴν κληρονομίαν αὐτοῦ) in Ps 105:40 LXX and saying "[you] made my inheritance into a detestable thing" (τὴν κληρονομίαν μου ἔθεσθε εἰς βδέλυγμα) in Jer 2:7 LXX.

has no explicit textual echo by which to decipher Paul's meaning. Most consider ἡ δόξα in Romans 9:4 a reference to the splendor of God, "the epiphany of the *Shekinah* in the historical and cultic sphere," according to Käsemann.[169] Alternately, Jewett suggests that it is a continuation of Paul's remarks on the future eschatological glory awaiting believers from Romans 8:17, 18, 21, 30.[170] Susan Eastman does so as well by implication; connecting the adoption and glory of the "sons of God" in Romans 8:19 to that of Israel in Romans 9:4, Eastman writes: "The future 'sons of God' are characterized by 'adoption' and 'glory' (8:17, 18, 21, 23). But in Rom 9:14, Paul says of the Jews, his kinsfolk according to the flesh, that to *them* belong ἡ υἱοθεσία καὶ ἡ δόξα."[171] Moo attempts to hold the two in tandem, suggesting that there is the "ultimate continuation of [God's presence with the people of Israel] (into the eschaton) that is the issue."[172] And, in contrast with the suppositions of most scholars, BDAG locates δόξα in Romans 9:4 under the category of "honor as enhancement or recognition of status or performance, *fame, recognition, renown, honor, prestige*."[173]

Contra Jewett and Eastman, the glory in Romans 9:4 does not refer to an eschatological glory, at least not an eschatological glory defined by that of Christ, as in Romans 8. With Newman and the majority of scholars, it is most likely that here, unlike elsewhere in Romans, Paul refers to God's theophanic manifestation in splendor in the exodus narrative. The primary reasons for this are twofold. The first is its occurrence in an unusual articular form, implying that it refers to something more specific than a general sense of honor or an exalted status: to Israel belongs "The Glory." It is here that Newman's glory tradition is appropriate. The second reason

---

[169]Käsemann 1980: 258-59. See Wilckens 1980: 188; Fitzmyer 1993: 546; Schreiner 1998: 484; Byrne 2007: 287; Kruse 2012: 371; Ortlund 2014: 121n47.

[170]Jewett and Kotansky (2007: 563) suggest that the arthrous δόξα refers back to the use of δόξα in Rom 8:18-19. They write: "Commentators overlook this function of the article, disregarding the connection with the immediately preceding chapter and referring instead to ancient Israel's concept of glory." Wright (2002: 629) and Barrett (1962: 178) omit comments on the presence of the arthrous δόξα altogether.

[171]Eastman 2002: 266.

[172]Moo 1996: 563; also Dunn 1988b: 526-27 and Schreiner 1998: 484.

[173]BDAG 2000: 257; emphasis original. Contrast this with BDAG's equally odd placement of δόξα in 1 Cor 15:43 under the category of being bright or shiny, which most commentators disagree with as well; see §4.2.2.1. Despite suggesting that the glory refers to the manifest presence of God, Fitzmyer (1993: 546) notes that "ancient commentators . . . sometimes understood *doxa* in the Hellenistic sense of Israel's honor or reputation in the world," listing Apollinaris of Laodicea and Gennadius.

is its placement within what Newman describes as a "litany of salvation-historical markers" particularly representative of the exodus tradition.[174] The exodus motif is difficult to miss or dismiss. I suggest that, with Newman and unlike in most places in Romans, Paul's reference to Israel's glory in Romans 9:4 is in fact a reference to the visible manifest presence of God in Israel.

This leaves then only the reference to Israel's glory in Romans 9:23 to consider. In Romans 9:22-24, Paul writes:

> What if God, desiring to show his wrath and to make known his power, has endured with much patience the vessels of wrath prepared for destruction; and what if he has done so in order to make known the riches of his glory for the vessels of mercy, which he has prepared beforehand for glory [καὶ ἵνα γνωρίσῃ τὸν πλοῦτον τῆς δόξης αὐτοῦ ἐπὶ σκεύη ἐλέους ἃ προητοίμασεν εἰς δόξαν;]—including us whom he has called, not from the Jews only but also from the Gentiles?

Paul's transition to the inclusion of Gentiles in Romans 9:24 makes clear that the "vessels of mercy" who are "prepared beforehand for glory" in Romans 9:23 refer to both Jewish and Gentile believers. As Esler rightly notes, "Paul now expressly states that the vessels of mercy include Israelites and non-Israelites"—the "children of God" and the "children of the promise."[175] While it would make sense to treat this verse in the following section where I treat the renewal of humanity's glory in Christ, Paul's focus on God's dealings with Israel in the preceding context makes this a better fit. Jews are guaranteed a future glory; God has prepared them for it beforehand (προετοιμάζω; see Wis 9:8; Eph 2:10).[176] Though the original glory was exchanged (indicated in the echoes of Ps 105 LXX and Jer 2 in Rom 1:23), they nevertheless have an eschatological glory awaiting them.

Further on in Romans 9, in Romans 9:23 Paul uses δόξα twice, once in reference to the "riches of God's glory" and once as that for which the "vessels of mercy" have been prepared beforehand. The phrase τὸ πλοῦτος τῆς δόξης αὐτοῦ occurs also in Ephesians 3:16, and a similar phrase, τὸ πλοῦτος αὐτοῦ ἐν δόξῃ, occurs in Philippians 4:19. Jewett suggests that

---

[174]Newman 1992: 217; see Moo 1996: 563.
[175]Esler 2003: 281.
[176]See Jewett and Kotansky (2007: 597-98) for a discussion of the predetermination motif latent in Rom 9:23.

the phrase in Romans "appears to be drawn from the tradition of liturgical participation in the numinous cloud or bright fire that was thought to surround the divine tabernacle (Exod 40:34f.) or throne (Ezek 1:26-28)."[177] I suggest, rather, that greater precedence exists for reading δόξα here not as anything associated with God's theophanic presence but as his honor, power, or character. The two terms, πλοῦτος and δόξα, are brought together throughout the LXX (e.g., 1 Kings 3:13; Eccles 6:2; Ps 3:4). I categorized this use as "a person's honor or status associated with his character, power, or wealth" in the concordance in the preceding chapter. Most appropriately, in 1 Chronicles 29:11-12 it is written: "Yours, O LORD, are the greatness, the power, the glory, the victory, and the majesty; for all that is in the heavens and on the earth is yours; yours is the kingdom, O LORD, and you are exalted as head above all. *Riches and glory come from you*, and you rule over all. In your hand are power and might; and it is in your hand to make great and to give strength to all." The phrase "the riches of God's glory" then refers to the magnitude of his power or character in salvation, his status as the one "exalted as head above all" who rules over heavens and earth; this is the glory of God made known to those who receive his salvation.

If this is the case, then the glory for which the "vessels of mercy" are prepared is perhaps not what Jewett calls the "divine glory," by which he means the presence of God,[178] or what Schreiner says "refers to the goal that is attained through God's foreordination: future splendor in the *eschaton*."[179] Nor can Newman's suggestion that it refers to "God's benefit" find support.[180] Rather, it is the "riches and glory (i.e., honor)" that the Chronicler says come from this King who saves.

Before turning to the renewal of glory to all believers more generally in Romans, one further point is necessary here in regard to the eschatological glory anticipated by Israel. Though certainly not present in Romans 9:23, precedence exists in the Qumran Scrolls for reading Israel's anticipated

---

[177]Jewett and Kotansky 2007: 597. Newman places it in the "left for consideration" category (1992: 160).

[178]Jewett and Kotansky 2007: 597; see also Fitzmyer 1993: 570.

[179]Schreiner 1998: 523.

[180]Newman 1992: 159-60. Rom 9:23b and 1 Cor 2:7, Newman says, are the two places where δόξα means God's "benefit." I find zero support for this reading. See also the note on Rom 2:7, 10 above.

eschatological glory with the fulfillment of Adam's original glory—a glory
that, according to the Scrolls, bears closer affinities to an exalted status
than to a garment of light.[181] In the Words of the Heavenly Lights (4Q504),
a liturgical text of prayers for the week, part of the first day's prayer reads:

> Rememb]er, O Lo[r]d that . . . Thou hast fashioned [Adam], our [f]ather in
> the likeness of [Thy] glory; Thou didst breathe [a breath of life] into his
> nostrils and with understanding a knowledge [Thou didst give him]. . . .
> Thou didst make [him] to rule [over the Gar]den of Eden which Thou didst
> plant . . . and to walk in the land of glory . . . he guarded. (4Q504 frag. 8)[182]

Genesis 1:26-28 is rewritten for the Qumran community and brings together
the motifs of God's image and glory. How exactly God's glory here should
be interpreted is unclear, but, given the range of uses of glory vis-à-vis
God noted above, it is not impossible that God's glory is his honor or
exalted status. Moreover, even if the author intends the reader to understand
God's glory as visible splendor, we are aware already of the fact that such
splendor symbolizes the presence of a particular God: the unsurpassed
God who rules over heaven and earth. Van Kooten adopts this balanced
approach: Adam's restoration to glory, or his creation in the image of God's
glory, "is an effulgence of God's glory, demonstrating the elevated status
of human beings above the rest of creation."[183]

Adam's glory fulfilled in Israel's eschatological glory is seen in several
other texts:[184]

---

[181]I am indebted to Wright 1992: 265; Keesmaat 1999: 87; Fletcher-Louis 2002: 92-97; and Macaskill 2013: 137-43 for these references. Unless otherwise noted, translations from Qumran
are taken from García Martínez 1996.

[182]Vermes 1987.

[183]Van Kooten 2008: 46-47. Van Kooten's statement is in response to the conclusions drawn by
Fletcher-Louis, who suggests that "given that the liturgy starts with Adam in the land of
Glory, as one made in the likeness of God's Glory, there seems also here to be a priestly
theology which grounded the prayer for God's restoration not simply in the Mosaic covenant
but also a pre-fall relationship of ontological affinity between God and his own humanity,
now summed up in Israel" (2002: 94). Specifically it is Fletcher-Louis's suggestion of an
"ontological affinity" that van Kooten critiques (2008: 21-22); see also Macaskill (2013: 119-21),
who rightly critiques Fletcher-Louis for his "slippage from his astute recognition of participation in heavenly liturgy to speaking of the angelomorphic divinity of human worshippers"
(p. 120), and, more generally, see Goff 2003.

[184]Considering Rom 3:23 and its commonly made associations with the Adam tradition represented in the Life of Adam and Eve, I suggest that, if indeed Paul was influenced by traditions
external to the LXX or MT, then those that bear the greatest theological similarity are these
from Qumran in which Adam and "the glory of Adam" occur frequently.

> For these are those selected by God for an everlasting covenant and to them shall belong all the glory of Adam. (1QS 4:22-23)

> You raise an [eternal] name for them, [forgiving them all] sin, eliminating from them all their depravities, giving them, giving them as a legacy all the glory of Adam and plentiful days. (1QH[a] 4:14-15)

> Those who remained steadfast in it will acquire eternal life, and all the glory of Adam is for them. (CD 3:19-20)

> Those who have returned from the wilderness, who will live for a thousand generations, in safety; for them there is all the inheritance of Adam and his descendants for ever. (4QpPs 37 3:1-2)

Macaskill rightly warns that these texts may not refer "to Adam as a person" but "to humanity more generally. None of the texts ultimately requires us to see a reference to the glory that Adam lost through sin, even if that is a possibility."[185] Rather, he states, "the phrase may point to the idea of the future rule of God's people over the nations of the world and the eschatological reversal of their fortunes."[186] His reading of these texts is similar to that of van Kooten: though the glory of God in which "Adam" is created is understood as the "glorifying presence of God,"[187] both scholars nonetheless recognize existing implications that bear on the "future rule of God's people," that is, Israel.

These motifs of glory will carry over into the following discussion of the renewal of glory in humanity throughout Romans. We will see that Romans 9:23 shares affinities with Romans 8:29-30, where God's adopted children are predestined (προώρισεν, Rom 8:30) to glorification (ἐδόξασεν, Rom 8:30)[188]—a glorification that (I will argue in the following section) refers to believers' exalted status.

---

[185]Macaskill 2013: 138.

[186]Macaskill 2013: 138.

[187]Macaskill 2013: 121. Macaskill uses this phrase to describe the glory of God mentioned in a range of texts on which Fletcher-Louis develops his argument for human transformation into angelic likeness in worship, texts that include but are not limited the "glory of Adam" texts noted here.

[188]Käsemann (1980: 271) also links Rom 9:23 with Rom 8:30, suggesting "eschatological glorification takes place already now in such a way that God's claim to lordship over the world . . . establishes itself over his creatures and restores the divine likeness (cf. 8:30) lost according to 3:23." This link between the texts is weak for Käsemann, however, given that his applied definition of δόξα in Rom 3:23 was not a "divine likeness" but "the radiance which . . . awaits the justified in heaven" (1980: 94).

3.3.3. God's children reinstated to glory. We turn now to the glorious climax, or more appropriately, the climax of glory in Paul's δόξα narrative in Romans. Paul uses δόξα and its cognates in seven key eschatologically focused verses: Romans 2:7, 10; 5:2; 8:17, 18, 21, 30. My comments here are intended primarily to demonstrate that Paul's use of δόξα and δοξάζω in these texts leading up to and in Romans 8 follows both the lexical and the narrative pattern I have argued for thus far.

Eschatological glory for God's people is first indicated in Romans 2:7: τοῖς μὲν καθ᾽ ὑπομονὴν ἔργου ἀγαθοῦ δόξαν καὶ τιμὴν καὶ ἀφθαρσίαν ζητοῦσιν ζωὴν αἰώνιον, and subsequently in Romans 2:10: δόξα δὲ καὶ τιμὴ καὶ εἰρήνη παντὶ τῷ ἐργαζομένῳ τὸ ἀγαθόν, Ἰουδαίῳ τε πρῶτον καὶ Ἕλληνι. In both verses the contrast is stark between the traditional denotation of human glory as the reflection of the visible presence of God—or "splendor," as Schreiner describes it[189]—and the understanding I am advocating, namely believers' share in God's honor or power as his image bearers.

The interpretative key undoubtedly lies in the triads of glory, honor, and immortality in Romans 2:7 and glory, honor, and peace in Romans 2:10. Commentators generally elaborate very little on the denotation of δόξα at this point, though most assign some element of synonymy with "honor."[190] According to Colin Kruse, it is "the reward for a good life," which I find ambiguous and unhelpful.[191] Most helpful is Jewett, who writes, "Paul is deliberately employing honorific categories that will appeal to his audience. . . . Both glory and honor are central motivations in the culture of the ancient Mediterranean world, where young people were taught to emulate the behavior of ideal prototypes. . . . That one should seek such honor and glory was simply assumed in Rome."[192] In an approach similar to Jewett's, Harrison contrasts the two triads

---

[189]Schreiner 1998: 113: "The personal benefits of those who are granted eternal life are emphasized in these words. They will experience splendor, honor, immortality, and peace."

[190]See, e.g., Dunn 1988a: 85; Fitzmyer 1993: 302; Moo 1996: 137n7; Byrne 2007: 86. As noted in my criticisms of Newman above, not once does he indicate how δόξα in Rom 2:7, 10 fits into his understanding of Paul's glory Christology, other than to suggest that they join forty-two other occurrences of δόξα "left for consideration" and yet never actually considered: 1992: 160.

[191]Kruse 2012: 228. At the point of Rom 5:2, Kruse offers a general taxonomy of believers' future glory throughout Paul's epistles, though it also is both too ambiguous and too brief to offer much usefulness here.

[192]Jewett and Kotansky 2007: 205.

with those mentioned by Sallust, a first-century Roman historian. Harrison writes:

> One of the interesting sidelights of Sallust's presentation of *Gloria* is his use of the word in triads that speak of political and social status. In contrast to Paul's eschatological triads of "glory, honour, and immortality" (Rom 2:7) and "glory, honour and peace" (2:10), Sallust articulates a different set of triads: "glory (*gloriam*), honour and power" (*Cat.* 11:1); "riches, honour and glory (*gloriam*)" (*Cat.* 58.8; 20.14); "honour, glory (*gloria*) and authority" (*Cat.* 12.1).[193]

Several discussions later, Harrison notes that

> Paul does not diminish the importance of the believer seeking "glory" (δόξαν), honour (τιμὴν) and immortality (ἀφθαρσίαν)" (Rom 2:7). For Paul, the Romans are correct in highlighting the importance of the quest for glory over against certain representatives of the Greek ethical tradition (e.g. Plutarch, Dio Chrysostom) who dismissed the acquisition of δόξα as misguided and ephemeral. But the allocation of δόξα for the believer is an eschatological gift and Paul differentiates his triads from Sallust and Cicero precisely by the addition of the parallel terms of "immortality" (Rom 2:7: ἀφθαρσία) and "peace" (Rom 2:10: εἰρήνη). Thus, according to Paul, the significance and worth of glory is not determined by the estimation of the Roman elite—as Sallust, Cicero and the Scipionic *elogia* proposed—but rather by the God who judges the secret thoughts of all (Rom 2:16).[194]

Given these parallels, it is difficult to imagine a Roman Gentile convert thinking in the first instance that δόξα refers to anything other than what it was considered by Sallust, Cicero, or any other Roman nobleman of societal honor and authority.

Further support for reading δόξα here as something other than believers' eschatological reflection of God's radiance is found in Paul's use of δόξα in 1 Corinthians 2:7: ἀλλὰ λαλοῦμεν θεοῦ σοφίαν ἐν μυστηρίῳ τὴν ἀποκεκρυμμένην, ἣν προώρισεν ὁ θεὸς πρὸ τῶν αἰώνων εἰς δόξαν ἡμῶν. On its own, δόξαν ἡμῶν could mean "the visible presence of God that we will reflect upon entering the heavenly realms" and that is made possible by God's wisdom. Oddly enough, Newman here suggests that our "glory"

---

[193]Harrison 2011: 209-10.
[194]Harrison 2011: 264.

is our "benefit."[195] However, it is not on its own, and the context demands an alternate reading.

The denotation of δόξα in 1 Corinthians 2:7 is made clear by the thematic emphases of 1 Corinthians 2:8 and Paul's reference to Jesus as the "Lord of glory." Here Newman suggests that the phrase κύριον τῆς δόξης stems from its only other known use: the apocalyptic throne vision of 1 Enoch 40:3.[196] Newman may be correct. Yet even if he is, it does not therefore imply that Paul is referring to Jesus as the embodiment of the theophanic presence of God. Jesus as the Lord of glory can equally refer to Jesus as the risen and exalted King who in his exalted status embodies the supreme Ruler on the throne in the apocalyptic vision. Van Kooten notes the work of B. Burrowes, who argues that it was neither Jewish literature nor the Damascus Christophany that led Paul to an understanding of Jesus as the image of God but the Hellenistic ruler ideologies. Burrowes's insights prove helpful here as well:

> Paul's conception of the Christ as the image of God derives from the Hellenistic ruler ideology. . . . In his vision of Christ, Paul experienced Jesus as the risen and enthroned kurios, since his most basic confession of faith is "Jesus is Lord" (Rom 10:9, 1 Cor 12:3). The exaltation of Jesus to universal lordship would naturally have brought comparison to secular rulers, specifically to the Roman emperors and the Seleucid kings of Antioch. In Hellenistic political philosophy, the ideal king was an image of the divine in the exercise of his power and in his moral character. As the only true Lord in contrast to the mere Roman and Seleucid pretenders, it is Jesus who is the true and faithful image of the divine.[197]

---

[195]Newman 1992: 159-60n14. Only twice does δόξα denote "benefit," according to Newman: in 1 Cor 2:7 and in Rom 9:23. He explains that in both verses the "construction features a verb + εἰς + δόξα in the accusative case with God being the one whom the verb benefits" (p. 160). Additionally, Newman notes that in both verses the emphasis on salvation history leads to God's actions being taken "'for his benefit' (εἰς δόξαν ἡμῶν)" (p. 160n15). It is unclear why Newman included ἡμῶν in his description, given that it seems directly to contradict his point (see also p. 209). In using ἡμῶν, Paul clearly refers to *believers'* ("our") glory/benefit. Moreover, this purpose-clause construction only confirms that it is for the purpose of someone or something and does not require that God be the recipient or the direction of the purpose. In the case of Rom 9:23, it is clearly the "objects of mercy" who are prepared beforehand for the purposes of glory, aka *their* glory, and the case is unequivocally the same in 1 Cor 2:7.

[196]Newman 1992: 235-39 with reference to the "Lord of Glory" in the apocalyptic throne vision of 1 En. 40:3 on p. 86.

[197]Burrowes 2007 quoted in van Kooten 2008a: 205.

Much the same can be said for Jesus as the glory of God. "Lord of glory," within Roman kingly and political ideologies, would naturally imply to Gentile converts the true King who has true power, honor, supreme dominion, as Harrison implies in his rhetorical question: "What would Paul's gospel of the 'Lord of glory' (1 Cor 2:8; 2 Cor 4:4, 6) have meant for Romans attached to the old republican perspectives of glory and for those who were grateful clients of the new imperial Lords of glory at Rome?"[198] Such Gentile converts may have recognized a further connection to Jewish apocalyptic throne visions, but even then, "glory" associated with a supreme deity on a throne would not lose its regal connotations. Moreover, Paul's emphasis in 1 Corinthians 2:8 is on the contrast between the "rulers of this age" and the true ruler, whom they crucified.

Paul's use of δόξα in 1 Corinthians 2:7, 8 fits first and foremost within this political and royal semantic field, and it is this same semantic field in which believers' eschatological δόξα fits in Romans 2:7, 10, as is made clear by the parallel triads of Sallust.

In Romans 2:7, 10 Paul only hints at believers' eschatological glory as the regained glory of God formerly exchanged or lost. He then refers explicitly to it in Romans 5:2: καυχώμεθα ἐπ᾽ ἐλπίδι τῆς δόξης τοῦ θεοῦ. The glory of God, Paul says, is believers' hope, their eschatological telos. But it is not at first obvious just how one should understand God's glory. In the realm of scholarship at this point, two oddities stand out. First, as in Romans 2:7, 10, Carey Newman makes very little of Paul's phrase here, including it in the forty-two occurrences of δόξα that require further consideration and that, other than one undiscussed mention of believers' hope of glory in Romans 5:2, are never again mentioned.[199] Second, Robert Jewett randomly links τῆς δόξης τοῦ θεοῦ with the כבוד יהוה traditions of the Hebrew Bible, referring to it as the glory of God "manifest in radiant holiness and in transcendent power to create and redeem," having not made such a link in either Romans 1:23 or Romans 3:23.[200]

The most common interpretation is that of a moral perfection or righteousness that classifies God and that classified the original "Godlikeness"

---

[198]Harrison 2011: 204.
[199]Newman 1992: 228.
[200]Jewett and Kotansky 2007: 352. They do add, however, that "only divine glory is perceived to be worthy of the highest possible honor."

of the prefall Adam. Moo describes it in this way: it is "that state of 'God-like-ness' which has been lost because of sin, and which will be restored in the last day to every Christian."[201] Schreiner develops this by saying:

> the already-not yet character of Paul's eschatology emerges in this para-graph. . . . We still await future glorification, which will involve moral per-fection and restoration to the glory Adam lost when he sinned. Believers are clearly not yet morally perfect, for otherwise they would possess God's glory now, and the growth in godly character described in verses 3-4 would be superfluous.[202]

Schreiner rightly notes that the glory of God in which believers hope is connected to the glory Adam lost, but that glory, as we have seen, is not a moral perfection. It is, rather, the exalted status gifted by God to all humanity and which Paul describes in the Adam motif in the following section, Romans 5:12-21, as having been rejected. As Dunn notes, "With the re-emergence of the theme 'the glory of God' Paul already before 5:12ff. reverts to the Adam motif—the divine purpose in salvation being understood in terms of a restoration (and completion) of fallen humanity to the glory which all now fall short of."[203] In fact, believers' hope of glory in Romans 5:2 stands as a thematic overview for the entire section to come, leading Moo rightly to note that "it is the topic of 'hope' and 'glory' that Paul elaborates on in 5:12-21 and 8:14-39."[204] To understand what the glory is in which believers hope in Romans 5:2, one must first understand the texts in which Paul further illustrates that glory: Romans 5:12-21 and Romans 8:17-30.

---

[201]Moo 1996: 302.

[202]Schreiner 1998: 254-55; see also Käsemann 1980: 134 and Byrne 2007: 165. Wolter (2015: 187-88) suggests "the meaning of 'glory' in [Rom 5:2; 8:18, 29-30] is in line with the use in the Old Testament and in Jewish writings outside of the bible. There this concept can be used as a comprehensive designation for the eschatic salvation that was expected [citing, e.g., Is 40:5; 60:1-2]. According to Rom 3:23, it is precisely 'God's glory' that humanity has lost because of their sin. Paul here picks up a traditional interpretation of the 'fall,' according to which Adam and Eve were the cause for humanity's loss of 'God's glory,' with which they originally were endowed." Two weaknesses of Wolter's assessment stand out: (1) with most scholars who comment on the phrase, he offers no rationale for why God's glory should be understood as God's salvation; and (2) if God's "glory" is God's "salvation" in Rom 5:2, and it is this glory that Adam and Eve lost in Rom 3:23, then this implies that Adam and Eve were endowed with a prefall "salvation"—a counterintuitive notion that requires further, but unoffered, explanation.

[203]Dunn 1988a: 249.

[204]Moo 1996: 297.

Given all that Paul has already said about humanity's relationship to the glory of God in Romans 1:23 and Romans 3:23, and presumably, though certainly less explicitly, in Romans 2:7, 10, the glory of God in which believers hope is not necessarily God's visible, manifest presence, nor is it God's moral perfection. It is Adam/humanity's honor or power associated with their status as the Creator's representatives called to steward his creation.

Romans 5:12-21 is often "treated as the ugly stepsister of the family of major sections in the letter to the Romans," according to Ciampa.[205] When valued as an expression of Paul's theology, it is viewed primarily as the basis of Paul's Adam Christology, and for good reason. Often overlooked, however, is that Paul primarily addresses the reason why God's people have hope in the glory of God (Rom 5:2). Adam was called to rule and to establish dominion on the earth and, as mentioned previously, allowed sin and death to reign in his stead (Rom 5:14, 17, 21).[206] But the story does not end there. Whereas Adam was disobedient, Jesus was obedient (Rom 5:19); and his obedience made it possible that God's people would again reign over the earth. Paul writes in Romans 5:17: εἰ γὰρ τῷ τοῦ ἑνὸς παραπτώματι ὁ θάνατος ἐβασίλευσεν διὰ τοῦ ἑνός, πολλῷ μᾶλλον οἱ τὴν περισσείαν τῆς χάριτος καὶ τῆς δωρεᾶς τῆς δικαιοσύνης λαμβάνοντες ἐν ζωῇ βασιλεύσουσιν διὰ τοῦ ἑνὸς Ἰησοῦ Χριστοῦ. Here is Paul's point in Romans 5:12-21: that believers will *reign in life* through the one man, Jesus Christ. It is a point often overlooked. In Jesus, God will restore humanity to their originally created vocation; humanity will again have the honor associated with dominion; they will again share in the glory of God of Romans 5:2.[207] Fitzmyer is one who misses the message: "Whereas in v 14 Paul spoke of the reign of death, now he replaces that with the *reign of life*, i.e., justified Christians enjoy the regal freedom of life eternal."[208] What replaces the reign of death is not life but those who receive God's abundant grace. As Dunn writes, "The opposite to the coldly final rule of death is the unfettered enjoyment of life—the life of

---

[205]Ciampa 2013: 103.

[206]See also Ciampa 2013: 111.

[207]Paul may be picking up Jewish traditions of restored rule: Dan 7:22, 26-27; Wis 3:8; 5:15-16; 1QM 12:14-15; 1QpHab 5:4-5; see also Mt 19:28; Rev 20:4, 6.

[208]Fitzmyer 1993: 420; emphasis mine. Surprisingly, Schreiner (1998: 291-92) omits any discussion of "reign in life," discussing the potential for an implied universalism instead; see also Schreiner 2001: 153.

a king."[209] Romans 5:17 is Paul's conclusion to the saga of Adam's rejection of his created vocation, his exchange of the glory of the immortal God (Rom 1:23).[210] God's people will again reign over the earth as Adam was meant to do, and, as Paul will make clear in Romans 8, they will do so as adopted children of God, sharing in the inheritance of the Firstborn Son.[211] To overlook this message in Romans 5:17 is to overlook the narrative of glory; to overlook this narrative of glory is to overlook the point of Romans 5:12-21; and to overlook the point of Romans 5:12-21 is to overlook what it is to boast in the hope of sharing in the glory of God in Romans 5:2—the theme to which Paul returns most climactically in Romans 8:17-30.

Finally, we turn to humanity's renewal of δόξα in Romans 8. Though Paul first introduces humanity's reinstatement to glory in Romans 8:17, followed closely by Romans 8:18, I begin this section in Romans 8:21. This verse is significant not only because it is difficult to translate but because it is the precise point at which Paul identifies the relationship between God's children and creation.[212] In fact, it is the reason Paul includes this otherwise ostensibly random focus on the cursed creation here at all. Romans 8:21 reads, beginning at the end of Romans 8:20: ἐφ᾽ ἐλπίδι ὅτι καὶ αὐτὴ ἡ κτίσις ἐλευθερωθήσεται ἀπὸ τῆς δουλείας τῆς φθορᾶς εἰς τὴν ἐλευθερίαν τῆς δόξης τῶν τέκνων τοῦ θεοῦ, translated by the Kingdom New Testament as "in the hope that creation itself would be freed from its slavery to decay, to enjoy the freedom that comes when God's children are glorified."[213] Tracing Paul's logic from present to future in Romans 8:17-21, we can deduce that:

> (Rom 8:20) though creation is currently subjected to decay,
>> (Rom 8:19) it waits for God's children to be revealed,
>>> (Rom 8:18) because their glory will then be reinstated,
>>>> (Rom 8:17) a glory that they have as God's heirs and co-heirs with Christ,

---

[209]Dunn 1988a: 282.

[210]See also Ciampa 2013: 114.

[211]See Ridderbos 1978: 559-62, who emphasizes believers' rule but not as a renewal of Adam's original glory. See also Morris 1988: 237-38; Byrne 2007: 179-80; Jewett and Kotansky 2007: 383-85; Wright 2013a: 890, 959, 1090.

[212]My argument for interpreting κτίσις as "creation" is given in §7.2.1.

[213]This is in contrast to creation obtaining "the freedom of the glory of the children of God" (ESV, NASB, NRSV) and "the glorious freedom of the children of God" (KJV and RSV, both with "liberty," NIV). These translations skew Paul's point: that creation obtains freedom from corruption when God's children are glorified. I will return to this text in more detail in §7.2.1.

at which point and, indeed, because of which,

(Rom 8:21) creation will again be free from its bondage to decay.

We can also deduce from Paul's logic that:

(Rom 8:21) if creation will be freed from its bondage

when

(Rom 8:18) God's children are reinstated to glory,

then

(Rom 8:20) creation was unwillingly subjected to decay

when

(Rom 1:21-23; 3:23 implicitly) God's children first forsook their inheritance

of glory.

According to Newman, humanity's eschatological glory in Romans 8:18, 21 refers to "a qualitatively new relational sphere of existence for the 'sons,'" which follows from the "ruptured relationship" implied in Romans 1:23 and Romans 3:23.[214] No doubt, a ruptured relationship is part of humanity's rejection of its created purpose, but a number of reasons exist for us to reject this thesis. (1) While Paul does emphasize the restored relationship between humanity and God through adoption in Romans 8 (esp. Rom 8:15),[215] he does not equate humanity's δόξα with that restored relationship. In fact, what Paul does equate humanity's eschatological glory with is its inheritance as children of God in Romans 8:17, a theme to which I will return at length in chapter six. (2) Humanity's eschatological glory as a restored relationship fails to explain the direct link between creation's restoration in Romans 8:21 and the restored relationship between God and man; what explicit impact does humanity's reestablishment in the presence of God have on the renewal of creation? (3) Newman's definition fails to explain why Paul includes a treatment of the restored creation here at all. In fact, if this is Paul's implicit understanding of δόξα, then his inclusion of the present groaning and future liberation of creation is inexplicable in its literary context.[216] (4) As I demonstrated in chapter two, the primary use of δόξα vis-à-vis humanity in the LXX is almost always in reference to a person's exalted or honored status, often associated with rule or authority.

---

[214]Newman 1992: 225-26.

[215]I will return to the motif of adoption in §6.1.

[216]I will return to this passage at length in §7.2.1.

(5) As noted above, the reference to humanity's δόξα in Romans 2:7, 10 bears far greater associations with the denotation I am suggesting than Newman's in Romans 8:18, 21, whose understanding of δόξα in Romans 2:7, 10 failed to make it into any denotative category.[217]

In response to (2) and (3) above, at least, if δόξα is understood as humanity's exaltation to a renewed status of honor associated with its created purpose of having dominion over creation, then creation's renewal as a result of humanity's restored δόξα makes sense, and Paul's inclusion of the restoration of creation at this point is no longer ostensibly random.[218] Humanity's renewed δόξα results in creation experiencing its own freedom from bondage, because in their glorification, creation itself is free to be what it was created to be, and humanity plays an integral role in making that happen. It is what humanity was created to do. Reasons (4) and (5) are self-explanatory; and, in regard to (1), because of the multiple critical and complex themes in Romans 8:17, 30, not least the significance of humanity's inheritance and the role that an interpretation of it plays in one's interpretation of δόξαζω, I hold off on many comments associated with the term in these two verses. I will return to them in full in chapter six.

3.4. Conclusion

This is the glory for which all God's people hope (Rom 5:2): this refitted, rejeweled, and replaced crown of glory originally bestowed on humanity in Psalm 8 (understood in tandem with Gen 1) and quickly rejected in Genesis 3. Through the Son, God would undo what Adam did, condemn sin in the flesh (Rom 8:3), and restore humanity's crown of glory. Though his point reaches its climax in Romans 8:30, nowhere does Paul make it more clear than in Romans 5:17: "If, because of one man's trespass, *death reigned through that one man*, much more will those who receive the abundance of grace and the free gift of righteousness *reign in life through the one man Jesus Christ*" (ESV). This is believers' "hope of glory," and, to arrive back at where we started, this is why δόξα and δοξάζω cannot be translated in Romans either as "splendor" or "radiance," even as words representing the visible presence of God, though these may exist in the

---

[217]See again Newman 1992: 160-61.
[218]See Wright 2013a: 1092.

background. To be glorified is to experience a transformation of status—to be exalted to a new status, one of honor associated with a representative reign over creation, crowned with glory and honor as Adam was meant to be and as the Messiah now is.

The significance of this introduction to Paul's use of δόξα and δοξάζω cannot be overstated. Understanding glory as humanity's honorable position associated with its dominion over the created order as God's vicegerent will be fundamental to understanding "conformed to the image of [God's] Son" in Romans 8:29b, both within the immediate context of Romans 8 and within the larger context of Romans 1–8. In the following chapter, I turn our attention to the theological motifs of union and participation in Pauline theology, motifs that underlie the premise of believers sharing in or being "coglorified" with the Son in Romans 8:17 and Romans 8:30, and thus ultimately being "conformed to the image of the Son" in Romans 8:29b.

4

PARTICIPATION IN
CHRIST'S GLORY

Before examining Romans 8:29b within its specific literary context of Romans 8, an assessment of one critical Pauline motif is necessary: participation with Christ. *Participation* is a term commonly applied to believers sharing in fellowship with Christ in which what is true of him becomes true of the Christian.[1] This motif of participation, which is part and parcel of Paul's incorporative language and which has recently regained popularity within discussions of Pauline theology, is central to Paul's use of συμμόρφος in Romans 8:29b.

This chapter and chapter six are intended to be read hand in glove: this chapter will comprise the glove into which chapter six will fit. In them I will argue that in the phrase συμμόρφους τῆς εἰκόνος τοῦ υἱοῦ αὐτοῦ Paul refers to believers' participation with the Firstborn Son in his rule over creation as adopted children of God. More specifically, I will suggest that in Romans 8:29 a *vocational* participation is implied. By "vocational participation" I mean that, on the basis of their union with Christ and thus transformed identities in him as the new Adam, believers therefore share with Christ in his resurrection life and glory, and thus fulfill their vocation as redeemed humans, representing God to his creation and interceding on behalf of creation to God. In this chapter I address the concept of

---

[1]McKim (1996: 201) suggests: "A general term to describe how the nature of one being can have effects on another."

vocational participation; the details of this vocation will be addressed in chapter seven.

Three discussions need to happen in this chapter. First, we need to examine the now commonly held idea that the concept of incorporation into Christ, whether expressed in union, representation, or participation, is a foundational motif in Pauline theology. In this first section, I will, first, provide a brief history of approaches to Paul's incorporative language and, second, articulate an implied "vocational participation" in union: believers who are glorified in the Messiah are therefore called to live out that glorification.[2] Second, we need to examine Paul's use of συμμόρφος as a term that connotes vocational participation in Philippians 3:21, a context that resembles Romans 8:29. Third, we need to examine Paul's use of εἰκών in 1 Corinthians 15:49 and Colossians 3:10, two verses with contexts wherein Paul presents believers as vocational participants with the Messiah in his cosmic rule. On the basis of these verses, I will establish the support for reading "conformed to the image of [God's Firstborn] Son" as implicative of believers' vocational participation in the Messiah as renewed humanity. In chapter six, then, I will establish this reading on the basis of Romans 8 itself. To begin, I turn our attention to the muddy waters of incorporative terminology.

4.1. PARTICIPATION AS A FOUNDATIONAL MOTIF IN PAULINE LITERATURE

4.1.1. History of incorporative language. Investigation of Paul's incorporative language is not a recent development in New Testament studies.[3] Between the late 1800s and today the motif has regained popularity within Pauline studies, and perhaps especially so since the mid-1970s. Beginning in 1892, Paul's incorporative language regained popularity in scholarship thanks to

---

[2] *Vocational* here should not be taken to imply "functional." It implies only an ontological reality expressed as a lived reality (being and act held inseparably).

[3] See Macaskill (2013: 54-72) for an overview of the Fathers' approach to incorporative language and Billings (2007) for an overview of Calvin's use of the motifs. For information additional to that presented here, see Campbell (2012: 31-58), who also notes Wilhelm Bousset (1970), John Murray (1955), Alfred Wikenhauser (1960), Fritz Neugebauer (1961), Michel Bouttier (1966), Karl Barth (1932–1968), Robert Tannehill (1967), W. D. Davies (1980), Richard Gaffin (1978), Michael Horton (2007) and especially Barth (1962); see also Macaskill (2013: 25-34), who notes N. T. Wright (1991 esp.) and Richard Hays (2002).

Adolf Deissmann.[4] Deissmann suggested that Paul's use of "in Christ" referred to a "Christ mysticism,"[5] in which "Paul lives 'in' Christ, 'in' the
living and present spiritual Christ, who is about him on all sides, and who
fills him, who speaks to him, and speaks in and through him."[6] Deissmann
distinguished Paul's "Christ mysticism," in which the person is not transformed into a deity or Christ, from what might be considered a technical
mysticism influenced by Paul's Hellenistic culture that blurs any distinction
between human and deity.[7]

Nearly four decades later, Albert Schweitzer argued in his 1930 work
Die Mystik des Apostels Paulus that, while Paul did have an ultimate mystical relationship with God in focus, it was a relationship mediated by a
mystical relationship with Christ in the present.[8] And, like Deissmann
before him, the mysticism of which Paul wrote, said Schweitzer, maintained
a distinction between the man and the deity.[9] Perhaps unlike those before
him, however, for Schweitzer, Paul's understanding of a mystical relationship
with Christ was the answer to a problem of eschatology. Campbell notes
that "Schweitzer regarded mysticism as the means by which Paul was able
to reconcile the otherwise contradicting elements of his eschatology. Redemption is future, and yet believers are able to experience Christ's death
and resurrection in their present existence because they share with Christ."[10]
Schweitzer's ideas were before their time and were for many years met with
quizzical dismissals.[11]

It was not only from within the New Testament guild, however, that
ideas of the corporate nature of Christ were developed. H. Wheeler Robinson
and his 1936 work on corporate personality in the Old Testament did as

---

[4]Wolter (2015: 221-22) notes several German scholars who alluded to the motif of "Christ
mysticism" before Deissmann.

[5]Deissmann 1912: 130-31.

[6]Deissmann 1912: 135-36; see Dunn 1998b: 391. Those who came after Deissmann and who also
focused much of their study of Paul's incorporative language on Paul's use of "in Christ"
include Best 1955; Neugebauer 1961; Kramer 1966; and Moule 1977: 54-69.

[7]Deissmann 1912: 149-53; see Macaskill 2013: 18-20. Campbell (2012: 34-35) and Macaskill
(2013: 20-21) also note that Deissmann's successor, William Boussett, also argued that Paul's
"mysticism" bears only vague resemblance to Hellenistic notions of mysticism; see Boussett
1970: 164.

[8]Schweitzer 1931: 3; see Macaskill 2013: 21-24.

[9]Schweitzer 1931: 15.

[10]Campbell 2012: 38.

[11]See Dunn 1998b: 391-93.

much to fuel conversations on the corporate nature of Christ as they did sociological conceptions of corporate identity in the Old Testament and Hebrew culture.[12] By "corporate personality" Robinson meant that "the whole group, including its past, present, and future members, might function as a single individual through any one of those members conceived as representative of it."[13] Robinson's work was criticized for its dependence on now-discredited theories of social anthropology,[14] its imprecise use of the term "corporate personality,"[15] and its lack of consideration for the emphasis on an individual's responsibility within Mosaic law.[16] Nevertheless, his work made a lasting impact on the study of both Old and New Testament understandings of corporate identity in the Old Testament[17] and theological themes of incorporation in and with Christ in the New Testament.[18]

Schweitzer's non-Hellenistic mystical understanding of "in Christ" stands in contrast to that later proposed by Rudolf Bultmann (1952). Whereas for Schweitzer, "in Christ" connoted a mystical unity, for Bultmann, the phrase referred to believers' "articulation into the 'body of Christ' by baptism," that is, becoming part of the church.[19] For Schweitzer, Paul was not influenced by the Hellenistic mystery religions; for Bultmann, the Gnostic redeemer myth was at the root of Paul's language.[20]

Though present in earlier years, conversations surrounding Paul's incorporative language intensified in the mid-1970s. During these years, the corporate nature of Christ slowly became coupled with a variety of other highly significant theological motifs: the role of covenant and the influence of Jewish apocalyptic literature on Paul's theology and letters, and, perhaps most theologically significant, justification (by faith), the economy of the

---

[12]See Macaskill (2013: 101-2) for a summary of Robinson's argument and its criticisms.

[13]Robinson 1981: 25.

[14]Powers 2001: 15; see Rogerson 1970: 9-12.

[15]Rogerson 1970: 1-16.

[16]Porter 1965: 361-80.

[17]See Kaminsky (1995) for a persuasive argument that, despite the weaknesses of Robinson's theory, ideas of corporate identity do exist and are significant in the Old Testament. Kaminsky focuses on deuteronomistic notions of corporate responsibility whereby the many are punished for the sins of the few—or the one, in the instance of a king—and the future generations bear the covenant curses of their ancestors. See esp. Kaminsky 1995: 47-54.

[18]See Best 1955 and Ridderbos 1975: 61-62.

[19]Bultmann 1952: 311; see Campbell 2012: 39.

[20]Bultmann 1952: 298.

atonement, and Pauline soteriology. The former two currently exist as themes at the center of discussions of participation, but the latter three have (primarily) occupied scholars' attention from the early 1970s onward. Each has its own history of interpretation, and to elaborate on all or even one would require more words than this project allows. What is important to say at this point is that one is hard-pressed to read publications on Paul's use of corporate language from 1970 onward that do not consider the motif in relationship to Paul's view of justification, the atonement, and/or salvation.

In 1971 Morna Hooker asked: "If Christ is identified with man's condition . . . how are the Jews set free from the curse of the law, and how does the blessing come to the Gentiles?"[21] The answer, she suggested, could be found in the term *interchange* or, more exactly, an "interchange of experience."[22] By *interchange* she suggested that "Christ shares in our experience, in order that we might share in his,"[23] or "Christ has become what we are in order that we might become what he is."[24] Interchange, for Hooker, is the key to interpreting Paul's incorporative language and its relationship to Paul's view of the atonement and salvation. Christ does not suffer on the cross as man's substitute but as his representative. As one whose identity is in Christ, man suffers with Christ.[25] This interchange of experience is at the heart of Paul's view of atonement, the reconciliation between God and man, and the relationship between creation and redemption—and the role and status of mankind in both.

Perhaps most famous for establishing the significance of Paul's incorporative language in more recent scholarship is E. P. Sanders. His 1977 release of *Paul and Palestinian Judaism* triggered a seismic shift within Pauline

---

[21]Hooker 1971: 351.

[22]Hooker 1971: 349-61, with "interchange of experience" on 353, 355.

[23]Hooker 1971: 352.

[24]Hooker 1971: 358. She argues that it is "in Christ" that Jews are set free from the law and Gentiles are brought into the Abrahamic blessing. More generally, Christ has become a curse for believers in order that they might become sons of God (Gal 2–3): p. 352; Christ has been sent in the likeness of sinful flesh in order that believers might be sons of God living in the Spirit (Rom 8:3, 14ff.): p. 354; Christ became human ("in Adam") in order that believers might "share what he is—namely—the true image of God" (Rom 8:3, 29): p. 355; "Christ humbled himself, becoming man, in order that by his humiliation we might become glorious in him" (Phil 2:6-11; 3:10, 21): p. 357.

[25]Hooker 1971: 358.

studies, the aftershocks of which continue to be felt throughout the disci-
pline. What Hooker said rather modestly through "interchange," Sanders
said with unequivocal abandon: "The heart of Paul's theology," Sanders
declared, "lies in the participatory categories" rather than juridical categories.[26] That is to say that "the main theme of Paul's gospel was the saving
action of God in Jesus Christ and how his hearers could participate in that
action."[27] This participatory salvation comes through being transferred into
the right union[28]—a union not characterized by enslavement and condemnation but a new union with Christ. Salvation comes through a union
characterized by participation in the death of Christ, freedom, transformation into a new creation, reconciliation, and justification/righteousness.[29]
This transfer from one union to the other comes from "*sharing* in Christ's
death" and thereby dying "to the *power* of sin or to the old aeon."[30] Sanders
argues that "the *purpose* of Christ's death was not simply to provide ex-
piation, but that he might become Lord and thus save those who belong
to him and are 'in' him" (Rom 14:8-9; 2 Cor 5:14-15; 1 Thess 5:10).[31] Christ's
death effected more than a verdict of "not guilty"; it effected a "*change in
lordship*"—a change that takes place through believers' participation in
Christ's death (Rom 6:3-11; 7:4; Gal 2:19-20; 5:24; Phil 3:10).[32]

Sanders draws heavily on Schweitzer's *Die Mystik* (1931), in which
Schweitzer had suggested more than forty years previously that Paul's gospel
centered on the mystical union of believers in Christ—a theme similar to
that of what Sanders called "participation." As indicated, however, Schweitzer's
work was premature. It was written at a time when currents within Pauline
scholarship were yet unfavorable to a new "center" of Paul's theology; that,
and he used the term *Mystik*, which perhaps carried connotations unin-
tended by Schweitzer.[33] Forty years on, however, the tide had turned, and

---

[26]Sanders 1977: 502, 520; see 431-523.

[27]Sanders 1977: 447.

[28]Sanders is not specific about who or what is the object of this former union, though he hints
at Adam in a brief synopsis of the Adam-Christ passages that refer to the salvation of all
humanity (e.g., Rom 5:18; 1 Cor 15:22): 472-74.

[29]Sanders 1977: 463-72.

[30]Sanders 1977: 467-68; emphasis original.

[31]Sanders 1977: 465; emphasis original.

[32]Sanders 1977: 465-66; emphasis original.

[33]Dunn (1998b: 394) notes that "'Christ mysticism' has become very much a 'back number,' the
lack of clear and consensual definition for its principal term and its esoteric overtones dis-
couraging the attention it deserves."

when Sanders published *Paul and Palestinian Judaism* and argued that the heart of Paul's soteriology is understood with participatory motifs, he also resurrected Schweitzer's previously rejected observations. Since 1977 Schweitzer has had no lack of audience, and *participation*, particularly in its relationship to other soteriological motifs, has now become a household word in Pauline studies.[34]

Dunn's 1998 *The Theology of Paul the Apostle* contains an entire section dedicated to "Participation in Christ,"[35] and, perhaps as a sign of the times, is categorized under the guise of the theme's relationship to Paul's views of justification and salvation.[36] Nevertheless, the interrelationship between the participation and soteriological motifs does not dominate his discussion. Dunn suggests that there are three primary ways of approaching and understanding Paul's "in Christ" language: (1) objectively, as the "redemptive act which has happened 'in Christ' or depends on what Christ is yet to do";[37] (2) subjectively, as believers being "in Christ";[38] and (3) where "Paul has in view his own activity or is exhorting his readers to adopt a particular attitude or course of action."[39]

Since the turn of the millennium, emphasis on incorporative language has reached new heights. The sheer number of works published with the sole purpose of addressing Paul's use of the motifs throughout his letters

---

[34]Sanders's emphasis on participation and union as key components of Paul's soteriology has led to an ever-expanding emphasis on Paul's incorporation language, particularly "participation with Christ," in relation to themes of justification and substitutionary atonement. To date, one of the most influential publications on the relationship between the two motifs, albeit only tangentially connected to Sanders's proposal regarding the relationship between judicial and participationist accounts of soteriology, in general, and the death of Christ, in particular, is Richard Hays's *The Faith of Jesus Christ* (2002 [1983]). Influenced by Sanders's emphasis on participation in Christ, Hays suggests that salvation comes through believers' participation in the faith/faithfulness of Jesus: 2002: xxvn12. He writes, "We are taken up into his life, including his faithfulness, and that faithfulness therefore imparts to us the shape of our own existence. . . . Ultimately, being united with Christ is salvific because to share his life is to share in the life of God": 2002: xxxii-iii. This participatory motif is only a secondary emphasis in *The Faith of Jesus Christ* but has nevertheless helped to solidify the increasingly popular argument that Paul's theology of justification by faith is linked with participation with Christ. See Macaskill (2013: 25-26, 31-34) for an extended discussion of Hays's "narrative participation." More recent works include Powers 2001 and Douglas Campbell's *The Deliverance of God* (2009).
[35]Dunn 1998b: 390-412.
[36]Dunn 1998b: 390-91.
[37]Dunn 1998b: 397.
[38]Dunn 1998b: 398.
[39]Dunn 1998b: 398.

demonstrates this increase.[40] Three scholars deserve mention in the more recent years of this historical survey: Michael Gorman (2001, 2009), Constantine Campbell (2012), and Grant Macaskill (2013). Gorman does not focus on the question of union and participation with Christ *in se* as much as he uses the concepts, particularly "participation," to put forth an argument that being "conformed to Christ" ultimately means participating in the life of God.[41] He suggests a union[42] between God and believers through what he calls *cruciformity*—believers' participation in the death of Christ[43] or, more semantically accurate, believers' conformity to the crucified Christ.[44] For Gorman, cruciformity is not limited to conformity to Christ but includes also conformity to God and the Spirit. *Cruciformity* means *theosis*, or "theoformity,"[45] which is "transformative participation in the kenotic, cruciform character of God through Spirit-enabled conformity to the incarnate, crucified, and resurrected/glorified Christ."[46] Because participation and conformity to Christ are key concepts for Gorman's argument, I will address a number of the finer points of his argument throughout the rest of this section.

The most comprehensive treatment of Pauline incorporative language to date is Constantine Campbell's 2012 *Paul and Union with Christ*. After systematically analyzing Paul's "in Christ," "with Christ," "through Christ," and so on language, Campbell discusses the notion of union with Christ in relation to other Pauline theological motifs. More so than most, Campbell attempts to distinguish between the commonly used terms *union*, *participation*, *identification*, and *incorporation*.[47] He suggests that "together these four terms function as 'umbrella' concepts, covering the full spectrum of Pauline language, ideas, and themes that are bound up in the metatheme of 'union with Christ.'"[48]

---

[40]A selection of monographs alone includes Powers 2001; Fowler 2005; Horton 2007; Billings 2007; Letham 2011; Billings 2011; White 2012; Campbell 2012; Macaskill 2013.

[41]Gorman 2009: 2.

[42]Though he does not use the term *union* specifically.

[43]Gorman 2001: 32.

[44]Gorman 2009: 4; see Macaskill (2013: 25-28) for an extended discussion of Gorman's understanding of *cruciformity*, *theosis*, and use of *likeness*.

[45]Gorman 2009: 4.

[46]Gorman 2009: 7.

[47]Campbell 2012: 406-13.

[48]Campbell 2012: 413; see Macaskill (2013: 38-40) for a summary of Campbell's conclusions.

One final work deserves mention. In *Union with Christ in the New Testament* (2013), Macaskill sets out to answer the question, "How is the union between God and those he has redeemed represented in the New Testament?"[49] Macaskill suggests in his central chapter that union with Christ is represented throughout the New Testament in "the paired images of the church as temple and body of Christ"—images that can be regarded "as core to New Testament theology."[50] This "pairing of images relates to participation" in that "it maintains the distinction between God and the creatures present in the temple, while allowing his glory to be shared with them; it is covenantal, and specifically related to the Spirit-promises of the new covenant; and it involves a particular union between believers and the Messiah."[51] Within the temple imagery, believers are the building and Christ is the cornerstone, and the union created by the two creates sacred space for the presence of the indwelling Spirit.[52] *Union with Christ* is the most extensive and in-depth analysis of the New Testament theme of union with Christ in scholarship to date, as well as the most comprehensive survey of union and participation in scholarship from the church fathers onward.

4.1.2. Defining and grounding the terms in Paul. With the exception of using the terms chosen by individual authors, I have thus far refrained from using terms other than "incorporative language" to describe Paul's "incorporative" motifs. There is an ever-present danger in overdefining such terms, but the danger of not defining words of such high significance is perhaps even greater.[53] For my purposes here, it is important only to

---

[49]Macaskill 2013: 1.

[50]Macaskill 2013: 12.

[51]Macaskill 2013: 12.

[52]Macaskill 2013: 147-59, but also picked up in detail throughout the study.

[53]See Wolter 2015: 221. The danger of not defining such terms is evident in the work of Johnson Hodge (2007), whose argument that the identities of Jews and Gentiles remain distinct from each other "in Christ" rests on a theology of union with Christ in which both Jews and Gentiles find their primary identities "in Christ" but also retain their ethnic distinctions (see esp. chap. 7, but the point is articulated throughout the work). A *theology* of union with/in Christ, however, is all but dismissed. She covers the theological interpretations of union with Christ of Deissmann, F. C. Porter, Dunn, and Sam K. Williams in four sentences, before suggesting that "each one seems to be based more on modernist theological reflection than on Paul's arguments" (p. 93). Failing entirely to qualify that statement, she then proceeds in the next sentence to suggest that "in Christ" language refers to "patrilineal descent," which she describes as the "notion that descendants are manifestations of their ancestors and that members of kinship groups share the same 'stuff'" (pp. 93-94); they are "in" their ancestors as Jews were "in" Abraham as his descendants. While patrilineal descent is probably correct on a fundamental level, in that it recognizes some element of kinship relationship between Jesus

articulate the relationship between *union* and *participation* as I am using the terms in this book.

Modern authors use *union* and *participation* synonymously at times, and at other times view the terms as separate but interrelated, with the intricacies of the interrelationship rarely explained. Hays argued in 1983 that believers participate in the faithfulness of Jesus but failed to articulate even once what he meant by *participate*.[54] Daniel Powers titled his 2001 dissertation *Salvation Through Participation* and yet mentioned participation no more than twice in the introduction, and not once to define the term. The case is much the same for the majority of recent scholars, particularly in reference to the relationship that exists between Christ and believers. The distinctions are important for our purposes here only because of the semantic use of *glory* or *glorification*, which I am suggesting stands behind Paul's use of the terms vis-à-vis humanity in Romans. It is important to flesh this out further.

Union. Paul's "in Christ" language operates in a variety of ways. According to Campbell, these include things achieved for/given to people, believers' actions, characteristics of believers, faith in Christ, justification, new status, contribution to trinitarian contexts, and paraphrases denoting someone as a believer.[55] Without disputing this list, I wish to emphasize here the transformation of believers' status and/or identity in union with Christ. For Paul, this transformed status and/or identity is communicated

---

and Gentiles (and I would suggest Jews, as well), disregarding the clearly theological aspects of Paul's "in Christ" language in which believers (on some level or in some way) share the experience of Christ's death and resurrection seems theologically reductionistic. This and other serious weaknesses that infect the entire work and thus prompt serious critique, particularly of her interpretation of Rom 8:29, will be addressed in §§5.3.2 and 6.1.

[54]Macaskill (2013: 26) notes this as well but suggests that it reflects a "deliberate move on Hays' part." I am less persuaded. More recently Hays tried to bring clarity of thought through an essay titled "What Is 'Real Participation in Christ'?" in a *Festschrift* dedicated to Ed Sanders (2008). There he identifies four suggestions for how to understand participation: belonging to a family, political or military solidarity with Christ, being the corporate body of Christ, and living within the Christ story, by which he means the narrative of redemption. Nevertheless, throughout the piece Hays hints that participation is somehow distinct from union, and yet at the very end he conflates the two: "These proposals [about 'real participation'] offer some ways of approaching the issue, but they hardly exhaust the matter; there remains something irreducibly mysterious about union with Christ" (p. 349).

[55]Campbell 2012: 67-199. He notes in conclusion (2012: 199): "It is, therefore, impossible to define the meaning of these idioms by a single description as though they are formulaic. Virtually the full range of lexical possibilities of the preposition ἐν is extant for ἐν Χριστῷ and its variations."

via a variety of metaphors: justified; adopted; free/redeemed from slavery to sin, death, and the law; reconciled to God; a new creation.[56] This new identity in Christ also includes being glorified: being identified by Christ's glory or having the honor that is Christ's. Justified,[57] adopted,[58] and glorified are the three transformations of a believer's identity most closely associated with Romans 8:17-30.

Wolter notes that Paul's descriptions of believers' "present status of salvation" (e.g., glorified, elect, children of God, no longer enemies of God, reconciled, etc.[59]) are all "semantically isotopic—they stand in a paradigmatic relationship and are therefore interchangeable among each other without limitation. The same thing is repeatedly said in different words."[60]

---

[56]For texts on being justified, see Rom 3:24, 26; 5:1, 9; 6:7; 8:1 (Paul does not use δικαιόω or δίκαιος in Rom 8:1, but the sentiment behind "no condemnation" is the same; see Wright 2009a: 234); Gal 2:16, 17. On being adopted, see Rom 8:15, 23; Gal 4:5; Eph 1:5. On being free/redeemed from slavery to sin, death, and the law, see Rom 6:1-10; 8:2; Gal 3:13-14; see Fee 2004: 52-55. On being reconciled to God, see Rom 5:10, 11; 2 Cor 5:19. On being a new creation, see 2 Cor 5:17. This short list of metaphors should in no way indicate that I am reducing them to a mere list of metaphors that talk about one's status "in Christ." Theologically and exegetically, each metaphor functions as and connotes much more than just this status. Together they form the larger narrative of creation, sin, exodus, exile, and redemption, all of which are rooted in Israel's past and Scriptures. As noted in the discussion of semiotics, metaphorical language does not imply metaphysical existence or nonexistence.

[57]The relationship between justification and union/participation, as indicated above, is often the center of the current discussions of Paul's incorporative language. Entering into the discussion here will not advance my larger argument, and thus I will refrain from so doing. I wish only to highlight and contest the proposal of Michael Gorman, who, with numerous contemporary scholars (see Gorman 2009: 41), suggests that justification by faith refers to a participatory soteriology. According to Gorman, Paul understands justification as "new life/resurrection via crucifixion with the messiah Jesus, or 'justification by co-crucifixion,' and therefore as inherently participatory" (Gorman 2009: 44). Gorman summarizes: "Justification is the establishment or restoration of right covenantal relations—*fidelity* to God and *love* for neighbor—by means of God's grace in Christ's death and our Spirit-enabled co-crucifixion with him. Justification therefore means co-crucifixion with Christ to new life within the people of God and the certain *hope* of acquittal/vindication, and thus resurrection to eternal life, on the day of judgment": Gorman 2009: 85-86; emphasis original. For a similar perspective, see Shauf 2006. The primary weakness I find with Gorman's description of justification is that in one line he suggests justification is "*by means of* . . . co-crucifixion" and in another he says justification "*means* co-crucifixion"; emphasis mine.

[58]Yarbrough (1995: 140) says that "for . . . Paul . . . adoption into the family of God is a key metaphor for the new status believers have obtained" (quoted by Burke 2006: 22). See Burke (2006: 120-23) on Paul's emphasis on adoption as a status made possible only through union with Christ. There Burke (p. 123) quotes John Murray, who says, "We cannot think of adoption apart from union with Christ . . . union with Christ and adoption are complementary aspects of this amazing grace. Union with Christ reaches its zenith in adoption and adoption has its orbit in union with Christ" (Murray 1961: 170).

[59]See Wolter 2015: 186.

[60]Wolter 2015: 186.

While "semantically isotopic" may be an overstatement, or perhaps even reductionistic, his recognition that the terms or phrases all describe salvation from different perspectives is correct. The same critique can be made of the important work of Michael Gorman.[61] As Gordon Fee notes, "although metaphors do indeed give expression to *one dimension of a reality*, no one of them is adequate to embrace *the whole of that reality*."[62] Each metaphor has its particular place in Paul's letters, and each speaks to believers' identity and location "in Christ." In this way, descriptions of a person's status in Christ are multivalent.

In furtherance to the brief comments I offered on ontological transformation in chapter two, I note here that, in terms of a believer's union with Christ, her glorification (as in Rom 8:30) or coglorification with Christ (as in Rom 8:17) *does* imply an ontological transformation—a transformation of the identity (which includes status) that characterizes her existence,[63] even if understood as honor or exalted status associated with rule: Christ's honor or exalted status becomes that of the believer. It is not as if the traditional understanding of glorification refers to an ontological transformation where the person becomes more like God, in the presence of God, and thus reflects the splendor of God, and this semantic use of glorification does not. Understanding human glorification as existing in or belonging to a status of honor is also ontological in that it belongs to a person's essential identity, which characterizes their existence.

Participation. Participation with Christ, as noted by Campbell, exists under the auspices of union with Christ. Participation is not somehow outside union with Christ or something different from union with Christ; it is a logical consequence of certain ontological transformations that take place in union with Christ, namely those that imply an active rather than passive reception of such transformations. For example, justification, sanctification, adoption, and traditional understandings of eschatological glorification "in Christ" are all passive. In each case, it is an ontological

---

[61]Throughout Gorman's work, a plethora of terms, including *union, participation, kenosis, theosis, cruciform, conform, transform(ation), holiness, justification, sanctification, suffering,* and *glory*, are used so frequently in mutual interpretation that, at the end of the argument, the reader is left to wonder how the terms can and should be distinguished one from the other.

[62]Fee 2004: 49; emphasis original.

[63]Refer back to my initial definition in §2.2.2.1 of how I am using *ontology* and *ontological* in this book.

transformation that happens in union with Christ and that implies no logically subsequent activity on the part of the believer.

On the other hand, being united with Christ in his suffering, crucifixion, death, and resurrection all imply sharing in an "activity" with Christ. This I am referring to as participation, and, more specifically, as vocational participation. It is the logical consequence of an ontologically transformed identity in Christ and occurs only because of that transformation.[64] In the case of glorification, if *glory* and *glorification* are used in Romans vis-à-vis humanity as they are in the LXX vis-à-vis humanity, then the semantic use of the terms as reference to honor, power, or authority associated with an exalted status of dominion implies an ontological transformation of status, which by definition also necessarily implies an associated action. To receive a status of honor associated with dominion or rule implies that the person will thus bear that honor in rule; as those glorified in Christ, they will actively participate in the glorious/honorable rule of Christ. As noted in chapter two, one's transformed identity logically includes "being" and "act"; one who is "in Christ" acts in ways that demonstrate that transformed identity.

A word of caution must be noted here. This ontological transformation that occurs in union with Christ is increasingly being referred to as *theosis*, a motif historically central to Eastern traditions and slowly making its way into Protestant traditions in the West.[65] Within these Protestant—primarily Pauline—circles, Michael Gorman has written on this transformation as *theosis*.[66] Gorman defines *theosis* as the "transformative participation in the kenotic, cruciform character of God through Spirit-enabled conformity to the incarnate, crucified, and resurrected/glorified Christ."[67] Gorman rightly emphasizes the role of the Spirit in this transformation, but, with Macaskill, I question Gorman's theological use of the term *theosis* and the interplay between becoming "like Christ" and "incorporation into the divine identity."[68] Participation in Christ does not blur the ever-present

---

[64]I reiterate that *vocational* is not somehow distinct from *ontological* but rather the teleological purpose to union with Christ. Karl Barth treated these distinctions similarly (though certainly not the same) to those I am presenting here. See Neder (2009: 15-28) for a succinct discussion of Barth's twofold (objective and subjective) form of participation.

[65]See Macaskill 2013: 42-82 on the church fathers' and Luther's understanding of *theosis*.

[66]Gorman 2009.

[67]Gorman 2009: 7.

[68]Macaskill 2013: 27-28.

distinction between God in Christ and believers in Christ. The glory in which believers participate is not innate to themselves; it originates in God alone and is received only as a gift from God in union with Christ.[69]

Within Pauline terms, these participatory activities that believers share with Christ, most significantly those of dying, rising, suffering, and sharing in glory,[70] are presented primarily through Paul's use of σὺν as an independent preposition and σὺμ-/σὺν-compounds.[71] Table 4.1 represents these participatory activities and the texts in which they are found.

Table 4.1

	Crucifixion/ Death	Burial	Suffering	Resurrection	Life	Glorification
σὺν Χριστῷ	Rom 6:8; Col 2:20				Col 3:3; Phil 1:23	
σὺν κυρίῳ					1 Thess 4:17	
σὺν αὐτῷ				1 Thess 4:14	2 Cor 13:4; Col 2:13; 1 Thess 5:10	Col 3:4
σὺν Ἰησοῦ				2 Cor 4:14		
σὺμ-/σὺν- compounds	Rom 6:6; Gal 2:20; Phil 3:10 (συμμορφίζω); 2 Tim 2:11	Rom 6:4, 5 (σύμφυτος); Col 2:12	Rom 8:17	Eph 2:6 Col 2:12; 3:1	Rom 6:8 Eph 2:5 2 Tim 2:11	Rom 8:17, 29 (σύμμορφος); Eph 2:6 (συγκαθίζω); Phil 3:21 (σύμμορφος); 2 Tim 2:12 (συμβασιλεύω)

Not every use of σὺν or every σὺμ-/σὺν-compound that has the believer as the subject and Jesus as the object of the preposition automatically signifies a participatory motif.[72] There are also two σὺμ-/σὺν-compounds

---

[69]See Macaskill 2013: 143.

[70]See Harvey 1992; Campbell 2012: 408.

[71]Dunn notes that there are approximately forty σύν-compounds found throughout the Pauline corpus that are the "real force" of the "with Christ" motif; see Dunn (1998b: 402-3) for the list of compounds and their respective locations throughout the letters. See McGrath 1952, who provides a lexical definition of twenty-four of the words.

[72]I include Phil 1:23 here for the sake of a less complex table, despite that it may not be the most appropriate category and that it may not refer to participation at all. Campbell includes Phil 1:23 as a reference to participation. I am not convinced, however, and consider Paul's "be with Christ" as emphasizing the physical proximity between the believer and Christ and thereby lacking the activity on which the participatory motif seems so dependent: 2012: 223. Intriguingly, Campbell does not include 1 Thess 4:17 in the list of participatory verses,

whose categories are not as obvious at first glance: συγκληρονόμος in Romans 8:17 (which I have not listed)[73] and σύμμορφος in Romans 8:29 (which I have and will defend shortly).

Space does not permit a full treatment of each of the motifs. I take as my starting point Robert Tannehill's analysis of believers' transfer from one dominion to another in Romans 6:

> The believers were enslaved to sin, but now they stand under a new master. This change has taken place through dying with Christ. The motif of dying and rising with Christ is important to Paul because it brings out this decisive transfer and connects it to the death and resurrection of Christ. Dying with Christ means dying to the powers of the old aeon and entry into a new life under a new power.[74]

Tannehill's analysis aligns with my suggestion above that believers are either in Adam or in Christ. Through participation in Christ's death and resurrection in baptism, believers are transferred from one dominion to another; they are transferred from one union to another. Or, as Esler describes it within his reading of Romans through the lens of social-identity theory, "Paul thus identifies baptism [in Rom 6:4-5] as the locus for the destruction of the old identity and the acquisition of the new."[75]

On the basis of this relationship between union and participation, the rest of this section will focus primarily on what I have defined above as a "vocational participation": sharing with Christ in his resurrection life and glory as redeemed humans. These vocational themes, I will demonstrate, are *a result of* dying and rising with Christ and *on the basis of* the newly formed union with Christ, and thus are a *vocational* participation with Christ/the new Adam as redeemed humanity. I will turn to Romans 8:29 shortly but before doing so will briefly examine the

---

suggesting that it has a "quasi-physical accompaniment with Christ rather than a conceptual or spiritual participation": 2012: 223. His description of 1 Thess 4:17 seems equally as apt for Phil 1:23.

[73] Eph 3:6 includes συγκληρονόμος and also συμμέτοχος—sharing the promise. In both cases, however, believers are fellow heirs or sharers in the promise with one another and not with the Messiah.

[74] Tannehill 1967: 21.

[75] Esler 2003: 214. Esler later writes (p. 217), "The reality that results [from baptism] can be described as 'union with Christ' and is communicated by the distinctive expressions beginning or associated with συν- ('with') that run throughout the passage and serve to align the experience of the Christ-follower with that of Christ."

participatory motifs in Romans 6:4-8 and Romans 8:17. Paul writes about believers' vocational participation with Christ in his resurrection in Romans 6:5,[76] his resurrection life in Romans 6:8,[77] and his glory in Romans 8:17, 29.[78]

I begin in Romans 6:4-8. Paul refers specifically to participation in Christ's resurrection in Romans 6:5 (albeit implicitly) and participation in Christ's resurrection life in Romans 6:8. In Romans 6:5 Paul says σύμφυτοι γεγόναμεν, meaning "planted together"[79] or, as most contemporary translations suggest, "united with."[80] Some may contend that Romans 6:5 does not contain participatory motifs, whether in reference to participation in the death or the resurrection of Christ, because Paul's reference is to a status or existence rather than an event. However, as Campbell rightly notes, "participation language remains apt since the verse refers to the state of being associated in common experience—the death of Christ. Thus, the phrase underscores the participation in which believers partake; they are joined with Christ in the co-experience of his death."[81] Campbell overlooks the participation in Christ's resurrection implicit in the second half of the verse, but the sentiment is the same: if believers share in or participate in Christ's death they will do so as well in Christ's resurrection.

This implicit point is made explicit in Romans 6:8. There Paul writes: εἰ δὲ ἀπεθάνομεν σὺν Χριστῷ, πιστεύομεν ὅτι καὶ συζήσομεν αὐτῷ. The only difference between Paul's sentiment in Romans 6:5 and Romans 6:8

---

[76]Implied; see also 1 Thess 4:14; Eph 2:6; Col 2:12; 3:1.

[77]See also 2 Cor 13:4; Col 2:13; 5:10; Eph 2:5; 2 Tim 2:11. Whether 1 Thess 4:17; Col 3:3; and Phil 1:23 belong here as well is unclear.

[78]See also Phil 3:21; Col 3:4; Eph 2:6; 2 Tim 2:12.

[79]KJV.

[80]ESV, NIV, RSV, NRSV. Fitzmyer (1993: 435) prefers "grown together with," and Dunn (1988a: 330-31) prefers "fused together with"; see Dunn (1998b: 329), where he uses a metaphor of two broken bones fused together at the ends. Interestingly, Byrne (2007: 191) uses "conformed to," a decision no doubt influenced by his reading of Rom 8:29. Most helpful here is Origen, who maintained the more lexically accurate "planted together with" in his commentary on Romans: "'Planted together' . . . must be understood of both. Consider how necessary it was for him to adopt the image of planting. For every plant, after the death of winter, await the resurrection of spring. Therefore, if we have been planted in Christ's death in the winter of this world and this present life, so too we shall be found in the coming spring bearing the fruits of righteousness from his root." Though the springtime resurrection is not necessarily a reference to "bearing the fruits of righteousness," the metaphor of "planted together" rather than "grown (or fused) together" makes more sense of Paul's argument: Origen, *Commentarii in Epistulam ad Romanos* 3.152, 154, 156, cited in Bray 1998: 157.

[81]Campbell 2012: 229.

is that in Romans 6:5 he refers to participation in the resurrection of Christ, and in Romans 6:8 he refers to the life of Christ. But both expressions refer to the same reality: the believer no longer participates in the dominion of sin but in the dominion of Christ. Believers are raised to new life in Christ and thus share in the vocation of Christ. Yet Paul's reference here is not to believers' status as those who have new life but to their active participation in the resurrection life of Christ. In dying *with Christ*, believers are raised *with Christ* to a life in which they actually *live with Christ*. And the life of Christ in which believers share is one in which Christ, the Messiah, reigns as such and as the new Adam. As indicated earlier, Paul has already stated this clearly in Romans 5:17.

This vocational participatory motif is more explicit in Romans 8:17 than elsewhere in the letter. Since I will address the participatory motifs of Romans 8:17 in the following chapter, here I note only the vocational nature of the motifs. Paul writes in Romans 8:17, "And if children, then heirs—heirs of God and co-inheritors of Christ [συγκληρονόμοι], if we suffer with him [συμπάσχομεν], in order that we might be glorified with him [συνδοξασθῶμεν]." Paul emphasizes participation with Christ, a result of being made children of God (see Rom 8:14-16). *If* God has already adopted the person and given her the status of child of God, *then* she is a co-inheritor with Christ, which is to say that she will be coglorified with Christ. The participation comes only as a result of or on the basis of the believer's adoption into God's eschatological family—a believer's change in status. Because the believer has received the Spirit of adoption (Rom 8:15) and her identity is that she is a child of God, she is a co-inheritor with Christ, which is to be glorified with Christ and thus share in his vocation as Messiah and new Adam.[82] Schreiner rightly notes that "the inheritance becomes a reality through union with Christ. . . . Those who are united with Christ share in the inheritance that he has gained for them."[83] Looking at the term through this lens of participation, one can readily see that it is a *vocational* participation.

---

[82]The details of this relationship between συγκληρονόμοι and συνδοξασθῶμεν will be examined in §6.2. Campbell (2012: 231) suggests that συγκληρονόμοι does not imply participation. The assumption is natural, especially if the reader does not see the relationship between συγκληρονόμοι and συνδοξασθῶμεν.

[83]Schreiner 1998: 428.

It would be natural to discuss the implied participation in σύμμορφος in Romans 8:29 at this point. For the sake of suspending conclusions until the end, however, I will refrain from doing so completely. I suggest here only that in Romans 8:29 Paul uses συμμόρφος, a σύν-compound literally meaning coformed to the image of the Son.[84] Similar to his use of συμμόρφος in Philippians 3:21 (examined below), here in Romans 8:29 Paul implies that believers participate in the image of the Son.[85] Believers do not become the image of the Son or the image of God in Christ. Humanity was created κατ᾽ εἰκόνα θεου in Genesis 1:27, and as those who are now in Christ, they now *bear* the image of the Son (as in 1 Cor 15:49; see below); it is the image that they bear and in which they participate and not the image that they are.

Saving the rest of what can and must be said on Romans 8:29 for later chapters, I will conclude this section with a brief word on Romans 8:32, where Paul writes, "He who did not spare his own Son but gave him up for us all, will he not also with him [σὺν αὐτῷ] give us all things [τὰ πάντα]?" Campbell says participation is not in view here.[86] His reading, I suggest, overlooks the larger context of Romans 8. What are the "all things" that God gives to his children that he has already given to the Firstborn Son? They are those "things" to which he has just referred, namely, believers' predestination, justification, and glorification (Rom 8:30), which God will bring to completion. More specifically, τὰ πάντα refers back to believers' inheritance in Romans 8:17. Jewett rightly notes that "τὰ πάντα ('the all') refers to the entire creation rather than the totality of salvation" and that this "is indicated by the article and suggested by the previous argument that believers inherit the promise to Abraham that his descendants should 'inherit the world'

---

[84]The reader will note that a number of other σύν-compounds exist in the context of Rom 8:16-26: "It is the Spirit himself bearing witness with [συμμαρτυρεῖ] our spirit" (Rom 8:16); "We know that the whole creation groans [συστενάζει] and suffers the pains of childbirth [συνωδίνει] until now" (Rom 8:22); "Likewise the Spirit helps us [συναντιλαμβάνεται] in our weakness" (Rom 8:26). These compounds, though they share the same context as the participatory compounds, are not themselves *participatory* compounds. They do not refer to the believer sharing with Christ or the Spirit in an activity.

[85]Byrne (2007: 272n29) notes that, because συμμόρφος is used with the genitive εἰκόνος, it has a substantival quality; see also Byrne 1979: n156, where he notes that this substantival use with the genitive denotes a "shared or taken part in."

[86]Campbell 2012: 224.

(4:13)."[87] God has already brought the predestination, justification, and glorification of the Firstborn Son to completion—the Son is *now* at the right hand of the Father (Rom 8:34). Paul says that God will do the same for all those who are "in him."

This section has served as an introduction to the motif of participation in Romans. More specifically, it has examined the motif of vocational participation: believers' participation as redeemed humanity in the new Adam's resurrection, life, and glory. Before turning specifically to Romans 8:29 within the context of Romans 8, three other passages demand our attention: Philippians 3:21, where Paul uses σύμμορφος in a participatory context; and 1 Corinthians 15:49 and Colossians 3:10, where Paul uses εἰκών in contexts of vocational participation. These texts and those examined in Romans 6:4–8:32 will provide insights into understanding "conformed to the image of [God's Firstborn] Son" in Romans 8:29 as believers' vocational participation with the Son in his glory. I will conclude with an examination of the role 2 Corinthians 3:18 and its context plays in the conversation.

4.2. PARTICIPATION ELSEWHERE

4.2.1. Conformed to Christ's body of glory in Philippians 3:21. Συμμόρφος appears only twice in the New Testament: in Romans 8:29 and Philippians 3:21.[88] Philippians 3:21 reads: ὃς μετασχηματίσει τὸ σῶμα τῆς ταπεινώσεως ἡμῶν σύμμορφον τῷ σώματι τῆς δόξης αὐτοῦ κατὰ τὴν ἐνέργειαν τοῦ δύνασθαι αὐτὸν καὶ ὑποτάξαι αὐτῷ τὰ πάντα. Paul declares that the believer will conform to "[Christ's] body of glory" in contrast to humanity's "body of humility." Despite his use of "body of glory" rather than "image of his Son," as in Romans 8:29b, the two phrases bear significant similarities. Interestingly, whereas the majority of recent translations suggest "conformed" for συμμόρφος in Romans 8:29, only the NASB and NRSV do so in

---

[87]Jewett and Kotansky 2007: 538; see further Wilckens 1980: 173-74; Dunn 1988a: 502; Scott 1992: 251-52; Wright 2002: 612; Byrne 2007: 276; contra Balz 1971: 119; Cranfield 1975: 437; Morris 1988: 336; Edwards 1992: 224; Fitzmyer 1993: 532, who understand τὰ πάντα as a reference to "all things necessary for salvation," and Käsemann 1980: 247; Barrett 1991: 161; Moo 1996: 541; Schreiner 1998: 460, who suggest a more all-inclusive referent.

[88]I am in general agreement with the arguments put forth by O'Brien as to why Phil 3:20-21 is not a pre-Pauline hymn. Paul perhaps borrowed language from earlier pieces, but the composition of the two verses is his own; see O'Brien 1991: 467-72.

Philippians 3:21. Most others, including the ESV, NIV, RSV, and KNT, all translate σύμμορφος as "be like." The KJV has "be fashioned like," and the NLT has "change them into."[89] This is partly due to the unclear grammatical use of the σύμμορφος in Philippians 3:21, where it stands as an accusative adverbial adjective with no substantive.[90] I suggest, however, that it is primarily due to the mistranslations of the two adjectival phrases and the failure to see the *embedded motif of believers' vocational participation in the Messiah's fulfillment of Psalm 8.* In the following discussion, I will examine the two elements of Philippians 3:21 that lead to this reading. First, Paul's use of δόξα here is consistent with what we have seen in Romans above. This will be demonstrated on the basis of Paul's use of ταπείνωσις and δόξα as contrastive possessive genitives and on the echo of Psalm 8. Second, the participatory motif behind the term σύμμορφος is consistent with Paul's language of participation elsewhere. Support for this will come in the link between Paul's morphic language in Philippians 2:6, 7; 3:21. Until conclusions can be drawn, I will translate σύμμορφος as "formed with."

4.2.1.1. Denoting δόξα. Paul's use of δόξα in Philippians 3:21 is identifiable on the basis of recognizing ταπείνωσις and δόξα as contrastive possessive genitives, and the implicit echo of Psalm 8. In this verse Paul contrasts two kinds of physical bodies: those of humanity, which he characterizes as τὸ σῶμα τῆς ταπεινώσεως, and that of the resurrected Jesus, characterized as τῷ σώματι τῆς δόξης αὐτοῦ. The two genitives are commonly read as adjectival genitives,[91] with τῷ σώματι τῆς δόξης αὐτοῦ usually translated as "glorious body"[92] and ταπείνωσις as "lowly," "weak," "vile," or even "wretched" body.[93] The two exceptions to this are the NASB, which renders the first phrase "body of our humble state," and the NRSV, which renders it "body of our humiliation." Both translate the second phrase as "body of his glory."

---

[89]Thurston and Ryan 2009: "change"; Hansen 2009: "be like" and "have the same form as."

[90]"The acc. adjective, when it is not dependent on a noun, almost defies classification. To discuss it under 'Adjectives' is somewhat misleading, as is a discussion of it under 'Accusative'": Wallace 1996: 200. The textual variant, εἰς τὸ γενέσθαι αὐτὸ, is clearly an attempt to smooth the difficult syntax caused by σύμμορφον. It is maintained in eight late manuscripts: D^I, Y, 075, 33, Û, sy; Ir, Ambr; see Silva 2005: 189; Reumann 2008: 580; Hansen 2009: 274n287.

[91]ESV, NIV, RSV, KJV, KNT.

[92]ESV, NET, NIV, RSV, KJV, NLT.

[93]"Lowly": ESV, NIV, RSV; "weak": GNB; "vile": KJV; "wretched": JB.

Σῶμα denotes the material body here, as it does in most places.[94] Yet its grammatical relationship to ταπείνωσις and δόξα suggests that believers' earthly or resurrection physicality is not Paul's emphasis, which is instead the characteristics by which each of the bodies is identified; the genitives are not merely adjectival (= "glorious body") but possessive (= "body that belongs to his glory").[95] Peter O'Brien suggests that "τῆς ταπεινώσεως is a genitive of quality, signifying not the body that is inherently evil (see AV, 'vile body') but that which *belongs to the state of humiliation* [what I have called 'possessive'] caused by sin and is thus always characterized by physical decay, indignity, weakness, and finally death."[96] As Joseph Hellerman notes, "unlike ταπεινοφροσύνη, which denotes an attitude or mind-set, ταπείνωσις signifies a 'state or condition.'"[97]

In contrast, in Philippians 3:21, the body of Jesus exists in a state of glory caused by resurrection and is thus characterized by imperishability, immortality, and power (see 1 Cor 15:42-43, 52-54, to which I will turn anon). Hellerman continues with, "Most take δόξης as 'radiant, glorious body,'[98] but given (a) the status connotations of the parallel ταπεινώσεως ('humble state or condition') and (b) the intended contrast with the pseudo-glory of those who set their minds on earthly things, the meaning 'fame, recognition, renown, prestige' is probably better."[99] Having been resurrected, Jesus' body exists within or belongs to his glorified or exalted state.[100] The bodies of believers continue to exist in a state of humility as ones not yet glorified.

---

[94]The four times σῶμα does not refer to the physicality of a human body are: (1) the metaphorical use of believers as the "body of Christ"—a "unified group of people," according to BDAG 2000: 984; see Rom 12:5; 1 Cor 10:17; 12:12-13, 27; Eph 1:23; 2:16; 3:6; 4:12, 16; 5:23, 30; Col 1:18, 24; 2:19; 3:15; (2) its reference to "slaves" in Rev 18:13; (3) its reference to plant and seed structures in 1 Cor 15:35, though here too it refers to the physical nature of them; and (4) its reference to substantive reality in Col 2:17. For the best treatment of the history of interpretation of σῶμα, see Jewett 1971: 201-50.

[95]This understanding of σῶμα should not be confused with that offered by Bultmann in his classic treatment of the word within Pauline anthropology (1952: 192-203), nor that of John A. T. Robinson's 1952 *The Body*, in which he dissents from Bultmann's treatment of σῶμα as the "me" rather than the "I": pp. 12-13n1.

[96]O'Brien 1991: 464; emphasis mine; see also Reumann 2008: 580; Hansen 2009: 274-75.

[97]Hellerman 2015: 224, noting also BDAG 2000: 990c.

[98]Citing BDAG 2000: 257a and Reumann 2008: 580.

[99]Hellerman 2015: 225.

[100]Schmisek (2013: 1) comes close to this reading but suggests that Christ's body of glory refers to "*Christ's presence with God,* rather than a descriptive phrase about properties of the resurrected body"; emphasis mine.

Support for this interpretation is found in Philippians 2:6-11, a text that overlaps in various ways with Philippians 3:10, 21.[101] The most notable overlap for our purposes here is the use of ταπεινόω in Philippians 2:8. Readers will undoubtedly be familiar with the labyrinth of studies done on this text. These studies and discussions will either be omitted in the following pages or relegated to footnotes if their relevance is obvious. My sole intent here is to discover how ταπεινόω functions within the passage.

In Philippians 2:6-8 Paul writes: ὃς ἐν μορφῇ θεοῦ ὑπάρχων οὐχ ἁρπαγμὸν ἡγήσατο τὸ εἶναι ἴσα θεῷ, ἀλλὰ ἑαυτὸν ἐκένωσεν μορφὴν δούλου λαβών, ἐν ὁμοιώματι ἀνθρώπων γενόμενος· καὶ σχήματι εὑρεθεὶς ὡς ἄνθρωπος ἐταπείνωσεν ἑαυτὸν γενόμενος ὑπήκοος μέχρι θανάτου, θανάτου δὲ σταυροῦ. To make sense of ταπεινόω in Philippians 2:8, we must first see its relation to the preceding clauses. In Philippians 2:6 Paul describes Christ as existing in the "form of God" and subsequently taking on the "form of a slave." Exactly what "form of God" means here in Philippians 2:6 is beyond our purview.[102] At a minimum, it means he shared the identity and activity of God in his equality with God (τὸ εἶναι ἴσα θεῷ);[103] as God, he possessed the sovereignty and power of God. Gorman and others note that "form of a servant" (Phil 2:7) should be read in direct contrast to "form of God," indicating therefore that being in the "form of a slave" means having the identity and activity of a slave.[104] In his equality with God in his power and sovereignty, he demonstrated that equality by his willingness to possess the status of a slave.[105] The result of or demonstration of this

---

[101]See Hooker 1975: 155; Hawthorne 1983: 169; Wright 1991: 59; Fee 1995: 382; Bockmuehl 1997: 235-36. On a purely lexical basis, the overlap of vocabulary is striking, including σύμμορφον (Phil 3:21) and μορφῇ (Phil 2:6); ὑπάρχει (Phil 3:21) and ὑπάρχων (Phil 2:6); μετασχηματίσει (Phil 3:21) and σχήματι (Phil 2:7); ταπεινώσεως (Phil 3:21) and ἐταπείνωσεν (Phil 2:8); δύνασθαι . . . ὑποτάξαι αὐτῷ τὰ πάντα (Phil 3:21) and πᾶν γόνυ κάμψῃ (Phil 2:10); κύριον Ἰησοῦν Χριστόν (Phil 3:20) and κύριος Ἰησοῦς Χριστὸς (Phil 2:11); δόξης (Phil 3:21) and δόξαν (Phil 2:11); contra Fowl 2005: 175n140.

[102]See O'Brien (2001: 205-16) for a survey of contemporary interpretations of the phrase; see also Hawthorne 1983: 110-14. For an extended discussion of the many uses of μορφή outside the Greek New Testament, see Martin 1967: 99-133; Behm 1975: 742-59; and, in part, Bockmuehl 1997.

[103]For evidence that ἐν μορφῇ θεοῦ refers to equality with God (τὸ εἶναι ἴσα θεῷ), see Hooker 1975; Hawthorne 1998: 101; Wright 1991: 83; Silva 2005: 100-101; Fowl 2005: 94; Gorman 2009: 19.

[104]Gorman 2009: 22.

[105]See O'Brien 2001: 224-25. The debate about how to understand ἁρπαγμός in Phil 2:6 is as deep as it is wide. For an overview of the main arguments, see Wright 1991: 62-90.

"form of a slave" is that he "became in the likeness of man" (Phil 2:7c), which is to say that he was "found as a man in his outward appearance" (Phil 2:8a); he became human.[106]

Most importantly for our purposes, in his status as a slave and in the mode of his being human, he "humbled himself [ἐταπείνωσεν ἑαυτὸν] by becoming obedient to the point of death" (Phil 2:8). Here Paul uses ταπεινόω, a word used only thirteen times elsewhere in the New Testament: Matthew 18:4, 23:12 (2x); Luke 3:5; 14:11; 18:14 (twice each in the latter two verses); 2 Corinthians 11:7; 12:21; Philippians 4:12; James 4:10; 1 Peter 5:6. With the exception of 2 Corinthians 12:21, every instance is clearly in reference to a low status. Given Paul's description of Jesus' obedience unto death in Philippians 2:6-8, the use of the term in Philippians 2:8 unequivocally denotes this low status as well. As Fee remarks, "In his human existence he chose, in obedience, to 'take the lowest place.'"[107] Jesus' humility was not a display of an attitude of meekness or unpretentiousness, nor was it the opposite of pride or arrogance, any of which can be denoted by *humility* or *humbleness* in modern terms. Rather, ταπεινόω here refers to his taking on a *status* of absolute subjection, a lack of any and all sovereignty or power over those who would crucify him; it was the status of being the most powerless even of slaves.

With this all-too-brief examination of Paul's use of μορφή and ταπεινόω in Philippians 2:6-8, I return our attention to Philippians 3:21 and its corresponding adjectives, δόξα and ταπείνωσις (returning to μορφή below). Given the connections Paul draws between the incarnate and now-resurrected body of Jesus in Philippians 2:6-8 and Philippians 3:21, it is clear that just as ταπεινόω did not mean the opposite of proud in Philippians 2:8, so also ταπείνωσις in Philippians 3:21 does not refer to an attitude of meekness or unpretentiousness. Contra John Paul Heil, it is not a reference to believers' "humbleness,"[108] which I take to be different from "humble

---

[106]See Hooker 1975: 160-62; O'Brien (2001: 224) suggests that the phrase ἐν ὁμοιώματι ἀνθρώπων γενόμενος identifies the manner by which Christ "emptied himself" rather than the manner by which Christ "took the form of a servant." This, however, is a false distinction, because, as O'Brien notes, since Christ's "emptying himself" refers to his "making himself powerless" (2001: 217), his "emptying himself" stands in apposition to his "taking the form of a servant"; thus, the incarnation is the manner by which both actions are accomplished.

[107]Fee 1995: 216.

[108]Heil 2010: 139.

state" (NASB), or "humiliation" (NRSV). And it certainly does not denote "weak," "vile," or "wretched." No, in Philippians 3:21 ταπείνωσις refers to believers' bodies, which belong to or exist in their state of humility[109]—as humans subject to the powers of this world, just as Jesus' body was in the incarnation (Phil 2:6-8).

It is this σῶμα τῆς ταπεινώσεως with which Paul contrasts σώματι τῆς δόξης. As Hellerman notes, scholars generally define *glory* here as Christ's heavenly radiance in connection with the presence of God,[110] if it gets defined at all.[111] Given this understanding of ταπείνωσις, and thus "bodies which belong to our state of humility," interpreting Jesus' resurrection body as the "body that exists in or belongs to his state of glory (i.e., sovereignty, power)" is hardly a stretch.[112] When understood in the light of Philippians 2:6-11, it becomes clear that the Messiah's glory in Philippians 3:21 is not the visible splendor of God but Jesus' own sovereignty and power over creation.[113] Paul does not yet know the "power of [Christ's] resurrection" (Phil 3:10), but he has participated with Christ in his death (Phil 3:10), and his citizenship is now in heaven (Phil 3:20). Until that citizenship is fully realized and his body is transformed, Paul's body and those of other believers with him remain in or belong to a state of humility characterized by subjection, suffering, and powerlessness over enemies.

I turn now to the second reason for reading Paul's use of *glory* in Philippians 3:21 as not the visible, manifest presence of God, usually conflated to "radiance" or "splendor," but the honor or power associated with the status of authority and sovereignty. At the close of Philippians 3:21 Paul describes the bodily transformation as happening κατὰ τὴν ἐνέργειαν τοῦ δύνασθαι αὐτὸν καὶ ὑποτάξαι αὐτῷ τὰ πάντα. Commonly accepted here

---

[109]Fee 1987: 785; Thiselton 2000: 1273.

[110]E.g., O'Brien (2001: 464n131): "'Glory,' as is often in Paul, denotes the active and radiant presence of God and here describes Christ's glorified body"; BDAG 2000: 257.

[111]E.g., Osiek (2000), though she hints at themes of royalty through suggesting echoes of Ps 110; Silva 2005; Thurston and Ryan 2005; Reumann 2008; Cousar 2009.

[112]Carey Newman's analysis runs similar to this, though he suggests that the power that characterizes Jesus' resurrection body indicates the christophanic presence of God: 1992: 210.

[113]See Hellerman (2015: 124-25) on the glory of God in Jesus in Phil 2:9-11: "Paul carries the themes of status, honor, and prestige through to the end of the narrative, where, through the exaltation of Jesus, God finally receives the public recognition that is his due."

is an echo of Psalm 8,[114] a text we have already seen to have implications for Paul's use of δόξα in Romans. In Philippians 3:21 Paul depicts Jesus as the son of man from Psalm 8 who is crowned with glory and honor and who has cosmic rule: ὑποτάξαι αὐτῷ τὰ πάντα. Since the motif of humanity's glory in Psalm 8 relates to humanity's creation in the image of God in Genesis 1:26-28, and both relate very closely to humanity's dominion over the created order, and Paul specifically alludes in Philippians 3:21 to the son of man's dominion over creation in Psalm 8, then Paul's echo of Psalm 8 in Philippians 3:21 should inform our interpretation of Paul's use of δόξα in Philippians 3:21.[115] Jesus' "body of his glory" refers to the body that exists in his glory, that is, his honor or power associated with his resurrection rule over all things. O'Brien rightly notes the echo and says that Christ "fulfils mankind's destiny" in subjecting all things to himself.[116] Jesus is the representative son of man in Psalm 8, the perfect human whose human body now belongs to or exists in the glory for which it was created. To this body of glory humanity will be "formed with."

---

[114]Tooman's and Hays's criteria are fully fulfilled here. (1) Uniqueness: the words in question are unique to Ps 8. (2) Volume, which includes elements of distinctiveness and multiplicity: three words or their cognates are found in both texts: δόξα, πάντα, and ὑπέταξας are found in and are distinctive to Ps 8, and δόξα, πάντα, and ὑποτάξαι are found in Phil 3:21. In each text, the three terms occur in very close proximity to one another. (3) Recurrence: Paul clearly quotes Ps 8:6 in 1 Cor 15:27, alludes to it in Eph 1:22, and, as seen above, implicitly echoes throughout Romans the motif of δόξα in Ps 8 and its link to the "image of God" in man in Gen 1:26-28. Additionally, Ps 8 was interpreted messianically by the writer of Heb 2:6-8. (4) Thematic correspondence: both texts describe the cosmic exaltation of the son of man, i.e., humanity and/or the messianic figure applied to Jesus.

[115]This is especially the case if an Adamic echo is present in Phil 2:6-11; see, e.g., Cullmann 1959: 174-81; Dunn 1989: 114-21; Hooker 1990: 96-100; Wright 1991: 58-62, 90-98; Hansen 2009. The argument rests in part on Paul's use of μορφή, in which Paul declares that Christ is not just according to the image of God (Gen 1:26; κατ᾽ εἰκόνα ἡμετέραν) as Adam was but that he was *equal* to God in being and in status. Whereas Adam was made according to the image of God, Christ is the image, i.e., form, of God (see 2 Cor 4:4; Col 1:15). Paul then develops this echo by emphasizing Jesus' obedience to God. Whereas Adam was disobedient (Gen 3:6; see Rom 5:19), Jesus was obedient (Phil 2:8; see Rom 5:19). Adam's disobedience forced him into a humble position of slavery and subjection; Jesus, in his obedience, *willingly* took on the form of a slave and *willingly* subjected himself to his crucifiers. Having done so, Paul writes that God therefore (διὸ) exalted him as Lord (Phil 2:9, 11) "in order that *at the name of Jesus every knee should bow*, in heaven and on the earth and under the earth." In his obedience to God, he became what Adam was meant to be—in a position of glory over creation. And again, van Kooten (2008a: 90) is unambiguous: "However one understands Philipp 2.6, the essential fact remains that this passage is part of Paul's Adam Christology, although [contra Dunn] the emphasis here seems to be on the pre-existent Adam from heaven." For objections to this reading, see Bockmuehl 1997: 9-11.

[116]O'Brien 2001: 466. See also, e.g., Reumann (2008: 600).

4.2.1.2. Σύμμορφος as "conformity." With this interpretation of Philippians 3:21, we are now in a position to make sense of Paul's use of σύμμορφος,[117] the primary (though not only) link between Philippians 3:21 and Romans 8:29. As mentioned previously, σύμμορφος is translated as "conformed to" in only the NASB and NRSV, while all other contemporary translations defer to "be like," "be fashioned like," or "change them into." Yet in nearly every contemporary translation of Romans 8:29, σύμμορφος is translated as "conformed to." Why does such a difference exist?

The primary reasons, I suggest, are the twofold issues noted above: the nature of glory in Philippians 3:21, and the genitives functioning as qualitative rather than adjectival are consistently misinterpreted or mistranslated; it is difficult to imagine participation in a radiant body. For this reason, Campbell translates σύμμορφος as "be like" and thus dismisses the participatory reference. On Philippians 3:21 he writes: "This σύν-compound is best not regarded as expressing participation with Christ per se. It conveys the idea that believers' bodies will be *like* Christ's, but this is distinct to sharing in his own body."[118] Campbell is correct; Paul does not describe

---

[117]A term used only twice in the New Testament: Phil 3:21 and Rom 8:29. It is part of Paul's transmorphic language. BDAG says "having a similar form, nature, or style" (2000: 958). The word is found only a few times elsewhere. In Nicander's *Theriaca* (line 321), from the second century BCE, σύμμορφος means "to resemble in physical form": Εὖ δ᾿ ἂν σηπεδόνος γνοίης δέμας, ἄλλο μὲν εἴδει αἱμορόῳ σύμμορφον, ἀτὰρ στίβον ἀντί᾿ ὀκέλλει, καὶ κεράων δ᾿ ἔμπλην δέμας ἄμμορον, ἡ δέ νυ χροιῇ οἵη περ τάπιδος λασίῳ ἐπιδέδρομε τέρφει (lines 320-23); "You would do well to recognize the form of the Sepedon, which in other respects resembles the Blood-letter in appearance, but it steers a straightforward path; moreover it is almost without horns, and its colour, like that of a carpet, is spread over a rough surface": translation from Gow and Schofield 1997: 49.

In Heraclitus Stoicus's *Quaestiones Homericae* (77, line 12), from 1 BCE to 1 CE, the meaning is ambiguous: ἔσπετε νῦν μοι Μοῦσαι Ὀλύμπια δώματ᾿ ἔχουσαι, οἵτινες ἡγεμόνες Δαναῶν καὶ κοίρανοι ἦσαν, ἢ πάλιν ἡνίκα τῆς Ἀγαμέμνονος ἀνδραγαθίας ἐνάρχεται τὸν τρισὶ θεοῖς ἥρωα σύμμορφον ὑμνῶν· (lines 8-12); "Tell me now, Olympian Muses, who have houses [or, Muses who live in Olympia], who were the leaders and rulers of Danaos; or again, when does he begin [telling] the heroic [deeds] of Agamemnon, while singing about the hero [who] is in the same shape as the three gods?" (my translation).

Origen uses it in *Contra Celsum* 2.69.15-16, where he comments on Phil 3:10 and 2 Tim 2:11. After these instances, the word is used only a handful of times over the next six centuries. See Kürzinger (1958: 296), who rightly notes: "Das Wort σύμμορφος ist also äußerst selten; wenn die Belegstelle aus Nikander sicher ist, braucht man nicht an eine Neubildung des Apostels zu denken. Aber auch dann hat er dem Ausdruck einen neuen Sinn gegeben." "The word σύμμορφος then is extremely rare. If the reference from Nikander is correct, then one does not have necessarily to think of it as a new formulation of the apostle. But even then, he gave the term a new meaning."

[118]Campbell 2012: 235; emphasis original. Similarly, in Phil 3:10 Campbell (2012: 234) writes: "Being conformed to Christ's death is distinct to sharing in Christ's death; the former

some form of mystical, physical union between Christ's body and those of believers. But this does not dismiss the notion of participation. Rather, Paul describes the transformation (μετασχηματίζω) of the body that will bear the resemblance of Jesus' resurrection body and that will participate in the mode of existence of Christ's resurrection body, namely, glory.[119] Paul's use of σύμμορφος in Philippians 3:21 bears the same participatory motifs as his σὺν-compounds do elsewhere. Being "like Christ" and participating with Christ is a false dichotomy. Walter Hansen sees what Campbell does not:

> A combination of 2:6-11 and 3:20-21 tells the complete story of the way of salvation that leads through suffering to glory. . . . The story of salvation tells us of a great "interchange" between Christ and us: Christ came to share in our suffering so that we would share in his glory. . . . The lines of his letter [lift] his readers to envision a bright future when all the humiliation of suffering will be transformed to glorious *participation in Christ's complete victory over all things.*[120]

With Hansen, Paul does express the theme of participation in Philippians 3:21, and given this I find no persuasive reason to translate σύμμορφος as "be like" rather than "conformed to."

Moreover, in Paul's use of σύμμορφος he describes the relationship between believers' present and future status and the Messiah's present status as a result of their union with Christ. Believers participate with Christ in his cosmological glory as those whose identity is shaped by their union with the Messiah—a Messiah who embodies the human vocation in Psalm 8. This is especially likely if van Kooten is correct. As noted previously, he suggests that Paul's morphic language (e.g., Phil 2:6-11; 3:10, 21) supports "one of the central tenets of his theology—his Adam Christology and, more precisely, his reflections on the image of God."[121] This is why Paul uses the

---

views his death as a pattern to which one may conform, while the latter involves participation in it."

[119]Contra Cohick (2013: 203), who writes: "Paul says, we participate in his (Christ's) suffering. But the glory is always and only Christ's. His is the victory over sin and death; ours is the sure hope of transformation to his likeness." On the contrary, believers share in that victory (see 1 Cor 15:57) and thus in the state of glory (even if it is ultimately a glory that belongs to Christ and in which believers participate through union with him).

[120]Hansen 2009: 276-77; emphasis mine.

[121]Van Kooten 2008a: 91.

word σύμμορφος in Philippians 3:21: to indicate, as a participatory σύν-
compound, believers' vocational fulfillment in their participation with the
Messiah in his cosmological reign over creation.[122] Though they are now
in subjection, this will not last; they will share in Christ's exaltation.[123] As
Christ participated in the human status of humility and subjection
(Phil 2:7-8),[124] those in Christ, having already participated in his death
(Phil 3:10), will thus also participate in his victory (Phil 3:21).

4.2.1.3. Συμμορφιζόμενος in Philippians 3:10. This reading of Philippians
3:21 is strengthened when it is read in the light of Philippians 3:10-11, where
Paul writes: τοῦ γνῶναι αὐτὸν καὶ τὴν δύναμιν τῆς ἀναστάσεως αὐτοῦ καὶ
[τὴν] κοινωνίαν [τῶν] παθημάτων αὐτοῦ, συμμορφιζόμενος τῷ θανάτῳ
αὐτοῦ, εἴ πως καταντήσω εἰς τὴν ἐξανάστασιν τὴν ἐκ νεκρῶν. Here Paul
uses συμμορφίζω, a semantic cousin of συμμόρφος and a hapax legomenon.
Different only in its grammatical function, συμμορφίζω serves in a semantic
role equal to that of its adjectival relative in Philippians 3:21 and, like
συμμόρφος in Philippians 3:21, is rarely translated as "conform to" in recent
translations. The ESV, NIV, NRSV, and RSV all provide "becoming like
him" in his death.[125] Hansen offers three common interpretations of the
phrase συμμορφιζόμενος τῷ θανάτῳ αὐτοῦ: (1) a reference to Paul's
martyrdom;[126] (2) a reference to "the inward experience of dying to sin by
being united with Christ in his death";[127] and (3) a reference to "Paul's
obedience in his faithful proclamation of the gospel of Christ."[128] Heil adds
a fourth: Paul desires to have the same "form" of humility in his own death
as that which Christ had in his, thus making him a "model of humility for

---

[122]Heil (2010) never suggests either a definition of σύμμορφος (or συμμορφίζω in Phil 3:10) or
a discussion of the term's relationship to Paul's other σύμ-/σύν-compounds elsewhere. The
closest he comes is on pp. 3, 127-28, 138-39, where, in every instance, "conform" is provided
with no explanation to meaning. This is unfortunate, not least because his work is titled
Philippians: Let Us Rejoice in Being Conformed to Christ.

[123]In Phil 3:21 this exaltation (aka glorification) of believers is purely future, as is made clear
through the future indicative μετασχηματίζω. The temporal element is less obvious in Rom
8:29-30 and will be treated in §7.2.2.

[124]See Tannehill 2007.

[125]Only the NASB provides "being conformed to his death" (also KJV: "being conformable to").

[126]O'Brien (1991: 409) suggests that this view "has been almost universally rejected," though see
Osiek 2000 and Thurston and Ryan 2009, who favor it.

[127]Silva 2005: 190; O'Brien 1991: 410; Hawthorne 1983: 145-46.

[128]Hansen 2009: 246-47.

the audience."[129] Hansen goes on to suggest that the three alternatives he notes may all reflect Paul's intentions behind the phrase.

True though this may be, I suggest that Paul primarily refers to his spiritual participation in the death of Christ—a death that thus brings him into unity with the Messiah. Three indications of this are obvious. First, in Philippians 3:10, as well as in Philippians 3:21, Philippians 2:6-8 stands in the background; the Messiah participated with humanity in its slave status (see Rom 8:3) in Philippians 2:7-8 and thus was exalted to the highest status. So also Paul wishes to participate in Christ's suffering in order that he might participate also in his exaltation (Phil 2:9-11; 3:11, 21; see Rom 8:17).[130] Second, Paul presents this two-stage participatory process of death and resurrection in Philippians 3:10-11: συμμορφιζόμενος τῷ θανάτῳ αὐτοῦ (Phil 3:10) εἴ πως καταντήσω εἰς τὴν ἐξανάστασιν τὴν ἐκ νεκρῶν (Phil 3:11). Paul does not use a participatory compound in Philippians 3:11, but the death-resurrection sequence fits the participatory mold found throughout his epistles, most obviously in Romans 6:4-8. Third, συμμορφιζόμενος as a present participle accords with the perfect-tense γεγόναμεν in Romans 6:5. Contra Hansen, who suggests the present-tense participle in Philippians 3:10 is the primary reason for not reading συμμορφίζω as participatory, Paul makes clear in Romans 6:5 that participation in Christ's death had a beginning and is ongoing. As O'Brien suggests, "Paul is continually being conformed to [Christ's] death as he shares in Christ's sufferings. The decisive break with the old aeon of sin and death must be continually maintained and affirmed, for the Christian is still exposed to the powers of that old aeon."[131] These three textual supports demonstrate that συμμορφίζω in Philippians 3:10 implies some form of participation in Christ. Moreover, only when this participatory reality is recognized will it make sense to translate συμμορφίζω like many other σὺμ-/σὺν-compounds in Paul where participation in the death or resurrection of Christ is in view. Here in Philippians 3:10, participation in the death of Christ is unequivocally in Paul's view.

Paul uses συμμόρφος in Philippians 3:21 and συμμορφίζω in Philippians 3:10 as participatory compounds with which he describes believers' participation

---

[129]Heil 2010: 127-28, 139.
[130]See Tannehill 1967: 114-23.
[131]O'Brien 1991: 410.

in Christ's death (Phil 3:10) and Christ's resurrection glory (Phil 3:21)—Christ's dominion over creation as the messianic son of man in Psalm 8. In Philippians 3:21 τῷ σώματι τῆς δόξης αὐτοῦ refers to the resurrection body of Jesus that exists in or belongs to his status of honor or power associated with his sovereign rule over creation. We may therefore conclude that σύμμορφος in Philippians 3:21 is intended to be understood as a participatory compound that refers to believers' vocational participation in the status and activity of the Messiah, who embodies the vocation of humanity in Psalm 8.

4.2.2. Paul's use of εἰκών in contexts of participation. As indicated in the introduction to this chapter, Paul's use of a σύμ-compound is not the only indication that he intends his reader to understand "conformed to the image of [God's] Son" as a vocational participation with Christ. Paul also does so with εἰκών. Given its use in Romans 1:23 and in Genesis 1:26-28, εἰκών is immediately recognizable as indicative of a vocational participation. In being "conformed to the *image* of [God's Firstborn] Son," believers—having been transformed into redeemed humanity in union with Christ—now participate with Christ in his resurrection life of vocation. This reading will be supported by an examination of Paul's use of εἰκών in 1 Corinthians 15:49 and Colossians 3:10, two texts thematically similar to Romans 8:29. In both texts Paul describes believers' transition from one image to another, that is, from participation in one domain to another. I conclude with an examination of the relationship between Romans 8:29 and 2 Corinthians 3:18.

4.2.2.1. First Corinthians 15:49. First Corinthians 15:49 and its context share textual affinities with both Romans 8:29 and Philippians 3:21 and their contexts. *Glory* has central importance in all three: Romans 8:17, 30; Philippians 3:21; and 1 Corinthians 15:40, 41, 43, as well as implicit glory in 1 Corinthians 15:21-28, not least due to the echo of Psalm 8. All three articulate a contrast between believers' pre- and postresurrection status: 1 Corinthians 15:35-53; Philippians 3:10-11, 20-21; Romans 8:23. Further, σῶμά occurs in all three contexts: 1 Corinthians 15:37, 44; Philippians 3:21; Romans 8:23. Finally, the identification of the Messiah/Son in all three passages is linked with a previously articulated, whether implicit or explicit, Adam-Christ typology: 1 Corinthians 15:21-28, 45-49; Philippians 2:6-11;[132] Romans 5:12-21.

---

[132]The presence of an Adam-Christ typology in Phil 2:6-11 is undoubtedly debatable. See the relevant footnote at the end of §4.2.1.2. If the typology is present, it is certainly implicit and thus different in emphasis from the typology presented in 1 Cor 15 and Rom 5. Nevertheless,

Recognizing these three-way similarities, I turn our attention to the most significant connection between 1 Corinthians 15:49 and Romans 8:29: Paul's use of *image* and *glory* within the context of an explicit Adam-Christ typology in 1 Corinthians 15:21-28, 45-49. After identifying the Son as the last Adam, Paul then responds to the Corinthians' question posed in 1 Corinthians 15:35 concerning the kind of bodies that will be raised (ποίῳ δὲ σώματι ἔρχονται), writing: καὶ καθὼς ἐφορέσαμεν τὴν εἰκόνα τοῦ χοϊκοῦ, φορέσομεν καὶ τὴν εἰκόνα τοῦ ἐπουρανίου.[133] The two sections are not unrelated. Throughout the verses, Paul does not use σύμμορφος or any other σύμ-compound in either 1 Corinthians 15:49 or the larger context, as he does in Romans. Nevertheless, when the phrase φορέσομεν καὶ τὴν εἰκόνα τοῦ ἐπουρανίου in 1 Corinthians 15:49 and the larger context of 1 Corinthians 15:21-58 are read as participatory, as I will demonstrate below, then it will become clear that, despite the omission of a σύμ-compound, Paul's use of εἰκών within 1 Corinthians 15:21-58 supports a motif of believers' participation in the new Adam and specifically in his glory.

The use of εἰκών in 1 Corinthians 15:49 rests on the Adam-Christ typology presented in 1 Corinthians 15:21-28, and so we begin our investigation there. In 1 Corinthians 15, Paul conflates Psalm 8 and Psalm 110, two psalms read messianically in the early church.[134] In 1 Corinthians 15:25 Paul makes an explicit allusion to the Davidic king of Psalm 110, whose enemies will be made a "footstool under [his] feet" (Ps 110:1). Then in 1 Corinthians 15:27 Paul links "footstool under [his] feet" from Psalm 110 with "all things are made subject under [the son of man's] feet" from Psalm 8:6.[135] In 1 Corinthians 15:28 Paul then conflates the subjects of the two psalms—the "son of man" in Psalm 8 and the (assumed) Messiah of Psalm 110—under the title "Son": "When all things are subjected to him [i.e., the son of man], then the Son [i.e., the Son of God] himself will also be subjected to him who put all things in subjection under him, that God may be all in all."

---

its presence in Phil 2 in no way limits the presence of the typology or its implications for Paul's anthropology presented in 1 Cor 15 and Rom 5.

[133]Whether Paul has in mind Philo's "Heavenly Man" in 1 Cor 15:44-49 (esp. 1 Cor 15:46-47) is beyond our purview here. For a list of the many possibilities, see de Boer 1988: 99-105.

[134]These two texts are also conflated in Mk 12:36; Mt 22:44; Eph 1:20-22; Heb 1:13–2:8; 1 Pet 3:22; and the letter of Polycarp to the Philippians 2:1-2; see Hengel 1995: 163-72; Hays 1989: 84.

[135]See Ciampa and Rosner 2010: 771-72; Collins 1999: 550.

Commentators regularly note Paul's use of both psalms in the passage, and most note Paul's messianic reading of Psalm 8.[136] Martin Albl writes:

> The whole of 1 Cor. 15:25-27, then, is a carefully adapted Christian reflection on the end times based on Ps. 110:1 and Ps. 8:7. Through textual conflations and the attribution to Christ of God's actions recorded in scripture, an eschatological narrative is produced in which Christ is portrayed as the Lord of all creation, triumphant even over death itself.[137]

More to the point, Wright notes:

> The passage in 1 Corinthians thus gives every indication that Paul had combined these great biblical themes: Adam, creation and the dominion of humans over the animals; the Messiah, his victory over the nations and his continuing rule until all are subject to him.... What this passage reveals further, albeit densely, is the intimate connection between those two (Adam and Messiah) in Paul's mind.[138]

The Messiah of Psalm 110 is the son of man of Psalm 8, according to Paul, and as both, he is the one in whom all humanity can find new life.[139] Also notable is that Paul collapses both figures under the title "Son" in 1 Corinthians 15:28.[140] The Son of God is the Messiah who is the new Adam, and he is so on the basis of both Psalm 8 and Psalm 110.

This is the foundation on which the reader is meant to read Paul's responses to questions concerning the body and its resurrection in 1 Corinthians 15:35-54. There Paul contrasts the earthly body and the resurrection body via a series of six antonyms: perishable/imperishable (1 Cor 15:42, 50, 53, 54); dishonor/glory (1 Cor 15:43); weakness/power (1 Cor 15:43); "natural"[141]/spiritual (1 Cor 15:44, 46; see 1 Cor 2:14); mortal/immortal

---

[136]In addition to those quoted below, see also Heil 2005: 205-20; Lee 2005: 217-19; Montague 2011: 273.

[137]Albl 1999: 223, also 228; see also Ciampa and Rosner 2010: 760-79; 2007: 745.

[138]Wright 2013a: 1064; also 733-37; see also Thiselton 2000: 1234-36.

[139]See also Wright 2003: 334; Ciampa and Rosner 2010: 771.

[140]Hays (1973: 109-10) examines all the texts in which the king of Ps 110 is associated with divine sonship: Barnabas 12:10; Mk 12:35-37 (Mt 22:41-46; Lk 20:41-44); Mk 14:61-62 (Mt 26:63-64; Lk 22:67-70); Heb 1:3-4, 13; 1 Cor 15:25, 28; 1 Clement 36:4.

[141]Much has been discussed regarding Paul's use of ψυχικός and its potential counter-Gnostic intent in 1 Cor 15:44. Scholars now agree that the contrast here is not between the material and nonmaterial. The only certainty is that he echoes Gen 2:7: καὶ ἐνεφύσησεν εἰς τὸ πρόσωπον αὐτοῦ πνοὴν ζωῆς καὶ ἐγένετο ὁ ἄνθρωπος εἰς ψυχὴν ζῶσαν, declaring so himself in 1 Cor 15:45a: "Thus it is written, 'the first man Adam became a living being,'" and then adding to

(1 Cor 15:53, 54); and earthly/heavenly (1 Cor 15:40, 47-49). He then concludes the series of antonyms with a final climactic adjective that will
characterize the resurrected body: victorious (1 Cor 15:57). These antonyms,
though contrasting the two representative bodies, are directly dependent
on Paul's contrast of the identity and actions of Adam and Christ in 1 Corinthians 15:21-28. Formerly God's people were identified by their participation
in Adam's death, as evidenced by their bodies' susceptibility to decay
(1 Cor 15:42), humiliation, and weakness (1 Cor 15:43). At the resurrection,
however, they will be identified by their participation in Christ's victory
over death (1 Cor 15:21-22, 57), as evidenced by their future bodies, characterized by incorruptibility (ἀθανασία) and immortality (ἀφθαρσία) in
1 Corinthians 15:53.

In distinguishing between the earthly and resurrection body, Paul says
believers do or will (see below) "bear the image of the heavenly man," the
last Adam, in contrast with the image they currently bear: that of the "man
of dust," the first Adam (1 Cor 15:49). No doubt, treatments of *image* here
vary. Collins and, surprisingly, Anthony Thiselton make little of its presence.
Collins's comments are summarized almost entirely with "Paul's words
express a christological and eschatological transformation of the image-
motif. For Paul the normative image is that of Christ, but it is an image
we must strive to bear even if it is a gift of God. Ultimately there is to be
conformity between human beings and the heavenly one."[142] Likewise,
Thiselton's comments in 1 Corinthians 15:49 are short, as if his extensive
discussion of the flesh/body, first Adam/last Adam contrasts in 1 Corinthians 15:35-48 has said all that is required. Indeed, it has come close to

---

it by stating in 1 Cor 15:45b: "The last Adam became a life-giving spirit." Paul is most likely
not refuting a Gnostic teaching but is simply using a cognate to ψυχὴν, which has its root
in Gen 1-3—a text from which he is forming not only his anthropology and Christology but
his eschatology throughout all of 1 Cor 15. For an extended look at Paul's use of σῶμα ψυχικόν
in 1 Cor 15:44, 46, see Wright 2003: 348-56; 2013a: 1400-1402.

[142]Collins 1999: 572; so also, e.g., Soards 1999 and Montague 2011. The majority of contemporary translations provide "to bear" for φορέω. With Thiselton, I believe Paul uses the
verb metaphorically, meaning "to wear"; see Thiselton 2000: 1289-90; also Kim 2004:
193-200; Ciampa and Rosner 2010: 825. Interestingly, Collins (1999: 570) translates it as
"conformity with": "A first implication [of Paul's Adamic Christology] is that living human
beings are in conformity with the first person; like the first person they are of dust. In
contrast, those who are in conformity with the last person are heavenly." Wishing to be
specific where the text is specific, I find it unhelpful to translate φορέω here as "conform
to" or any variation thereof.

doing so. Yet as helpful as his preceding discussion is, his comments on the role of εἰκών in the parallel phrases of 1 Corinthians 15:49 are left wanting. There he equates the "image of the man of dust" with "*being human*," which is to say being "*vulnerable, fallible, and fragile*," and "the image of the man of heaven" with "a mode of existence wholly like that of the raised Christ in glory."[143] Thiselton is correct, but his treatment of *image* would be more complete had he brought forward his discussion of Paul's Adam-Christ typology from the preceding verses.

Fee rightly notes that, in the context of Adam and Christ as prototypical representatives,[144] the use of *image* may reflect Genesis 1:26-27.[145] This seems a strong possibility, not only because of the Adam-Christ typology at play, but also because of the importance of "image of God" language within that typology, and that Paul cites Genesis 2:7 in the verse just previous, placing the reader already in the primal motif. Fee writes: "Since believers have all shared the existence of the first Adam, they are being called to bear the image of the last Adam, which in its eschatological expression will be a 'heavenly' body such as he now has."[146]

Determining how we read the phrase φορέσομεν καὶ τὴν εἰκόνα τοῦ ἐπουρανίου is partially dependent on whether φορέσομεν is read as an aorist subjunctive, "let us bear," or a future indicative, "we shall bear." The external evidence highly favors the subjunctive.[147] On the grounds of internal evidence (i.e., Paul's clear emphasis on the resurrection body of believers throughout the context), however, the NRSV, REB, NIV, NJB, RV, AV/KJV, the fourth edition of the UBS, and the majority of commentators opt for the future indicative. Hans Conzelmann suggests that "the context demands the indicative."[148] Contra Conzelmann, however, I am persuaded by Fee's analysis of the external evidence, which seems to demand the subjunctive: "It is nearly impossible to account for anyone's having changed a clearly understandable future to the hortatory subjunctive

---

[143]Thiselton 2000: 1290; emphasis original.
[144]See also Conzelmann 1975: 288.
[145]Fee 1987: 794.
[146]Fee 1987: 788.
[147]P[46], ℵ, C, D, F, G, Latin VSS, Coptic, Bohairic, Clement, the Latin of Irenaeus, Origen, and Gregory of Nyssa. The future indicative is supported only by B and a few minuscules, with the Coptic, Sahidic, Gregory Nazianzus.
[148]Conzelmann 1975: 280n3.

so early and so often that it made its way into every textual history as the predominant reading."[149]

If therefore Paul says that believers should now bear the image of the man from heaven, what does bearing that image in a preresurrection state mean? Can the internal evidence be so overlooked? Fee's answer is that Paul is not only referring to a future bodily likeness but "Paul is here intending also a broader sense, including behavioral implications, involved in their sharing in his likeness now."[150] He goes on to write that Paul's "exhortation is not that the Corinthians try to assume their 'heavenly body' now. . . . Rather, they are being urged to conform to the life of the 'man of heaven' as those who now share his character and behavior."[151] Richard Hays follows a similar line of thought.[152] And though Thiselton favors the future indicative, his recognition that the "image" believers (will) bear is not purely the physical body but a "mode of existence"[153]—a mode that could plausibly be operative in either the present or the future.

In line with both Fee and Hays, I suggest that Paul is exhorting believers to live out the new identity or participate fully in the new identity that is already present within them and that will be brought to its completion with the future transformation of the body. Though also opting for the future indicative, Ciampa and Brian Rosner nevertheless recognize this participatory element at work in the text, here commenting on 1 Corinthians 15:47: "[Paul] will build on the Adam/Christ distinction to distinguish between what it means to participate in Adam's kind of humanity and what it means to participate in the new (renewed) humanity Christ has brought about through his resurrection from the dead."[154] Campbell also identifies the motif: "The notion of bearing *the image of the heavenly man* is at least suggestive of union with Christ, though it is unusual language for the concept."[155] Bearing the image of the heavenly man, or participating in the "new (renewed) humanity," is not reducible to having the same body

---

[149]Fee 1987: 794-95. See Collins 1999: 572; Fee 2007: 119, 519.
[150]Fee 1987: 794.
[151]Fee 1987: 794-95.
[152]Hays 1997: 273.
[153]Thiselton 2000: 1290.
[154]Ciampa and Rosner 2010: 822.
[155]Campbell 2012: 314; emphasis original.

as the heavenly man; it must incorporate, as Fee suggests, the "life" of the heavenly man, the last Adam, even now in union with Christ.

What is assured in all this is that believers will be raised with Christ and their bodies will be transformed to bear the likeness of that of the last Adam. Those bodies will be characterized by imperishability, power, and immortality. The body will also be "raised in glory" (1 Cor 15:43; ἐγείρεται ἐν δόξῃ).[156] Conzelmann writes that "σῶμα is not the stuff of the body, but the form, and δόξα is its state. . . . σῶμα always exists in a specific mode of being."[157] This surely is not far from what we saw to be the case in Philippians 3:21. The question, then, is how one is to conceive of the state of glory in which the body will exist. BDAG places the word under "the condition of being bright or shining."[158] Ironically, most scholars disagree with BDAG here, or at least they do not suggest this definition in the first instance. Rather, they recognize that δόξα in 1 Corinthians 15:43 refers to a state of honor. According to Ciampa and Rosner, "The word's antithetical relationship with 'dishonour' in this verse clearly indicates that glory in the sense of (majestic) honor is in mind, not luminescence, although it will certainly involve magnificent splendor as well."[159] And, according to Fee and Thiselton, not only should the term not be understood as splendor or luster, but the ἀτιμία of 1 Corinthians 15:43 should be rendered "humiliation" or "lowly position," as both scholars note it is in Philippians 3:21.[160]

This recognition that, contra BDAG, δόξα in 1 Corinthians 15:43 refers to a state of honor is all the more striking given that Paul uses δόξα just previously in 1 Corinthians 15:40, where the general consensus is that the term does mean "splendor, radiance, or luster," as suggested by BDAG. That most commentators regard δόξα to have two semantically different

---

[156]Newman (1992: 160-61) places 1 Cor 15:43 in the category of the forty-two occurrences of δόξα "left for consideration" rather than the category of "social status" or "honor," in which he includes only 1 Cor 4:10; 11:15; 2 Cor 6:8; 1 Thess 2:6 and notes that in three of the four occurrences, "Paul contrasts δόξα with ἄτιμος in the immediate context." He mentions 1 Cor 15:43 for a second time in the footnote of the following sentence, in which he says, "There does not seem to be any observable syntactical pattern to this profile." Yet later, on p. 194, he writes in reference to 1 Cor 15:43 that "[the body] is raised in/by eschatological Glory."

[157]Conzelmann 1975: 282.

[158]BDAG 2000: 257.

[159]Ciampa and Rosner 2007: 814; see Conzelmann 1975: 283.

[160]Fee 1987: 785; Thiselton 2000: 1273.

meanings, and that these meanings are separated by only three verses here in 1 Corinthians 15:40-43, is testimony to the fact that δόξα has a variety of semantic uses and that Paul utilizes those distinct uses throughout his letters. This is a generally recognized fact but seems often to be forgotten in practice, as can be seen in how δόξα is treated in, for example, Philippians 3:21, and, as I have argued throughout this book, in Paul's letters more generally.

To return then to the notion of participation in the future life of the last Adam, one characteristic of that life will be glory: a state of honor or exalted status. Macaskill rightly notes that there is no indication here that Paul is referring to the glory of the first Adam.[161] I suggest nevertheless that Paul is highlighting the glory of the last Adam—the son of man of Psalm 8 who now has victory over death (1 Cor 15:21-28). The physical body of the resurrected Christ, which is imperishable, immortal, glorious, and powerful, represents his victory (1 Cor 15:57) over the powers and rulers of this age and declares that he alone is the Lord of glory (1 Cor 2:8). It is this life of dominion, of victory, in which believers will share in total transformation in the resurrection, and in which they participate through union with Christ already.[162] The "life" of the heavenly man, as suggested by Fee above, goes hand in hand with the glory of the heavenly man and his dominion over creation as the last Adam.[163] This is why Paul states in 1 Corinthians 15:50 that only those who wear the "image of the man of heaven" can "inherit the kingdom of God." Moreover, it is why Paul can write in 1 Corinthians 15:54-57: "Death is swallowed up in victory. . . . Thanks be to God, who *gives us the victory*

---

[161]See Macaskill 2013: 143.

[162]One may question the duration of the Son's dominion within the kingdom, and thus believers' participation in that dominion, on the basis of 1 Cor 15:24, 28. As Payne (2009: 134-35) correctly argues, however, it is best not to see a subordinationist theology at work in these two verses but to recognize that in 1 Cor 15:28 Paul transitions from designating God as the Father (1 Cor 15:24) to God as the Godhead (1 Cor 15:28)—"so that God may be all in all." Christ does not lose his authoritative or exalted position, as Paul makes clear in Rom 9:5; Eph 1:20-22. Thiselton too (2000: 1237) notes that we must "recall that the purposes of God and of *Christ* remain *one*, and that any differentiation occurs within the framework of a source, mediate cause, agency, means, and goal which *do not compete* but belong to what Paul and other NT writers (not least John) express as a shared purpose"; emphasis original.

[163]Ciampa and Rosner (2010: 813-14) recognize an echo of Ps 8 here. Unfortunately, they blend Adam's glory as honor or rule in the psalm with that of Adam's glory as splendor in some early Jewish literature.

[τῷ διδόντι ἡμῖν τὸ νῖκος] through our Lord Jesus."[164] With the resurrection body—a body that exists in or belongs to a new "mode of existence," the resurrection glory, the "image of the heavenly man"—believers
will participate in the Messiah's subjection of all God's enemies (1 Cor
15:27-28; see Rom 8:37). They will participate in the Messiah's victory
over death, and their resurrection bodies will be living proof of that
participation; they will be remade in the "image of the heavenly man,"
the new Adam.[165]

   4.2.2.2. Colossians 3:10.[166] Participation in Christ is a characteristic motif
of Colossians though is a motif noticed less often here than, for example,
in Romans. Marianne Meye Thompson is one of the few to acknowledge
the motif explicitly: "[Believers] participate [with Christ] in his death,
resurrection, and parousia. They are identified with Christ in his death,
resurrection, and ultimate revelation in glory. What they have, they have
in him and from him, a reality which Paul summarizes in the metaphor
that their lives are hidden with Christ in God."[167] Ben Blackwell has argued
that participation with Christ, a phrase that he says implies "attributive
deification," stands behind Colossians 2:9-10: "In him all the fullness of
deity dwells bodily, and you are filled in him."[168] Blackwell's conclusions
will prove helpful for my purposes here—purposes that focus not on Colossians 2:9-10 but on the participatory language that builds up to the
image language of Colossians 3:10. There the believer is described as "being
renewed in knowledge according to the image of its creator." In this section,

---

[164]Collins (1999: 583) notes Christians' victory in 1 Cor 15:57 but does little with it. Ciampa and
   Rosner (2010: 837) again helpfully write: "Here Paul makes it clear that God's victory is also
   our victory. It is the victory that God *gives us . . . through our Lord Jesus Christ.* In a strange
   paradox, the Christian needs to learn that 'it's not about me' but about Christ the Lord and
   his agenda. Once that has been properly grasped, one may go back and recognize that, as it
   turns out, God's agenda has been that of redeeming us (and the rest of his creation) and
   giving us the ultimate victory over the enemies of his righteous reign"; emphasis original.
[165]See further Rowe 2005: 302-6.
[166]I am persuaded that Paul wrote Colossians, or that he at least had a direct hand in its creation.
   I regard the often-noted theological, lexical, and stylistic distinctions between Colossians and
   the undisputed Pauline epistles to be less significant than they are commonly assumed to be.
   With O'Brien (1982: xlix), I believe the differences that exist between Colossians and the
   undisputed Pauline epistles "are best interpreted as being called forth by the circumstances
   at Colossae."
[167]Thompson 2005: 69; see further Lohse 1971: 103-5.
[168]Blackwell (2014) clarifies that, in attributive deification, "believers take on divine attributes
   through an ontological transformation but remain distinct from the divine essence" (104).

I wish briefly to highlight the language of participation used to characterize believers as those who were once identified by the "old man" and are now identified by the "new man," their new identity in Christ. Because recognition of the identity of this "new man" is dependent on recognition of the identity of Christ, I begin there.

In Colossians, Christ is depicted as the cosmic victor, beginning in Colossians 1:15-20, a text traditionally regarded as the Colossian hymn.[169] Here too the Son is described with εἰκών-language: in Colossians 1:15 as ὅς ἐστιν εἰκὼν τοῦ θεοῦ τοῦ ἀοράτου, πρωτότοκος πάσης κτίσεως and in Colossians 1:18 as ὅς ἐστιν ἀρχή, πρωτότοκος ἐκ τῶν νεκρῶν. Scholarship generally recognizes a literary dependence on Wisdom traditions here, particularly those rooted in Proverbs 8:22 and Wisdom of Solomon 7:26.[170] The Messiah, God's Son, is referred to in the terms with which Wisdom was personified in Jewish tradition.[171] R. M. Wilson points out the two often-recognized divisions or strophes in the hymn, Colossians 1:15-17, 18-20, with the former focused on creation and the latter focused on redemption.[172] This identity of the Son gets folded into the rest of Colossians, where, as David Garland rightly notes, Paul's primary focus is undoubtedly on the

---

[169]For a survey of discussions on Col 1:15-20, see O'Brien 1982: 32-37; Hay 2000: 50-66; Wilson 2005: 123-26.

[170]See also Philo's reference to Wisdom as "beginning," "image," and "vision of God" in *Allegorical Interpretation* 1.43. For an extended treatment of Wisdom texts that exist here as possible background motifs, see Lohse 1971: 46-56.

[171]In accordance with most scholarship, Dunn suggests that the Messiah is presented as the preexistent God who is sovereign over creation in terms of Wisdom in Col 1:15. Yet he diverges from the mainstream in his reading of Col 1:18. There Dunn suggests that, while the Wisdom motifs in Col 1:15 emphasized Christ's "*primordial* primacy," in Col 1:18 they emphasize his primacy as a result of the resurrection, particularly Christ's work of reconciliation as the last Adam; see Dunn 1996: 98-99, as well as Barrett 1962; Martin 1974: 59; and Davies 1980: 36-51, who picks up the work of C. F. Burney, who read the hymn as an exposition of *Bereshith* in Gen 1:1 (*JTS* 27: 1926). Determining whether Dunn is correct is not critical for this discussion of participation in Christ. I am not arguing in this section that Paul's reference to the "old man" and "new man" in Colossians are references to the first and last Adam. If Paul has an implied Adam Christology at work in Colossians, it is far less perspicuous than in Romans and 1 Corinthians. That being said, I do not disregard it as a possibility worth exploration, particularly given the complexities of terminology used in the text, not least *image*, *firstborn*, *creator*, and the characterization of a person as either "old" or "new," which no doubt bears some semblance (whether or not the semblance is intentional in Col 3:9-10) to Paul's description of Christ as the "last/second man" opposed to Adam as the "first man" in 1 Cor 15. See also the treatment of the "image of God" motif in Ridderbos (1975: 68-78), who suggests that little separation can ultimately be made between the different interpretations of Christ as the image of God.

[172]Wilson 2005: 126-27.

incarnate "image of the invisible God," the man Christ who through his death and resurrection is now established as sovereign of creation.[173] Paul's focus in Colossians is on the resurrection Christ (πρωτότοκος ἐκ τῶν νεκρῶν, Col 1:18) and what that resurrection has accomplished: through him God "reconciled all things to himself" (Col 1:20);[174] Christ became the "head over every power and authority" (Col 2:10), having "disarmed the rulers and authorities" and "making a public spectacle of them" (Col 2:15), and is now "seated at the right hand of God" (Col 3:1) in glory (Col 3:4).

Blackwell argues that it is the death and resurrection, along with these consequences of the resurrection, that form the expression of Christ's divinity. He rightly and persuasively argues (on the basis of Bauckham's work, noted previously[175]) against the division between "functional" and "ontic" categories for Christ, recognizing instead that Christ's divinity is expressed in his actions and accomplishments. Blackwell further argues that these actions, particularly the death and resurrection, are the attributes of Christ in which believers participate (or "embody") and are thus "deified."[176] While I appreciate Blackwell's distinction between attributive and essential deification, I find it unnecessary to extend beyond the terminology of participation and union I have outlined above, not least because Blackwell's definition of *attributive deification* aligns closely with my use of *participation*. Nevertheless, with Blackwell, it is these actions and accomplishments of Christ in which believers' identity is shaped and in which they thus participate with Christ.

Paul's participatory language begins in Colossians 1:13-14 with "He has rescued us from the power of darkness and transferred us into the kingdom of his beloved Son, in whom we have redemption, the forgiveness of sins." Believers exist as those who are redeemed and who now belong to or are identified by their existence in the kingdom of the Son. He goes on to say in Colossians 1:21-22a that believers were formerly "alienated and hostile in mind, doing evil deeds" and are now reconciled to God in Christ. The motif of transfer from one identity to another is part and parcel of believers'

---

[173]Garland 1998: 90.

[174]For a persuasive summary of why "all things" in Col 1:20 refers to humans, angels, and creation, see Peterson 2010.

[175]See §2.2.2.1.

[176]Blackwell 2014: 105-11.

union with Christ in Colossians. Eduard Lohse suggests that "the aorist forms ἐρρύσατο (delivered) and μετέστησεν (transferred) point to baptism as the event through which the change from one dominion to another has taken place, in that we have been wrested from the power of darkness and placed in the 'kingdom' of the beloved Son of God."[177] And, as Wilson rightly notes, the aorists indicate "an accomplished fact."[178] Believers belong now to the kingdom of the Son.

The reality of this transfer and its implications are elaborated throughout Colossians. Moreover, the language used to do so bears significant resemblance to Paul's language in Romans 6:4-8; 8:17-30, where he describes the new union through the various σύμ-/σύν-compounds that pertain to dying, being buried, rising, living, and sharing glory with Christ. Interestingly, few commentators acknowledge the significance of these σύμ-/σύν-compounds for Paul's (or the writer's) theology in Colossians.[179] As in Romans 6:4, participation with Christ occurs through believers dying with Christ (Col 2:20; ἀπεθάνετε σὺν Χριστῷ), being buried with the Son (συνθάπτω) in baptism, and "raised with him [συνεγείρω] through faith in the power of God" (Col 2:12; 3:1). Believers were formerly dead in their sins and are now alive with Christ (Col 2:13; συζωοποιέω); their lives are now "hidden with Christ" (Col 3:3; κέκρυπται σὺν τῷ Χριστω). And having been raised with Christ (συνεγείρω), believers can expect to appear in glory with Christ (Col 3:4; σὺν αὐτῷ φανερωθήσεσθε).

O'Brien helpfully notes,

When the preposition σὺν ("with") is compounded with certain verbs it relates to past events and resulting present experiences so that this close union with Christ is already a present reality. Both the phrase and related verbs are employed in Colossians to describe the death and resurrection with Christ as a past event and the resulting new experience for the Christian: it is his life with Christ.[180]

---

[177]Lohse 1971: 38.

[178]Wilson 2005: 115.

[179]The significance of this literary and theological overlap between Colossians and Romans is testimony to Pauline authorship of Colossians. Dunn (1996: 158) suggests that it is "characteristically Pauline." Even if it was written after Paul, it was done so by someone who knew the apostle's mind well. See also O'Brien 1982.

[180]O'Brien 1982: 170-71; Dunn (1996: 208) describes it as "identification (not just association) of Christ with the (real) life of believers ('who is our life')."

Indeed, from Colossians 2:6–3:4 but also more sporadically elsewhere, Paul highlights believers' participation with Christ as the logical result of their union with Christ, their redemption in him (Col 1:14) and new existence in his kingdom (Col 1:13). In Blackwell's words: "Through a variety of images, Paul returns again and again to the embodiment of Christ's death and life—through baptism, circumcision, forgiveness, triumph over powers, mindset, and clothing. In all these things, embodying the Christ narrative is the central soteriological experience for believers."[181]

These participatory motifs build up to Colossians 3:5, where Paul transitions ("therefore"; οὖν) from illustrating the fact of believers' position in Christ in his kingdom to their lived expression of that fact. Paul says believers should embrace their new identities in Christ. They should live not as the "old man" (τὸν παλαιὸν ἄνθρωπον, Col 3:9), the man who lived under the power of darkness (Col 1:13), but as the "new man," the man "being renewed in the image of its Creator" (Col 3:10, τὸν ἀνακαινούμενον εἰς ἐπίγνωσιν κατ᾽ εἰκόνα τοῦ κτίσαντος αὐτόν). But just who are this "old man" and "new man"?

Τὸν παλαιὸν ἄνθρωπον and τὸν νέον are often translated as "old self" and "new self"[182] rather than "old man" and "new man." But this overlooks Paul's anthropology in Colossians, which is so firmly rooted in Christ, the firstborn of the dead who reigns in his kingdom in glory as the perfect human. Wilson rightly suggests that "the 'old man' is their former preconversion way of life, which they have now left behind."[183] Similarly, Wright describes the "new man" as "the new humanity" that "is the solidarity of those who are incorporated into, and hence patterned on, the Messiah who is himself the true Man. . . . At last, in Christ, human beings can be what God intended them to be."[184] Though it is not explicit in the text, Frank Matera nonetheless suggests that "they are grounded in the Adam Christology of Romans and 1 Corinthians. Whereas the old self is indebted to Adam (the old human being), the new self draws its life from Christ (the new human being), the eschatological Adam."[185] Whether Paul intends his

---

[181]Blackwell 2014: 117.
[182]ESV, NASB, NIV, NRSV; MacDonald 2000: 137.
[183]Wilson 2005: 251.
[184]Wright 1986: 138.
[185]Matera 2012: 78. See also Moule 1958: 119; Carson 1960: 84; Martin 1974: 107; Dunn 1996: 222; Seitz 2014: 159. See also Johnson (1992), who argues that the two occurrences of εἰκών

readers to hear echoes of Adam in the "old man" is unclear, and unfortunately space does not allow what would surely be a helpful investigation;[186]
but Matera is nonetheless correct in recognizing Paul's emphasis on believers'
new identity in Christ.

This new life in Christ is not simply analogous to the resurrection life
of Christ; it is instead a believer's transformed identity in Christ. Believers
are not therefore divine like Christ, but the depth of their humanity is
shaped by that of Christ as they embody his same human experience.[187]
For this reason Paul can say that the new man "is being renewed in the
image of its Creator." In the use of εἰκών in Colossians 3:10, the reader is
taken back to the description of the Son in Colossians 1:15-20. Again,
Blackwell's parallel conclusions ring true: "The nature of the 'image' is clear:
Christ is the image of God who created the world (1:15-16), and he is the
one who died and who was raised from the dead (*passim*). Thus, being
renewed according to this image is dying and rising with Christ or, in the
language of the immediate context, stripping off the old self and putting
on the new self."[188] In their solidarity as redeemed humanity, believers are
patterned on the image of the Creator, the image that is Christ—the firstborn
of creation and the firstborn of the dead. According to Colossians 3:10,
then, believers participate in the Son's kingdom through taking off or
disarming their "old man" loyalties and putting on those of Christ. Indeed,
those who are in the kingdom of the Son have already "put on" the image
of the Creator and those characteristics that identify them with him.[189]
Transformation has happened and is happening in Christ, that is, in believers'

---

in Col 1:15; 3:10 reflect an Adam-Christ typology in which the image of God is understood
primarily as a functional concept (i.e., dominion) that is restored in humanity in the eschaton. While I am sympathetic to his argument, I do not find it persuasive on the basis of the
basic (reductionistic?) Adam-Christ typology Johnson presents for Colossians.

[186]See my note above on Col 1:18. Lohse (1971: 142) writes, "God's eschatological new creation
is described here with reference to Gen 1:26f. To be sure, this reference does not consist of
an explicit Scripture citation, but originated in the adopted catechetical tradition which in
turn relied on Gen 1:26f."

[187]See Blackwell 2014: 119-20: "Christ and believers have a similar experience but distinct on-
tologies. Though Christ is *homoousios* with humanity, he is also *homoousios* with the Father,
and believers are not. They participate in the divine life through Christ, but they do not (and
cannot) become a member of the holy Trinity."

[188]Blackwell 2014: 117.

[189]O'Brien (1982: 189) notes that the two aorist participles in Col 3:9, 10 are used to connote
completed actions, just as aorist participles or aorist indicatives often do in Colossians: Col
1:6, 7, 13, 22; 2:6, 7, 11-15, 20; 3:1, 3.

participation with Christ in his kingdom and in the continuous expressions of their new identities.

4.2.2.3. Second Corinthians 3:18; 4:4. Before concluding this chapter, I address the role that 2 Corinthians 3:18; 4:4 play in interpreting Romans 8:29b. Scholars consistently link Romans 8:29 to 2 Corinthians 3:18, and they primarily do so on the basis of the presence of εἰκών (here also 2 Cor 4:4), δόξα (also 2 Cor 3:7, 8, 9, 10, 11; 4:4, 6, 15, 17), and morphic language in both texts.[190] 2 Corinthians 3 is a significant passage for the helpful work of both Seyoon Kim and Carey Newman. Nevertheless, caution must be exhibited when comparing 2 Corinthians 3:18 with Paul's image, glory, and morphic language elsewhere. I suggest in this final section that, while Paul's image, glory, and morphic language in 2 Corinthians 3–4 is significant and cannot be dismissed, Paul nonetheless uses each term differently than he does in, for example, Romans, Philippians, and 1 Corinthians, and that the two passages should therefore not be forced into a mutually interpretative relationship.

I begin with Paul's image language in 2 Corinthians 3:18; 4:4. In 2 Corinthians 4:4, the Messiah is presented as the "image of God" (ἐν οἷς ὁ θεὸς τοῦ αἰῶνος τούτου ἐτύφλωσεν τὰ νοήματα τῶν ἀπίστων εἰς τὸ μὴ αὐγάσαι τὸν φωτισμὸν τοῦ εὐαγγελίου τῆς δόξης τοῦ Χριστοῦ, ὅς ἐστιν εἰκὼν τοῦ θεοῦ), and it is into this "image" that believers are transformed in 2 Corinthians 3:18 (ἡμεῖς δὲ πάντες ἀνακεκαλυμμένῳ προσώπῳ τὴν δόξαν κυρίου κατοπτριζόμενοι τὴν αὐτὴν εἰκόνα μεταμορφούμεθα ἀπὸ δόξης εἰς δόξαν καθάπερ ἀπὸ κυρίου πνεύματος). The image motif here, as in 1 Corinthians 15:49; Colossians 1:15; 3:10; and Romans 8:29, is significant for Paul's Christology. But, as seen above in Paul's use of εἰκών in Colossians 1:15; 3:10, εἰκών can be used in a variety of ways and with a variety of referents.

The question surrounding Paul's use of εἰκών in 2 Corinthians 3:18; 4:4 regards whether its use implies an Adam Christology, a Wisdom Christology, both, or neither.[191] Those who suggest an implicit Adam Christology naturally

---

[190]E.g., Käsemann 1980: 244-45; Best 1987: 35; Dunn 1988a: 483-84; Morris 1988: 333; Segal 1990: 59; Fitzmyer 1993: 525; Schreiner 1998: 453; Garland 1999: 200; Gorman 2001: 337, 347; Wright 2002: 602; Matera 2003: 102; Keener 2005: 170; Byrne 2007: 272; Jewett and Kotansky 2007: 530; Litwa 2008; van Kooten 2008a; Gorman 2009: 6, 32, 169.

[191]For a recent survey of the numerous suggestions on the textual backgrounds, particularly of the use of the mirror, including Greek magic, Dionysian mysteries, "vision mysticism," and Greco-Roman mythology, among others, see Litwa 2012. Litwa himself suggests the rabbinic

link εἰκών to Genesis 1:26-27, suggesting therefore that Christ is the perfect image of God in contrast to the fallen image in humanity.[192] Others suggest that, as is commonly seen in Colossians, Paul is dependent here on Wisdom traditions, especially that seen in Wisdom 2:23; 7:26.[193] The majority, however, suggest that both Wisdom and Adamic texts form the background to the designations "image of the Lord" in 2 Corinthians 3:18 and "image of God" in 2 Corinthians 4:4.[194] According to M. D. Litwa, "Paul assumes no sep-aration between Christ as theological image and anthropological image in 2 Cor. 3:18 or elsewhere in his undisputed letters."[195]

I sympathize with those who wish to see a reference to both Genesis and Wisdom texts in 2 Corinthians 3:18; 4:4. But contra Litwa, Paul does distinguish between the human and divine images of Christ, through the employment of his Adam-Christ typology. Unlike in Romans and 1 Cor-inthians, where Paul explicitly describes an Adam-Christ typology, little evidence exists in 2 Corinthians 3:18; 4:4 to suggest that Paul is reflecting on that typology. Rather, Paul here is primarily dependent on Wisdom traditions, as he is in Colossians 1:15, texts that place the emphasis on Christ's relationship to the "divine" image, in Litwa's terms. Paul's image language cannot be so easily reduced to an all-of-the-above approach, as van Kooten demonstrates in *Paul's Anthropology in Context*.[196] Recognizing this scholarly desire for both Adam and Wisdom, and the common pro-pensity to treat Paul's image language consistently throughout the epistles, Barrett writes:

---

reading of Num 12:8, which linked the vision of God through a mirror with the Sinai tradi-tion. This last option also includes Wright's suggestion that the "image" that one sees in the mirror in 2 Cor 3:18 is the reflection of Christ in other believers, a suggestion rejected by most today; see Wright 1987: 147. It can also be applied to those who, though not following the suggestion of Wright, nevertheless omit any reference to either Genesis or Wisdom texts; e.g., Martin (2014), who simply says on 2 Cor 3:18, "Christ is the living embodiment of God's revelation" (p. 214), and on 2 Cor 4:4, "Christ is not only the full representation of God but the coming-to-expression of the nature of God, the making visible . . . of who God is in himself" (p. 223), and Harris (2005), who says the image is "Christ as God's glory or God in Christ" (p. 315) without reference to background texts.

[192]E.g., Jervell 1960: 173-76; van Kooten 2008a: 91; Seifrid 2014: 184, 197-98.

[193]E.g., Barrett 1973: 125; Thrall 1994: 293; Sampley 2000: 70.

[194]E.g., Barnett 1997: 207; Garland 1999: 200; Matera 2003: 102; technically Litwa 2008 fits here in his argument that Christ as the image of God in 2 Cor 3:18; 4:4 implies Christ as both the "theological" (i.e., "divine") and the "anthropological" (i.e., "human") image, though he does not base such categories on Wisdom or Genesis texts respectively.

[195]Litwa 2008: 123.

[196]Litwa's article and van Kooten's book were both published in 2008.

> It is impossible to draw together into a unity the various occurrences in the Pauline writings of the word *image*. Paul was aware of its use in the Old Testament creation narrative, and in the Wisdom literature. . . . In for example 1 Cor. xi it is the creation narrative that is in mind; here in 2 Cor. iv (and in Col. i. 15) he uses the concept of Wisdom as the means by which the unknown God is revealed. . . . Wisdom was God's agent in creation (Prov. viii.22, 30; Wisd. vii. 21), and also "entered into holy souls making them friends of God and prophets" (Wisd. vii. 27)—that is, Wisdom was also the agent of conversions.[197]

I echo this sentiment wholeheartedly, both with regard to Paul's use of εἰκών and δόξα and to his choice morphic language, to which I now turn.

Paul uses δόξα in 2 Corinthians 3–4 more frequently than any other place in his letters. In 2 Corinthians 3:1-18 Paul contrasts his ministry in the new covenant of Christ with that of Moses' ministry of the old covenant. In 2 Corinthians 3:7-18 he draws imagery from Exodus 34:29-35, where, after seeing the glory of the Lord, Moses needed to veil his face in order to, according to Paul, "keep the people of Israel from gazing at the end of the glory that was being set aside (or fading)" (2 Cor 3:13). Paul's use of δόξα in this section unequivocally stems from the semantic use of δόξα that refers to the visible splendor of God's presence in theophany, what Newman classifies as part of the Sinaitic glory construal.[198] Moses reflected God's glory, his visible, manifest presence on Mount Sinai. But, as Harris notes, that glory also becomes a symbol of the impermanence and permanence of the old and new covenants (2 Cor 3:10, 13).[199] Indeed, Paul uses the term in various ways throughout the passage.[200] In 2 Corinthians 3:18 the glory that Paul said once characterized the old covenant and now characterizes the ministry of the Spirit is now the glory that characterizes the believer who is being transformed into the image of God in Christ "from glory to glory" (ἀπὸ δόξης εἰς δόξαν), from one degree of divine transformational presence to another.[201]

---

[197]Barrett 1973: 125.

[198]Newman 1992: 107-12.

[199]Harris 2005: 300.

[200]I highlighted this issue in §3.1.1, where I offer some inadequacies of Newman's "Glory-Christology" for application to Romans.

[201]Seifrid (2014: 182) rightly notes three distinct differences from Ex 34 to 2 Cor 3:18: this vision of the divine glory is now unmediated, it is for all who believe, and it is seen in the image, which is Christ.

"Transformation" (μεταμορφόω) or, more literally, "metamorphosis" into the image of God in Christ (τὴν αὐτὴν εἰκόνα μεταμορφούμεθα), van Kooten says, results in the "gradual growth of the 'inner man'" in 2 Corinthians 4:16 and the "renewal of the mind," given the shared terminology with Romans 12:2.[202] Paul Sampley writes: "As believers gaze upon the glory of the Lord, therefore, they actually look to their source and at the same time to their goal to which, gradually, as they become more like Christ, God's glory reflected, they become more identified with the glory of God."[203] For van Kooten and Sampley, as for the majority of scholars who comment on this verse, including Litwa, who argues against the majority of scholarship on the verse,[204] this "identification with the glory of God" indicates a progressive metamorphosis into the moral likeness of God (i.e., sanctification, or what Litwa describes as "a mode of being that is manifested in concrete acts").[205]

Amid the many questions that surround this difficult passage, what is beyond questioning is how δόξα functions semantically: in 2 Corinthians 3 δόξα unequivocally refers to God's theophanic splendor, which symbolizes his presence with and in his people, in particular the Christ, who is the perfect image of God. And yet, δόξα in 1 Corinthians 15:41 clearly means "brightness" or "luminosity" and nothing more, and δόξα in 1 Corinthians 15:43 means a status or position of honor and victory. Δόξα indisputably spans the semantic range throughout Paul's letters. With Barrett above, we need to allow Paul's words to mean what they mean in their own contexts, without imposing a one-size-fits-all definition on them.

---

[202]Van Kooten 2008a: 203-4; see also van Kooten 2008a: §7.3.

[203]Sampley 2000: 71.

[204]Litwa tries to argue that this transformation is a transformation into Christ's divinity as much as it is his humanity. Against Scott Hafemann (2005) in particular, but the majority of scholarship on 2 Cor 3:18 in general, Litwa argues that, because Paul does not distinguish between the "theological" and "anthropological" images of Christ (according to his reading), when believers are transformed into "the same image," they are thus transformed into *both* the "anthropological" and "theological" (divine) images of Christ. They "will truly share in God's [the divine] reality" (p. 129), which, for Litwa, is the "life of joyful obedience to God's commands" (p. 129). Litwa's argument strikes me as reductionistic and unnecessary. It is reductionistic because it reduces the "divine" image of God in Christ to Christ's "joyful obedience"—the logical conclusion to arguing that humanity's transformation into Christ's "divine" image results in their "joyful obedience" to God. It is unnecessary because Litwa basically arrives at the same conclusion as those whom he is arguing against (e.g., Hafemann): the human fully transformed into the image of God in Christ is a human who is fully and "joyfully obedient" and thus perfectly sanctified.

[205]Litwa 2008: 129.

Additionally, Paul's use of εἰκών differs in 2 Corinthians 3–4 from its use in contexts of an Adam-Christ typology, as in Romans 8:29 (see below) and 1 Corinthians 15:49. In 2 Corinthians 3:18; 4:4 εἰκών more closely resembles his use of εἰκών in Colossians 1:15—a Wisdom Christology.[206] While it is understandable at first glance that readers should connect 2 Corinthians 3:18 (also 2 Cor 4:4) to Romans 8:29, caution must be exercised in doing so. The similarities no doubt exist, but they are nevertheless outweighed by the subtle but present differences. I simply suggest that no conclusions regarding Romans 8:29 can be drawn on the basis of 2 Corinthians 3:18 or 2 Corinthians 4:4 or their larger context.

4.3. Conclusion

Romans 8:29b is indicative of Paul's larger theology of participation, evidenced by his use of συμμόρφος as a participatory compound and his use of εἰκών in reference to Jesus. But it is more specifically indicative of a vocational participation: believers' participation in the resurrection life and rule of the Messiah over creation in fulfillment of God's originally intended Adamic vocation. This motif of vocational participation is evident also in Paul's use of συμμόρφος in Philippians 3:21, where Paul implies believers' eschatological participation with Christ in his cosmological glory. And the motif is also evident at times in Paul's use of εἰκών, namely in 1 Corinthians 15:49 and Colossians 3:10. In all three texts, Paul emphasizes believers' vocational participation in the Messiah's present reign over creation. And, in the case of Philippians 3 and 1 Corinthians 15, this cosmological rule of Christ and believers' participation in that rule is in fulfillment of Psalm 8, the psalmist's vision of Genesis 1:26-28.

On the basis of these conclusions, it is reasonable to make a preliminary suggestion: "Conformed to the image of [God's Firstborn] Son" in Romans 8:29 means believers' vocational participation with the Son. And now the question remains: Can this preliminary conclusion be defended on the basis of Romans itself and specifically on the basis of Romans 8? The heart of this project lies in this question and its implied answer, to which we now turn in the second half of this book.

---

[206]Contra Rowe, who, though he highlights Paul's emphasis on believers' participation in the image of Christ, nevertheless does not distinguish Paul's Wisdom Christology from his new Adam Christology, nor Paul's distinctive use of εἰκών in both contexts (2005: 304-5).

PART
2

ROMANS 8:29

5

IMAGE OF THE SON

We are now in a position to investigate Romans 8:29b within the literary and theological context of Romans 8 itself. In the following two chapters I will investigate the notion of believers' participation in the image of the Son (chapter six) and then conclude with an examination of the relationship between believers' conformity to the image of the Son and the calling and purpose of God (chapter seven). Here I take up the phrase itself, τῆς εἰκόνος τοῦ υἱοῦ αὐτοῦ, and address the identity of the person whom Paul refers to as God's Son. I will argue that behind the designation of "Son" in Romans 8:29 stands both the long-awaited Davidic Messiah and the new Adam, the image of redeemed humanity. His messianic identity, I will argue, is established in subtle echoes of the Davidic royal ideologies of Psalms 89; 110 in Romans 8:29, 34, respectively. I will suggest that his identity as the new Adam lies in Paul's use of εἰκών and πρωτότοκος within the context of an already-established Adam-Christ typology in Romans 5:12-21. There the Messiah's identity as the new Adam is clearly linked to his designation as the Son of God in Romans 5:10. Before turning to Romans 8:29, I offer a brief survey of scholarship on "son of God" backgrounds and a few comments on my primary presupposition: the significance of Jesus' messianic identity for Paul.

5.1. SON OF GOD BACKGROUNDS

The designation "Son of God" or "Son" originated long before its ascription to Jesus.[1] In Jewish literature the title was ascribed to King David's son in 2 Samuel 7:12-14 and Psalm 89, and ascribed to the Davidic heir of Psalm 2. It is also found in particular Jewish texts of the Second Temple period. In ancient Near Eastern accounts, Egyptian, Mesopotamian, and Canaanite literature all testify to the use of "Son of God" as a designation of the king.[2] Roughly contemporary with Jesus, Roman emperors ascribed to themselves the title, beginning with Caesar Augustus.[3] The literature on "Son of God" in each of these contexts is vast and will not be engaged here. My purpose in this section is to provide an all-too-brief account of the trajectory of scholarship on the background of Paul's use of the title.[4]

I begin with the *religionsgeschichtliche Schule* and its proposal that "Son of God" has parallels within Hellenistic literature.[5] William Bousset argues in *Kyrios Christos* that early Christianity was influenced by Hellenistic mythology[6] and that Paul's use of "son of God" stemmed from pagan mystery religions and Gnostic redeemer myths known throughout the empire.[7] Bousset writes, "The title 'the Son of God' does not at all fit in with the sensitivities of Old Testament piety. It has a much too mythical ring which stands in contradiction with the rigid monotheism of the Old Testament,"[8] and then later, "When [Paul] speaks of the Son of God, it may once more be stressed, he has in view the present exalted Lord whom

---

[1]In this chapter I assume that when Paul refers to Jesus with υἱός, υἱός is shorthand for the full title, υἱὸς τοῦ θεοῦ. Likewise, I assume that when Paul read 2 Sam 7:14 and Ps 2:7, he understood υἱός as υἱὸς τοῦ θεοῦ.

[2]Yarbro Collins and Collins 2008: 3-11.

[3]Questions remain regarding a possible distinction between *deus* and *divus*. See Peppard (2011: 32, 41-42), who argues that the former distinctions of *deus* as "god" and *divus* as "deified" (and therefore less honorable) have now been overturned by recent archaeology and understandings of the emperor cult; see also Wright 2013a: 327n205.

[4]The most comprehensive short survey of "son of God" remains that of Jarl Fossum 1992: 128-37.

[5]See Baird 2007: 222-53.

[6]Bousset 1970: 93-97, 206-10.

[7]Bousset 1970; see also Hurtado 1993: 901; Peppard 2011: 14-17. Peppard (p. 15) summarizes Bousset's overarching thesis: "*Kyrios Christos* charts the development of early Christian veneration for Jesus, from the primitive Palestinian community's acclamation of the 'son of man' as a pre-existent, heavenly Messiah to the later Gentile communities' confession of Jesus as 'Lord.'"

[8]Bousset 1970: 93.

the Christians venerate in the cultus."[9] In today's scholarship the tide has turned. The Hellenistic mythologies are deemed irrelevant to Paul's theology, as Larry Hurtado summarizes: "It is difficult to find true Greco-Roman parallels that would account for Paul's view of Jesus as God's 'Son' or render it more intelligible to Paul's Gentile converts. The human race could be referred to as offspring of Zeus or other gods, but this generally seems irrelevant to the particular significance Paul attached to Jesus as God's unique Son."[10]

This tide turned in the mid-1970s with Martin Hengel's publication of *Son of God*.[11] He argues there that the origin of Paul's Christology, particularly his use of "Son of God," was not influenced by pagan traditions but by Hellenistic Jewish literature. Hengel traces "Son of God" language through Sirach, Wisdom of Solomon, Joseph and Aseneth, Qumran Scrolls in which royal messianic traditions of the Old Testament are found, 3 Enoch, the Prayer of Joseph, Wisdom traditions, and Philo.[12] A number of scholars have followed Hengel's lead,[13] and today the conversation of "Son of God" backgrounds in relation to Paul's use of the term remains focused on Jewish literature. I argue in this chapter that, of the Jewish texts originally surveyed by Hengel, several in particular are the key influences on Paul's use of "Son of God," at least as a designation for Jesus in Romans. These influences are those Old Testament texts that feature a royal Messiah: 2 Samuel 7:12-14 and Psalms 2; 89. More will be said about each text in its turn. For now, one additional background to Paul's use of "Son of God" must be mentioned: the emperor cult.

Bousset and others in the *religionsgeschichtliche Schule* originally considered the emperor cult as part of the Hellenistic sphere of influence, though they afforded it little weight compared with that of the mystery cults and other pagan traditions. Unlike the rest of the Hellenistic influences, emperor worship and the designation of the emperor as the "son

---

[9]Bousset 1970: 209.

[10]Hurtado 1993: 900; see also Hengel 1976: 23-41.

[11]Hengel's publication was anticipated by Samuel Sandmel's 1961 SBL presidential address, later published as "Parallelomania" in *JBL* 18 (1962).

[12]Hengel 1976: 42-56.

[13]E.g., Dunn 1989; Wright 1991; Dunn 1998b; Wright 2003; Yarbro Collins and Collins 2008. More generally on Jesus' identity understood through Jewish texts, see, e.g., Hurtado 1999; Longenecker 2005; Fee 2007; Bauckham 2008.

of god" have recently resurfaced as backgrounds to the title. After surveying the trend in scholarship from Bousset until today, Michael Peppard examines "son of God" as a metaphor dependent on first-century practices and milieus. He proposes that the majority of Christian scholarship is too dependent on Nicene-era presuppositions and phraseology when analyzing Paul's first-century use of the title.[14] He writes that "son of God has received some treatment as a topic that connects Jesus Christ and the emperor, but the studies have been thin; the imperial 'son of God' title has been often noted but rarely elaborated."[15] Octavian's designation of himself as the "son of god," Peppard argues, meant that Paul's designation of Jesus as the "Son of God" created an unmistakable contrast between the two rulers.[16]

Not all agree that the imperial designation "son of god" is as significant as Peppard claims. Hurtado writes: "Any influence of Roman emperor devotion upon early Christology was probably much later than Paul and likely involved Christian recoil from what was regarded as blasphemous rather than as something to be appropriated."[17] N. T. Wright, one of the few advocates for the significance of both Jewish literature and the Roman imperial context, makes an important distinction between "derivation" and "confrontation." He argues that while Paul did not derive the title "Son of God" from the Roman imperial context, he may have nevertheless used it to confront the bold claims of Caesar;[18] there was one ruler of the world, and Caesar was not it. I acknowledge that the Roman imperial use of "son of God" would no doubt have come to mind when Paul's letter to the Romans was read. Nevertheless, I will argue that Paul's primary inspiration came from his reading of the royal ideologies attached to the Davidic dynasty.

---

[14]Peppard 2011: 29-30. He concludes this discussion with: "Recent scholarship on emperor worship has catalyzed a new understanding of divinity in the Roman world. A focus on material culture and ritual practices, combined with a rejection of old presuppositions, illuminates a conception of divinity as a status based on power, not an essence or nature. The old 'problem' of emperor worship—was he a man or a god?—has turned out to be a mirage, which vanishes when the background horizon is altered": 2011: 40.
[15]Peppard 2011: 45, also 30. He lists as examples: Kim 1998; Yarbro Collins 2000; Mowery 2002.
[16]Peppard 2011: 46-49.
[17]Hurtado 1993: 901; see also Hengel 1976: 28-30, 62-63.
[18]See Wright 2013a: 1272.

5.2. Christ as Messiah—A Presupposition

Before looking at Paul's use of "Son of God" in Romans 8, let me acknowledge and address my primary presupposition. In this chapter (and throughout this book) I presuppose that Paul uses χριστός as a reference to Jesus as the Messiah. For Paul, Jesus Christ is the long-anticipated Davidic King and Redeemer of the Jewish people—what Wright has deemed "the very heart of Paul's theology."[19] Because the conversation is as deep as it is wide, my intent here is simply to provide a survey of the classic arguments posed against reading χριστός as more than a proper name interchangeable with Ἰησοῦς and those more recently posed in support of it.

5.2.1. Arguments against Χριστός as a messianic reference. Within Romans, χριστός is found sixty-five times.[20] In comparison, Ἰησοῦς is found thirty-six times,[21] κύριος is found seventeen times,[22] and υἱός is found seven times.[23] Despite—or for some, because of—the number of occurrences of χριστός, many scholars are disinclined to ascribe to it any significance beyond that of a denotative name.[24] One classic opponent of a messianic reading is Martin Hengel, who notes six reasons why χριστός should be interpreted as a proper name in Pauline literature: (1) In Paul's letters, χριστός as a title was simply "taken for granted"; (2) Paul was an apostle to the Gentiles, a race of people without a historical or theological relationship to the term; (3) given Paul's difficult typological interpretations of Scripture (e.g., 1 Cor 10:1-11), it is probable that he had already explained to his readership at a previous point the significance of the term χριστός for the person of Jesus; (4) χριστός was a unique term and, when used alongside Jesus, a common name, served to identify that particular Jesus as the Messiah; (5) "Kyrios," because of its replacement of the tetragrammaton,

---

[19]Wright 2013a: 816.

[20]Rom 1:1, 4, 6, 7, 8; 2:16; 3:22, 24; 5:1, 6, 8, 11, 15, 17, 21; 6:3, 4, 8, 9, 11, 23; 7:4, 25; 8:1, 2, 9, 10, 11, 17, 34, 35, 39; 9:1, 3, 5; 10:4, 6, 7, 17; 12:5; 13:14; 14:9, 15, 18; 15:3, 5, 6, 7, 8, 16, 17, 18, 19, 20, 29, 30; 16:3, 5, 7, 9, 10, 16, 18, 25, 27. The case is much the same throughout the Pauline corpus. Within Paul's seven undisputed letters χριστός occurs 270 times: Novenson 2012: 64.

[21]Rom 1:1, 4, 6, 7, 8; 2:16; 3:22, 24, 26; 4:24; 5:1, 11, 15, 17, 21; 6:3, 11, 23; 7:25; 8:1, 2, 11, 34, 39; 10:9; 13:14; 14:14; 15:5, 6, 16, 17, 30; 16:3, 20, 25, 27.

[22]In clear reference to Jesus: Rom 1:4, 7; 4:24; 5:1, 11, 21; 6:23; 7:25; 8:29; 10:9; 13:14; 14:14; 15:30; 16:18, 20.

[23]In clear reference to Jesus: Rom 1:3, 4, 9; 5:10; 8:3, 29, 32.

[24]See particularly Chester 2007: 382-96.

was the stronger of the titles/names so that, ultimately, the association of Jesus and Messiah was overshadowed by the fact that "Jesus Christ" was the "Lord";[25] and (6) Paul's use of χριστός is dependent on the historical fact that Jesus went to the cross as the Messiah.[26]

Each of these suppositions is contestable on different grounds. (1) It is impossible to know that the messianic designation was simply "taken for granted," when, in fact, the sheer frequency of occurrences indicates that it was not. As John Collins contends, "If this [frequency of occurrences] is not ample testimony that Paul regarded Jesus as messiah, then words have no meaning."[27] (2) The Gentiles may not have had a historical or theological relationship to the term χριστός, but that does not relegate its use within Romans or elsewhere to a mere name, especially since, (3) having never met the majority of his readers, Paul would be dependent on others not only to understand the significance of χριστός but also to assist in making its use clear on a historical and theological basis (as in Rom 15:8-13) to those less familiar with the issues.[28] (4) "Jesus" was a common name, but that does not necessitate the diminishment of χριστός as a term indicative of something more. (5) If "Kyrios" truly did nullify any messianic expression of χριστός, then one should expect the frequency of both terms to be reversed. (6) The historical event of the crucifixion in no way undermines the significance of either the historical role of the Messiah within Israel's history of redemption or the theological role of Jesus as that Messiah within Paul's letters.

N. Dahl takes a philological approach. He contends that, because χριστός is "never a general term but always a designation for the one Christ, Jesus"; nowhere a predicate; never governed by a genitive or a possessive pronoun; and never in an appositional structure ('Ιησοῦς ὁ Χριστὸς), χριστός should therefore be understood as a proper name.[29] Unlike Hengel, Dahl does well to base his arguments on the text, but he nevertheless fails to

---

[25]Zetterholm (2007: 33-56) also emphasizes Jesus' identity as Lord over that of Messiah, but he does so on the conviction that it was Paul's way of keeping the Gentiles from associating themselves too closely with Israel's Torah.

[26]Hengel 1983: 71-76.

[27]Collins 2010: 2 cited in Wright 2013a: 818n130.

[28]Galatians also lacks an explanation of χριστός, a term used thirty-eight times in reference to Jesus. Yarbro Collins and Collins (2008: 106) argue that Paul most likely had already explained the term. See also Wright 2012.

[29]Dahl 1974: 37-40.

demonstrate that, because these semantic patterns exist in Paul's letters, they therefore *necessitate* that χριστός neither should be nor cannot be considered a messianic designation.[30]

5.2.2. Arguments for Χριστός as a messianic reference.

Paul's use of χριστός as more than a name cannot be dismissed as freely as some are inclined to do. My purpose here is not to make a case for reading χριστός as a messianic designation in Paul, nor do I wish even to build on the footings poured by others, most recently that of Matthew Novenson.[31] Due to the importance of his work, however, I briefly note Novenson's primary contribution to the discussion. In his recent study on the lexical and semantic use of χριστός within patterns of speaking, Novenson concludes that Paul used χριστός as neither a proper name nor a title but as an honorific, much like Caesar took the honorific Augustus. Novenson writes:

> Paul's ostensibly idiosyncratic use of χριστός is not really idiosyncratic, at least not in a formal sense. Granted, it is neither a proper name nor a title of office, but it is not therefore an onomastic innovation. Rather, it fits a known onomastic category from antiquity, namely the honorific. Honorifics, which are amply attested in Greek, Latin, and Hebrew in the Hellenistic and Roman periods, were typically borne by rulers. An honorific was taken by or bestowed on its bearer, usually in connection with military exploits or accession to power, not given at birth. It was formally a common noun or adjective (e.g., hammer, star, savior, manifest, august, anointed), not a proper noun. In actual use, it could occur in combination with the bearer's proper name or stand in for that proper name. It was not a uniquely Semitic-language convention but one shared among ancient Mediterranean cultures and even translated from one language to another. It is not coincidental that these are the very features of Paul's use of χριστός that have so vexed his modern interpreters.[32]

I consider Novenson's work the principal treatment of Paul's messianic use of χριστός. On the basis of it and that of others,[33] I presuppose in this chapter the messianic significance of χριστός for Paul.

---

[30]For an assessment of Dahl's four arguments, see Novenson 2012: 98-115.

[31]Novenson 2012.

[32]Novenson 2012: 95-96.

[33]See especially Wright 1991: 41-55; 2013a: 815-911; 2014b: 3-23. Moreover, I presuppose messianic significance on the basis of pre-Christian messianic expectations: e.g., 2 Sam 7:16; Ps 89:3-4, 19-37; Is 11:1, 10; Jer 23:5-6; 30:9; 33:14-18; Ezek 34:23-24; 37:24-25. Other texts that could be

My primary aim here is to illuminate the most obvious reason for interpreting Paul's use of χριστός as an honorific for the Messiah in Romans. This
reason is that Paul clearly and purposefully presents Jesus as the human
descendant of David at two significant points in the letter, and he does so on
the basis of Old Testament texts fundamental to Jewish messianic expectations:

περὶ τοῦ υἱοῦ αὐτοῦ τοῦ γενομένου ἐκ σπέρματος Δαυὶδ κατὰ σάρκα (Rom 1:3)

γὰρ Χριστὸν διάκονον γεγενῆσθαι περιτομῆς ὑπὲρ ἀληθείας θεοῦ, εἰς τὸ
βεβαιῶσαι τὰς ἐπαγγελίας τῶν πατέρων (Rom 15:8)

Ἡσαΐας λέγει· ἔσται ἡ ῥίζα τοῦ Ἰεσσαὶ καὶ ὁ ἀνιστάμενος ἄρχειν ἐθνῶν, ἐπ᾽
αὐτῷ ἔθνη ἐλπιοῦσιν (Rom 15:12)

In the letter's introduction the Son of God is presented as the "seed [σπέρμα]
of David according to the flesh" (Rom 1:3). Paul does not echo any particular text here, but no doubt certain texts would ring out as background
motifs of Davidic sonship, most importantly 2 Samuel 7:12-14 and
Psalm 89:3-4.

> When your days are fulfilled and you lie down with your fathers, I will raise
> up your offspring [σπέρμα] after you, who shall come from your body, and
> I will establish his kingdom. He shall build a house for my name, and I will
> establish the throne of his kingdom forever. I will be to him a father, and
> he shall be to me a son. (2 Sam 7:12-14 ESV)

> You have said, "I have made a covenant with my chosen one; I have sworn
> to David my servant: 'I will establish your offspring [σπέρμα] forever, and
> build your throne for all generations.'" (Ps 89:3-4 ESV)

At the outset of Romans, Paul declares that the Son of God is the descendant
of David, the long-awaited Messiah of Israel whom YHWH had promised
would be higher than all earthly kings (Ps 89:27) and whose throne would
be established forever. Adela Yarbro Collins and John Collins write, "It is
striking that Paul gives more information about Jesus as son of God and
messiah in the address and greeting of Romans than he gives anywhere in
his other letters."[34]

---

noted are Pss. Sol. 17.23 (21); 4Q161; 4Q252; 4Q174. Also, as Wright points out, the messianic
florilegium from Qumran Cave 4 includes Ps 2:7 and 2 Sam 7:14. See Collins 2007: 1-20 for
a full survey of pre-Christian messianic expectations.
[34]Yarbro Collins and Collins 2008: 116.

Though David is mentioned by name only once in relation to the Messiah (Rom 1:3),[35] David is also the implicit referent in Romans 15:8, 12 as the "root of Jesse," quoting Isaiah 11:10 LXX.[36] The "root of Jesse" (Rom 15:12) unequivocally refers to David, the Israelite king who rose to rule the nations (ὁ ἀνιστάμενος ἄρχειν ἐθνῶν, Is 11:10) and in whom "the nations will hope" (ἐπ᾽ αὐτῷ ἔθνη ἐλπιοῦσιν). This "root of Jesse" is not David alone, however, even in Isaiah, as it is he who will lead Israel and the nations when God chooses to gather the remnant of his people (Is 11:11). For Paul, as it was for Jews in the Second Temple period,[37] the root of Jesse is the Messiah.[38] The semantic dependence of Romans 15:12 on Romans 15:8 demonstrates this:[39]

> Christ became a servant to the circumcised . . . (Rom 15:8)[40]
>> and [he did so in order that][41] the Gentiles might glorify God.
>>> As it is written . . . (Rom 15:9)
>
> "The root of Jesse will come, even he who arises to rule the Gentiles;
>> in him will the Gentiles hope." (Rom 15:12)

For Paul, the "root of Jesse" is Jesus as the Son of God, sent to redeem God's people and, moreover, to rule over the Gentiles *as their hope*.[42]

---

[35]David is also mentioned by name in Rom 4:6; 11:9 but in no direct association with the Messiah at these points.

[36]Paul is clearly quoting Is 11:10 LXX, which differs from the MT at a particularly crucial point. While the LXX records that the root of Jesse will "rise to rule the nations," the MT has "who will stand as a sign for the nations" (אשר עמד לנס עמים).

[37]4Q285 frag. 5; 4QpIsaᵃ frags. 7-10; Pss. Sol. 17:21-25; see further Collins 2010: 52-78.

[38]This is consistent with the reading of the Isaiah Targum at this point. Tg. Isa. 11:1 reads: "And the king will come forth from the sons of Jesse, and the Messiah from his sons' sons will grow up." Tg. Isa. 11:6 reads: "In the days of the Messiah of Israel peace shall be multiplied in the earth. The wolf shall dwell with the lamb"; and in Tg. Isa. 11:10: "And there shall be at that time a son of the son of Jesse, who shall stand for an ensign of the people; kings shall obey Him, and the place of His dwelling shall be in glory"; texts taken from Pauli 1871: 39-40. See also Chilton 1983: 88, 89, 113.

[39]See esp. Jewett and Kotansky 2007: 896-97; also Fitzmyer 1993: 707-8; Schreiner 1998: 757-58; Wright 2002: 748-49; Byrne 2007: 430. Contra Dunn (1988b: 846, 850), who acknowledges the messianic reference, particularly in Rom 15:12, but suggests Paul is emphasizing Jesus as the risen Christ in both Rom 15:8 and Rom 15:12.

[40]The NA²⁷ lists Ps 89:3 as an allusion in Rom 15:8b.

[41]I take the δὲ at the start of Rom 15:9 to coordinate the adverbial infinitive in Rom 15:9 (τὰ . . . δοξάσαι) with the εἰς + τὸ + infinitive construct in Rom 15:8b, thus making Rom 15:9a a purpose clause stemming from Rom 15:8a. This reading is supported by most contemporary translations and commentators. Contra Wagner (1997: 473-85), this reading is supported by the semantic structure of Rom 15:8-12 as a unit, a structure Wagner does not consider.

[42]See Novenson 2012: 160.

This reading is further confirmed by the fact that Romans 15:7-13 has a claim to be the summation of Paul's theological argument—an argument that began with the messianic identity of the Son in Romans 1:3-4.[43] In Romans 1:3 and Romans 15:8-12 Paul says that Jesus is the Messiah, the descendant of David. It is difficult to imagine on what basis Hengel made his observation that "nowhere does Paul advance a proof that Jesus is the anointed one and bringer of salvation promised in the texts of the Old Testament. Of course he presupposes that Jesus is the Davidic Messiah . . . but he never employs this in the course of his argument."[44] Paul establishes his terms at the very beginning: the Son of God is the Messiah, the promised Davidic heir to the throne, who will redeem Israel and the Gentiles too, and in whom the nations will hope. Contrary to Hengel's suggestion that "the traditional messianic proof texts of the Old Testament do not play any direct or essential role in his letters,"[45] Paul does employ these messianic texts of the Hebrew Scriptures with absolute directness and they play *the* essential role in his letters, at least in that to Rome. Through the course of this chapter, this messianic emphasis will become all the more evident, particularly in Paul's identification of the Son as the Messiah in Romans 8.

5.3. SON OF GOD AS THE DAVIDIC MESSIAH

In Romans 15:5, 12 Paul employs Isaiah 11 to designate the Son of God as the long-awaited Davidic Messiah—a designation he gave the Son, albeit more subtly, already in Romans 1:3-4. But Jesus' messianic identity as the Son of God is also perspicuous throughout the letter, and it is especially so in Romans 8, where three of the seven references to Jesus as God's Son occur in Romans (Rom 8:3, 29, 32), the others being Romans 1:3, 4, 9; 5:10. I suggest that at two critical points in Romans 8 Paul echoes two messianic psalms, and each psalm occurs at a point in Romans 8 where Paul designates Jesus as the Son of God. The two psalms are Psalms 110; 89, and they occur in Romans 8:34, 29 respectively. The first is virtually indisputable, and the second is probable but not without nuance. I begin on the most stable terrain.

---

[43]See esp. Jewett and Kotansky 2007: 891, 896; also Wright 2002: 746, 748.
[44]Hengel 1983: 67.
[45]Hengel 1983: 67.

5.3.1. The right hand of God—Psalm 110. Psalm 110 is a Davidic psalm in which the Davidic king is told to sit at the right hand of (the LORD) until his enemies are made a footstool for his feet (Ps 110:1). Collins notes that, with Psalms 2; 89, Psalm 110 is an enthronement psalm used in Israelite coronation ceremonies.[46] Whether the psalm was originally intended as a messianic psalm is debatable. "Messiah" is not used, but given that it is an enthronement psalm of the Davidic king, Novenson suggests that the reader can assume the king in reference is Israel's Messiah.[47] Echoes of this reading are possibly supported by Daniel 7:9-14 and by R. Akiba,[48] and rabbinic literature after the second half of the third century CE also interpreted the king of Psalm 110:1 as the Messiah.[49] But according to Albl, it was the New Testament writers who established Psalm 110 as a messianic psalm.[50]

Paul unmistakably echoes Psalm 110—the "most cited scriptural text in the NT"[51]—in Romans 8:34. There he writes: Χριστὸς [Ἰησοῦς] ὁ ἀποθανών, μᾶλλον δὲ ἐγερθείς, ὃς καί ἐστιν ἐν δεξιᾷ τοῦ θεοῦ, ὃς καὶ ἐντυγχάνει ὑπὲρ ἡμῶν. The echoed phrase is κάθου ἐκ δεξιῶν μου in Psalm 109:1 LXX. Most commentators notice the echo; of those who do, however, few draw any christological significance from it.[52] In this case, only the word δεξιός is

---

[46]See Collins 2010: 25. Other royal psalms include Ps 2; 18; 20; 21; 45; 72; 101; 110; 132; 144; see Gunkel 1998: 99-120; Collins 2013.

[47]See Novenson 2012: 145-46.

[48]b. Sanhedrin 38b.

[49]A messianic reading of Ps 110 is attested, but it was one among many: David, Abraham, Hezekiah, and the Hasmonean rulers were also understood as the one at the right hand of God. See Hay (1973: 26-28) for an extended list of the literature, and Juel (1988: 137-39), who reiterates and updates Hay's discussion of Ps 110 in Jewish literature; see also Hengel 1995: 119-225, esp. 137-63.

[50]Albl 1999: 222; see Collins 2010: 142.

[51]Byrne 2007: 280. The NA[27] lists Mt 22:44; Mk 12:36; Lk 20:42; Acts 2:34; 1 Cor 15:25; Col 3:1; Heb 1:13; 5:6; 7:17, 21 as direct quotations, and Mt 26:64; Mk 14:62; 16:19; Lk 22:69; Rom 2:5; 8:34; 11:29; Eph 1:20; Col 3:1; Heb 1:3; 5:10; 6:20; 7:3, 11, 15; 8:1; 10:12 as allusions; see also Lee 2005: 214-16.

[52]E.g., Cranfield 1975; Käsemann 1980; Morris 1988; Fitzmyer 1993; Schreiner 1998; Witherington 2004; Byrne 2007; Jewett and Kotansky 2007. Seifrid offers a slightly extended commentary (2007: 635), and, intriguingly, not even the basic fact of Jesus' placement at the right hand of God makes an appearance in Wright's commentary (2002: 612-14), not to mention the resulting omission of Paul's allusion to Ps 110—and just where one might expect to find a whole paragraph dedicated to the Son's messianic fulfillment of a highly regarded Old Testament messianic text! Though in the *Paul for Everyone* series (2004b: 160) he does suggest an allusion in Rom 8:33-34 to the Servant Song in Is 50:4-9. More recently in *Paul and the Faithfulness of God*, Wright mentions on p. 1066, albeit very briefly, the significance of Paul's use of Ps 110 at Rom 8:34 for establishing Jesus' messianic identity.

common between the two texts, and it is certainly not a word on its own that is distinct or unique to Psalm 109 LXX. Nevertheless, the *similarity of the two phrases* and the *thematic correspondences* between the two texts make the echo unmistakable. While δεξιός on its own bears no significance, "the right hand" or "being at the right hand [of God]" is a commonly noted reference to power or to a position of power, honor, or exaltation throughout the LXX (Ex 15:6, 12; Deut 33:2; Job 40:9; Ps 17:7; 18:35; 97:1; Is 41:13).[53] The phrases "sit at my right hand," spoken by God to the Messiah, and "at the right hand of God," Paul referring to the Messiah in his resurrection state of exaltation and victory, certainly correspond thematically. Moreover, given the *significance and recurrence* of Psalm 110 as a messianic psalm throughout the New Testament witness, especially in 1 Corinthians 15:21-28,[54] according to the criteria established by Hays and Tooman, the burden of proof rests on those who would argue against the presence of an echo of the psalm in Romans 8:34.

Recognition of the echo of Psalm 109:1 LXX, then, establishes once again in Romans that Paul considers the Son of God to be the Davidic Messiah. His description of the Messiah here stems from that of the Son in Romans 8:32 (ὅς γε τοῦ ἰδίου υἱοῦ οὐκ ἐφείσατο ἀλλὰ ὑπὲρ ἡμῶν πάντων παρέδωκεν αὐτόν). The Son, who was "given up on behalf of us all" (Rom 8:32) and who rose again (Rom 8:34), is *now* at the right hand of God the Father, ruling as God's Son—the Messiah. Dunn suggests the significance behind Paul's "obviously deliberate" allusion to the psalm is, in part, "a highly honorific way of asserting that Israel's king was appointed by God as, in effect, God's vice-regent over his people."[55] Moo also notes the echo, saying, "The language is, of course, metaphorical, indicating that Jesus has been elevated to the position of 'vicegerent' in God's governance of the universe."[56] The Son is the Davidic King who, at his resurrection, is exalted to a position of regency at the right hand of God and over the kings and nations of the earth (Ps 110:5-6).

5.3.2. The Firstborn Son—Psalm 89. The Son's messianic identity in Romans 8 is also presented in Romans 8:29, where believers are conformed

---

[53]See Dunn 1988a: 503.

[54]Peppard 2011: 99: "Paul makes clear that Jesus' divine sonship is constitutive of his being the eschatological Messiah (e.g., 1 Cor 15:20-28). 'Son of God' is a royal title."

[55]Dunn 1988a: 503-4.

[56]Moo 1996: 543.

to the Son *in order that* (εἰς τὸ εἶναι) he might be the *"firstborn among many siblings"*: πρωτότοκον ἐν πολλοῖς ἀδελφοῖ. Dunn rightly notes that υἱός and πρωτότοκος are coterminous, with υἱός made explicit by its modifier, πρωτότοκος;[57] the Son of God is, more specifically, the Firstborn Son of God, and it is to this Son that God's people are conformed. The primary question needing to be addressed here is whether πρωτότοκος signifies something beyond itself, and, if so, what? Before doing so, however, I raise briefly the question of the identity of the ἀδελφοὶ in Romans 8:29, a question to which I will return at length in the following chapter.

Caroline Johnson Hodge argues in *If Sons, Then Heirs* (2007) that the ἀδελφοὶ are Gentile believers who, through baptism into union with Christ, are adopted as children of God, having received the Spirit of adoption. According to Johnson Hodge, Gentiles alone constitute Jesus' siblings in Romans 8:29 because they alone are in need of a kinship connection to Abraham. Arguing primarily against traditional (i.e., Lutheran) readings of Paul in which those "in Christ" constitute a "universal, 'non-ethnic'" identity of God's people, Johnson Hodge suggests that Paul does not eradicate ethnic distinctions between Jews and Gentiles in Christ. Jews are connected to Abraham by birth and thus are already established as his descendants; they are already recipients of the promises and therefore do not require a kinship with Jesus in order to be made children of God. The "central theological problem of [Paul's] writings," she argues, is that "gentiles are alienated from the God of Israel," and Paul's solution is that "baptism into Christ makes gentiles descendants of Abraham."[58] I will take up Johnson Hodge's argument again in the following chapter when I turn to the motif of adoption and participation in the Son's inheritance. Here I

---

[57]Dunn 1988a: 483; see Hughes 2001: 27; Byrne 2007: 272n29; Hasitschka 2010: 353.

[58]Johnson Hodge 2007: 4. As a reader of Paul who is also heavily dependent on Stowers, as well as John Gager and Lloyd Gaston, Pamela Eisenbaum (2009: 173) posits something similar: "The most important theological force motivating Paul's mission was a thoroughgoing commitment to Jewish monotheism and how to bring the nations of the world to that realization as history draws to a close." Also with Johnson Hodge, though without a nod to her, Eisenbaum (2009: 207) similarly argues that "the purpose of Paul's mission is to integrate all these various non-Jewish peoples into the Abrahamic family. Like Abraham, Jesus' faithfulness benefits others, in this case, Gentiles in particular. Jesus' great act of faithfulness enables the integration of Gentiles into the lineage of Abraham, so that now Jews and Gentiles are all the heirs of God's promises. Paul's mission is about helping God keep God's promises." Certainly this is the case, but Paul is also about helping to keep God's promises for the rescue and renewal of Israel.

note only some perennial weaknesses that stand at the heart of her overall thesis and will prompt further discussion anon.

(1) As noted earlier, Johnson Hodge is uncritically reliant on Stowers's thesis that Paul's "encoded audience" is exclusively Gentile—a perspective that clouds nearly every part of her work.[59] (2) The identity or role of Jesus as the Jewish Messiah is never articulated, a fact that then leads to two highly significant but also unanswered questions:[60] *Why* is Christ as the seed of Abraham the "perfect candidate for passing the blessings on to the gentiles"?[61] What is Jesus' identity as the Son of God in both Romans 1:4 and Romans 8:29, and how does that identity affect her understanding of his siblings? (3) The relationship between the Jew and Christ is never fully articulated, other than a few scattered suggestions that the Jew is also "in Christ" through baptism, an oversight that also prompts a number of related but unanswered questions: What does it mean to be "in Christ," or what is her theology of "union with Christ"? What do Jews gain from being baptized into Christ? What is her theology of baptism? What is her theology of sin/salvation? What is her theology of Jesus' death and resurrection? What is the Jew's relationship to the disobedience of Adam and obedience of Christ? What is the Jew's relationship to sin, or the Jew's need of salvation through the death and resurrection of Christ? (4) How can she argue that Gentiles' alienation from God is "the central theological problem of his writing," when issues such as these just listed are never discussed, most importantly Paul's hamartiology and soteriology? (5) What is the Jew's relationship to the Spirit, particularly if Jews are not in need of the Spirit of adoption? (6) What is the reason for Paul's tribulations in 2 Corinthians 11:24 if he does not advocate

---

[59]Here, too, Stowers's words are just below the surface (1994: 283): "As Christ was appointed 'a son of God' or 'the son of God' (Paul's language is ambiguous), so also gentiles in Christ will be designated sons of God. . . . The gentile communities that are thus 'conformed to the image of his [God's] son' (8:29) have been destined, called, and justified as part of God's plan to reconcile the world." See Dunn's (2009: 644-45) unfortunately short critique of Johnson Hodge here, where he writes, "The disproportionate influence of Stowers is understandable but skews an otherwise valuable thesis." It is helpful to note here that an argument for an exclusively Gentile "encoded" or implied audience does not predetermine this reading of the brothers of Christ in Rom 8:29. Mark Nanos maintains that the letter has a "primarily, if not exclusively" (1996: 84) Gentile audience and yet includes both Jewish and Gentile followers of Christ in the identity of the Son's siblings in Rom 8:29. See Nanos 1996: 112 for a helpful table of distinctions.

[60]The most description she provides is that Jesus is "a messianic agent of God" (p. 4).

[61]Johnson Hodge 2007: 104.

a "universal" family of God on the basis of the faithfulness of Christ rather than the law or one's ethnic identity?[62]

Because these questions are not addressed by Johnson Hodge, her argument that the ἀδελφοὶ of Romans 8:29 are exclusively Gentiles baptized into Christ and who are thus children of God as siblings of Jesus can only be deemed unsound. Gentiles are undoubtedly included in the family of God through baptism into Christ, as I have argued before, but little evidence exists to suggest that Jews are not also included as those made part of the family of God on the basis of Christ's faithfulness. As Alan Segal argued nearly two decades before Johnson Hodge: "The idea of two separate paths—salvation for gentiles in Christianity and for Jews in Torah—does not gain support from Paul's writings."[63] Johnson Hodge posits that "traditional scholarship . . . has tended to ignore or make abstract Paul's kinship language," a tendency that has "allowed interpreters to wrench the words out of a first-century context by subsuming the passage under the later Christian theological categories of predestination, personal salvation, and the restoration of God's image."[64] While the argument I am presenting agrees with her assessment, in part, the suggestion that the restoration of God's image is a "later Christian theological category" has no basis.[65] Moreover, the dichotomy she creates between the restoration of God's image and Paul's emphasis on kinship to Christ is a false dichotomy. It is kinship with Christ that Paul articulates, but it is a kinship of both Jews and Gentiles and a kinship that restores the image. I will return to Johnson Hodge's thesis throughout this chapter and the next. For now I return our thoughts to who Jesus is as the πρωτότοκος.

It is possible to regard πρωτότοκος as a reference to Paul's Wisdom Christology, as is the case in Colossians 1:15.[66] Ironically, though it is possible to link Romans 8:29 to Colossians 1:15, rarely is Paul's use of πρωτότοκος in Romans 8:29 linked to Jewish Wisdom speculation in particular. Even the link to Colossians 1:15 is made more often on the basis of Paul's use of εἰκών, which I discuss below, rather than πρωτότοκος. Unlike in

---

[62]On this last point, see also Barclay 1995: 651 and Hays 1996: 40 in response to Stowers.

[63]Segal 1990: 130.

[64]Johnson Hodge 2007: 110.

[65]The weakness of her argumentation on the "image of God's Son" here is evident in the fact that van Kooten's work fails even to appear in the bibliography.

[66]See §4.2.2.2.

Colossians 1:15, where Paul's emphasis is on Christ's preexistent agency in creation as the "firstborn," the larger context of Romans 8 and indeed Romans 5–8 is on the eschatological renewal of God's people in their relationship to Christ in his incarnate and resurrection state. In this way, Paul's use of πρωτότοκος in Romans 8:29 is closer to his use of πρωτότοκος in Colossians 1:18.

With the support of numerous scholars, I suggest that πρωτότοκος functions in Romans 8:29 in two ways. First, it functions as an echo of Psalm 89, a text that itself exists as part of the larger Old Testament trope of Israel as God's "firstborn."[67] Second, Paul designates the Son of God as the new Adam, the firstborn of the new humanity. The two backgrounds are not as unrelated as they may at first appear, as will be seen. I will return to the new-Adam designation below but take up here the notion of the Son as the firstborn of God's eschatological family.

The designation πρωτότοκος was applied most explicitly to Israel in Exodus 4:22 (cf. Jer 31:9; Hos 11:1) and is taken up by the psalmist in Psalm 89:27.[68] Whereas in Exodus 4:22 it is a designation that all of Israel bore as the redeemed family of God from their slavery in Egypt, in Psalm 89 the term is limited to the son of David, the "one chosen from the people" (Ps 89:19; see also Ps 89:3). This chosen Son from among the people would be established as King and would inaugurate worldwide renewal on behalf of Israel. At Psalm 89:26-29 the psalm reads: "He shall cry to me, 'You are my Father, my God, and the Rock of my salvation!' I will make him the firstborn, the highest of the kings of the earth. Forever I will keep my steadfast love for him, and my covenant with him will stand firm. I will establish his line forever, and his throne as long as the heavens endure." The Davidic king, depicted as a son of God in Psalm 89:26, is established as God's royal representative: κἀγὼ πρωτότοκον θήσομαι αὐτόν ὑψηλὸν παρὰ τοῖς βασιλεῦσιν τῆς γῆς (Ps 88:28 LXX). He is the Son of God (Ps 89:26; cf. 2 Sam 7:14a), is appointed as a Davidic descendant or as a chosen one among Israel (Ps 89:3, 19; cf. 2 Sam 7:12), and is given an everlasting

---

[67]See, e.g., Dunn 1988a: 484; Scott 1992: 254; Moo 1996: 535; Schreiner 1998: 453-54; Byrne 2007: 269; Jewett and Kotansky 2007: 529; Hultgren 2011: 329.

[68]The majority of instances of πρωτότοκος in the LXX refer to individual humans or animals born first in the succession of births. Ex 4:22 and Jer 31:9 are the only instances of the term used as a reference to the body of God's people, and Ps 89 is the only reference to a king.

throne (Ps 89:4, 29, 36-37; cf. 2 Sam 7:13). In Psalm 89:27, the firstborn is the Son of God (Ps 89:26) who will rule over the earth (Ps 89:25) as the "highest of the kings of the earth" (Ps 89:27). Worldwide renewal will come through this Firstborn Son, the Davidic king, and it will come on behalf of all God's children, Israel.

Here in Romans 8, at the climax of the entire epistle thus far, Paul's focus is on the Spirit-led children of God (esp. Rom 8:14-17) and their renewal as God's family in the Firstborn Son (Rom 8:17, 29), as indicated by the adverbial infinitive, εἰς τὸ εἶναι, indicating purpose.[69] In his use of πρωτότοκος, neither Exodus 4:11 nor Psalm 89:28 is very distant. Though he does not include Exodus 4:11, James Scott likewise concludes that "πρωτότοκος in Rom. 8:29c alludes to God's promise that the Davidic Messiah would be adopted as son to rule as chief among other rulers of the world (Ps. 89:28)."[70] According to Fee, the significance of πρωτότοκος and υἱός appearing here together for the first time in Paul's epistles indicates that Exodus 4:22-23 and Psalm 89 are in the background. He writes, "God's Son is also his 'firstborn' (=has the rights of primogeniture), who in Paul's understanding has assumed the role of the messianic king, who in turn had come to stand in for God's people."[71] The two texts exist together in Romans 8:29, analogous to their relationship in the Old Testament, though Paul's focus in Romans 8:29 is undoubtedly on the firstborn Son of God as the messianic Son to whom all other sons are conformed.[72] As Arland Hultgren writes, "He is the πρωτότοκος (the 'firstborn') 'among many brothers and sisters,' the new humanity, and that company of brothers and sisters, fellow heirs, is devoted to him as its Lord."[73]

---

[69]Wallace 1996: 590-91.

[70]Scott 1992: 254.

[71]Fee 2007: 250.

[72]Johnson Hodge (2007: 115) provides a very limited sample of the use of *firstborn* in the Old Testament: vis-à-vis the eldest son of a family (Ex 13:1-2), Israel as God's firstborn (Ex 4:22), and the Levites as God's firstborn (LXX Num 3:11-13). She fails to note Ps 89. After dedicating one sentence to each (sentences primarily composed of the verse itself), she concludes by stating: "Thus when Paul describes Christ as the 'firstborn among many brothers,' he is simultaneously linking Christ to the gentiles in a kin relationship and setting him apart as one who particularly belongs to God." I fail to see her logic. Based on these verses and the ambiguous logic linking them to "thus," at a minimum, Christ should be linked with the physical descendants of Abraham in a kinship relationship rather than with Gentiles.

[73]Hultgren 2011: 329. Hultgren goes on in the text to note Ps 89 as the background to Paul's imagery.

Based on the criteria set by Hays and Tooman, the presence of Psalm 89 in Romans 8:29 finds its needed support. It is not heavily supported in terms of volume, with only πρωτότοκος linking the two texts. Additionally, it is true that πρωτότοκος occurs in a variety of texts throughout the LXX and is thus not unique to Psalm 89 or Exodus 4. That being said, πρωτότοκος is certainly distinctive to Psalm 89:28, as well as Exodus 4:11 (also Jer 38:9 LXX), despite its various applications throughout the LXX. Moreover, its associated use with Psalm 89 is recurrent in the New Testament most clearly in Revelation 1:5: ἀπὸ Ἰησοῦ Χριστοῦ, ὁ μάρτυς, ὁ πιστός, ὁ πρωτότοκος τῶν νεκρῶν καὶ ὁ ἄρχων τῶν βασιλέων τῆς γῆς. Most of all, the thematic correspondence between the preeminent Sonship of the Firstborn in Psalm 89 and the associated sonship of God's people in Exodus 4 is a primary theme of Romans 8, especially Romans 8:14-17, 29. I will return to these themes in chapter six. Romans 8:29 is at least partially about the renewal of God's eschatological family in the Firstborn Son, the Messiah, the one who is now exalted to the right hand of God in Romans 8:34.

5.4. SON OF GOD AS THE NEW ADAM

We have seen thus far that the Son of God in Romans 8:29 is the long-awaited Davidic king. But, as noted in the introduction to this chapter, the Son of God is also the new Adam, the representative of a new humanity. Though the Son is not named as the new or last Adam in Romans 8:29, as he is in Romans 5:12-21 or 1 Corinthians 15, implicit reference to his role as such is nonetheless present. This is demonstrable on the basis of Paul's own identification of the Son as the new Adam in Romans 5, and the use of εἰκών and πρωτότοκος within the context of an Adam-Christ typology.

5.4.1. *Romans 5:10.* I return our attention to the Adam-Christ typology explicit in Romans 5:12-21.[74] Despite the fact that Romans 5:12-21 is usually considered a self-contained pericope,[75] it is important to note that Paul's identification of the new Adam in Romans 5:12-21 (Rom 5:15, 17, 19) is but a continuation of his identification of the "Lord Jesus the Messiah" (Rom 5:11),

---

[74]See §3.3.1 above.
[75]This pericope is based on the break created by the διά clause at the beginning of Rom 5:12.

whom Paul identified as the Son of God in Romans 5:10. Though separating Romans 5:1-11 from Romans 5:12-21 is now commonplace, the reader should not be bound by such contemporary divisions. This Son of God, Paul says in Romans 5:10-21, is the new Adam who ended the dominion of death (ὁ θάνατος ἐβασίλευσεν, Rom 5:17) and the reign of sin in death (ἐβασίλευσεν ἡ ἁμαρτία ἐν τῷ θανάτῳ, Rom 5:21; also Rom 5:12-14; cf. Rom 6:6, 12) inaugurated by the first Adam. Unlike the first man, the new Man was not disobedient to the will of God but was obedient (Rom 5:19); and through his obedience, the powers of sin and death were defeated. All that the new Man, the new Adam, does or accomplishes in the pericope is a direct reflection on his Sonship in Romans 5:10. This new Man is the Son of God, the Messiah, who now stands as the new royal representative over the created order, wearing the crown of glory and ruling over every created thing (Rom 8:34; see Rom 8:17; 1 Cor 2:8; Phil 3:21).

The link Paul creates between his identification of Jesus as the Son who is the eschatological Adam in Romans 5:10-21 is essentially the same as the link Paul creates between the two names in 1 Corinthians 15. As noted above, in 1 Corinthians 15:21-28 Paul conflates Psalm 8:6 and Psalm 110:1 in 1 Corinthians 15:27. Then in 1 Corinthians 15:28 he conflates the subjects of the two psalms: "When all things are subjected to him [i.e., the son of man], then the Son [i.e., the Son of God] himself will also be subjected to him who put all things in subjection under him, that God may be all in all." Based on 1 Corinthians 15:21-28 and Romans 5:10-21, it is no problem to equate the title of Son of God with the new Adam. In both passages, the Son serves as the redeemer of a new humanity, in whom is life and victory (1 Cor 15:57) and rule (Rom 5:17) for all God's people.

5.4.2. Εἰκών and the Adam-Christ typology. Paul identifies the Son in Romans 5:10 as the new Adam. It is now incumbent on me to establish that the identification of the Son in Romans 8:29 also bears that function. I suggest that the Son's role as the new Adam is expressed in Paul's use of εἰκών and πρωτότοκος within the continuing context of the Adam-Christ typology he established in Romans 5:[10]12-21. I will first highlight the evidence that suggests that this typology has not receded from Paul's purview and then discuss his use of εἰκών within that context. A discussion of πρωτότοκος within that same context will follow.

Dahl rightly notes that Romans 8:31-39 establishes a bookend to the
section that began in Romans 5:1-11.[76] Moreover, a number of motifs that
exist in either or both of these sections are also picked up throughout
Romans 5–8 as a whole. These motifs include God's enemies/those hostile
to God (Rom 5:10; 8:7); justification (Rom 5:1, 9; 8:30, 33); reconciliation
(Rom 8:10, 11; and Rom 8:39, albeit implicitly); the Son's death (Rom 5:6,
8, 11; 8:3, 32, 34); the Son's resurrection/life (Rom 5:10; 8:11, 34); the presence
of the Holy Spirit (Rom 5:5; 8:2-16, 26-27); the Christian's suffering (Rom
5:3; 8:17, 18, 35-36); the Christian's glory (Rom 5:2; 8:17, 18, 21, 30); hope
(Rom 5:4, 5; 8:20, 24, 25)—all summarized in the love of God (Rom 5:8;
8:35, 37, 39). More extensive yet, Dunn argues that Romans 8:18-30 stands
as the bookend to what Paul started in Romans 1:18.[77] His scope and suc-
cinctness compel me to quote him in full:

> [Romans 8:18-30] is the climax to chaps. 6–8, and indeed of 1:18–8:30. Paul
> presents this cosmic outworking of salvation in strong Adam terms, as the
> final reversal of man's failure and climax of his restoration. Hence the verbal
> links back to 1:18ff.: κτίσις (1:20, 25; 8:20-22), ματαιότης (1:21; 8:20); δοξάζειν
> (1:21; 8:30); δόξα (1:23; 8:18, 21); εἰκών (1:23; 8:29); σώματα degraded (1:24)
> and redeemed (8:23). And above all the dominance of the whole Adam
> motif—with restoration of creation cursed for Adam's sin and dependent
> on man's own restoration (8:19-23) providing final answer to the dismal
> analysis of 1:18-32, and the salvation-history sweep of 8:29-30 with its strong
> Adam-Christology insertion matching the similar sweep of 5:12-21, and
> bringing the argument back to that point with the issues of chaps. 6–8 having
> been clarified.[78]

Indeed, given Paul's assessment of the sinful state of humanity in Romans
1:18–3:20 and his rationale for that state in Romans 5:12-21, it is not a stretch
of the imagination to see the death and resurrection of the Son of God as
restoring that state of humanity (and creation) to its divinely intended
purposes. That Paul says the Son was sent in order to deal with sin in
Romans 8:3 speaks to the fact that the impact of the first Adam's transgression has not faded, at least not fully, into the background. Just as Paul
uses the Adam-Christ motif in 1 Corinthians 15 to establish the importance

---

[76]See Dahl 1952: 37-48.
[77]See also Fee 2007: 249.
[78]Dunn 1988a: 467; see also van Kooten 2008a: 342.

of the Son's resurrection victory over death, and thus the guarantee of new life for believers, he also does so in Romans 5–8. The sin and death that came from the first Adam are replaced by the life that comes to those who have received the Spirit of adoption into the new family of God on the basis of the obedience of the new Adam (Rom 8:5-17). And in Romans 8:29-30, Dunn rightly notes, Paul picks up that "salvation-history" sweep of Romans 5:12-21 and declares that it is not according to the sonship of the first Adam that believers are made children of God but in the Sonship of the new Adam. In him God creates a new humanity of God worshipers— a new family of God.[79]

How then should one understand Paul's use of εἰκών in Romans 8:29? It should be noted first that, as Philip Hughes rightly suggests, τῆς εἰκόνος and τοῦ υἱοῦ in Romans 8:29 should be taken as mutually explicative, so that the verse reads "be conformed to the image (that is) [God's] Son" (see 1 Cor 15:49).[80] The image is neither external to the Son nor an attribute of the Son that can theoretically be removed or replaced; the image is the Son himself, the perfect representation of Sonship. On this note, I turn our attention to the meaning of the phrase "image of his Son."

Among scholars, the consensus generally lies in one of four areas:

1. "Image of his Son" refers to the image of the eternally preexistent Son who is the absolute image of God, similar to Paul's use of εἰκών in Colossians 1:15.[81] Käsemann writes, "In reality Christ as the manifestation of eschatological divine likeness is the divine image in the absolute, as in 2 Cor 4:4; Heb 1:3. He is thus the mediator of creation as in Col 1:15 and the prototype of every creature."[82] Cranfield suggests that "the thought of man's creation 'in the image of God' (Gen. 1:27) and also the thought (compare 2 Cor. 4:4; Col. 1:15) of Christ's being eternally the very 'image of God'" both stand behind the phrase in 8:29.[83] Interestingly, while this use of εἰκών in Colossians 1:15 is commonly associated with Paul's Wisdom Christology, the same connection is rarely made by commentators on Romans 8:29.

---

[79]I will return to these themes at length in the following chapter.

[80]Hughes 2001: 27; see also Dunn 1988a: 485; Fitzmyer 1993: 525; Moo 1996: 534.

[81]See §4.2.2.2 above.

[82]Käsemann 1980: 244.

[83]Cranfield 1985: 205; see Murray (1959: 319), who recognizes a similar tension in the text.

2. In the phrase "image of his Son," Paul employs the broad Jewish motif of mankind being made in the image of God.[84] The motif is demonstrated elsewhere in the New Testament in 1 Corinthians 11:7 and James 3:9. Jewett notes that the idea of humanity bearing the image of God "was derived from ancient kingship ideology, in which the ruler was thought to represent divine sovereignty and glory. Paul joins the OT tradition of democratizing this ideology by extending the restoration of sovereignty and glory to all those conforming to Christ's image."[85] In this view no one particular text from within the motif stands out as significant for Romans 8:29, and scholars are generally prone to link Paul's εἰκών-language to any of its other occurrences we have examined (i.e., 1 Cor 15:49; Col 3:10; 2 Cor 3:18; 4:4). Often, though not always, Colossians 1:15 is excluded from the list. Always omitted in this category, though, is the designation of the Son as the new Adam.

3. In the phrase "image of his Son," Paul specifically employs his Adam-Christ typology on the basis of Genesis 1:26-27 (ἐποίησεν ὁ θεὸς τὸν ἄνθρωπον κατ᾽ εἰκόνα θεοῦ ἐποίησεν αὐτόν; Gen 1:27 LXX).[86] Recognizing that the motif of humanity being made in the image of God is present throughout the various Old Testament texts, Genesis 1:26-27 is nonetheless of greater significance for Paul, and, according to Herman Ridderbos, "the idea of Christ as the second Adam is predominant."[87] Matera writes that Paul "refers to him as 'the image of God,' 'the eschatological Adam,' 'the new human being.'"[88] According to Moo, "The language Paul uses here . . . suggests a (negative) comparison with Adam. Now it is God's purpose to imprint on all those who belong to Christ the 'image' of the 'second Adam.'"[89] Though being an "imprint" is perhaps not the most accurate synonym for being "conformed," Moo's suggestion is indicative of the general consensus of those who support this new-Adam reading. Peter Stuhlmacher, too,

---

[84]E.g., Gen 1:27; Sir 17:2-4; Wis 2:23; Testament of Naphtali 2.5; Apoc. Mos. 10.3; 12.1; 33.5; 35.2; LAE 14.1-2; 37.3; 4 Ezra 8.44; Ps 8:6-7 is often included in the list. See, e.g., Fitzmyer 1993; Jewett and Kotansky 2007.

[85]Jewett and Kotansky 2007: 529. Jewett nevertheless notes Jervell's (1960: 197-256) argument that in early baptismal traditions, the image that was lost at the fall was understood to be regained through the baptismal union of the believer to the image of Christ.

[86]Dunn 1988a; Moo 1996; Schreiner 1998; Hughes 2001; Byrne 2007.

[87]Ridderbos 1975: 225.

[88]Matera 2012: 80.

[89]Moo 1996: 534.

recognizes the "image of the Son" in Romans 8:29 as a reference to the Son as the last Adam.[90] And, as we have seen above, van Kooten suggests that Paul's letters that contain an explicit Adam Christology (esp. 1–2 Corinthians and Romans for van Kooten) as well as εἰκών-language "also contain the designation of Adam as the image of God, be it Adam I or Adam II."[91]

4. For some, "image of his Son" is not a phrase that can be parsed into divine, anthropological, or Adamic emphases. The identification of the Son as the last Adam is inseparable from the Son as the eternal Son of God; both identities or roles of the Son are wrapped up in him being the "image of God" in Romans 8:29. Attempting to maintain this tension he sees as implicit in the text, Fee writes: "The one who as divine Son perfectly bears the divine image, in his humanity also perfectly bore the true image intended by God in creating human beings in the first place. The second Adam, in his becoming incarnate and through his death and resurrection, has restored what the first Adam defaced."[92]

Adjudication between the options rests once again on the criteria established by Hays and Tooman. In terms of volume, uniqueness, and distinctiveness, all four depend on the sole use of εἰκών and its relationship either to the use of εἰκών in the Wisdom traditions or the texts that reflect the motif of humanity being made in the image of God, whether Genesis 1:26-27 is made primary or not; εἰκών as a single term is neither unique to or distinctive of one or the other category. Likewise, all four also find support elsewhere in the New Testament in terms of recurrence, though when viewed in the light of their thematic correspondences, the support they share here is perhaps not spread equally. In Romans 8:29, how to understand εἰκών depends primarily on the final criterion of thematic correspondence, and here, I suggest, understanding εἰκών as an implicit reference to Genesis 1:26-27 finds greater support than the alternatives.

The idea that in Romans 8:29 believers are conformed to the preexistent divine image of God who was present with God as mediator of creation (category one above) finds little thematic support in Romans 8. This is

---

[90]Stuhlmacher 1994: 136.

[91]Van Kooten 2008a: 75 (pp. 71-75).

[92]Fee 2007: 251. See also Ridderbos (1975: 77), who writes, "In a word, his Sonship and his Redeemership are in Paul's preaching nowhere abstracted. For this reason *even in the glory of his pre-existence he can be designated by the name of the last Adam* and he can already be ascribed by the disposition that would characterize him as the second man"; emphasis mine.

certainly Paul's emphasis in Colossians 1:15, where the image of God is also the Firstborn of all creation, that is, the beginning of all creation as the eternally preexistent image of God. Likewise, with Fee and supporters of category four above, it is unequivocally the case that the incarnate and resurrected Son can never be identified as somehow distinct from the eternal Son who *became* incarnate; and thus, theologically, the eternally preexistent Son is always behind Paul's references to the Son in his incarnation and resurrection (e.g., Rom 8:3). That said, when interpreting Paul's specific uses of the phrase within their particular literary contexts, it should go without saying that Paul may give precedence to one aspect of the Son's identity over another. This is clearly seen in the differences between his image language in Colossians 1:15 and in 1 Corinthians 15:49. And in Romans 8:29, as in 1 Corinthians 15:49, Paul's emphasis is obviously on the resurrected, incarnate Son as the image to which believers are conformed, not the preexistent divinity, as is reflected in Colossians 1:15.

It is this emphasis on the resurrected, exalted Son as the image of God in Romans 8:29 that propels most scholars to cast their vote toward either the general motif of humanity being made in the image of God (category two), or the new-Adam imagery that is specific to Genesis 1:26-27 in particular (category three). But are these two options very different from each other? Both focus on a renewed humanity in the resurrected image of the Son who represents God's children as the preeminent Son. What is altered in the interpretation when the Son is identified as the last Adam, the resurrected representative of a renewed humanity—as he clearly is in 1 Corinthians 15:49, the text to which supporters of the general motif commonly link Romans 8:29? I suggest that identifying the representative of a renewed humanity as the last Adam alters the interpretation very little.

Those who identify the general motif of humanity's creation in the image of God are therefore correct. But I suggest precedent exists within Romans for identifying the Son as the new Adam on the basis of Paul's use of εἰκών in Romans 8:29. First, as suggested above, the role of the Son as the new Adam, established in Romans 5:10-21, has not receded completely into the shadows. In Romans 8, Paul continues to elaborate on the reconciliation and renewal of life that is established on the basis of the death and resurrection of the Son, the new Adam of Romans 5. Second, as Catherine McDowell has recently demonstrated, humanity's creation in the "image of God" in Genesis 1:26-27 implies humanity's kinship with God, and, more specifically, humanity's sonship with God (as is supported by the image language of Gen 5:3). McDowell writes that the ancient Near Eastern accounts

> demonstrate that image and likeness terminology was indeed used in the ancient Near East to define the relationship between a god and his offspring as one of sonship. . . . I suggest, therefore, this is how these terms are functioning in Genesis 1. That is, the nature of the divine-human relationship as it is presented in Genesis 1 has three major components that are intimately related to one another: kinship, kingship, and cult.[93]

McDowell's thesis no doubt has implications for interpreting Paul's εἰκών and sonship language in Romans 8:29.

At this point also, Johnson Hodge is both on target and yet far off center. For her, "conformed to the image of God's Son" refers to sharing the form of Jesus' sonship, similar to Aristotle's claim that "the male seed shapes the fetus 'after its own pattern.'"[94] She writes that "the language of Romans 8:29 is connected to procreation in the context of scientific and philosophical discussions of embryology, succession, and the relationship between parents and offspring."[95] Like many scholars on Romans 8:29, Johnson Hodge rightly picks up on the image language of Genesis 1:26-27; 5:3.[96] She also rightly notes the connection between image and sonship, particularly in Genesis 5:3—an interpretation now well attested by McDowell. However, unlike most scholars on Paul's use of εἰκών, particularly van Kooten, Johnson Hodge limits the use of εἰκών to kinship and procreation, ignoring its Pauline applications elsewhere. In Romans 8:29 εἰκών is clearly used in the context of kinship, but the same cannot be said so easily of its use in, for example, Romans 1:23 and 1 Corinthians 15:49. Moreover, because she fails to identify what it means for Jesus Christ to be the "Son of God" in Romans 8:29, her criticism that Romans 8:29 is not about the restoration of God's image is weakened all the more. Paul's εἰκών-language here does indeed

---

[93]McDowell 2015: 136.
[94]Johnson Hodge 2007: 113.
[95]Johnson Hodge 2007: 113.
[96]Johnson Hodge 2007: 111.

carry kinship connotations, but the term's use elsewhere in Paul and outside Paul suggests that its applications extend beyond kinship relationships.

Third, the other occurrence of εἰκών in Romans is in Romans 1:23, where, as demonstrated above, Paul echoes Genesis 1:26-28. And, as noted previously, in Romans 1:23 Paul does not highlight the fall of Adam but the created purpose of humanity in Adam (again, see Gen 5:2 LXX)—the same purpose Jewett suggests in his non-Adamic explanation of Romans 8:29: "to represent divine sovereignty and glory."[97] The created purpose of human governance as God's vicegerents runs throughout Romans, from Romans 1:23 to Romans 3:23 to Romans 5:17 to Romans 8:29, where that purpose finds its fulfillment in the new Adam (already hinted at in Rom 5:17). This is why Byrne can suggest that "implicit in the present description of God's plan for human beings is the sense of Christ, as risen Lord and 'Last Adam' (1 Cor. 15:45), displaying and 'modelling' for the new humanity the original design of the Creator according to which human beings 'image' God before the rest of creation (Gen 1:26-28; Ps 8:5-8)—the role in which the 'First' Adam failed."[98] Likewise, it is why Schreiner can write, "The use of the term 'image' signifies that Jesus as the second Adam succeeded where the first Adam failed. Human beings were created to rule the world for God and to live under his lordship, and we know Adam failed in this endeavor. . . . The second Adam has secured what the first Adam failed to accomplish."[99] Indeed, the category with the greatest textual support is also that which finds the greatest scholarly support: in "the image of [God's] Son" Paul employs his Adam Christology, identifying the Son of God as the exalted image of an eschatologically redeemed humanity.

5.4.3. Πρωτότοκος and the Adam-Christ typology. What then does one make of Paul's use of πρωτότοκος? I suggested above that little in the context of Romans 8:29 supports reading it as part of a Jewish Wisdom motif, as Paul uses it in Colossians 1:15. I also suggested above that πρωτότοκος in Romans 8:29 likely picks up the Old Testament motif of Israel being the "firstborn" of God's children, with special emphasis on the firstborn of Psalm 89, the "one chosen from among [Israel]" to serve as Israel's representative ruler. I now suggest that, in addition, πρωτότοκος,

---

[97]Jewett and Kotansky 2007: 529.
[98]Byrne 2007: 272n29.
[99]Schreiner 1998: 454.

with εἰκών, picks up the new-Adam motif that Paul explicitly employs in Romans 5. Much of the evidence for this has already been discussed in the paragraphs above, but a brief word is nonetheless useful.

Those who identify Paul's image language as referring to the Son as the image of God who is the archetype of all redeemed humanity generally also find πρωτότοκος as a reference to his resurrection status as the representative new Adam.[100] As Barrett rightly notes, πρωτότοκος in Romans 8:29 more closely resembles the use of πρωτότοκος in Colossians 1:18 than in Colossians 1:15.[101] In Colossians 1:18 he is the πρωτότοκος ἐκ τῶν νεκρῶν, the first to rise into the transformed existence of resurrection life. Ridderbos suggests that a parallel metaphor likewise exists in 1 Corinthians 15:20: Νυνὶ δὲ Χριστὸς ἐγήγερται ἐκ νεκρῶν ἀπαρχὴ τῶν κεκοιμημένων, followed by 1 Corinthians 15:23: Ἕκαστος δὲ ἐν τῷ ἰδίῳ τάγματι· ἀπαρχὴ Χριστός, ἔπειτα οἱ τοῦ Χριστοῦ ἐν τῇ παρουσίᾳ αὐτοῦ.[102] In his resurrection from the dead, Christ is the "firstfruits" of those who sleep, that is, the first to experience the resurrection life of those who have died. Perhaps most significant, at least in terms of the early church witness to Paul's use of πρωτότοκος here in Romans 8:29, is the use of πρωτότοκος in Revelation 1:5: Ἰησοῦ Χριστοῦ, ὁ μάρτυς, ὁ πιστός, ὁ πρωτότοκος τῶν νεκρῶν καὶ ὁ ἄρχων τῶν βασιλέων τῆς γῆς. I noted it above in discussion of the importance of Psalm 89 at this point, but here we can see also its significance for the Son's being the first human to rise from the dead. John conflates the two ideas: Jesus is the first to rise from the dead, and, as that Firstborn, he fulfills Psalm 89:27. Πρωτότοκος is not limited as a reference to either one (Ps 89) or the other (representative of a new humanity).[103]

---

[100]E.g., Ridderbos 1975: 81; Dunn 1988a: 483-84; Moo 1996: 534; Byrne 2007: 269; Jewett and Kotansky 2007: 529.

[101]Barrett 1971: 170; see Dunn 1988a: 484.

[102]Ridderbos 1975: 56; see also, e.g., Moo 1996: 535.

[103]Mounce (1997: 49) writes on Rev 1:5 that Jesus' messianic kingship stems from Ps 89:27. He further notes that "as the risen Christ now exercises sovereign control, so also will the faithful share in his reign (Rev. 20:4-6)." Beale (1999: 191), too, recognizes the significance of Ps 89 here for both Jesus as the Messiah and those who share in his messianic reign: "John views Jesus as the ideal Davidic king on the escalated eschatological level, whose death and resurrection have resulted in his eternal kingship and in the kingship of his 'beloved' children." Neither Mounce nor Beale describes the Messiah as a representative of a new humanity or the king's descendants as a new humanity, but their recognition that the Davidic promises of rule extend to believers on the basis of Ps 89 is nevertheless similar to the motif of believers sharing in the Messiah's reign as Son in Rom 8:29.

Though the discussion at this point is not directly related to the reuse of Scripture, the criteria we have established can prove helpful here as well. In terms of those applicable criteria, πρωτότοκος recurs in Colossians 1:15, 18 and Revelation 1:5, but according to the thematic correspondences, only Colossians 1:18 and Revelation 1:5 can be deemed similar to Romans 8:29. Support for reading πρωτότοκος as reference to the firstborn of a new humanity also exists in the parallel metaphor of ἀπαρχή in 1 Corinthians 15:20, 23.[104] Given these correspondences between texts, particularly with ἀπαρχή in a context with an explicit Adam-Christ contrast, I suggest that the implicit identity of the Firstborn in Romans 8:29 is the new Adam: it is how Paul identifies Jesus as the ἀπαρχή in 1 Corinthians 15; it bears close proximity to a thematically similar use of εἰκών; it occurs in a context in which the role of the new Adam is not far removed; and it is the logical and christological (in this context) result of declaring the Son to be the representative of a new humanity.

The Son in Romans 8:29 is the first to rise from the dead of those who would become God's eschatological family: πρωτότοκον ἐν πολλοῖς ἀδελφοῖς, or what O'Brien describes as "a new eschatological race of people."[105] Whether his Sonship is one of temporality or primacy, however, is debatable. Dunn writes that "although there is a clear sense that the sonship of believers is *derived* from Jesus' sonship, is a sharing in *Jesus'* sonship, there is no clear implication that the sonship of believers is of a different order from Jesus' sonship. If anything, the thought is rather of Jesus as the eldest brother in a new family of God."[106] Contra Dunn, however, Ortlund rightly notes that πρωτότοκος does not merely designate the Messiah as the Son born first in a long line of sons.[107] This temporal element of πρωτότοκος is intrinsic to the term, no doubt, and the temporal connotations are certainly primary in the parallel metaphor in 1 Corinthians 15:23. But in Romans 8:29, *firstborn*

---

[104]For an extended discussion of the relationship between πρωτότοκος, ἀπαρχή, and ἀρχή, see Ridderbos 1975: 54-55.

[105]O'Brien 1993: 303. Dunn (1988a: 485) refers to it as a "new family of humankind." The nature of this eschatological family is of course contested but is anticipated by Paul in Rom 2:25-29 and indeed in most of Rom 4. In both passages, God's eschatological family includes both Israel and humanity as one new and unique group of people.

[106]Dunn 2004: 114; emphasis original. See also Byrne 1979: 118; 1996: 269; Barrett 1991: 159; Hasitschka 2010: 353.

[107]Ortlund 2014: 118; see also, e.g., Kürzinger 1958; Schreiner 1998: 453-54; Hultgren 2011: 329; Kruse 2012: 357.

primarily indicates a position of supremacy and agency. Hurtado writes, "The one divine Son here is the prototype as well as the agent through whom others are enfranchised as sons of God. The uniqueness of Jesus the Son is not restrictive but redemptive."[108] Jesus' identity as the Firstborn Son—the representative of a new humanity in whom God's people find new life, the Davidic Messiah who rules over the kings of the earth and who represents Israel as God's Firstborn—can be nothing other than redemptive and restorative.

5.5. Conclusion

In Romans 8:29 in particular, Paul refers to Jesus as God's Son, designating him as the firstborn of God's eschatological family. Paul picks up the motif of Israel as God's firstborn, a designation that is applied to the Davidic Messiah of Psalm 89: the one called from among God's people in order to represent them as God's firstborn, the highest of the kings of the earth. This messianic identity is supported by the echo of Psalm 110:1 in Romans 8:34, where the Son is described as being at the right hand of God. But Paul does not present Jesus only as the long-awaited Davidic king. Paul also presents Jesus as the new Adam, the paradigmatic and preeminent representative of a new, redeemed humanity. Jesus is the perfect image of God, who in his resurrected and exalted state is the firstborn of both a new humanity and an eschatological family of God—brothers and sisters who participate in the life of this resurrected Son. And it is to this participation in sonship in Romans 8 that we now turn.

---

[108]Hurtado 1993: 905.

6

PARTICIPATION IN THE
FIRSTBORN SON'S GLORY

In chapter four I made a preliminary argument that Romans 8:29b refers to believers' vocational participation with the Messiah in his exalted status of rulership. I made this argument on the basis of Paul's use of σύν-compounds in Romans 6–8 and on the basis of his use of συμμόρφος in Philippians 3:21 and εἰκών in 1 Corinthians 15:49 and Colossians 3:10. In chapter five, I argued that "the image of [God's] [Firstborn] Son" refers to the Son's identity as both the exalted messianic king, who serves as the firstborn of all God's people, and as the new Adam, the representative of a new humanity. We are now in a position to examine Romans 8:29b as a reference to believers' vocational participation in the Son's exalted status within the context of Romans 8 itself. In this chapter I will argue that συμμόρφους τῆς εἰκόνος τοῦ υἱοῦ αὐτοῦ *means* the participation of believers in the Firstborn Son's honorable status of power and authority over creation as adopted members of God's eschatological family and as renewed humanity.

This chapter will consist of three parts: (1) an examination of believers' adoption into God's eschatological family, a theme that forms a new-exodus motif in Romans 8:1-16 and the basis for Romans 8:17-30, which follows; (2) an examination of Romans 8:17 and in particular the relationship between believers as co-inheritors and those who are coglorified with Christ; and (3) an examination of δοξάζω in Romans 8:30.

6.1. ADOPTION INTO GOD'S ESCHATOLOGICAL FAMILY: THE BASIS OF CONFORMITY

Romans 8:17-30, and specifically Romans 8:29, can be understood only in the light of Paul's references to sonship and adoption in Romans 8:14-16. But even this connection between Romans 8:14-16 and Romans 8:17-30 must first be established on the transition Paul makes from Romans 8:1-13 to Romans 8:14-16. In Romans 8:1-13 Paul reiterates from Romans 6 the transfer of believers from their status as slaves to the law of sin and death (Rom 8:2) in the realm of the flesh (Rom 8:12-13) to the life found in the realm of the Spirit (Rom 8:10-13). Esler rightly notes that "when Paul describes members of the Christ-movement as those 'who walk . . . according to the Spirit' (8:4) he is designating them with respect to the unique and exciting realm of the Spirit-charged to which they were admitted on baptism."[1] Then for the first time in Romans, in Romans 8:14 (see Gal 3:26) Paul refers to those in Christ as "sons of God": ὅσοι γὰρ πνεύματι θεοῦ ἄγονται, οὗτοι υἱοὶ θεοῦ εἰσιν, who in Romans 8:15 have received the Spirit of adoption: πνεῦμα υἱοθεσίας[2] (Rom 8:23; 9:4; Gal 4:5; Eph 1:5). Because this is the first time Paul mentions the theme of adoption/sonship, Otto Michel infers that Paul's sudden emphasis on sonship or adoption at Romans 8:14 does not follow the logic of the passage.[3] What does the metaphor of sonship have to do with freedom from the flesh? In part, Michel's confusion is understandable. Not only is there no obvious link between the two sets of motifs, but Paul mentions neither believers' sonship nor adoption at any point previously in the letter.

The answer to Michel's question, I suggest, lies in the context from which Paul draws the term υἱοθεσία. The term is used in the New Testament only by Paul, and only in Romans 8:15, 23; 9:4; Galatians 4:5; and Ephesians 1:5. It is not found once in the LXX, nor is it a word or a practice with roots

---

[1] Esler 2003: 246.
[2] Ὑιοθεσία is omitted in P[46], D, G but is probably original. Discussions surrounding Paul's use of πνεῦμα υἱοθεσίας in Rom 8:15 are plentiful but cannot be a focus here. With Jewett and Kotansky (2007: 498), I suggest the genitive indicates purpose ("a Spirit which produces sonship" or "effects sonship" [à la Dunn 1988a: 452] or "constitutes sonship" [à la Fitzmyer 1993: 498]); contra Byrne (1979: 100), who suggests the genitive should be translated as a Spirit that "goes with" or "pledges" adoption.
[3] Michel 1966: 196-97; see Leenhardt 1961: 213-14.

in Jewish culture.[4] It is, however, a term and practice common within first-century Greco-Roman society. For this reason, scholars suggest that Paul derives his understanding of the term from the socio-legal context of adoption in his imperial world.[5] Fitzmyer suggests that Paul borrows the word from the Greco-Roman setting, in which legal adoption was a common practice, and applies it metaphorically to the formation of God's family, composed of Gentile and Jew.[6] The place of adoption and sonship within the Greco-Roman milieu has been investigated in detail and will therefore not be a focus of our study here.[7] Not all are convinced, however, that the Greco-Roman environment, whether in mythological or legal categories, provided the impetus for Paul's use of the term. Scott suggests that the one possible Greco-Roman legal context, the Roman ceremony of adoption "in which the minor to be adopted was emancipated from the authority of his natural father and placed under the new authority of his adopted father," lacks any close parallel context in Paul's letters to make it likely.[8]

Despite the paucity of references to adoption in the Old Testament, the possibility that Paul draws his material from his Jewish roots has recently grown in popularity. James Scott has provided the most detailed argument, suggesting that, even in texts such as 2 Samuel 7,[9] what the author describes is essentially what the first-century Romans understood as adoption, despite the nonuse of the term and the prevalence of the practice in the Hebrew culture.[10] Υἱοθεσία, he suggests, not only is a Jewish motif but

---

[4]Fitzmyer (1993: 500) helpfully notes: "There is practically no evidence of it in the OT. Normally, one could not be taken into a Jewish family in order to continue the line of the adopter. Although a form of adoption seems attested in Gen. 15:2; 48:5; Jer. 3:19; and 1 Chr. 28:6, these are instances of either slaves in the *familia* or other cases about which we know little in detail. For otherwise either polygamy or Levirate marriage was the substitute for it. Philo of Alexandria knows of the institution, but does not use the word *huiothesia*; he refers to the institution to express figuratively the relation of the wise man to God (*De somn.* 2.41 ss273). Later rabbinic Judaism was aware of men who brought up the children of other parents (Str-B 3.340), but it is far from clear that such children ever had filial rights."

[5]E.g., Bruce 2003: 157; Dunn 1988a: 452; Fitzmyer 1993: 500; Esler 2003: 247; Burke 2008: 266.

[6]Fitzmyer 1993: 500.

[7]See Scott 1992: 3-60; Lindsay 2009; Peppard 2011. Scott (1993: 16) lists examples of Greco-Roman mythological adoption, none of which use υἱοθεσία: the adoption of Heracles by Hera (Diodorus Siculus, *Bibliotheca historica* 4.39.2); Alexander the Great by Amon-Zeus (Plutarch, *Alexander* 50.6); Solon by Fortune (Plutarch, *Moralia* 318c); and Libyan goddess "Athena" by Ammon-Zeus (Herodotus, *Historiae* 4.180).

[8]Scott 1993: 16.

[9]For Scott (1992), in fact, 2 Sam 7 is Paul's single key Old Testament text; see Burke 2006: 29.

[10]Scott 1992: 3-114; 1993: 15-18. Before him, Theron 1956: 6-14.

must always be translated as "adoption." In this, however, Scott stands rather alone.

Trevor Burke suggests with Scott that Paul derives his understanding of this new family of God from the Hebrew Scriptures but disagrees that Paul does so on the basis of the concept of adoption itself. Rather, he suggests, Paul does so on the Old Testament motif of Israel as the son of God.[11] Burke notes that, rather than adoption, "a much more important theme on the landscape of the Old Testament . . . which permeates the entire canon of Scripture, is the *general notion of sonship*, and if there is any Old Testament background to Paul's adoption term, it is more likely to be found here."[12] Sonship is a dominant theme at particular points of Israelite and Jewish history,[13] and, more specifically, that of Israel (or the eschatological Israel) as the children/sons of God.[14] In chapter five I argued that Paul presents Jesus in Romans 8:29 as the Firstborn Son of Psalm 89 in conjunction with Exodus 4:22 (Sir 36:17; Pss. Sol. 18:4). Here in Romans 8:14-17, it is those who are "in Christ" who are the sons of God (Rom 8:14) or children of God (Rom 8:16, 17).

With Fitzmyer above, Paul likely derived the term υἱοθεσία from the socio-legal practices of Rome and the empire. He applied the term, however, to the historical narrative of God and God's family, and theologically to his understanding of believers' union with the Firstborn Son. As those who are "in Christ," the Firstborn Son, believers are adopted as God's children. "In him" believers are made sons of God;[15] their legal and social status has changed. Yet their sonship is not a natural sonship. Couched between Romans 8:3 and Romans 8:29, believers' sonship is only in relation

---

[11]See Burke 2006: 46-71.

[12]Burke 2006: 71; emphasis original.

[13]See Fossum 1992: 128-37.

[14]Fitzmyer 1993: 497. See Deut 32:6, 7, 20, 43 (τῶν υἱῶν αὐτοῦ [LXX] compared with עבדיו [MT]); Deut 14:1; Ps 28:1 LXX (υἱοὶ θεοῦ compared with בני אלים [Ps 29:1 MT]); Is 1:2, 4; 43:5-7; 45:11 (τῶν υἱῶν μου καὶ περὶ τῶν θυγατέρων μου [LXX] compared with בני [MT]); Is 63:8; 64:7; Jer 31:9 (LXX 38:9); Jer 31:20 (LXX 38:20); Ezek 16:21 (MT) (בני ["my sons"] compared with τὰ τέκνα σου with σου referring to Israel [LXX]); Hos 1:10 (2:1 LXX; see Rom 9:26); Hos 11:1; Sir 36:4; Wis 9:7; 12:6, 21; 14:3; 16:10, 26; 18:4, 13; 19:6; Pss. Sol. 13:9; 17:27; 18:4; Jub. 1:24, 25; 2:20; Sibylline Oracles 3.702; 5.202; T. Mos. 10.3; 1 En. 62:11; 4 Ezra 6:58; 2 Bar. 13:9; LAB 18.6; 32:10; 4Q504 3.4-6; 3 Macc 6:28.

[15]Byrne (1979: 81) notes that, given the emphasis on sonship in the Hebrew Bible, "Paul's contribution would not consist in coining a new metaphor but rather in extending a traditional way of speaking about the privilege of Israel to the Christian community, composed of Jews and Gentiles alike."

to that of the Messiah's Sonship, whose Sonship forms his original identity. Believers, however, are *granted* sonship, solely on the basis of their union with the Son (Rom 8:17). For this reason Byrne suggests that it is best to keep the metaphor clear in Romans 8:15, 23 by translating υἱοθεσία as "adoption" rather than merely "sonship"[16] or even "adoptive sonship."[17] This combination of Greco-Roman legal practices and Jewish notions of sonship indicates the context from which Paul derived his use of υἱοθεσία, a derivation that may be, as Burke suggests, "Paul's own unique and creative thinking on adoption, where he provides novel insights to serve his own theological purposes."[18]

The most extensive treatment of the phrase "Spirit of adoption" and the themes of sonship and inheritance in Romans 8:14-17 is that of Sylvia Keesmaat's doctoral dissertation, "Paul and His Story" (1999).[19] She suggests that underlying Romans 8:14-17 is a new-exodus narrative. Keesmaat does not interact with Paul's use of υἱοθεσία at any length, but she nevertheless argues that the themes of freedom, slavery, life, sonship, and Spirit in Romans 8:14-16, and thus the context surrounding υἱοθεσία, as well as inheritance and glory in Romans 8:17, are direct allusions to the exodus traditions from the Hebrew Bible. She suggests that Paul uses the exodus traditions to retell the continuing story of the formation of God's people (Ex 6:7; Lev 26:12; see Jer 31:33)—that they are/would be his son(s) (Ex 4:22; see Is 45:11; 43:6; Hos 1:10). Keesmaat traces the themes in Romans 8:14-17 back to the various accounts and retellings of the exodus in Jewish history[20] and then interprets Romans 8:18-30 on the basis of that rereading.[21] Her argument is that Paul uses the exodus traditions in ways similar to

---

[16]NIV and RSV in Rom 8:15, though these decisions probably have more to do with Paul's use of the phrase πνεῦμα υἱοθεσίας than they do the use of υἱοθεσία as a metaphor.

[17]Byrne 2007: 252. This represents a change of thinking from Byrne's 1979 work on the text, where he preferred *sonship* over *adoption* because *sonship* reflects Paul's emphasis on status rather than action.

[18]Burke 2006: 71.

[19]Unfortunately, few commentators since the publication of her work have taken up her argument. The one exception is N. T. Wright, who, using Keesmaat's suggestion as a launch pad, has continued the investigation into Paul's use of the exodus tradition in Romans. He argues that, beyond Rom 8:14-17, the entirety of Rom 3–8 contains rethought elements of the exodus motif: Wright 1999: 160-68; 2002. See also Thielman (1995: 169-95), who argues that the narrative of Israel forms part of Paul's argument in Rom 5–8, despite the lack of explicit references to Israel or the biblical text.

[20]Keesmaat 1999: 60-74.

[21]Keesmaat 1999: 97-154.

his predecessors: with the prophets, Paul says the believers, like Israel, are called "sons of God" and therefore "they have both an identity and calling to obedience,"[22] and that they are passing through the wilderness en route to their inheritance. However, Keesmaat also argues that Paul shapes the tradition to fit the new context: the new exodus is now taking place, the law is no longer "central in this new exodus event,"[23] and God's people find their identity in a suffering Messiah rather than Torah.[24]

Keesmaat's thesis is insightful and offers a plausible explanation for Paul's references to sonship and adoption in Romans 8:14-17. Paul's metaphor of adoption provides the basis for believers' conformity to the image of the Son, because it is in their adoption that they are made coheirs with Christ and therefore are coglorified with him (Rom 8:17). Because of the Messiah's victory over the powers, God's people are redeemed from the "Egypt of sin and death" and are united with Christ. As Esler also notes, "Paul invokes sonship and heirship of God as a further means of designating the new identity they have achieved in Christ, now using imagery from the realm of kinship and household, the arena of social relations most characterized by its intimacy and fidelity."[25] After Romans 8:30 Paul does not drop the themes of sonship or adoption but declares that, for those who are God's adopted children—those redeemed from slavery to the powers of sin and death—there is no power, great or small, that can undo what Christ has done (Rom 8:31-39). There will be no return to Egypt; victory is theirs in Christ (see 1 Cor 15:57). Victory is theirs because they are adopted sons of God, the motif that dominates the entirety of Romans 8.

Two final words on the motif of adoption in Romans 8 are necessary before taking a closer look at Romans 8:17 in particular. The first regards the proleptic nature of adoption expressed in Romans 8:23. Believers' adoption in the Spirit dominates Romans 8:14-17 before Paul turns to the plight of creation. He then refers to adoption again in Romans 8:23: οὐ μόνον δέ, ἀλλὰ καὶ αὐτοὶ τὴν ἀπαρχὴν τοῦ πνεύματος ἔχοντες, ἡμεῖς καὶ αὐτοὶ ἐν ἑαυτοῖς στενάζομεν υἱοθεσίαν ἀπεκδεχόμενοι, τὴν ἀπολύτρωσιν

---

[22]Keesmaat 1999: 153.
[23]Keesmaat 1999: 141, 153-54.
[24]Keesmaat 1999: 153.
[25]Esler 2003: 248.

τοῦ σώματος ἡμῶν. The motif of adoption as both a present and a not-yet-complete reality in Romans 8 is made clear in the contrast between Romans 8:14-17, 23a, 23b: those in union with the Messiah *now* have the Spirit of adoption (Rom 8:15)—the firstfruits[26] of their adoption (Rom 8:23a)—and look forward to their full adoption as children of God (Rom 8:23b) when their bodies also are fully redeemed. Fee suggests that "the larger context and the nature of the argument indicate that verse 23 is the main point of everything in vv. 18-27."[27] I broadly agree with this; however, it is not the redemption of the body that is the "main point of everything" but the completion of believers' adoption to the full status of sonship *and all that that entails*, including possessing the inheritance/glory (Rom 8:17) and the redemption of the body (Rom 8:23).[28]

Second, I return to the work of Johnson Hodge on adoption in Romans 8. In the previous chapter I raised a number of questions regarding her argument that only Gentiles are "in Christ" as adopted children of God. Space does not allow for a comprehensive treatment of her work here or of the critical unstated points that permeate it. Our focus must rest on her reading of Romans 8:14-17 and the associated argument that Gentiles alone are recipients of the Spirit of adoption. Her thesis that Jews are not included is more stated than it is argued, as indicated by the pressing but unanswered questions I posed above.

According to Johnson Hodge, Paul indicates in Romans 9:4 that Jewish followers of Jesus are those who already bear the adoption and sonship of God[29] and are therefore not in need of receiving the Spirit of adoption in

---

[26]Esler (2003: 262) suggests that the reference to the "first fruits" of the Spirit in Rom 8:23 is "undoubtedly to the exciting array of charismatic phenomena, such as miracle working, prophecy, and glossolalia, that characterized the early communities of Christ-followers." Certainly the "charismatic phenomena" were associated with the reception of the Spirit at baptism, but there is little in Rom 8:23 to suggest that Paul refers specifically to these benefits of the Spirit. A more cautious reading that emphasizes the status and benefits of adoption associated with the Spirit is likely more appropriate at this point.

[27]Fee 1994: 572.

[28]Susan Eastman's (2002: 268-70) suggestion that the singular *body* in Rom 8:23 refers to the metaphorical body of Christ, a transition from the reference to individual *bodies* in Rom 8:11, is interesting but also ultimately unpersuasive. In fact, the link between the physical redemption of creation in Rom 8:19-22 and the physical redemption of the body in Rom 8:23 makes a metaphorical reference not only difficult to argue for but also superfluous within the context. The suggestion only obfuscates what the context makes obvious.

[29]Johnson Hodge 2007: 50-51, 71.

their baptism into Christ.[30] The assumption made here is that Israel is thus not in need of spiritual renewal and reform. Surely, though, this was the exact message of the prophets, including that of Ezekiel, whom Johnson Hodge suggests Paul "has in mind" in Romans 8:14-16, albeit only for the Gentiles. It is worth quoting her in full at this point:

> It is possible that Paul has in mind several biblical texts which associate the spirit with a creation or restoration of a relationship with God. These passages contain a cluster of related themes: God issuing the spirit upon his people, the people renewing their commitment to the Law, and the reestablishment of the relationship between God and his people.[31]

She goes on to quote Ezekiel 36:26-28;[32] Testament of Judah 24:3;[33] and Jubilees 1:23-24[34] before continuing with:

> These passages . . . describe moments of God taking back those who have already been his people and renewing a covenant with them. In each one, as in Romans 8:15 and Galatians 4:6, the people receive some sort of spirit which establishes an ethnic or kinship tie with God. Part of this new relationship is a commitment on the part of God's people to follow his laws. *In the case of Paul who is talking about gentiles*, he does not exhort them to follow the Law in the same way *Ioudaioi* do, but he instructs them to live the life of the spirit, so that the "just requirements of the Law" are fulfilled in them (Rom 8:4). The spirit enables the gentiles to live as the Law requires. The goal seems to be the same for Jews and gentiles (to live as the Law requires), but the means are different (*life in the spirit for gentiles*; faithful practice of the Law for Jews). In the Testament of Judah and Jubilees passages, God takes the Israelites on as his children, just as in

---

[30]What baptism symbolizes for Jews and why they would need to be baptized into Christ are two questions left unanswered, other than in articulating their identity "in Christ" as their primary identity (pp. 117-35). Why this identity is needed is also left unstated.

[31]Johnson Hodge 2007: 73.

[32]"A new heart I will give you, and a new spirit I will put within you; and I will remove from your body the heart of stone and give you a heart of flesh. I will put my spirit within you, and make you follow my statutes and be careful to observe my ordinances. Then you shall live in the land that I gave to your ancestors; and you shall be my people, and I will be your God" (NRSV).

[33]"And he shall pour out the spirit of grace upon you; And you shall be to him sons in truth, and you shall walk in his commandments first and last."

[34]"And I will create in them a holy spirit, and I will cleanse them so that they shall not turn away from me from that day to eternity. And their souls will cleave to me and to all my commandments, and they will fulfill my commandments, and I will be their father and they shall be my children."

Romans and Galatians the gentiles become adopted children of God. Paul's adoption passages use the language of these Jewish texts, asserting that there is some connection between the spirit, kinship, and a new standing before God.[35]

As Johnson Hodge rightly acknowledges, the three texts clearly and specifically describe the coming "life in the spirit" *for Israel*. However, though Paul unequivocally includes the Gentiles in this new life in Christ by the Spirit, there is no indication that Israel, too, was not also in need of the Spirit. And it certainly cannot be argued on the basis of Romans 9:4. The adoption, glory, covenants, law, worship, and promises of Romans 9:4 were Israel's during the exile, but Ezekiel's exilic prophecy was no less necessary. The same can be said for Jeremiah's prophecy of the coming new covenant (Jer 31:31-33): the covenants belonged to Israel, but Jews were nevertheless in need of a new covenant. And just as they were in need of the new covenant in Christ Jesus, so also Jews were in need of the Spirit of adoption in Christ Jesus.

Johnson Hodge also limits the Jewish need of the Spirit of adoption when she notes the "pedigree of the firstborn son" as she sees it in Romans 1:4. Here she writes:

> Christ is both a descendant of David "by birth" (or "according to the flesh") and he was made the son of God by the spirit. These two kinships (shared blood and kinship by spirit) converge to make Christ a *particularly capable agent of gentile salvation*. Because he *is made a son by the spirit*, Christ is a model for how the gentiles will be adopted as younger siblings. Because he is a descendant "by birth," however, Christ serves as the necessary link to the lineage of David and Abraham.[36]

A number of unanswered questions pose themselves here. (1) What does it mean for Christ to be a "son of God by the spirit"? If other Jews do not need to be made such, why did Christ, and how was he therefore different from other Jews? (2) How does being a son by the spirit make Christ a "particularly capable agent of gentile salvation"? (3) What is "gentile salvation," and how is it different than Jewish (Jews') salvation? (4) Most

---

[35]Johnson Hodge 2007: 74; emphasis mine.
[36]Johnson Hodge 2007: 115; emphasis mine. These two sentences are taken from a four-sentence paragraph that precedes the chapter conclusion and is left entirely unsupported.

importantly, why is Jesus' "kinship by spirit" beneficial only for Gentiles and not also Jews?[37]

Johnson Hodge's arguments in both Romans 8:14-17 and Romans 1:4 that only Gentiles require adoption by the Spirit are left, for all intents and purposes, unexamined and unsupported. My argument here will therefore continue to interpret Paul's theology of adoption to sonship as one that includes both Jew and Gentile.[38]

6.2. PARTICIPATION IN THE SON'S INHERITANCE AND GLORY IN ROMANS 8:17

It is as those who are led by the Spirit and adopted into God's family by the Spirit of adoption that believers in Romans 8:17 are said to be children of God. And, as children of God, they are heirs of God and coheirs with Christ, as well as coglorified with Christ, if they share also in Christ's suffering: εἰ δὲ τέκνα, καὶ κληρονόμοι· κληρονόμοι μὲν θεοῦ, συγκληρονόμοι δὲ Χριστοῦ. εἴπερ συμπάσχομεν ἵνα καὶ συνδοξασθῶμεν. This participation in the Son's inheritance, suffering, and glory in Romans 8:17 is the continuation of the new-exodus motif established in Romans 8:1-16, as well as the introduction to Romans 8:17-30.[39] As Wright correctly notes, "[Rom 8:17] is the fulcrum about which the whole discourse now pivots."[40]

---

[37]These are the omissions that permeate Johnson Hodge's work and that must be answered if she wishes her argument to stand. Hays's (1996: 42) critique of Stowers is that his work "is insufficiently theological." The criticism can be applied to the arguments of Johnson Hodge as well.

[38]Hays's (1996: 38) challenge to Stowers regarding the inclusion of the Jew in Rom 1:16 is applicable to Johnson Hodge's thesis here as well. The Jew cannot be excluded from Paul's theology of adoption in Christ until Rom 1:16 is treated adequately, something Johnson Hodge, like Stowers, fails to do.

[39]Like all passages of Scripture, particularly in Paul's letters, this proposed structure of Rom 8 is debated. Most agree that Rom 8:31-39 stands as a unit and that Rom 8:17 creates a transition point between Rom 8:1-16 and Rom 8:18-30, with Rom 8:17 usually added to the end of Rom 8:1-16. Scholars have suggested a variety of subparagraph divisions within the sections Rom 8:1-17 and Rom 8:18-30, most of which do not impact the narrative in a significant way. The one exception is the placement of the transitional Rom 8:17. Most often, Rom 8:17 is combined with the first primary section of the letter, Rom 8:1-17. Nevertheless, a number of reasons exist for why it should be read as the start of Rom 8:17-30: (1) the explicit role of the Spirit ends in Rom 8:16; (2) the δὲ in Rom 8:17 indicates a shift or development in Paul's thought; (3) Paul introduces themes of being heirs and coheirs, suffering and glory—themes Paul will develop in Rom 8:18-30; and (4) the semantic relationship between Rom 8:17 and Rom 8:29-30, which encloses the unit. See Cranfield 1975: 404-5.

[40]Wright 2002: 594.

The reader will recall that I examined Paul's use of δόξα in Romans 8:18, 21 as part of the conclusion to the implicit narrative of glory that climaxes in Romans 8, and there deferred examination of the verbal cognates in Romans 8:17, 30. Having now discussed Paul's Adam Christology in Romans and elsewhere, his implicit theology of believers' union and participation with Christ throughout his letters, and the messianic and Adamic identity of the Son in Romans 8:29, we are now prepared to examine the occurrences of δοξάζω in Romans 8:17, 30. I begin in Romans 8:17, where believers' coglorification with Christ is closely associated with their co-inheritance with Christ.

6.2.1. Participation in the Son's inheritance in Romans 8:17. We begin with the inheritance believers share with the Son in their role as children of God: εἰ δὲ τέκνα, καὶ κληρονόμοι (Rom 8:17a; see Gal 3:29; 4:7).[41] The inheritance due to them, however, is not their own; it is their brother's, the Firstborn's inheritance: κληρονόμοι μὲν θεοῦ, συγκληρονόμοι[42] δὲ Χριστοῦ (Rom 8:17ab). As children of God and therefore God's heirs, those adopted into God's eschatological family are given the privilege of sharing with the Firstborn in the family inheritance. Thus, to know what it means to be co-inheritors with the Messiah, we must first know what it is that the Messiah inherits.

Paul does not explicitly state what the Son's inheritance is in Romans 8. Nor is Paul's source for the term immediately obvious. Hultgren writes that "Paul takes for granted that Christ is an 'heir of God,' which would have its basis in various OT texts concerning God's declaring the king (messiah) to be his son (2 Sam 7:14; Ps 2:7; 89:27 [LXX 88:28])."[43] Given the links to Paul's use of πρωτότοκος in Romans 8:29, Hultgren's suggestion seems warranted. According to Burke, κληρονόμος stems from Roman law, in much the same way as he claims the term υἱοθεσία is derived from the Roman sociopolitical context.[44] I submit that, while Hultgren's suggestion certainly has merit, κληρονόμος stems from Paul's understanding of the Abrahamic promises, given his use of the term already in Romans 4, where

---

[41]See Hermann and Foerster 1965: 768-69 for a full treatment of the term's background.
[42]See Jewett and Kotansky 2007: 502 for a list of pre-Pauline uses of the term; also BDAG 2000: 952.
[43]Hultgren 2011: 316.
[44]Burke 2006: 97.

he identifies those promises.[45] There Paul's focus is on the patriarch, God's promise to him regarding his seed, and the seed's inheritance of the world. A closer look will be helpful.

In Romans 4 Paul reminds his readers of how God promised Abraham[46] that he and his offspring would "inherit the world" (τὸ κληρονόμον αὐτὸν εἶναι κόσμου, Rom 4:13) and that his descendants would swell to the size of "many nations" (Rom 4:17-18; Gen 17:4-5). In his reuse of Scripture here Paul adjusts the original promise given by God to Abraham in Genesis 15. In Genesis 15:5 God promises Abraham that he will make his descendants as "numerous as the stars," and in Genesis 15:7 that God "will give [Abraham] [the] land to possess" and the same to his descendants (Gen 15:18). These promises are in addition to the promise God made at Abraham's calling: "In you all the families of the earth shall be blessed" (Gen 12:2-3; 18:18). Esler suggests that Paul's reference to Abraham's descendants inheriting "the world" is a summary statement of these three promises noted throughout Genesis 12–22.[47] Undoubtedly, all the promises included in the Abrahamic covenant are for Abraham's descendants, but it is probably best to recognize in Paul's use of κόσμος in Romans 4:13 a reference to the specific promise of land rather than a general reference to all the promises. In Genesis, the hope of the nations is in Abraham's family, Israel, and Israel's hope is to possess and rule the land from Egypt to the Euphrates. In Romans 4:13, however, the land that extends from Egypt to the Euphrates has disappeared and is replaced by "the world" (κόσμος). According to Paul, Abraham and

---

[45]Wright, Byrne, Keesmaat, Scott, and Johnson Hodge are among those who have either noticed or developed this connection. Interestingly, Wright says very little about Rom 8:17 in his commentary, given that it is "the fulcrum" of the passage. He does not describe what the inheritance is, nor does he link it to the covenantal promises given to Abraham in Rom 4. In his recent "Paul and the Patriarch" (2013b: 554-92), however, he presents a persuasive argument that Paul intended the inheritance in Rom 8:17 to be understood in the light of its relation to Abraham in Rom. 4.

[46]In this section I recognize that previous to Gen 17, Abraham is more accurately called "Abram." However, because Paul refers to Abram as Abraham in Rom 4, I do so as well here.

[47]Esler 2003: 191-92. Nanos (1996: 140n138) takes a similar approach, though on the basis of what Paul writes elsewhere in Romans rather than the Genesis text: "What did Abraham expect to inherit? The focus Paul gives in Romans variously describes it as righteousness (4:22-25); forgiveness (4:3-8, 25; 3:23-26); salvation (1:16; 13:11); justification (3:24-26; 4:25); and the glory of the children of God, the redemption of our bodies that the very creation waits to share in (8:16-25)." Paul undoubtedly recognized such gifts as the ultimate result of the Abrahamic promises, but the suggestion that Abraham himself considered these as part of the promises is textually indefensible.

his offspring would inherit the world, which is to say that Israel would possess and thereby rule the world.

This reading of Romans 4:13 is supported by other texts that demonstrate that the expansion of the land in Genesis was not Paul's creation. In Psalm 2, David expands the implied promises of God to include the "nations" and the "ends of the earth" as part of the Son's inheritance: δώσω σοι ἔθνη τὴν κληρονομίαν σου καὶ τὴν κατάσχεσίν σου τὰ πέρατα τῆς γῆς (see also Ps 72:8). Moreover, the expansion of the land had grown popular throughout the intertestamental period (see Jub. 22:14-15; 32:19; Pss. Sol. 14.5-10;[48] 1 En. 5:7; 40.9; 2 En. 9.1;[49] 4 Macc 18.3[50]; 4 Ezra 6.59; 2 Bar. 14.19).[51] On the basis of these texts, Byrne notes that "'inheritance' came eventually to embrace the whole complex of eschatological blessings promised to Israel,"[52] an understanding of the covenantal promises given to Abraham that Paul picks up in his letters. Most noticeable in Romans 4:13 is not the spiritual adaptation but the physical expansion. In Genesis 12:7; 15:7, 18 LXX Abraham is promised "this land" (τὴν γῆν ταύτην), a specific region of the physical earth. "This land," then, Paul expands by declaring that Abraham and his descendants shall inherit the world, ὁ κόσμος, in Romans 4 (see Rom 1:20). Abraham's offspring shall inherit everything in existence.

The expansion of the land to the world is not Paul's only adaptation of the original promises. He also narrows the identity of Abraham's descendants from Israel to Jesus. In Romans 4:13 Abraham's offspring (τῷ σπέρματι αὐτοῦ), the same collective singular as is used by the writer of Genesis, should be read as a singular, given that "heir [κληρονόμον] of the world" is singular. This "heir" could refer to Abraham, though the emphasis in Genesis is on Abraham's descendants, and Paul's emphasis likely reflects that. Paul makes this insight more explicit in Galatians 3:16, 19 than he

---

[48]Here the inheritance of Israel is life: οἱ δὲ ὅσιοι κυρίου κληρονομήσουσιν ζωὴν ἐν εὐφροσύνῃ (Pss. Sol. 14:10).

[49]The terms *inheritance* and *heir* are not used, but the anticipated eschatological place mentioned is "Paradise," a level of heaven prepared for and guaranteed to the righteous; see Charlesworth 1983a: 116 note K-L.

[50]This text is ambiguous as to whether the inheritance (here θείας μερίδος) is of a spiritual or physical nature.

[51]Cf. Hermann and Foerster 1965: 776-81; Byrne 1979: 68-69; Schreiner 1998: 427; Keesmaat 1999: 82-83.

[52]Byrne 2007: 251. Johnson Hodge (2007: 70n10) also acknowledges Paul's return to Rom 4:13 and suggests that "Paul incorporates various promises (land, descendants, gentiles) into a larger vision of the promise, in which Abraham and his seed inherit the world."

does in Romans 4:13. In Galatians 3:16 (see Gal 3:29) the seed of Abraham is unequivocally the Messiah, who exists as the corporate representative of Israel.[53] The singular descendant is present in Romans 4:13 nevertheless. For Paul, Israel will inherit the world, but the inheritance will pass through Abraham's offspring, Jesus (the) Lord (Rom 4:24). The Messiah, as Israel's representative, is Abraham's descendant and the heir of the world.

Returning, then, to the theme of inheritance in Romans 8:17, we see that Paul speaks not in terms of the Abrahamic family but of God's family.[54] Jesus (the) Lord (Rom 4:24) is no longer the heir of Abraham but, as the Son of God, is the heir of God. For Cranfield this shift in emphasis from Abraham's children in Romans 4 to God's children in Romans 8 is the exact reason why the inheritance in Romans 8:17 is *not* the Abrahamic inheritance: believers will share "not just in various blessings God is able to bestow but in that which is peculiarly His own, the perfect and imperishable glory of His own life."[55] So also Scott concludes that "since coming into the Abrahamic inheritance thus depends on being a son of God, Paul can say that the sons of God are heirs 'through God' (διὰ θεοῦ [Gal. 4:7]) or even heirs 'of God' (8:17)."[56] Yet this overlooks Paul's theological narrative that underscores the entire epistle, and it especially overlooks the connection between believers' inheritance in Romans 8:17 and the inheritance of Abraham's offspring in Romans 4:13. Against Scott, children of God are not heirs "of God," as if to say that God is the object of believers' inheritance,[57] but they are heirs "of God" in that they receive the inheritance that God gives: that is, the promises originally given to Abraham. The inheritance behind Romans 8:17 is the same inheritance to which Paul refers in Romans 4 and Galatians 3–4; it is the land promised to Abraham

---

[53]See Longenecker 1990: 131-32; Schreiner 2010: 228-30; Moo 2013: 229-30.

[54]"The 'inheritance' in question is unquestionably the whole world, as in Psalm 2 and as in the explosive promise about creation's renewal in Romans 8:18-24. Interestingly, several of Paul's uses of the *klēronomos* root occur when he is talking about 'inheriting God's kingdom,' which goes closely with the 'messianic' theme at least in the basic text of Psalm 2": Wright 2013a: 819.

[55]Cranfield 1975: 407. Cranfield (1975: 406) draws a distinction between being an heir "through God" (διὰ θεοῦ) in Gal 4:7 and an heir "of God" (θεοῦ) in Rom 8:17. Despite these slight syntactical differences, the overlap of the motifs of Abraham, Messiah, son(s), and inheritance between Rom 4; 8; and Gal 3; 4 are too great to discount.

[56]Scott 1992: 249, 251; Burke 2008: 272.

[57]See Moo 1996: 505; contra Schreiner 1998: 427; Cranfield 1975: 406-7; Burke 2006: 98.

and his descendants in Genesis 15 and extended in Romans 4 to include the world.

This is the case not least because believers' sonship and thus inheritance is directly dependent on their being co-inheritors in union with the Firstborn Son. Hurtado refers to believers' sonship as a "derived sonship": "Paul consistently refers to the sonship of Christians as derived sonship, given through and after the pattern of Jesus, whereas Jesus is the original prototype, whose sonship is not derived from another."[58] Through the Spirit of adoption and their freedom from slavery to the former reigns of sin and death, God's children are co-inheritors with the Firstborn Son, and as sons of God themselves they are guaranteed the reception of the same inheritance (Gal 3:26-29).[59] As Scott writes, "The Abrahamic heirs are those who participate in Christ, who is the 'seed' of Abraham and heir of the promise *sensu stricto*."[60] Abraham's promised children, those led by God out of the Egypt of sin and death and declared to be his own sons, will participate with the Messiah in ruling over the promised inheritance on the basis of their participation in his Sonship.[61]

The question remains then as to the nature of the inheritance. What does it mean to inherit "the world"? Jewett suggests the inheritance is more relational than it is about "ownership of property":[62] "So in the case of the children of God in Paul's discourse, every promise and possession once granted to Israel are now granted in a new and symbolic sense to each and every believer and to each believing community."[63] This relational and spiritual emphasis, however, is difficult to square with Paul's connection of "the world" to the original promises of the physical land in Romans 4, now realized in the Messiah, or with Paul's emphasis on the relationship

---

[58]Hurtado 1993: 906. In indirect counterpoint to Hurtado's description, Peppard (2011: 102) writes: "The context of the verse in Romans suggests that, in any case, Paul is not trying to *separate* the divine sonship of Christ from the divine sonship of Christians. On the contrary, he draws them as closely together as he can. 'Conformed to the image of his Son' and 'firstborn of many brothers' are meant to unify all those who share in the spirit of the resurrection, the family spirit that binds them under one father."

[59]See Schreiner 1998: 428.

[60]Scott 1992: 249, 251.

[61]See Byrne 2007: 253n17; Scott 1992: 244.

[62]Jewett and Kotansky 2007: 501; see Morris 1988: 317. Jewett and Kotansky (2007) do not suggest that Paul returns to Rom 4 at Rom 8:17, nor do they say what the inheritance is other than the relationship.

[63]Jewett and Kotansky 2007: 501-2.

between humanity and the physical world in Romans 8:19-22.[64] Even Byrne,
who draws the connection between Romans 8:17 and Romans 4:13, spiri-
tualizes the inheritance into eternal life:

> With the sonship status established, v. 17 moves on to the deduction that as
> sons of God we are also heirs. It is at this stage that the ζήσεσθε of v. 13
> finally receives its full support from vv. 14-17 considered as a whole. To be
> an "heir (of God)" is to be one destined to receive the inheritance of eternal
> life from his hands. The progress from the idea of sonship to that of in-
> heritance is a natural one and one may think that Paul here simply pursues
> an image that comes easily to mind. However, the description of the eschat-
> ological blessings and specifically eternal life in "inheritance" terms is char-
> acteristic of the Jewish background.[65]

Eternal life is certainly one of the many blessings given by God to his
eschatological family, but it is not a result of their adoption as sons—not,
at least, in Romans 8:13. Rather, like adoption, the gift of eternal life is a
result of the Spirit's indwelling of the believer. No longer is the believer
enslaved to death but is granted freedom and life. The inheritance and
eternal life are certainly not unrelated; but they are not, as Byrne suggests,
synonymous. Instead, the inheritance is the physical world, the physical
land of Genesis 12; 15, now expanded to include the cosmos and everything
in it. God's family will possess the creation that bears his name.[66] Bringing
together the Abrahamic and Davidic promises, Scott recognizes the fulfillment of both in believers' co-inheritance with the Messiah, which he
describes as "universal sovereignty"

> when the Son will be the first-born among many brothers and sisters
> (Rom 8:29; cf. 2 Ps 89:27). At that time the sons of God will share in the

---

[64]I will return to this relationship in §7.2.1.

[65]Byrne 1979: 101-2. Byrne's emphasis on the recourse to eternal life in Rom 8:13 is muted in
his Romans commentary. There his understanding of Paul's dependence on Rom 4 is more
developed than it was in 1979. He writes, "The motif . . . occurs very frequently with regard
to the promise God made to Abraham regarding possession of the Land; in the later tradition,
with the broadening of the 'Land' promise to embrace both the present and future world,
'inheritance' came eventually to embrace the whole complex of eschatological blessings promised to Israel": 2007: 251.

[66]Jesus picks up this theme in the Beatitudes, saying, "Blessed are the meek, for they shall inherit
the earth" (Mt 5:5). Closer yet to Paul's terms elsewhere, those who are children of God will
inherit the kingdom of God (1 Cor 6:9, 10; 15:50; Gal 5:21), a metonym for God's sovereign
rule over all that exists.

Abrahamic promise of universal sovereignty as fellow-heirs with Christ the
Messiah (Rom 8:17; cf. Rom 4:13; 8:32; Gal 4:1). Hence the present and future
aspects of *huiothesia* in Romans 8 reflect successive stages of participation
in the Son by the Spirit and, as such, constitute ways that believers share
with the Son in the Davidic promise.[67]

Indeed, in their adoption as children of God in the Firstborn Son of God,
believers are given their portion of the inheritance: participation in the
Messiah's "universal sovereignty."

6.2.2. Participation in the Son's glory in Romans 8:17. With this understanding of συγκληρονόμος in Romans 8:17, Paul's passive use of συνδοξάζω
becomes all the more obvious. In this section I draw together what I have
already established in previous chapters, namely, that believers' final glorification in Romans is their reinstatement to Adamic rule over creation
and that the Firstborn Son of God already reigns over creation as the
Messiah who is the new Adam. As believers share in the Firstborn Son's
inheritance, his possession of the world, so also believers share in the
Firstborn Son's eschatological rule over that world as God's reigning representatives.[68] This is the heart of Romans 8:17-30 and Romans 8:29b
and is thus the heart of my argument: as children of God, believers are
coheirs with the Son of God and thus share in his glory: they are conformed to the image of the Son, who rules as God's firstborn and as
humanity's representative.

I note first that, just as believers' sonship is what Hurtado calls a "derived
sonship," and thus their inheritance is a derived inheritance, so also is
believers' eschatological glory. As Paul makes clear through the use of the
passive in Romans 8:17 (συνδοξασθῶμεν), believers' glory is not something
intrinsic to themselves, but it comes to them as part of their union with
Christ. As those who share in the Sonship of the Firstborn Son, they too
are "made to share" in Christ's glory. As Bruce rightly notes, believers "are
fellow heirs with Christ because the glory which they are to inherit by
grace is the glory which is his by right (*cf.* Jn. 17:22-24)."[69]

---

[67]Scott 1993: 17.

[68]I will discuss the temporal aspects of believers' glorification in §7.2.2.

[69]Bruce 2003: 159. He says very little about Rom 8:17 otherwise, making no mention of the
Abrahamic promises, the nature of either glory or inheritance, or the way in which believers
demonstrate their inheritance and glory.

Again, I return to the example offered by Newman in his now-classic treatment of δόξα and its cognates in Paul's letters. On the use of συνδοξάζω in Romans 8:17, Newman writes: "The passive form of συνδοξάζω in Rom. 8:17 refers to a metamorphosis into Glory and therefore relates the verb to a paradigmatic field of words and constructions for spiritual transformation (e.g., μεταμορφόομαι, Rom. 12:2; 2 Cor. 3:18)."[70] He suggests additionally that, in both Romans 8:17 and Romans 8:30, "The verb can also be used to denote eschatological transformation of the state of possessing divine presence."[71] And though I emphasize Newman's interpretation here, he is certainly not alone. Hultgren, for example, writes, "To be 'glorified with Christ' . . . means to share in his glory in the presence of God, made possible by resurrection."[72]

I find a number of weaknesses in this understanding of believers' eschatological glorification in Romans 8:17. First, to suggest that it is part of a "paradigmatic field of words of constructions for spiritual transformation" is simply unfounded. Newman gives no support for this suggestion, other than to say that it shares similarities with μεταμορφόομαι in Romans 12:2 and 2 Corinthians 3:18. Μεταμορφόομαι does fall into a field of "transformation" signifiers, as van Kooten demonstrates;[73] συνδοξάζω, however, does not, even in a passive form. Second, Newman's analysis overlooks the significance of Paul's συν-compounds throughout this section and particularly the fact that συνδοξάζω is one—the participatory importance being suggested all the more by the relationship to συγκληρονόμοι and συμπάσχω in the same verse. Third, the relationship between συγκληρονόμοι and συνδοξάζω is strikingly close. Whether designated as coterminous or synonymous, the meaning of συγκληρονόμοι has direct impact on the meaning of συνδοξάζω. And, as I demonstrated above, to be a co-inheritor with Christ is to share in his universal sovereignty. Finally, I demonstrated in chapter three that Paul's use of δόξα in Romans 8:18, 21 implies believers' exalted status as humans designated to have dominion over creation, and not, contra Newman, a restored relationship between humanity and God.

---

[70]Newman 1992: 158.
[71]Newman 1992: 158. On 2 Thess 1:10 Newman (1992: 159) writes: "The ideas of God's (i) future (ii) self-manifestation are (iii) coordinated with the believer's transformation into Glory."
[72]Hultgren 2011: 317.
[73]See van Kooten 2008a: 69-91.

If such is the case in Romans 8:18, 21, where the semantic function stems from the verbal cognate in Romans 8:17, then the verbal cognate should bear the same or at least a similar semantic function.

In Romans 8:17, where believers' shared inheritance with the Son implies their participation in the Son's universal sovereignty by means of their union with Christ, the best designation for believers' shared glory with the Son is their participation in his glory as the Son of God. Though Esler does not examine this verse, he nevertheless insightfully translates the final clause, ἵνα καὶ συνδοξασθῶμεν, as "in order that they might be honored with him"—a translation that more closely resembles my proposed interpretation of συνδοξάζω than Newman's. Believers are reinstated to glory on the basis of their position as children of God, sharing in the inheritance of the Son, who as the Messiah and new Adam is already crowned with glory and honor.

6.2.3. Participation in the Son's sufferings in Romans 8:17. Before turning to the glorification of believers in Romans 8:30, a brief note on the relationship between συμπάσχω and συνδοξάζω in Romans 8:17 is necessary. Paul refers to the fact that believers "rejoice in tribulation" (καυχώμεθα ἐν ταῖς θλίψεσιν) in Romans 5:3. In Romans 8:17 the reference is to believers' shared suffering with Christ (συμπάσχομεν) and in Romans 8:18 to believers' sufferings of the present time (τὰ παθήματα τοῦ νῦν καιροῦ). In each case suffering is closely linked with glory: the "hope of glory" in Romans 5:2, participation in the Messiah's glory in Romans 8:17, and future glory in Romans 8:18.

Paul does not articulate the nature of the suffering in Romans 5:3 and Romans 8:17-18. Recent commentators either offer no comments on the nature of the suffering[74] or suggest the sufferings in these texts refer to the general hardships of preresurrection life.[75] Burke suggests, along with Moo[76] and others: "For God's children who live on this side of eternity,

---

[74]E.g., Byrne (2007) on Rom 8:17, 18; Schreiner (1998) on Rom 8:17, 18; Wright (2002) on Rom 5:3; 8:17. Intriguingly, Gorman (2009) never references Rom 5:3 and only mentions Rom 8:18 in relation to the theme of Rom 8:18-25.

[75]E.g., Moo 1996: 302-3 on Rom 5:3 and p. 511 on Rom 8:18. Käsemann (1980: 231) suggests only that the suffering in Rom 8:18 is shared between believers and creation.

[76]If Moo sees a connection between Rom 5:3 and Rom 8:17, then he contradicts himself in Rom 8:17 by stating that "the suffering Paul speaks of here refers to the daily anxieties, tensions, and persecutions that are *the lot of those who follow the one who was 'reckoned with the transgressors'* (Luke 22:37)": 1996: 506; emphasis mine. He specifically says on Rom 5:3 that the

sufferings may be manifested through persecution, illness, bereavement and, of course, death itself."[77] Of those who suggest something more general, a number point out the sufferings expected at the end times, as in Mark 13:7-8, 19-20 (see Jas 1:2-4; 1 Pet 1:6-7);[78] others note the list of tribulations at Romans 8:35-39;[79] but most do all of the above throughout the three verses. Jewett suggests that the suffering in Romans 5:3 and Romans 8:17-18 refers specifically to the persecution of Roman Christians. This, he argues, is indicated by Paul's inclusion of the article in Romans 5:3—ταῖς θλίψεσιν and ἡ θλῖψις.[80]

What is important for our purposes here, though, is not the nature of the suffering but the implied relationship between suffering and glory. Paul writes: συγκληρονόμοι δὲ Χριστοῦ, εἴπερ συμπάσχομεν ἵνα καὶ συνδοξασθῶμεν. The εἴπερ is most commonly taken as conditional: "We will be glorified with Christ *provided that* we first suffer with Him."[81] Within traditional interpretations of glorification, the implied assumption then becomes that cosuffering with Christ progresses into coglorification with Christ; suffering produces sanctification, which in its most completed form is glorification. In recognition, then, of the semantic relationship between Romans 8:17 and Romans 8:29, 30, believers' conformity in Romans 8:29 is understood to refer to both suffering and glory. This is the reason why Gorman can write:

---

sufferings experienced are not limited to "those sufferings caused directly by the believer's profession of Christ."

[77]Burke (2006: 182) on Rom 8:18, who goes on to cite Loane. Loane, however, seems to argue a point more similar to Jewett than Burke is: "St. Paul's basic idea was that suffering in one form or another belongs to the experience of *all who are members of God's household.* . . . Not all are martyrs; not all are captives; not all are driven into exile for Christ's sake; not all are in fact called upon to bear insult, scorn, or assault on the open stage of the world's hostility. Many indeed are still called, just as many were called when St. Paul wrote these words, for the world is no more in love with God and his *children* now than it was before. And yet even those whose path has been most sheltered in the goodness of God will be called to endure suffering somehow, some time, in the course of this life, if they . . . live as *sons of God*": Loane 1968: 76; emphasis mine.

[78]E.g., Käsemann (1980: 134), who suggests θλῖψις in Rom 5:3 is the "end-time affliction which comes on the Christian as a follower of the messiah Jesus"; see Beker (1980: 146) on Rom 5:3; Byrne (2007: 166) on Rom 5:3; Schreiner (1998: 255) on Rom 5:3.

[79]Byrne (2007: 166) on Rom 5:3; Wright (2002: 595) on Rom 8:18.

[80]Jewett and Kotansky 2007: 353.

[81]See, e.g., Käsemann 1980: 229; Dunn 1988a: 456; Fitzmyer 1993: 502; Byrne 2007: 254; Moo 1996: 505-6; Schreiner 1998: 428; Dunn 1998b: 485; Burke 2008: 285; Ortlund 2014: 126.

Paul, then, experiences hope in the midst of suffering, but he understands his suffering not merely as something to be endured or conquered because it enables him to participate in the sufferings of Christ, the final end of which is glory. This is cruciform hope: conformity to the image of God's Son (Rom. 8:29) in suffering and glory, in the present and the future.[82]

In this reading conformity in the present is represented by suffering, and conformity in the future will be represented by glorification.

Gorman is correct to suggest that hope resides in the midst of suffering; he is, however, incorrect to suggest that the end of suffering is glory, as if the terms function on the same plane, the suffering side of which is in the present age and the glory side of which is in the future age. Undoubtedly Paul is speaking in Romans 8:17 to the future glorification of believers with Christ, and it is probably correct to read the εἴπερ as conditional,[83] but this does not warrant a reading in which suffering progresses into glorification, and it certainly does not warrant a reading of Romans 8:29 that suggests that present conformity is represented by suffering and future conformity is represented by glorification, that is, a complete(d) sanctification. I will argue in the following chapter that glorification, at least in Romans 8:30, does not imply only a future glorification. If glorification is understood as I have proposed here, namely, as being placed in an exalted status or status of honor associated with a position of authority or rule, and that status is the Firstborn Son's as the Messiah and new Adam, then suffering is not a preresurrection version of being glorified with Christ, as Gorman suggests. Rather, it is a present reality contemporaneous with present glory (Rom 8:30) and is a reality that will cease when glorification is experienced in its fullness in the future (Rom 8:17). This will become more clear in the following chapter when I discuss the present aspects of glorification in Romans 8:30.

Much the same can be said for the relationship between suffering and glory in Romans 8:18: Λογίζομαι[84] γὰρ ὅτι οὐκ ἄξια τὰ παθήματα τοῦ νῦν καιροῦ πρὸς τὴν μέλλουσαν δόξαν ἀποκαλυφθῆναι εἰς ἡμᾶς. Paul's reference to suffering here likely refers to the participatory suffering just mentioned in Romans 8:17, and so also for the glory. With Gorman and others, Moo

---

[82]Gorman 2001: 329-30.
[83]Contra Jewett and Kotansky 2007: 502-3.
[84]Moo 1996: 511: Paul uses λογίζομαι "with the connotation of 'realize from the standpoint of faith'"; see Rom 2:3; 3:28; 6:11; 14:14; 1 Cor 4:1; 2 Cor 10:7, 11; 11:5; Phil 3:13; 4:8.

suggests that "Paul is not so much interested in [suffering's] relationship to glory as he is in their sequence": suffering now, glory later.[85] Though this sequential aspect is clearly part of Romans 8:17-18, where Paul just happens to refer to believers' *final* and *absolute* glorification, contra Moo, in Romans 8:17-18 the intrinsic relationship between the two is no less important. If glory in Romans 8:18 is not "a qualitatively new relational sphere of existence for the 'sons,'" as suggested by Newman,[86] but humanity's renewed status as sons of God and thus participants in the new Adam, then no reason exists to read Paul as saying that suffering will be replaced by glory in the eschaton, as if glory in the future is the completion of suffering in the present.

6.3. A Reglorified Humanity in Romans 8:30

Paul returns to this theme of believers' glory in Romans 8:30, and here Paul's narrative of glory comes to its glorious climax—or rather climax of glory. From Romans 1:23 and Romans 3:23, and with Romans 2:7, 10; 5:2; 8:17, 18, 21 in the middle, Paul has come around full circle in Romans 8:29-30 in describing humanity's response to God's intentions for it.[87] Because the majority of what could be said about the semantic function of δοξάζω in Romans 8:30 has already been adumbrated elsewhere, I will keep my comments here brief.

Newman's treatment of συνδοξάζω in Romans 8:17 applies equally to his treatment of δοξάζω in Romans 8:30: it denotes believers' transformation into the manifest presence of God. BDAG classifies it under "to cause to have splendid greatness, *clothe in splendor, glorify*."[88] Dunn writes on both Romans 8:17 and Romans 8:30, "Since δόξα describes the radiance of heaven and of God in particular, in contrast to the duller shades of earth, it is natural to describe the hoped-for transformation to heaven in terms of

---

[85]Moo 1996: 508-9.

[86]Newman 1992: 225-26.

[87]See Ortlund 2014. Van Kooten (2008a: 203) recognizes the connection between Rom 1:23 and Rom 8:29/30, though not in terms of glory but of image: "Whereas pagans have 'exchanged the glory of the immortal God for the likeness of an *image* of a mortal human being or birds or four-footed animals or reptiles' (Rom 1.23), it is through being predestined to become of the same form as the *image* of Christ, God's Son (Rom. 8.29) that man is able to overcome the downfall of humanity"; emphasis original.

[88]BDAG 2000: 258.

δόξα."[89] And Fitzmyer simply describes "glorification" as "the final destiny for all who put faith in Christ Jesus."[90] Interestingly, many scholars fail to define δοξάζω in either Romans 8:17 or Romans 8:30. In his examination of the temporal aspects of δοξάζω in Romans 8:30,[91] Ortlund helpfully writes, "The point is that *Romans 8:30 restores what was lost according to Rom 3:23.* Having been born in Adam and thus into sin, lacking the divine glory that was ours in Eden (3:23), in union with Christ that glory is restored: 'we are glorified' (8:30). That is, we are restored to 'the image of his Son' (8:29), the new Adam."[92] Unlike most, Ortlund is aware of the various approaches to understanding glory, particularly that which is possessed by or characterizes humanity. He continues:

> In systematic theological terms glory is generally thought of as a visible resplendence or beauty, as seen especially in the writings of such thinkers as Augustine, Jonathan Edwards, or Hans Urs van Balthasar. This should certainly be acknowledged as a connotation of glory as used by Paul and other biblical writers. Yet our investigation indicates that if glory is often referring to what humans (and not only God) possess, Paul would define glory as that which visibly represents a beautiful God. One thinks, for example, of the theophanic cloud of glory that was the tangible representation of Yahweh. Such a definition of glory acknowledges the close connection between image and glory, since image is clearly that which visibly represents God on earth—namely, humanity, supremely in Christ and derivatibly in those united to him. . . . Glorification, then, is the restatement of the divine image. It is to be rehumanized.[93]

Despite his recognition of the connections between Romans 8:23, glory, image, and believers' rehumanization in the new Adam in Romans 8:30, the glory nevertheless remains for Ortlund the "divine glory," namely the theophanic presence of God.

Here again I wish to contest this interpretation of believers' eschatological glory and to suggest, rather, that believers' eschatological glory, or transformation into glory, is best understood as their transformation into an exalted

---

[89]Dunn 1988a: 456-57.
[90]Fitzmyer 1993: 526.
[91]I will return to this topic in the following chapter.
[92]Ortlund 2014: 121; emphasis original.
[93]Ortlund 2014: 129-30.

status as those who participate in the sovereign rule of Christ. First, the end of Paul's "golden chain" is δοξάζω, which is parallel to Romans 8:29b, conformity to the image of the Son.[94] If Romans 8:29b is participation in the image of the Son, who is the representative kingly figure, then so also is believers' glorification in Romans 8:30. Second, glorification in Romans 8:30 picks up coglorification in Romans 8:17, where coglorification is directly related to being co-inheritors; and, as discovered, being co-inheritors refers to participating in the Son's universal sovereignty. Third, it is consistent with not only συνδοξάζω in Romans 8:17 but also believers' δόξα in Romans 8:18, 21, both demonstrated to refer to believers' exalted status. Fourth, it is consistent with Paul's depiction of humanity's rejection of glory in Romans 1:23 and Romans 3:23 and picks up humanity's hope for glory in Romans 2:7, 10; 5:2. Fifth, like Romans 8:17, it follows the LXX use of *glorification* for humanity. Finally, Paul's reference to σύμμορφος in Romans 8:29 and δοξάζω in Romans 8:30 is similar to his use of σύμμορφος and δόξα in Philippians 3:21. There I demonstrated that the text refers to believers' conformity to the resurrection body of Christ, which exists in a state of glory, that is, a position of sovereign rule over the cosmos in fulfillment of Psalm 8. The evidence strongly suggests that believers' glorification in Romans 8:30 entails a transformation of status through participation in the exalted rule of Christ.

Before concluding the treatment of δόξα and δοξάζω in Romans, from Romans 1:23; 2:7, 10; 3:23; 5:2; 8:17, 18, 21, to now Romans 8:30, I wish to return briefly to Ortlund's helpful critique of common approaches to interpreting glory in the Bible. He is right to distinguish between those approaches made by systematicians and biblical theologians, as in the quote above. He further writes on Romans 8:30 in particular (but applicable to each of the examined texts here),

> Rom 8:30 should *first* (not *only*) be read through a disciplined lens of biblical theology, in which we strive to let the text inform our system rather than (in an unhealthy way) our system inform the text. To be sure, it is not only impossible but undesirable to read any given text without a systematic framework. Yet our mindset must be one of self-consciously letting the text tinker with the framework rather than the framework with the text.[95]

---

[94]This connection will be analyzed more fully in the following chapter.
[95]Ortlund 2014: 128; emphasis original.

This is a sentiment that I wholeheartedly echo, along with his further recognition of the importance of "the need for theological formulation that is self-consciously controlled by the text, context, and thought-world of the biblical author, rather than importing connotations of specific words or concepts (such as glorification) into the domain of biblical theology."[96] Ortlund is, of course, speaking to the previous distinctions between systematic and biblical approaches to interpretations of glory and glorification. But I find his important words applicable within the field of biblical scholarship itself and, more specifically, within Pauline scholarship. What I have argued throughout this book is just this: that "importing connotations of specific words or concepts (such as glorification)" into the domain of Paul's epistles—epistles with different contexts, themes, and messages—can only lead to an oversight of what is actually a highly *varied* application of δόξα and δοξάζω throughout his epistles.

In short, what I have argued here in Romans 8:29-30 is that Paul sees that those conformed to the image of the Son are those who, though once participants in the Adamic submission to the powers of sin and death, now participate in the reign of the new Adam over creation. Mankind's position on earth as God's vicegerents to his creation is now restored, though now through the image of the Son of God, who reigns as God's preeminent vicegerent.[97] The depiction of humanity being crowned with glory and honor and established with dominion over creation in Psalm 8 is now again a reality, through both the Firstborn Son of God and those who participate in his exalted status, that is, his glory. Byrne notes that this is the "full arrival at the goal of God's intent for human beings" in Romans 8:29.[98] Those conformed to the image of God's Son participate in the

---

[96]Ortlund 2014: 129.

[97]See Jewett and Kotansky 2007: 529-30. Cranfield (1975: 432) mentions this connection but does not develop it.

[98]Byrne 2007: 268-69; see Byrne 2007: 253n17: "For Paul the risen Christ, as 'Last Adam' (1 Cor. 15:45), is heir already in possession of the inheritance (Phil. 2:9-11); believers are heirs in waiting, and enjoy this status solely in virtue of their union with him (see also Gal. 3:16, 26-29). In 1 Cor. 3:21b-23 Paul states that 'all things' belong to Christians in that they 'belong' to Christ; their union with the risen Lord as 'Last Adam' sets them in line to come into that lordship of the universe which, in the development of Gen. 1:26-28 (cf. also Psalm 8) in the Jewish tradition, represents God's original design for human beings"; see also Byrne 2007: 272-73n29. Byrne's reading of the passage has changed considerably since his publication of *Sons of God—Seed of Abraham* in 1979. His comments in *Romans* include themes of ruling,

Firstborn Son's sovereign position over creation as adopted members of God's eschatological family and, *as such*, as a reglorified humanity.

6.4. CONCLUSION

This chapter has focused on the restoration of believers' glory through their adoption into the family of God and thus their participation in the inheritance and glory of the Firstborn Son. From Romans 8:1-16 Paul traces believers' transition from bondage to sin (Rom 8:1-4) to life in the Spirit (Rom 8:5-13) to adoption into God's family (Rom 8:14-17) on the basis of a new-exodus motif. In Romans 8:17 Paul presents the theme of believers sharing in the inheritance and glory of the Son, both of which refer to believers participating in the universal sovereignty of the Son. These themes are picked up again in Romans 8:29-30. In Romans 8:30 in particular, glorification follows the pattern set previously in Romans vis-à-vis humanity's eschatological glory. Believers' conformity to Christ in Romans 8:29 and glorification in Romans 8:30 entails a transformation of status in Christ. We are now poised to address, as a final word on the topic, the temporal aspects of this transformation.

---

reigning, and sovereignty, as well as connections with Gen 1:26-28 and Ps 8, none of which feature in the earlier publication.

PURPOSED FOR CONFORMITY

U p to this point I have for all intents and purposes ignored the majority of Romans 8:28-30 that surrounds Romans 8:29bc; it is too deep a canyon for us to walk incautiously along its rim. Some risks, however, must be taken. In this seventh and final chapter, I turn our attention to the placement of Romans 8:29b within Romans 8:17-30 more generally and Romans 8:28-30 in particular. I will suggest that "conformity to the image of [God's Firstborn] Son," that is, vocational participation in the Firstborn Son's exalted position over creation, is the task for which believers are called and purposed *in the present as well as the future*. This seventh chapter consists of two parts. First, I will briefly outline the embedded structure of Romans 8:28-30 and discuss the role of κλητός in Romans 8:28 and καλέω in Romans 8:30 within that structure; and second, I will argue that, contrary to the majority of scholarship, believers already manifest their decreed calling and purpose by participating in the Son's glory in the present.

7.1. GOD'S ETERNAL DECREE: CALLED WITH A PURPOSE: ROMANS 8:28-30

I first examine the notion of believers as τοῖς κατὰ πρόθεσιν κλητοῖς οὖσιν in Romans 8:28c and again in Romans 8:30. Both Romans 8:28 and Romans 8:30 are pithy, yet pregnant with theological and narratival weight. For Paul, the narrative of God's commitment to his covenant begins and ends with the purposes of God's calling. People in Christ are God's children, Paul declares, on the basis of God's eternal decree, "rooted in God's inscrutable will."[1] God has foreknown and predestined his eschatological family; he has called them, justified them, and glorified them *according to his purpose.*

The history of interpretation of Romans 8:28-30, particularly with a view to the *ordo salutis* or the "golden chain," is too vast to recount here.[2] Nor do I wish to provide an individually focused treatment of each of the heavyweight terms. My goal here is only to highlight these verses as a bold brushstroke on Paul's canvas of Romans. I suggest that the three verses work together to form a composite whole with an often-overlooked internal structure—a structure by which Paul tells the creational and covenantal narrative of redemption. God calls his people because of a commitment to his creation and his covenant, which includes his commitment to accomplishing his aims through a redeemed humanity. The structure of Romans 8:28-30 makes this clear.

7.1.1. *Romans 8:28-30 and its structure.* Romans 8:28-30 reads:

Οἴδαμεν δὲ ὅτι τοῖς ἀγαπῶσιν τὸν θεὸν (Rom 8:28a)

πάντα συνεργεῖ εἰς ἀγαθόν, (Rom 8:28b)

τοῖς κατὰ πρόθεσιν κλητοῖς οὖσιν. (Rom 8:28c)

ὅτι οὓς προέγνω, καὶ προώρισεν (Rom 8:29a)

συμμόρφους τῆς εἰκόνος τοῦ υἱοῦ αὐτοῦ, (Rom 8:29b)

εἰς τὸ εἶναι αὐτὸν πρωτότοκον ἐν πολλοῖς ἀδελφοῖς· (Rom 8:29c)

οὓς δὲ προώρισεν, τούτους καὶ ἐκάλεσεν· (Rom 8:30a)

καὶ οὓς ἐκάλεσεν, τούτους καὶ ἐδικαίωσεν· (Rom 8:30b)

οὓς δὲ ἐδικαίωσεν, τούτους καὶ ἐδόξασεν. (Rom 8:30c)

Despite its significance for this project and theologically within Romans 8:28-30, Romans 8:29b is not Paul's main point—at least not directly. Paul's main point is Romans 8:28b: God has called his people with the ultimate goal of fulfilling his purposes through them. In Romans 8:29a, then, Paul steps back even behind God's calling and says that God's people were foreknown and predestined by God with the ultimate end of being "conformed to the image of [his Firstborn] Son," which he identifies as glorification in Romans 8:30. In all the verses there is divine action with an ultimate goal and a specific means to that goal. Structurally, it looks like this:

---

[1]Wright 2004a: 93; see Hurtado 1993: 905.
[2]See Muller 1985: 215-16 and esp. Fahlbusch 2003.

Rom 8:28   called ...   according to his purpose.

Rom 8:29   foreknew—predestined ...   to be conformed to the
                  image of his Son.

In Romans 8:30, then, Paul brings together Romans 8:28-29, albeit now
with *called* occurring after *predestined*:

Rom 8:30   predestined—called—justified—glorified

With Romans 8:30 the reader realizes that the two ultimate goals of
Romans 8:28 and Romans 8:29 (i.e., fulfilling God's purposes and conformity
to the Son) are not only the same but are the same as the final divine
action in Romans 8:30 (i.e., glorified):

Rom 8:28   called ...   according to his purpose.

Rom 8:29   foreknew—predestined ...   to be conformed to the
                  image of his Son.

Rom 8:30   predestined—called—justified ...   glorified.

If the embedded sequence of divine actions and ultimate goals is brought
to the fore and rearranged according to their logical and theological or-
dering, particularly with regard to *called*, the three verses take new shape:

Romans 8:28-30   foreknew—predestined—called (and justified) according
                  to ...

     his ultimate purpose (general)
     which is to say, being:
     conformed to the image of his Son (implicit)
     or
     glorified (explicit)

Fee correctly identifies "the key element in this recital of divine purpose:
what God had in mind from the beginning was that human redemption
should take the form of our being 'conformed to the *image* of his *Son*, so
that he [the Son] might be the *firstborn* among many brothers and sisters,'"[3]
or, put another way around, that they might be "glorified." My emphasis
here is on the *ultimate* goal of the calling, which Paul makes clear is not
believers' justification, contrary to much of Protestant post-Reformation

---

[3]Fee 2007: 249; emphasis original.

theology. The goal is a redeemed people through whom God brings redemption to the rest of the cosmos. The embedded structure of Romans 8:28-30 makes this clear.

7.1.2. Romans 8:28-30: A calling of God's people. As indicated in the structure examined above, Paul emphasizes in Romans 8:28-30 that God has "called" his people according to his "purpose." And despite the amount of ink used to discuss the importance of προγινώσκω,[4] προορίζω,[5] and, dare I add, δικαιόω in Romans 8:29-30 and in Pauline theology in general, their importance in Romans 8:29-30 is relative to that of κλητός in Romans 8:28 and καλέω and δοξάζω in Romans 8:30. Paul uses προγινώσκω and προορίζω merely to modify and enhance the sense of calling as a divine initiative.[6] With Gaffin, I suggest that "the center of Paul's teaching is not found in the doctrine of justification by faith or any other aspect of the *ordo salutis*. Rather, his primary interest is seen to be in the *historia salutis* as that history has reached its eschatological realization in the death and especially the resurrection of Christ."[7] Because I have already examined in detail Romans 8:29bc and Romans 8:30c, and because Romans 8:29a (foreknown and predestined) and Romans 8:30a (predestined) are not Paul's emphases, my focus here will be on Paul's understanding of God's calling and purposing of his people.

Along with the majority of commentators on Paul's use of κλητός in Romans 8:28 and καλέω in Romans 8:30,[8] Byrne suggests that it is the

---

[4]BDAG (2000: 866) suggests it means in Rom 8:29 "to choose [someone] beforehand," opposed to *knowing* beforehand or in advance; emphasis mine. Byrne (2007: 272n29) notes that, as in Rom 11:2, προγινώσκω "reflects a biblical idiom where 'foreknowledge' connotes 'choice' and 'election' as well; see Gen. 18:19; Jer. 1:5; Hos. 13:5 (Hebrew); Amos 3:2; also 1QH 9:29-30)"; see 1 Pet 1:20, and though προγινώσκω is not found in Eph 1:4, the sense is "election" "before the foundation of the world" and thus shares the same meaning.

[5]BDAG (2000: 873) suggests "decide upon beforehand, *predetermine*"; emphasis original. Burke (2006: 78) quotes Liefeld (1997: 38), who says, "We are not merely predestined but predestined *for* or *to* something"; emphasis mine. Contrary to Burke's (2006: 78) suggestion, that to which believers are predestined is not adoption but glory, the result of adoption (Rom 8:17).

[6]See Hasitschka 2010: 353.

[7]Gaffin 1987: 13; see also 29: "It may be maintained here as a working principle, subject to further verification, that whatever treatment Paul gives to the application of salvation to the individual believer is controlled by his redemptive-historical outlook."

[8]Within Romans itself, Paul makes this purpose of calling explicit. Paul is called to be an apostle (Rom 1:1; see 1 Cor 1:1); believers are called to belong to Jesus (Rom 1:6) and to be saints (Rom 1:7; see 1 Cor 1:2). Elsewhere in Paul, believers are called to freedom (Gal 5:13), to peace (1 Cor 7:15; Col 3:15), to hope (Eph 1:18; 4:4), to a calling (Eph 4:1; 2 Tim 1:9), to holiness/obedience (1 Thess 4:7), to salvation (2 Thess 2:14), to eternal life (1 Tim 6:12).

formation or the creation of a people called out for God and as God's children.[9] This association of calling and sonship is recurrent in Jewish literature.[10] In the same way that Paul uses καλέω in Romans 4:17 ("[who] calls into existence things that do not exist") to denote an act of creation, so also is Israel's formation as the descendants of Abraham (Gen 12:2) and as a nation called out of Egypt (Hos 11:1)—a connection made previously when I examined Paul's references to sonship and adoption as exodus motifs in Romans 8:14-16. Additionally, numerous references exist in Deutero-Isaiah to God's calling of Israel as his people (Is 41:9; 42:6; 43:1; 48:12).[11]

Yet, in contrast to the use of κλητός and καλέω in Jewish literature, and in contrast to the arguments highlighted previously of Stowers and Johnson Hodge regarding the identity of Gentiles alone as the adopted children of God and siblings though Christ, Paul's use of κλητός and καλέω in Romans 8:28, 30 is not exclusive. Rather, the calling of believers in Romans 8:28, 30 implies God's faithfulness to his eschatological family—a family now composed of both Jew and Gentile (see Zech 2:11). Rosner recognizes what Stowers and Johnson Hodge do not. He writes,

> With respect to the election of Israel, in Romans Paul opposes the notion
> that the Jews . . . constitute the people of God. . . . Instead, the church com-
> prises the new people of God, whom he describes as the elect (8:33); called
> (1:6-7; 8:28, 30; 9:7, 12, 24-28); beloved (1:7; 9:25); saints (1:7); beloved children
> of Abraham (4:11-12, 16-17); and the true circumcision (2:28-29).[12]

Likewise, Byrne notes that "the 'call' that has gone out as the first stage in the realization of God's plan refers to the summons contained in the gospel. By means of the gospel God has 'called' into being a People of God, made up of Jews and Gentiles (cf. 9:24; 1 Cor. 1:26), destined to display God's original design for human beings."[13] As Byrne hints, this understanding of καλέω is certainly present in Romans 9:24.

---

[9]Byrne 2007: 273n30.

[10]Hos 1:10 (MT, LXX 2:1); 11:1; Sir 36:17; Jub. 1:25; Ps-Philo 18:6; 4 Ezra 6:58; 4QDibHam 3:4-5. See Byrne 2007: 273.

[11]Israel is referred to as God's elected or chosen people at numerous points in Jewish history: Deut 7:6; 14:2; Ps 105:6; Is 43:20; 45:4; Sir 46:1; 47:22; Wis 3:9; 4:15; Jub. 1:29; 1QS 8:6; CD 4:3-4.

[12]Rosner 2013: 218.

[13]Byrne 2007: 269; see also Burke 2006: 172.

Nevertheless, though this new identity is unequivocally part of Paul's underlying paradigm, it is not Paul's emphasis in Romans 8:28, 30. With καλέω, rather, Paul affirms God's faithfulness to his covenant people. God promised Abraham a family (Gen 18:19; 21:1; see Rom 4:21) and Israel the land as their inheritance (Ex 12:5; 32:13; Deut 9:28; 12:20; 19:8; 27:3; Josh 23:5; see Acts 7:5). Paul picks up these promises in Romans 4:21: "[Abraham was] fully convinced that [God] was able to do what he had promised." Likewise, God also promised Israel, saying, "I will take you to be my people, and I will be your God" (Ex 6:7 ESV; see Lev 26:12; Deut 26:19; 29:13; Jer 7:23; 11:4; 30:22; Ezek 36:28).[14] Rather than emphasizing that God is doing something new in believers' calling in Romans 8:28, 30, Paul declares that God has actually done something quite rooted in the past. God has brought to fruition an ancient element of Israel's history—his covenantal promises to Abraham and to Israel as a people set apart for God. In this case, God has done so by calling believers to be his own, bringing them into a life of faith and obedience to God.[15]

7.2. Called with a Present Purpose: Romans 8:17-30

Up until this point I have discussed conformity and glorification with an undefined time. We now must ask, "At what point are believers conformed to the image of the Son?" Or, "When are God's children glorified?" The answer to this question is not easy to secure, particularly in Romans 8, where Paul's articulation of the redemptive narrative is decidedly *inter tempora*. In Romans 8:17-18, the glory of believers is yet to come; according to Romans 8:30, believers are already glorified. The same scenario exists with believers' adoption: in Romans 8:15 believers have already received adoption, but in Romans 8:23 that adoption is yet to come. I will return to this conundrum below. Dunn remarks that "what complicates things for Paul is the fact that, contrary to conventional Jewish apocalyptic expectation, these two 'ages' have not followed each other in orderly sequence;

---

[14]See Deut 1:11; 6:3; 15:6.

[15]See Jer 7:23; 11:4; Eph 4:1; 1 Thess 4:7; 1 Pet 2:21. See Wright (2004a: 93), who notes that "'call' denotes the event that people often refer to as 'conversion,' though of course whereas 'conversion' draws attention to the change of heart and mind in the person concerned, the word 'call' draws attention to God's action and hence places that change of heart and mind already in the category of 'obedience' as well as 'faith' (see e.g. Rom. 1:5)."

they in fact overlap and co-exist at the present time."[16] Yet because the ages overlap and the eschatological age has come in the present, if not yet fully, those currently in the Messiah have also been raised with the Messiah. As Ortlund posits, "We are indeed only glorified with the dawning of the eschaton, the *Endzeit—and this dawning has already broken onto the world stage*, at Christ's coming and particularly at his resurrection."[17] Byrne also rightly notes, "This means that, as far as relations with God are concerned and as attested by the gift of the Spirit, believers already live the life of the new age. As far as their bodily existence is concerned, however, they are still anchored in the present age."[18]

Philip Esler questions the traditional, proleptic "now but not yet" reading of Paul's eschatological framework. He suggests that the Mediterranean culture recognized a trajectory of history in which what comes in the future stems from what exists in the present, rather than as a future age launched at some point in the recent past.[19] The notion of a "now" and "not yet," he writes, is "an unnecessary modern intrusion on Paul's thought."[20] Distinctions are important, no doubt, but on this point, the present reality for Paul is the same either way: the present and future are intricately connected; one reflects a version of the other. As Byrne is noted above as saying, believers' reception of the restored physical body may not occur in the present age, but their participatory lives in Christ have nevertheless begun. The argument, I will suggest, is the same for believers' glorification.

The reader would expect the greatest clue as to when believers are glorified to come in Romans 8:29b or Romans 8:30c itself. Romans 8:29b is of no assistance, however, given that σύμμορφος is an atemporal adjective.[21] Moreover, because the adjective is linked in a cause-effect relationship with Romans 8:29c, σύμμορφος is at least partially ruled by the infinitival purpose clause (εἰς τὸ εἶναι) that determines Romans 8:29c. Neither is interpreting Paul's use of the aorist ἐδόξασεν in Romans 8:30 a straightforward endeavor.

---

[16]Dunn 1998b: 464; see Byrne 2010: 85.
[17]Ortlund 2014: 131; emphasis original.
[18]Byrne 2010: 85.
[19]Esler 2003: 260-65.
[20]Esler 2003: 265.
[21]Nevertheless, Byrne 1979: 118; Barrett 1991: 159-60; Scott 1992: 247 all suggest an entirely future dimension of conformity.

According to traditional grammar rules of Greek, the use of the aorist implies that God has already glorified believers, just as he has already foreknown, predestined, called, and justified his children. For many commentators, though, this use of the aorist is difficult to reconcile with what seems to be a present reality.

Most agree that Paul writes as if he himself were standing in the eschaton and looking back, and the glorification of believers in real time and space has not yet begun.[22] Witherington is representative when he writes, "The verb tenses make it clear that Paul is looking at things from the eschatological end of the process, with even glorification already having transpired. *Doxa*, 'glory,' here refers to the future glory of resurrection."[23] Without qualification, Moo assumes that it is a future glorification: "What makes this interesting is that the action denoted by this verb is (from the standpoint of believers) in the future, while the other actions are past."[24] Moo says that Paul "touches on the ultimate source of assurance that Christians enjoy, and with it he brings to a triumphant climax his celebration of the 'no condemnation' that applies to every person in Christ."[25] Dunn also makes this end-time viewpoint and believers' assurance of salvation the basis for understanding Paul's use of the aorist: "This probably explains the exceptional use of the aorist here ('we were saved'); only in the later Paulines do we find comparable language (Eph. 2:5, 8; 2 Tim. 1:9; Tit. 3:5). . . . Its use here . . . mirrors the character of hope: assured hope assures of completed salvation. The aorists of 8:29-30 reflect the same confidence: God's purpose as seen from its assured end."[26] Schreiner simply says, "The glorification posited here does not begin in this life."[27] Even Esler himself arrives at a similar conclusion, though he does so via a different pathway. Esler writes on *glorified* in Romans 8:30: "If one adopts a more Mediterranean view of time that locks present and future far more closely together, a different solution suggests itself. Now the

---

[22]E.g., Murray 1959: 321; Calvin 1960: 182; Cranfield 1975: 433; Barrett 1991: 160; Scott 1992: 295; Stuhlmacher 1994: 137; Moo 1996: 535-36; Dunn 1998b: 484-86; Witherington with Hyatt 2004: 230. For a comprehensive list, see Ortlund 2014.

[23]Witherington with Hyatt 2004: 230.

[24]Moo 1996: 535-36.

[25]Moo 1996: 536.

[26]Dunn 1998b: 438n129; see also 467.

[27]Schreiner 1998: 454; see Schreiner 2001: 277.

glory is forthcoming, rather than future, and has a direct, organic connection with present experience. It exists on the horizon of the present, even if it is not already here."[28] How this "solution" is different from those posed above is unclear. Though the glory has an "organic connection with present experience," it is nevertheless still "forthcoming" and "not already here." These attempts to make sense of the aorist ἐδόξασεν in Romans 8:30 are typical.

Contrary to Schreiner, Witherington, Moo, and others who maintain this guaranteed future reality, there is no indication within the context of Romans 8:30 that Paul writes from this future standpoint. Assurance alone is not a strong rationale for assuming Paul is writing about believers' guarantee of glorification from a future perspective. I suggest that scholars take this view because their presupposed definition of δόξα requires it: God's people have clearly not yet been brought fully into the divine glory; therefore, the only explanation of the aorist is that, because it is so assured in the future, it can be spoken of as if it were a reality already in the present. This anticipatory interpretation, however, is unsupported.[29]

Dane Ortlund (whose criticisms of particular theological uses of *glory* were noted at the end of the last chapter) has most recently advanced the conversation, arguing thoroughly—though neither exhaustively nor without oversight—that ἐδόξασεν refers to an inaugurated reality.[30] He argues on the basis of several factors: (1) Paul's inaugurated eschatological framework, which dominates throughout Romans 8; (2) the relationship between Romans 8:29b and glorification in Romans 8:30 on the basis of the relationship between δόξα and εἰκών throughout Paul's epistles; (3) justification, just preceding glorification, is primarily regarded as inaugurated;[31] (4) according to Romans 6, believers are united to "the glory-resurrected Christ"; (5) believers' glory is spoken of in the present elsewhere in the New Testament; (6) Psalm 8 speaks of human glory being a present glory and is a text that links δόξα and εἰκών as Paul does. Ortlund's argument is well substantiated on a number of levels, and I direct my readers to his article.

---

[28]Esler 2003: 265.

[29]Moreover, reading the aorist on the basis of verbal aspect theory, while perfectly warranted, by its nature offers no solution. See Porter 1993: 83-109.

[30]Ortlund 2014.

[31]See also Byrne 2007: 269.

In the following paragraphs, I wish to add to Ortlund's contextual reading of Paul's use of the aorist in Romans 8:30. Before doing so, however, I note one point of clarification. On the basis of my proposed interpretation of the denotation of glorification, I too suggest that believers' glorification has already taken place, as have the other aorists in Romans 8:30. But I do not suggest that ἐδόξασεν in Romans 8:30 should be understood as an ingressive aorist. As Ortlund rightly notes on this: "Our argument is not simply that the aorist ἐδόξασεν should be read as an ingressive aorist, indicating the beginning of a process that will one day be completed. Such a reading allows for a beginning of glorification but retains a focus on the future, and understands glorification as a process instead of a single event in two phases."[32] Glorification, according to my working definition, occurs in two stages. On the basis of believers' union with Christ, glorification is a present reality, at least in part. They are free from the powers of sin and death and have received the Holy Spirit, the firstfruits of their adoption. When believers' bodies are resurrected to share in the glory of Christ, as in Philippians 3:21, then they will do so fully.

With this in mind, I wish to add to Ortlund's contextual argument, though on the basis of grounds untouched in his work. I suggest here that believers' present glorification is attested not only on the basis of the six areas presented by Ortlund but also in the immediately preceding verses: Romans 8:26-28 and their relationship backward to Romans 8:17-25 and forward to Romans 8:29-30. The traditional readings of Romans 8:26-27 and Romans 8:28 need rethinking. All three verses are generally read as assurance for believers that, in the midst of suffering, their ultimate good will come, either from the Spirit's intercessory work (Rom 8:26-27) or God who works all things for their good (Rom 8:28). Before looking at these three verses, however, I must return our attention to the hope of creation in Romans 8:18-25. I noted earlier in discussing humanity's glory in Romans 8:18, 21 that it is in Romans 8:18-21 that Paul says believers have a job to do.[33] I now return to the hope of creation

---

[32]Ortlund 2014: 132-33. Contra Byrne (2007: 270), who emphasizes the present hiddenness and future public revelation of glory. Also Jewett and Kotansky (2007: 530), though Jewett does so only in agreement with Käsemann's suggestion of a baptismal tradition (1980: 245), following Eltester (1958: 24-25, 165).

[33]Refer back to §3.3.3.

in Romans 8:18-21 with a view to examining more closely the relationship between creation's anticipated freedom and humanity's glory—a relationship that is then linked to Paul's subsequent points in Romans 8:26-27, 28, 29-30.

7.2.1. The hope of creation.

Thinking back to the narrative of glory that I demonstrated in chapter two, it is here in Romans 8:18-27,[34] framed by Romans 8:17, 28-30, that the final act of Paul's soteriological drama is properly acted out. Here the hope of God's people and the hope of creation are aligned. But what is the hope of creation? And first, what is the κτίσις to which Paul refers? With the majority of recent commentators, I suggest that Paul's use of κτίσις in Romans 8:19-22 is a reference to the nonhuman creation, that is, "nature."[35] The rationale for understanding κτίσις as the subhuman creation is expressed in a number of points. (1) This is the sense behind Paul's use of the word in Romans 1:25; 8:39. (2) This is the sense of κτίσις in the LXX (whether collectively: Wis 2:6; 16:24; 19:6 or in reference to individual creatures: Tob 8:15; Sir 43:25).[36] (3) The personification of nature in the Old Testament, similar to that of κτίσις in Romans 8:19-22,

---

[34]The structure of Rom 8:18-27 is debated. The nuances of the argument will add little to our investigation here, but a brief word is perhaps useful. The structure of Rom 8:18-27 is primarily dependent on one's reading of the threefold use of συστενάζω in Rom 8:22, 23, 26. If the three uses of συστενάζω are parallel, then Rom 8:18-27 is divisible into Rom 8:19-22, 23-25, 26-27. Hahne (2006: 173) suggests that, because the "groaning" of creation in Rom 8:22 and the "groaning" of believers in Rom 8:23 both imply an anxious and thus negative groaning, and the groaning of the Spirit in Rom 8:26 is one of intercession and thus a positive groaning, Paul therefore does not intend a threefold parallel structure; see also Hahne 2006: 175 for an alternate structure. Contra Hahne, Byrne (2010: 88) suggests that the ὡσαύτως at the beginning of Rom 8:26 indicates a parallel use of συστενάζω, despite the differences between Rom 8:22, 23, 26; see Burke (2006: 180), who draws on Byrne (1979: 104). With Byrne, I am persuaded that the ὡσαύτως at the start of Rom 8:26, as well as the sheer presence of a third occurrence of συστενάζω, is evidence enough that the three sections are thus parallel.

[35]This reading began as early as Irenaeus (*Adversus Haereses* 32.1; 5.36.3) and Chrysostom (*Homiliae in epistulam ad Romanos* 14) and continues more recently with Barth 1933: 306-8 (though his shorter commentary on Romans supports κτίσις as "humanity": Barth 1959: 99); Dodd 1954: 108; Cranfield 1975: 411-12; Sanders 1977: 473; Wilckens 1980: 152-53; Morris 1988: 322; Dunn 1988a: 469; Fitzmyer 1993: 506; Moo 1996: 551; Wright 2002: 596; Hahne 2006: 177; Byrne 2007: 256; Jewett and Kotansky 2007: 511. Because the "cosmic" view is the most accepted today, I refer to Cranfield (1975: 411), Christoffersson (1990: 19-21, 33-36), and Hahne (2006: 177-78) for discussions of the less-accepted suggestions and their supporters. Two recent suggestions are not included in these three sources: (1) Fewster's 2013 linguistic work on κτίσις, in which he argues that the term serves as a metaphor for "the body"; and (2) Susan Eastman's suggestion (2002: 273-76) that κτίσις refers to the subhuman creation and nonbelievers who are primarily Israel.

[36]Hahne 2006: 180.

is frequent.[37] (4) Paul echoes the creation narratives of Genesis 1–3.[38] As Adams notes, "Paul is reworking the Genesis story,"[39] which thus limits κτίσις to the subhuman creation. (5) With Fee and Keesmaat, Paul here is picking up the new-exodus motifs of Isaiah 40–66: "God is about to do a 'new thing' (Isa. 43: 18-19), and in the end will establish 'new heavens and a new earth' (Isa. 65: 17; 66:23-3)."[40] (6) Jonathan Moo convincingly argues that in Romans 8:19-22 Paul echoes the cosmic judgment and redemption of the earth and its inhabitants in Isaiah 24–27.[41] (7) Moreover, as numerous commentators point out, κτίσις cannot include nonbelievers because nonbelievers do not wait for the revelation of the sons of God (Rom 8:19).[42] These seven reasons provide strong support for reading κτίσις in Romans 8:19-22 as the nonhuman creation. Now we must ask, "What is its hope?"

Paul writes: τῇ γὰρ ματαιότητι ἡ κτίσις ὑπετάγη, οὐχ ἑκοῦσα ἀλλὰ διὰ τὸν ὑποτάξαντα, ἐφ᾽ ἐλπίδι ὅτι καὶ αὐτὴ ἡ κτίσις ἐλευθερωθήσεται ἀπὸ τῆς δουλείας τῆς φθορᾶς εἰς τὴν ἐλευθερίαν τῆς δόξης τῶν τέκνων τοῦ θεοῦ (Rom 8:20-21).[43] First, contrary to Hahne and the majority of recent scholars,[44] the hope of creation is not to share in the glory of the children

---

[37]Hahne (2006: 181) writes: "Various aspects of nature are frequently ascribed emotions, intellect and will (Pss. 77:16; 97:4-5; 114:3-8; Isa. 1:2; see Luke 19:40). The earth and other parts of nature have sorrow or pain due to human sin (Gen. 4:11; Isa. 24:4, 7; Jer. 4:28; 12:4). They rejoice at human righteousness, the display of God's glory, the vindication of God and the presence of the righteous in the messianic kingdom (Pss. 65:12-13; 98:4, 7-9; Isa. 14:7-8; 55:12). The OT also describes the suffering of the natural world due to human sin (Gen. 3:17; Isa. 24:4-7; 33:9; Jer. 4:4, 11, 26-28) and the transformation of nature in a future golden age of righteousness (Isa. 11:6-9; 65:17-25; 66:22-23)."

[38]The effects of sin on nature are recorded elsewhere in Jewish literature: 4 Ezra 7:11; 1 En. 51:4-5; 2 Bar. 29:1-2, 5-8. See also Is 65:17-19.

[39]Adams 2002: 28.

[40]Fee 2004: 47; see Keesmaat 1999: 97-135; Wright 2004a: 100.

[41]Moo 2008: 83-89; Moo and White 2014: 105-8.

[42]Contra Eastman 2002: 273-76.

[43]On the question of causality and subjection in Rom 8:20, the majority of scholars understand God to be the primary cause of creation's subjection to futility. Byrne (2010: 89) suggests an appropriate balance between God and Adam as the "cause" of creation's subjection: "God was the agent of the subjection (the *hypotaxanta* corresponding to the divine passive in *hypetagē*); Adam was its cause in the sense of meriting this punishment; creation, as the instrument of the divine retribution, was compelled to be the innocent victim in the entire transaction." This is a softening of his previous stance, in which he, against the majority of opinions, considered Adam to be the primary cause of creation's subjection in Rom 8:20: Byrne 2007: 261-62n20.

[44]E.g., Burke (2008: 285): "If Paul here is reworking the Genesis story—which undoubtedly he is—then just as the non-human order had a share in humanity's fall (Gen. 3:17-19) so it will have a share in the future glory through the final revelation of the adopted children of God."

of God, or more pointedly, to be glorified with the children of God. Hahne writes: "Romans 8:19-22 looks forward to the eschatological glory of creation. Even though it traces the present plight of creation to the fall, it does not use the language of a return to paradise or the restoration of pre-fall conditions. Rather, creation will gain more than it lost due to the fall and will have greater glory."[45] The problem with this interpretation is threefold.

First, it assumes that τῆς δόξης τῶν τέκνων τοῦ θεοῦ in Romans 8:21 refers to believers' bodily redemption. David Horrell notes that "if the impact of Adam's sin was universal, bringing decay and death throughout creation, then, so Paul's logic seems to run, God's work of redemption, restoring what was lost, can and must encompass the whole created order, or else it remains only a very partial reversal of the earlier pattern of decay and death."[46] Jeremy Law makes the same point when he states that "redemption cannot be conceived as something which separates and distinguishes between humanity and nature: 'In physical terms, believers are bound together in a common destiny with the whole world and all earthly creatures. So what they experience in their own body applies to all other created things.'"[47] These observations are accurate, but they do not warrant reading creation's hope as sharing in the glory of humanity, as if humanity's glory were merely the redemption of a person's body. No doubt, humanity's glory will include the physical redemption of the body, as in Romans 8:23 (and as seen previously in Phil 3:21 and 1 Cor 15:43), but it certainly is not limited to physical renewal. Creation, too, will be physically redeemed; but, like humanity, creation's hope rests in the results of that physical redemption, that is, freedom.

Second, in Romans 8:18 Paul says that the glory to be revealed is the glory "in us" (εἰς ἡμᾶς). The prepositional phrase should be translated "in us"[48] or "for us" but is usually translated "to us." It is not a glory that believers view from a distance but is, rather, a glory in which they are active participants.[49] Either way, the glory is revealed in relation to the human and not the created order.

---

[45]Hahne 2006: 216 with similar sentiments on 171, 173, 219, 228.
[46]Horrell 2010: 77. See Hahne 2006: 215. See Is 11:6-9; 43:19-21; 55:12-13; Ezek 34:25-31; Hos 2:18; Zech 8:12; 1 En. 45:4-5; 51:4-5; cf. 1 En. 72:1; 4 Ezra 8:51-54; 2 Bar. 29:1-8; Sibylline Oracles 3:777-95.
[47]Law 2010: 232 quoting Moltmann 1985: 68. See also Jervell 1960: 271-84.
[48]The NIV rightly translates the preposition "in"; most other translations elect "to us."
[49]See Murray 1959: 301; Jewett and Kotansky 2007: 510.

Third and most importantly, the text says that in the eschaton creation will obtain not glory but freedom. The genitival relationship of τὴν ἐλευθερίαν and τῆς δόξης is one of means—creation will receive a freedom that comes *by means of* or *by way of* the glory of the children of God. What Paul says in Romans 8:21 is that *when* God's children are glorified, *then* the creation will be liberated from its bondage to corruption. The glorification of God's children will directly result in the freedom of creation. This is why "the creation waits with eager longing for the revealing of the children of God" in Romans 8:19.[50] Creation's hope, therefore, is not to receive glory or physical renewal—though physical renewal is *a hope* of creation's far more than glory is—but freedom. Just as humanity's physical renewal in Romans 8:23; 1 Corinthians 15:49; and Philippians 3:21 will enable men and women to have full dominion over creation as they were intended, so also creation's physical renewal will enable it to be the creation it was intended to be before it became subject to corruption (Rom 8:20). Physical redemption for both creation and humanity is a means to a much greater end: freedom to fulfill God's purposes.[51] Only when God's children are reinstated to their original throne—their crown of glory and position of dominion over creation as expressed in Psalm 8:5-8—will the creation be liberated.

This fits the interpretation of Romans 8, especially Romans 8:17, 29, 30, that I have offered throughout this book. Freedom is one of a number of themes that, following on the narrative started in Romans 5, is prevalent in Romans 8. Believers are free from sin and death (Rom 6:18, 22; 8:2; see Gal 5:1), and creation is set free from futility (ματαιότης)[52] in Romans 8:20 and corruption (φθορά) in Romans 8:21. And the freedom that both believers and creation receive is a freedom to fulfill the purpose of God or, as Hahne rightly notes, "The futility of nature will be removed *so that* it fulfils the purpose for which it was created."[53] So also Byrne, quoting Cranfield: "It is probably safest to see [ματαιότης] retaining its basic sense

---

[50]See Byrne 2010: 90.

[51]This is primarily (though not solely) in opposition to Witherington, who overemphasizes physical renewal as the goal of humanity throughout this section, including "conformed to the image of [God's] Son" in Rom 8:29; refer back to §1.4.2.

[52]Ματαιότης has the sense of "worthlessness" or "purposelessness": BDAG 2000: 621.

[53]Hahne 2006: 215; emphasis mine.

of 'inability to attain its true purpose.'"[54] What the purpose of creation is, Paul does not say. One possible solution is the common Jewish motif of creation's praise of its Creator (e.g., Ps 148).[55] Whatever the true purposes of creation are, as long as it remains in its current state of corruption, those created purposes are thwarted.

7.2.2. Believers' glory and the redemption of creation.

Having now introduced the hope of creation in Romans 8:19-22, I turn our attention to God's calling of believers for his purposes in the present. If the hope of creation is to experience the freedom of fulfilling its created purpose under the glory of God's children, who participate in the glory of the Firstborn Son, how does this contingent relationship work itself out in the present? Or does it? I suggest that, though God's children have not yet fully received their adoption as sons and thus are not yet in full possession of the inheritance, they are nevertheless called with the purpose of cooperating with God to bring restoration to his creation in the present. Discussions regarding humanity's responsibility toward the nonhuman creation are increasingly popular, particularly within discussions surrounding the intersection of ecological concerns and theology.[56] Byrne even goes so far as to suggest that "the future of the world (salvation) does to some extent lie in human hands."[57] He continues by stating, "Hope for the future in this sense takes human action into account. It remains hope in God but it is also hope in the prevailing power of God's grace *working through*, not around or above human cooperation."[58]

This view is not without opposition, however. In direct response to these suggestions, Horrell writes that "Paul does not explicitly tell believers to 'care for the whole creation or to value and preserve non-human creatures'"[59] and "Paul does not say here, at least not explicitly, that humans have a role to play in helping to 'liberate' the creation. The main thrust of the text is to encourage a suffering, vulnerable minority group to endure their

---

[54]Byrne 2010: 89 quoting Cranfield 1975: 413-14. Witherington writes that the best translation is "'ineffectiveness,' inability to reach its goal and raison d'être": 2004: 223.

[55]See Ps 66:1-4; 96:1, 11-12; 97:1; 98:4-9; Is 44:23; 55:12; Joel 2:21-22. See Fretheim (2005: 267-68) for an extended list, most of which are psalms; see Horrell 2010: 134.

[56]Though for an earlier treatment, see Jervell 1960: 282-85; more recently, see Moo 1996: 474, 484; Wright 2002: 602; Bauckham 2010; Byrne 2010; Horrell 2010; Moo 2014.

[57]Byrne 2010: 93.

[58]Byrne 2010: 93; emphasis original.

[59]Horrell 2010: 75.

suffering, with a sure hope that God will bring final deliverance."[60] Horrell is primarily keen to renounce any suggestion that humanity has a God-given right to dominate the earth or to exploit it to its benefit,[61] an emphasis shared by the majority of those who recognize the *positive* role of humanity in creation's redemption.[62]

I also acknowledge with Horrell that Paul does not state directly that humanity plays a role in the redemption of creation. Nevertheless, I propose that Paul does, at a minimum, intimate humanity's cooperation with God within the context, particularly in Romans 8:26-30. This cooperation then is additional support for reading *glorified* in Romans 8:30 as a present reality and not merely as a guarantee of a future reality. More specifically, this cooperation is seen, first, in Romans 8:26-27, where the task of believers is to intercede on behalf of creation, a task made possible only by the help of the Spirit; and, second, in Romans 8:28, where the good that God brings is brought in cooperation with humanity and for the benefit of both humanity and the nonhuman creation. Let's consider each of these in its turn.

Romans 8:26-27: Interceding for the creation. In Romans 8:26-27 Paul writes: Ὡσαύτως δὲ καὶ τὸ πνεῦμα συναντιλαμβάνεται τῇ ἀσθενείᾳ ἡμῶν· τὸ γὰρ τί προσευξώμεθα καθὸ δεῖ οὐκ οἴδαμεν, ἀλλὰ αὐτὸ τὸ πνεῦμα ὑπερεντυγχάνει στεναγμοῖς ἀλαλήτοις· ὁ δὲ ἐραυνῶν τὰς καρδίας οἶδεν τί τὸ φρόνημα τοῦ πνεύματος, ὅτι κατὰ θεὸν ἐντυγχάνει ὑπὲρ ἁγίων.[63] Commentators stumble over these verses because they either misread Paul's point in Romans 8:18-25 that what creation hopes for is physical redemption and/or glory, or because they understand Romans 8:18-25 but misread Romans 8:26-27 as tangential verses on believers' prayer life and therefore fail to make the connection between Romans 8:18-25 and Romans 8:26-27. W. Sanday and A. C. Headlam understand Paul to provide an excursus on prayer, as in *how* to pray,[64] and Käsemann takes it to refer to glossolalia in worship (see 1 Cor 14:14).[65] Neither suggestion offers a rationale for Paul's transition from the hope of creation and God's people in Romans

---

[60]Horrell 2010: 79; see 86-87.
[61]Church of England Report: 2005; Horrell 2010: 136.
[62]Bauckham 2010; Moo 2014.
[63]See Ps 44:21.
[64]See Sanday and Headlam 1902: 213.
[65]Käsemann 1971: 239-41. See Fee 1994: 577-86. Cranfield denies this possibility: 1975: 420-24, as do Schreiner (1998: 445) and Wright (2002: 599).

8:18-25 to two seemingly random verses on prayer. Some commentators, in fact, neglect even to offer a hypothesis for how Romans 8:26-27 relates to Romans 8:18-25 at all.[66]

Most understand the reference to the Spirit's intercession *on behalf of* believers (ὑπὲρ ἁγίων) at the end of Romans 8:27 as *for the benefit of* believers. In other words, that for which believers ought to pray in Romans 8:26 is their own benefit—they ought to pray for themselves. But they themselves are not yet fully redeemed and thus struggle with weakness (ἀσθένεια). This weakness is commonly understood as believers' inability to know what particulars to pray for, whether because the particulars are too great and too extensive for the human mind and heart or because the human mind and heart themselves remain in such great need of restoration.[67] Therefore the Spirit intercedes for them. The result, presumably, is that the Spirit's intercession is efficacious for the benefit of the believer. This interpretation flows smoothly into the traditional interpretation of Romans 8:28, which I examine below. But I suggest that it also contributes to the oft-created unnatural division between Romans 8:18-25 and Romans 8:28-30 and is the reason why it can be seen as an excursus on prayer.

I propose that nothing in the text warrants reading τὸ γὰρ τί προσευξώμεθα καθὸ δεῖ οὐκ οἴδαμεν in Romans 8:26 as a reference to the prayers believers should make only on their own behalf. Instead, what believers ought to pray for in Romans 8:26 and what the Spirit intercedes for in Romans 8:27 is not *only* for the believers' own good but is *also* for the good of the creation, which currently groans, hence Paul's transition from creation to believers in Romans 8:22-23. If this is the case, then the prepositional phrase ὑπὲρ ἁγίων is not *on behalf of the saints* but is *for the benefit of* both the groaning saints and the groaning creation. Wright captures Paul's point here well: "In this condition they do not even know what to pray for, how it is that God will work through them to bring about the redemption

---

[66]See Murray 1959: 310-11. Schreiner suggests Rom 8:26-27 is connected to Rom 8:19-22, 23-25 by linking the idea of hope in Rom 8:19-25 and the Spirit's sustainment of that hope in prayer in Rom 8:26-27; also Moo 1996: 522-23. For a comprehensive overview of differing approaches, see Jewett and Kotansky 2007: 521-24.

[67]Käsemann 1971: 127-28; Cranfield 1975: 421; Dunn 1988a: 477; Fee 1994: 575, 579; Schreiner 1998: 443; contra Jewett and Kotansky (2007: 522), who suggest the weakness is the same as the suffering of Rom 8:18.

of the world."[68] But the Spirit does. The Spirit knows the will of God and thus is able to help (συναντιλαμβάνομαι) believers in their weakness to fulfill their task of interceding (ὑπερεντυγχάνω in Rom 8:26 and ἐντυγχάνω in Rom 8:27) for the groaning creation. Wright continues:

> The point Paul is making . . . is that the Spirit's own very self intercedes within the Christian precisely at the point where he or she, faced with the ruin and misery of the world, finds that there are no words left to express in God's presence the sense of futility (v. 20) and the longing for redemption. It is not . . . that the Spirit intercedes "for us"; that misses the point, and makes Paul repeat himself in the following verse. What Paul is saying is that the Spirit, active within the innermost being of the Christian, is doing the very interceding the Christian longs to do, even though the only evidence that can be produced is inarticulate groanings.[69]

God's children are tasked with the role of participating in God's restoration process in creation through the practice of prayer. In this way they participate with the Son's rule over creation as those whose new identity is in Christ. Just as the Son intercedes on behalf of the saints in his glory in Romans 8:34, so also the saints demonstrate their sonship, and thus their participation in the Son's glory, in the present. And they do so not in domination but in a Christ-modeled dominion (e.g., Phil 2:6-11) that leads to redemption. But because of their weakness, they can only fulfill this role with the help and intercession of the Spirit.

Romans 8:28: Cooperating with God for the good of all things. Paul may refer to believers' ultimate glory in Romans 8:17, 18, 21, but, as with most motifs present in Romans 8 (e.g., adoption, new life), Paul can write just as easily about present realities as he does about future realities. The reading of Romans 8:26-27 just proposed demonstrates the present glorification of believers, and it flows into Romans 8:28, where, I suggest, Paul's focus is on just this—believers' present glorification. There Paul writes: Οἴδαμεν δὲ ὅτι τοῖς ἀγαπῶσιν τὸν θεὸν πάντα συνεργεῖ εἰς ἀγαθόν, τοῖς κατὰ πρόθεσιν κλητοῖς οὖσιν. As with Romans 8:26-27, Romans 8:28 is usually separated from the verses that precede it, especially Romans 8:19-22. But as with Romans 8:26-27, I suggest that the traditional interpretations or translations

---

[68]Wright 2002: 599; see also Dunn 1988a: 480.
[69]Wright 2002: 599; see 606.

have obscured the implicit thematic continuity from Romans 8:17-30 and thus also believers' present glorification.

These oversights are due to a number of exegetical issues in Romans 8:28, those most frequently discussed having to do with the textually suspect ὁ θεὸς and, related, the identity of the subject of the verb. There are a handful of commonly accepted ways to take the dense phrase πάντα συνεργεῖ εἰς ἀγαθόν. And each way revolves around the question of the subject of the verb, συνεργεῖ, and whether πάντα is read as an accusative of specification, the direct object, or whether it itself is the subject of the verb. The question of the subject is partly complicated by the possible omission or addition of ὁ θεὸς in various manuscripts.[70] If ὁ θεὸς is accepted as original, then God is the explicit subject of the verb. The best witnesses, however, are those that do not include the subject. But even if ὁ θεὸς is not accepted as original, God can still be the implied subject of the verb. This is supported by the relationship of Romans 8:28 to Romans 8:29-30, where God is the subject.[71] The subject of the verb may also be the Holy Spirit, supported by the relationship between Romans 8:28 and Romans 8:26-27, where the Spirit is the subject. Few support this option, with Robert Jewett and Gordon Fee being notable among those who do so.[72] Also contributing to complications is the ambiguity of πάντα, which can be read as an accusative of specification: "in all things"; a direct object: "God/the Spirit works all things"; or the subject of the verb: "All things work together." These options leave us with five possible combinations:[73]

1. God (whether explicit or implicit) works all things for good (NASB)

2. The Spirit works all things for good

3. In all things God works for good (NIV, RSV)[74]

4. In all things the Spirit works for good

5. All things work together for good (ESV, KJV, NKJV, NRSV, NET)

---

[70]The best witnesses are those that do not include the subject, namely, ℵ, C, D, F, G, Ψ, 3, 1739, 1881, M, latt, sy, bo, Cl, while those that do are limited to P⁴⁶, A, B, 81, sa.

[71]See Bertram 1971; Morris 1988: 331; Wright 2002: 600.

[72]NEB; Fee 1994: 588-90; Jewett and Kotansky 2007: 527.

[73]Most commentators provide three or four of these possibilities, but the majority omit number four.

[74]BDAG 2000 suggests accusative of specification.

These are significant issues to discuss, no doubt, but the resultant underlying message is the same either way: eventually everything works out for God's people. In fact, many commentators and grammarians find it necessary to comment on this point in particular, that the "good" is specifically for believers. Schreiner states: "What is remarkable . . . is that even suffering and tribulation turn out for the good of the Christian," noting Chrysostom's *Homilies on Romans* 15 (on Rom 8:28), who says "God uses painful things in this way to show his great power."[75] It is this emphasis on the good that comes to believers and these subject-focused exegetical discussions that have broken the obvious link between Romans 8:28 and Romans 8:19-22.

What we need to reconsider, I suggest, is the meaning of συνεργέω and how to render the appositional dative participles τοῖς ἀγαπῶσιν and τοῖς . . . κλητοῖς οὖσιν. These participles are almost always translated as either *for* those who love/are called or *to* those who love/are called. They are translated as datives of advantage or as the indirect object. But these are not the only possibilities.

I suggest that the dative participles should be read as datives of instrumentality, "by means of," or as datives of association, "with." Support for this reading already exists in abbreviated form in the NJB and the RSV. The NJB translates the verse as "We are well aware that God works *with* those who love him, those who have been called in accordance with his purpose," though the editors tack on at the end "and turns everything to their good." The RSV is more true to the text. It translates Romans 8:28 as "We know that in everything God works for good *with* those who love him, who are called according to his purpose." The RSV clearly identifies the dative participles as datives of association. Daniel Wallace notes that the dative of association and dative of instrumentality/means are closely linked, though distinctions can still be maintained.[76] In Romans 8:28 the distinction is dependent on how one translates the verb, συνεργέω.

There are two primary denotations of the verb. Συνεργέω can denote a sense of "working together"—as in "working toward" or "progressing toward" completion, as is the case in translation number five above.[77] The

---

[75]Schreiner 1998: 449.
[76]Wallace 1996: 159-61.
[77]E.g., ESV, NASB, NRSV.

most common meaning, however, is to "work with" or "cooperate with," as in two parties working in partnership. BDAG suggests the verb in Romans 8:28 means to "help (or work with) someone to obtain something or bring something about." Liddell and Scott's lexicon provides "work together with, help in work, co-operate, co-operate with, or assist." Louw and Nida in their lexicon suggest that συνεργέω means "to engage in an activity together with someone else" or "to work together with, to be active together with."[78] The story is not much different in *Theological Dictionary of the New Testament* or older lexicons. The point here is that, while it is possible to translate συνεργέω as "work together," as in "progressing toward something," as about half of the major English translations of Romans 8:28 do, its primary denotation is "work with" or "cooperate with" someone or something.

The verb's use in the New Testament tells the same story. Elsewhere in the New Testament συνεργέω is used only four times, all of which are clearly understood as a working partnership or cooperation between two entities. In Mark 16:20 we find: "And they went out and proclaimed the good news everywhere, while the Lord *worked with them* and confirmed the message by the signs that accompanied it" (NRSV). In James 2:22 it is written: "You see that his *faith* worked with his *actions*": ἡ πίστις συνήργει τοῖς ἔργοις αὐτοῦ. Like in Romans 8:28, συνήργει is used in conjunction with a dative of association. And, in addition to Romans 8:28, Paul uses it twice elsewhere: in 1 Corinthians 16:16, where he writes, "I urge you to put yourselves at the service of such people, and of everyone *who works and toils with them*," and in 2 Corinthians 6:1 with "As we *work together with him,* we urge you also not to accept the grace of God in vain." In Mark 16; 1 Corinthians 16; and 2 Corinthians 6, the dative "with them" or "with him" is supplied by the translators. In James 2, as in Romans 8, the dative is included as an obvious dative of association. In every instance, two entities cooperate with each other to produce a final result, and, where a dative is explicit rather than implied, it is a dative of association.

These two denotations, then, provide the distinction between rendering the dative participles in Romans 8:28 as datives of association or datives of instrumentality. If συνεργέω is rendered "work together," in the sense

---

[78]Louw and Nida 1989: 42.15.

of either God progressing all things toward an end or all things progressing toward an end under God's providence, then the datives are likely datives of instrumentality. If συνεργέω is taken as it is most commonly found, that is, "work with" or "cooperate with" another entity, then the datives are likely datives of association. Additionally, Wallace notes that "frequently, though not always, the dative [of association] will be related to a compound verb involving σύν."[79] Given this fact, and given that συνεργέω is primarily understood as two entities working together, a strong chance exists that what Paul is saying is not simply that God is working all things for good for the benefit of his people. Rather, I suggest two alternate possibilities from those commonly provided for reading Romans 8:28. These are: (1) συνεργέω as "work toward completion" or "progress toward completion" + dative of instrumentality:

> All things work together for good (in God's providence) *by means of* those who love God, who are called according to his purpose.

> God works all things together for good *by means of* those who love God, who are called according to his purpose.

Or, more likely: (2) συνεργέω as "work with" or "cooperate with" + dative of association:

> In all things God works for good *with those* who love God, who are called according to his purpose.

> God works all things for good *with those* who love God, who are called according to his purpose.

Whichever translation is chosen, the good that is done is not for the believer but is done by God *and* the believer on behalf of "all things."

I have argued thus far that this is confirmed both by the definition of συνεργέω and by the common datives associated with such συν-compound verbs. This reading is additionally supported by the meaning of πάντα. No matter how πάντα is treated grammatically, it is always understood as little more than a synonym for "unpleasant circumstances." More specifically, it is understood as little more than a synonym for believers' difficult or unpleasant circumstances. Cranfield suggests that πάντα refers to "the sufferings

---

[79]Wallace 1996: 159.

of the present time" from Romans 8:18, which he says is confirmed by believers' assurances in Romans 8:35-39.[80] While Moo is unwilling to restrict "all things" to human suffering and includes even that of humanity's sin, he unfortunately limits the term to that which affects humanity.[81] I suggest that this is a myopic misreading of πάντα and that πάντα does not refer specifically to believers' sufferings and unfortunate situations; rather, it is a metonym for every entity and circumstance in existence. "All things" in Romans 8:28 really is "all things": everything in existence, both entities and circumstances that are not "good" or that are in need of being declared "good." "All things" includes the sufferings of believers from Romans 8:18 *and* those of the physical creation in Romans 8:20-22, as I argued above is the case for Romans 8:26-27 as well.

If the datives in Romans 8:28 are taken as I have suggested, then not only is the translation grammatically sound, but the link between Romans 8:19-22 and Romans 8:28 is obvious: the good that God brings to all things comes in part through his cooperation with believers, a theological reality that parallels Paul's statements in Romans 8:19-22 about the redemption and liberation of creation that comes when God's children are glorified. Moreover, Romans 8:28, then, is not a part of a semidetached three-verse section, whether it be the end of Romans 8:26-27 or the beginning of Romans 8:29-30 (thus leaving Rom 8:26-27 as its own semidetached section) but is a transitional verse uniting Romans 8:17-30 as one very clear unit on the glory/glorification believers receive. God's children *will receive this glory in full* when their own redemption and adoption is complete, but they also *are currently glorified,* even if *in part.* This is the reason believers are predestined, called, and justified: that, as God's eschatological family, his children might be used by God to bring redemption to the world around them, in part by action and in part by prayer (Rom 8:26-27). This participation is the *now* of believers' glorification, the present purpose for which they were called (Rom 8:28, 30). Believers are not yet glorified entirely or completely, but they nonetheless participate in the Son's glory in the present as those whose new identity is established in the Messiah, the Son of God.

---

[80]Cranfield 1975: 428; see also Schreiner 1998: 449; Byrne 2007: 267.
[81]Moo 1996: 529; see Schreiner 1998: 449; Wright 2002: 600.

Paul's use of the aorist ἐδόξασεν in Romans 8:30c, therefore, does indeed speak to a present reality, as Ortlund persuasively argues (though he does not share the reading of Rom 8:28 I have proposed here). Believers are glorified, which is to say that believers are *now* "conformed to the image of [God's Firstborn] Son," at least in part. As Jewett insightfully notes on the relationship between Romans 8:28-29: "The transformation is currently manifest, at least in part, as believers cooperate with the Spirit to achieve the good (Rom 8:28); to restrict the bearing of this passage to future transformation in the resurrection overlooks the significance of the aorist verbs."[82] Believers' conformity will not be complete until they too rise from the grave with redeemed bodies (Rom 8:23); but, as Ortlund rightly argues, if believers are now in union with the Messiah, so too they are now participants in his eschatological glory.

7.3. CONCLUSION

In this seventh and final chapter, I have suggested that "conformed to the image of [God's Firstborn] Son," that is, glorified, is the ultimate task for which God purposed and called his children. In the first part of the chapter I outlined the structure of Romans 8:28-30 and demonstrated that Paul's placement of Romans 8:29b within the three verses makes conformity to the Firstborn Son the eternally decreed conclusion to that narrative; it is what believers are purposed to do. This ultimate goal of conformity, that is, glory, is not only a purpose of the future. Rather, believers are called even in the present to represent God within creation and to cooperate with God to bring redemption to that creation. Believers are children of God and coheirs with Christ. They are conformed to the image of God's Firstborn Son, participating in his role as the reigning representative of God within the cosmos.

---

[82]Jewett and Kotansky 2007: 529.

8

CONCLUSION

8.1. ALTERNATIVE PROPOSALS

Before marching directly to some final thoughts, it will be good to remind ourselves once again just how the argument for Romans 8:29 that I have presented here is on many levels different from what is commonly assumed. Though the themes of each of the alternative proposals were introduced in chapter one and are subsequently interwoven throughout my argument, a brief word on each will be nevertheless quite helpful at this point.

8.1.1. Resurrected bodily conformity. Unequivocally, part of believers' resurrection redemption is the renewal of the body, as it is in Philippians 3:21; 1 Corinthians 15:43; and as Paul clearly states in Romans 8:23: οὐ μόνον δέ, ἀλλὰ καὶ αὐτοὶ τὴν ἀπαρχὴν τοῦ πνεύματος ἔχοντες, ἡμεῖς καὶ αὐτοὶ ἐν ἑαυτοῖς στενάζομεν υἱοθεσίαν ἀπεκδεχόμενοι, τὴν ἀπολύτρωσιν τοῦ σώματος ἡμῶν. That being said, Paul's emphasis in Romans 8:29c is on sonship, a holistic identity rather than a corporeal identity. The case is the same for Paul's entire discussion of adoption and sonship in Romans 8:14-17, 23. Understanding the phrases "adoption as sons" and "redemption of our bodies" in Romans 8:23 as epexegetical not only ignores the parallels with the Abrahamic promises in Romans 8:17 but thereby suggests that the inheritance is the redemption of the body. As in Philippians 3:21 and 1 Corinthians 15, the Messiah's Sonship is not showcased by the sheer presence of his body but by what he does *with* the body. The Son of God was raised with an incorruptible body, but, as in 1 Corinthians 15, the body is only an indication of the fact that the Messiah now reigns over the powers of sin and death. Paul's point is that the Son reigns in glory over his inheritance with his new body, and believers, with their renewed bodies, will do the same.

8.1.2. Transformation in holiness. As with the resurrected body, believers' holiness will also be transformed. But this does not warrant Gorman's assertion that Romans 8:29; 12:2 are speaking to the same realities. Gorman writes on Romans 12:2: "That this holiness is in fact Christlikeness is clear from the assertion that the *telos* of salvation in Romans is conformity to 'the image of his [God's] Son' (8:29) rather than conformity to this age (12:1-2)."[1] As noted above, Gorman is correct to suggest that Paul refers in Romans 12:2 to moral transformation, that is, holiness/sanctification. This contrast of verses, however, has two problems. The first problem is exegetical. Gorman oversteps linguistic bounds when he applies the themes of Romans 12:2 (and 2 Cor 3:18) to Paul's use of σύμμορφος in Romans 8:29.[2] Σύμμορφος does not occur in Romans 12:2, nor do the majority of the other themes that surround Paul's use of σύμμορφος in Romans 8. As I have noted on several occasions, one cannot read Paul's morphic language, image language, and glory language throughout his epistles as all referring to the same reality. They must be interpreted on the basis of their use within their particular lexical and theological contexts. The second problem is theological. The "telos of salvation"—especially if it is understood on the basis of Romans 8:29-30—is not holiness but glorification, which I will turn to below. My reader will be aware by now that I find no reason to suggest that believers' glorification refers to their transformed sanctity, at least not in Romans 8. Holiness, while certainly a significant aspect of a believer's redemption, is nowhere in Paul made the "end all" of redemption in Christ.

8.1.3. Suffering with Christ. As Paul clearly states in Romans 8:17, suffering with Christ is part of the life of the believer this side of eternity. But

---

[1]Gorman 2009: 111, also 113.

[2]Gorman 2009: 111, also 113. Second Corinthians 3:18 is also often linked with Phil 3:21 due to a similar emphasis on transformation. In Phil 3:21, however, Paul uses μετασχηματίζω, a term we should not assume means "moral transformation." It is found elsewhere only in 1 Cor 4:6, where it means "apply," and in 2 Cor 11:13, 14, 15, where it means "disguise."

this does not mean that suffering with Christ is part of the telos of salvation. To emphasize the connection between Romans 8:17 and Romans 8:29 and thereby to suggest that σύμμορφος must include suffering with Christ is to deny the much stronger semantic structure of the passage linking Romans 8:29b to *glorified* in Romans 8:30, which is linked to *coglorified* and *coheirs* in Romans 8:17. According to this semantic structure or logic of discourse, σύμμορφος is not linked with the suffering but with the glory. In fact, conformity to the image of the Son is the exact opposite of suffering with Christ, contra Käsemann, who refuses to suggest any future aspect of conformity,[3] and Keesmaat, who suggests that "suffering is the so-far-unarticulated centre of the whole passage."[4] As Byrne rightly notes, "Conformity to the total 'career' of Christ—suffering as well as glory—is certainly implicit in the overall Pauline view (cf. esp. v. 17c). But Paul is spelling out here the *goal* of the divine *prosthesis*—the end God has in view for us . . . rather than the stages on the way."[5]

8.1.4. Restoration to the presence of God. Throughout this book I have interacted with Newman's glory Christology as the commonly used paradigm for interpreting Paul's use of δόξα and δοξάζω throughout Romans. This was not because I wished to refute his work completely; I have made it clear that, while criticizing it, there is much to learn from it, as I suggested in chapter three. Rather, I chose Newman's work because it demonstrates the complexities behind the terms throughout Paul's letters and serves as a cautionary word not to allow one denotation of *glory* or *glorification* to become master of them all. Moreover, as I indicated throughout, Newman does not interact heavily with Paul's glory language in Romans and thus served as a good conversation partner for doing just that. That being said, of all the suggestions for interpreting Romans 8:29b, the proposal that it indicates the restoration of glory or the presence of God comes the closest. It is rightly made in recognition that Romans 8:29b aligns with *glorification* in Romans 8:30 and with *coglorification* in Romans 8:17c. What is overlooked, however, is that, in the LXX, δόξα and δοξάζω—vis-à-vis humanity—primarily denote a status of honor associated with power, authority, or rule. And Paul's glory language in Romans—again, vis-à-vis humanity—follows

---

[3]Käsemann 1980: 244-45.
[4]Keesmaat 1999: 88.
[5]Byrne 2007: 272-73n29.

more closely the LXX use of the terms than it does the theophanic tradition of God's manifest presence made visible in splendor.

These four suggestions are the most pronounced among scholars' references to Romans 8:29b. Nevertheless, when a reference to the phrase occurs in an argument, it more often than not occurs as evidence for semirelated issues, and rarely with an eye to Paul's implied *meaning* of the phrase; "conformed to the image" is itself a chameleon, adaptable to almost any argument, or so it would seem.

8.2. CHAPTER CONCLUSIONS

I have argued for an alternative interpretation of the phrase, one that takes into account the function of Romans 8:29b within the context of Romans 8:17-30 and within Romans 1–8 as a whole. My argument was divided into two halves. The first half served to establish the larger motifs of glory and glorification in the LXX and in Romans as well as to establish the motif of vocational participation throughout Paul's letters. The second half focused on Romans 8:29b within its immediate context of Romans 8:17-30 and examined three key elements of the verse: the phrase "image of [God's] Son," believers' participation in the Son's glory, and the implicit notion of believers' present glorification. I will briefly summarize the argument of each chapter and thus draw the overarching argument into a concise whole.

After introducing the problem—the lacuna of focused treatments of Romans 8:29b—and the most commonly suggested interpretations of the phrase "conformed to the image of [God's] Son," I turned our attention in chapter two to the semantic uses of δόξα and δοξάζω in the LXX. The discussion centered on the significance of semiotics and the recognition that words function in various ways, often figuratively as metaphor, metonymy, or symbol within connotation chains or "orders of significance." I suggested that these basic elements of semiotic theory must be applied when articulating the function of words in the Old Testament, particularly to the analogous and symbolic language used to describe God. With this basis of semiotic theory in place, I turned our attention to the work of George Caird and Millard Berquist on the primary functions of כבוד as it is used throughout the Hebrew Bible. Independent of each other, Berquist and Caird arrived at three conclusions: (1) when associated with mankind,

כבוד refers to a person's status or honor; (2) the most extensive use of כבוד associated with God *does not mean* a theophanic revelation; and (3) the theophanic revelations that do occur symbolize God's status, power, or character. Using their investigations into כבוד as a basis, I then turned our attention to the semantic function of δόξα and δοξάζω throughout the LXX, analyzing Muraoka's lexical entry on the terms and providing a lexical entry and concordance of my own.

In categorizing the concordance according to semantic domains and connotations that exist within those domains, I demonstrated that δόξα and δοξάζω are used in various ways throughout the LXX in reference to both God and humanity. I drew four primary conclusions about the word when used in reference to God: (1) δόξα does not primarily mean "splendor"; (2) God's glory is commonly associated with his status or his identity as king; (3) the "glory of the Lord" does not always refer to God's theophanic manifestation; (4) when the glory of God does indicate the visible, manifest presence of God, that presence must be recognized as only part of the equation. Likewise, I drew three conclusions for the term's function in reference to humanity. First, *glory* (and its cognates) primarily bears its denotative meaning of status/honor associated with power, authority, character, or riches. In nearly every instance it is a reference to the exalted status or honor the person possesses or in which they exist, rather than a visible splendor after the likeness of God's theophanic splendor. Second, humanity's glory and glorification as exalted status or possessed honor is often associated with the person's status as king, ruler, or person of authority. Third, glorification of a person is never indicative of the transformation of a person's sanctity.

Chapter two concluded with a brief examination of how *glory* and its cognates functions in Daniel and 1 Enoch, two important examples of apocalyptic imagery. After noting the symbolic nature of the literature, which arose out of a historical context, possibly one of resistance, I then offered a concordance of the terms in both pieces of literature and a brief analysis of the general themes that arose out of those concordances. For Daniel, conclusions included (1) with two exceptions for δόξα, both δόξα and δοξάζω in Daniel unequivocally mean either possessing or being placed in a position of honor, power, or an exalted status associated with some form of rule or governance that is possessed by God or people; (2) the One Like a Son of Man in Daniel 7:14 clearly is given glory understood as power, authority, honor associated with a status of rule. From 1 Enoch, I drew a number of inferences, the most important of which include (1) the two most frequently recurring uses of *glory* are for the name of God, which is often closely associated with his identity as King, and in the genitival relationship with *throne* or *seat*; (2) only once does a person have a radiant glory (the infant Noah in 1 En. 106:6); (3) only once is someone "glorified"—the Elect One in 1 Enoch 51:4—and there it is clearly in reference to his exaltation to a status of rule/dominion.

In chapter three, then, I turned to Paul's use of δόξα and δοξάζω in Romans. There I suggested that the common glosses of "splendor" or "radiance" are inadequate for understanding Paul's use of the terms in Romans. I also suggested that Carey Newman's *Paul's Glory-Christology*, in which he argues that the visible manifestation of God in theophany in the Old Testament was present in the person of Jesus Christ, though insightful for many of Paul's letters, is less helpful for understanding the semantics of believers' glory or glorification in Romans. By his own admission, Newman's study rests almost exclusively on the כבד-δόξα word group as it related to God (rather than humans) throughout the Hebrew Bible/LXX. Moreover, Newman's study rests almost exclusively on Paul's use of the terms outside Romans. Paul's "Glory-Christology," as Newman calls it, as well as the more traditional glosses of "splendor" or "radiance," does little to explain believers' expectation of glory in texts such as Romans 2:7, 10, where δόξα is clearly a reference to honor or an exalted status. This alone warranted a reexamination of Paul's use of the terms elsewhere in Romans.

Before reexamining Paul's use of δόξα and δοξάζω in Romans, I offered some brief considerations on key issues that pertain to the investigation. Most notable of these considerations is the significance of Psalm 8 within the discussion of Paul's use of *glory*. First, Psalm 8 highlights the semantic use of δόξα as part of the motif of humanity's honor or exalted status in which that honor or status is clearly associated with rule or dominion. Second, Paul reads Psalm 8 messianically in his letters, most explicitly in 1 Corinthians 15:27, which indicates his recognition of its significance for the incarnate Son of God as the new Adam. Furthermore, the relationship between humanity's glory as caretakers of creation in Psalm 8 is closely associated with humanity's role as image bearers and thus caretakers of creation in Genesis 1:26-28, a fact that also leads to the noncoincidental overlap of δόξα and εἰκών throughout Paul's letters. On the basis of these factors, I suggested that it is at least a *possibility* that Psalm 8 and the crowning of Adam with glory and honor was a possible textual backdrop to δόξα at various points in Paul's letters. A second notable consideration regarded the likelihood that Paul echoes Adam at all in Romans, especially in Romans 1:23; 3:23. I suggested that, while many scholars rightly reject an echo of Genesis 3 and the fall narrative, there is undoubtedly an echo of Genesis 1:26-27 in Romans 1:23 that gets carried over into Romans 3:23. I argued that in Romans 1:23 the echo is of corporate humanity in Adam (אדם) from Genesis 1:26-27, and Paul uses it to emphasize not Adam's transgression of God's command from Genesis 3 but the identity as God's royal representative that Adam (and all humanity with him) was intended to demonstrate. This echo of humanity's created purpose is at the heart of Paul's anthropology and new-Adam Christology throughout Romans.

Finally in chapter three, I examined the texts in Romans in which Paul refers to the glory or glorification of humanity (Rom 1:23; 2:7, 10; 3:23; 5:2) and Israel (Rom 1:23; 9:4, 23), with the exception of a close analysis of those in Romans 8. In doing so, I offered what I referred to as Paul's "narrative of glory"—an underlying narrative of eschatological renewal, of humanity, Israel, and creation—implicit in Romans. In this section I argued that Paul echoes humanity's rejection of its created purpose as God's representatives in Romans 1:23; 3:23, which he then elaborates on in Romans 5:12-21. Though δόξα and δοξάζω are both absent from the passage, Adam's abdication of his throne is not. Here Paul uses βασιλεύω to describe death's dominion, which existed in place of Adam's (and all humanity's in Adam) intended dominion over creation. Had humanity in Adam not "exchanged the glory of the immortal God" (Rom 1:23) and come to "lack the glory of God" (Rom 3:23), humanity would reign and sin and death would be nonexistent. And, yet, though the first Adam allowed death to exercise dominion, the obedience of the new Adam ensures that believers will again "reign in life" (Rom 5:17). They have a renewed "hope of glory" (Rom 5:2) and can look forward to glory, honor, immortality, and peace (Rom 2:7,

10). These themes underlie Paul's emphasis on believers' eschatological glory in Romans 8, a discussion that by necessity was primarily relegated to chapters six and seven of this book. At this point in chapter three, I further articulated the inadequacy of Newman's glory Christology for understanding the relationship between creation's renewed freedom and believers' renewed glory—or why Paul would address this relationship at all—in Romans 8.

In chapter four, the final chapter in the first half of the book, I examined the Pauline motif of participation in Christ, a motif with significance for Paul's emphases in Romans 5–8 in general and Romans 8:29 in particular. There I argued that Paul articulates a vocational participation, in which believers' participation in the resurrection life and glory of Christ is a fulfillment of their intended vocation as God's earthly representatives—those whose identity is now in the new Adam, the representative Son of Man of Psalm 8. This vocational participation, I argued, is most clearly identified in Romans 6:4-8, where Paul says believers are transferred in baptism from their identity in Adam to their new identity in Christ. Being united with Christ, believers thus participate in the resurrection life of Christ; they actively share with Christ in his messianic and new Adamic reign. This motif of vocational participation in Jesus' reign arises again in Romans 8:17, where Paul describes it in terms of being co-inheritors and coglorified with the Son. On the basis of believers' adoption to sonship (Rom 8:14-16) and thus their change in identity, as children of God believers participate with the Son of God in his inheritance and glory—his vocational rule over the world as the Firstborn Son of God.

In the second half of chapter four I examined Philippians 3:21, where Paul uses σύμμορφος in a participatory context, and 1 Corinthians 15:49; Colossians 3:10; and 2 Corinthians 3:18; 4:4, where Paul uses εἰκών in contexts of vocational participation. In Philippians 3:21 I argued that, contrary to common interpretations, Christ's "body of glory" (τῷ σώματι τῆς δόξης αὐτοῦ) should not be read as adjectival, that is, "glorious body," but as possessive, that is, "his body that exists in glory." On the basis of Christ's status of humility and status of exaltation in Philippians 2:6-11, Paul's reference to "bodies of humility" in Philippians 3:21 should also indicate "bodies that exist in [the status of] humility." Believers' conformity to Christ's "body that exists in glory," then, should be viewed as their transformation into and vocational participation with Christ in his δόξα, a glory that both denotes an exalted status or power and that is associated with his rule over creation, as indicated by—or, in fact, is necessitated by—the echo of Psalm 8 at the end of Philippians 3:21.

Though σύμμορφος is not used in 1 Corinthians 15, Paul nevertheless articulates a motif of vocational participation through his use of εἰκών and δόξα, both of which occur within the context of the explicit Adam-Christ typology in 1 Corinthians 15:45-49, a typology that continues the contrast between the first Adam and last Adam of 1 Corinthians 15:21-28, where Christ's sovereignty is established, again, on the basis of Psalm 8. In 1 Corinthians 15:49 Paul writes that believers bear the "image of the heavenly man," indicating the future resurrection body to be characterized by immortality and incorruptibility but also indicating a present union and participation with Christ in his victorious rule. The body that will be raised to bear the image of the heavenly man (1 Cor 15:49) will also be characterized by δόξα—a term used in contrast with ἀτιμία (1 Cor 15:43) and which therefore does not denote "splendor" or "radiance." Throughout 1 Corinthians 15:21-28, 45-49, Paul highlights the glory of the last Adam—the Son of Man of Psalm 8 who now has victory over death itself (1 Cor 15:54-57). It is this life of dominion, of victory, in which believers will share in total transformation in the resurrection and in which they participate through union with Christ already (1 Cor 15:57).

The motif of vocational participation is also found in the context of Colossians 3:10, where the believer is described as "being renewed in knowledge according to the image of its creator." Paul's participatory language is expressed in Colossians through various σύμ-/σύν-compounds (Col 2:12, 13, 20; 3:1, 3, 4), through which Paul highlights believers' participation with Christ as the logical result of their union with Christ, their redemption in him (Col 1:14) and new existence in his kingdom (Col 1:13). Because believers have been transferred into Christ's kingdom, they should live not as the "old man" (Col 3:9), the man who lived under the power of darkness (Col 1:13), but as the "new man," the man "being renewed in the image of its Creator" (Col 3:10). This is to say that believers should live in solidarity as redeemed humanity, having been patterned on the image of the Creator, the image that is Christ—the firstborn of creation and the firstborn of the dead. According to Colossians 3:10, then, believers have taken off or disarmed their "old man" loyalties and put on those of Christ, thus becoming full and active participants in his kingdom.

Before concluding chapter four, I suggested that a certain level of caution should be exhibited in drawing any conclusions on Romans 8:29 on the basis of 2 Corinthians 3–4. There are, at first glance, a number of lexical similarities between the two texts, but on closer inspection, the correspondences become less obvious. Paul's morphic language of "transformation" (μεταμορφόω) corresponds more closely to Romans 12:2, where Paul emphasizes the renewal of the mind, than it does to Romans 8:29, where σύμμορφος falls within a context dominated by the motif of vocational participation. Likewise, Paul's use of εἰκών differs in 2 Corinthians 3–4 from its use in contexts of an Adam-Christ typology (e.g., 1 Cor 15:49). In 2 Corinthians 3:18; 4:4 εἰκών more closely resembles Paul's use of the term in Colossians 1:15 than it does its occurrence in Romans 8:29. Colossians 1:15 clearly echoes a Wisdom Christology—a use of εἰκών that few scholars propose for Romans 8:29. Perhaps of greatest dispute is Paul's use of δόξα (or its cognates) in the contexts of both 2 Corinthians 3 and Romans 8. In 2 Corinthians 3 δόξα unequivocally refers to God's theophanic splendor, which symbolizes his presence with and in his people, in particular the Christ who is the perfect image of God. But this in no way necessitates that the term shares the semantic function elsewhere. Paul uses δόξα in various ways throughout his letters: in 1 Corinthians 15:41 it clearly means brightness or luminosity and nothing more, and just two verses later the term means a status or position of honor and victory. Even within 2 Corinthians 3 itself, δόξα takes on various nuances. Δόξα indisputably spans the semantic range throughout Paul's letters, and therefore it should not be assumed that Paul's use of the term in Romans 8:29 is the same as his use of the term in 2 Corinthians 3.

Having established in the first half of the book the semantic range of δόξα and δοξάζω in the LXX, Paul's use of δόξα and δοξάζω with regard to humanity in Romans, and the motif of vocational participation in Christ in Paul's letters, I then focused in the second half on an examination of Romans 8:29b within the literary and theological context of Romans 8. I argued in chapter five that behind the designation of "Son" in Romans 8:29 stands both the long-awaited Davidic Messiah and the new Adam, the image of redeemed humanity. Before examining the two identities more closely, I offered a brief treatment of "son of god" backgrounds. There I suggested that, though the Roman imperial use of "son of god" would have been a common association for Paul to make, his primary inspiration for the designation likely came from his reading of the royal ideologies attached to the Davidic dynasty. Additionally, I offered a brief treatment of my primary working presupposition in chapter five and throughout this book: that Paul uses χριστός as a reference to Jesus as the Messiah, the long-anticipated Davidic King and Redeemer of the Jewish people.

The majority of chapter five was dedicated to an examination of Jesus' designation as the Son of God, in which I argued that, through subtle echoes of Psalms 89; 110 in Romans 8:29, 34, respectively, Paul suggests that Jesus is the promised Davidic King. In Romans 8:34 Paul echoes Psalm 109:1 LXX, a clear reference to the messianic king. As the messianic King, Jesus is at the right hand of God and over the kings and nations of the earth. This echo of Psalm 109 LXX in Romans 8:34 illuminates the echo of Psalm 89, another messianic psalm, in Romans 8:29. Jesus is the Firstborn Son of God of Psalm 89:26; he is appointed as a Davidic descendant, the chosen one among Israel who is established as God's royal representative. It is in this Davidic king, the Firstborn of Israel, that the Spirit-led children of God are renewed as God's family.

In addition to the Son's identity as the Davidic Messiah, I also argued that Paul designates the Son as the new Adam, the representative of a new humanity. He does so, I argued, through the use of εἰκών and πρωτότοκος within the context of an already-established Adam-Christ typology in Romans 5:12-21, a typology that stems from Paul's designation of Jesus as the Son of God in Romans 5:10. In Romans 8 Paul continues to elaborate on the reconciliation and renewal of life that is established on the basis of the death and resurrection of the Son, the new Adam of Romans 5. Furthermore, the other occurrence of εἰκών in Romans is in 1:23, where, as I argued in chapter three, Paul does not highlight the fall of Adam but the created purpose of humanity in Adam. This created purpose of human governance as God's vicegerents runs throughout Romans, from

Romans 1:23 to Romans 3:23 to Romans 5:17 to Romans 8:29, where that purpose finds its fulfillment in the new Adam (already hinted at in Rom 5:17). Likewise, the Son as the πρωτότοκος also implies that he is the firstborn of the dead, as it does in Colossians 1:18. He is the first to rise into the transformed existence of resurrection life. That πρωτότοκος can refer to both the Davidic King and the "firstborn of the dead" is demonstrated in Revelation 1:5, where John conflates the two ideas in a way similar to Paul in Romans 8:29.

Chapter six functioned as the heart of this book. In it I argued that συμμόρφους τῆς εἰκόνος τοῦ υἱοῦ αὐτοῦ *means* the vocational participation of believers in the Firstborn Son's honorable status of power and authority over creation as adopted members of God's eschatological family and as renewed humanity. The argument is predicated on believers' Spirit-led adoption into sonship as God's children, who are redeemed from the "Egypt of sin and death" and united with Christ in his Sonship (Rom 8:1-16). This union is then articulated in terms of believers' vocational participation with Christ in his inheritance, suffering, and glory in Romans 8:17, and ultimately in believers' conformity to Christ in Romans 8:29 and glorification in Romans 8:30.

Turning to συγκληρονόμος in Romans 8:17, I argued that Paul returns to what he established in Romans 4, where Paul expands the original inheritance of Abraham's offspring from the land to the world (Rom 4:13). According to Paul, Abraham and his offspring would inherit the world, which is to say that Israel would possess and thereby rule the world. For Paul, Israel would inherit the world, but the inheritance passed through Abraham's offspring, Jesus (the) Lord (Rom 4:24). In Romans 8:17, then, Paul speaks not in terms of the Abrahamic family but of God's family. Jesus (the) Lord is no longer the heir of Abraham but, as the Son of God, is the heir of God, and it is in his Sonship and inheritance of the world that the adopted children of God will thus also share.

Believers' participation in the Son's inheritance parallels believers' participation in his glory in Romans 8:17 and is linked also to their glorification as children of God in Romans 8:30. On the basis of συγκληρονόμος in Romans 8:17 and Paul's use of δόξα and δοξάζω for believers elsewhere in Romans (chapter three above), I argued that Paul's passive use of συνδοξάζω in Romans 8:17 and δοξάζω in Romans 8:30 means believers' vocational participation (chapter four above) in the inheritance of the Son, who as the Messiah and new Adam (chapter five above) is already crowned with glory and honor. Believers' final glorification in Romans is their reinstatement to Adamic rule over creation through union with the Firstborn Son of God, who already reigns over creation as the Messiah and the new Adam. Mankind's position on earth as God's vicegerents to his creation is now restored, though now through the image of the Son of God, who reigns as God's preeminent vicegerent. The depiction of humanity being crowned with glory and honor and established with dominion over creation in Psalm 8 is now again a reality, both through the Firstborn Son of God and those who participate in his exalted status, that is, his glory. This is the heart of Romans 8:17-30 and Romans 8:29b and is thus the heart of my argument: as children of God, believers are coheirs with the Son of God and thus share in his glory: they are conformed to the image of the Son, who rules as God's Firstborn and as humanity's representative.

Having brought the examinations of chapters two through five together in chapter six, in chapter seven I argued that "conformity to the image of [God's Firstborn] Son," that is, vocational participation in the Firstborn Son's exalted position over creation, is the task for which believers are called and purposed in the present as well as the future. I argued first that, structurally and theologically, Paul's main point in Romans 8:28-30 is not Romans 8:29b but Romans 8:28b: God has called his people with the ultimate goal of fulfilling his purposes through them, his purposes of creating a redeemed people through whom he would bring redemption to the rest of the cosmos. Paul articulates this creation of a people through his use of κλητός in Romans 8:28 and καλέω in Romans 8:30; God has brought to fruition an ancient element of Israel's history—his covenantal promises to Abraham and to Israel as a people set apart for God—and he has done so by calling believers to be his own, bringing them into a life of faith and obedience to God.

I argued additionally that believers already manifest their decreed calling and purpose by participating in the Son's glory in the present. Adding to Dane Ortlund's contextual argument, though on the basis of grounds untouched in his work, I argued that believers are called to participate in this restoration process in Romans 8:26-27 and in Romans 8:28, both of which are intricately connected to the relationship between the nonhuman creation and the children of God in Romans 8:18-21. There Paul writes that the "creation waits with eager longing for the revealing of the children of God" (Rom 8:19 NRSV) because, *when* God's children are glorified, *then* the creation will be liberated from its bondage to corruption (Rom 8:21). Believers cooperate with God to bring restoration to the nonhuman creation, and they do so, Paul continues to articulate, in two ways. First, Paul says in Romans 8:26-27 that God's children play a role in God's restoration process in creation through the practice of prayer. Though believers' prayers in Romans 8:26 are often understood as referring to the prayers believers make on their own behalf, nothing warrants this conclusion. Instead, what the believer ought to pray for in Romans 8:26 and what the Spirit intercedes for in Romans 8:27 is not *only* for the believers' own good but is *also* for the good of the creation, which currently groans; hence Paul's transition from creation to believers in Romans 8:22-23. Just as the Son intercedes on behalf of the saints in his glory in 8:34, so also the saints demonstrate their sonship, and thus their participation in the Son's glory, in the present through intercession.

Second, I argued that Paul articulates believers' present glorification in Romans 8:28, where he describes believers' cooperation with God for the good of all things. Though συνεργέω can denote a sense of "working to-gether," as in "working toward" or "progressing toward," in its four New Testament occurrences elsewhere συνεργέω clearly denotes a working partnership or cooperation between two entities (Mk 16:20; Jas 2:22; 1 Cor 16:16; 2 Cor 6:1). Likewise, while the appositional dative participles are typically rendered as datives of advantage or as indirect objects, I argued that they should be read as datives of instrumentality, "by means of," or as datives of association, "with." Finally, I suggested that, while typically understood as little more than a synonym for believers' difficult or un-pleasant circumstances, πάντα truly indicates "all things": everything in existence, including the sufferings of believers from Romans 8:18 *and* those of the physical creation in Romans 8:20-22. In Romans 8:26-28, then, Paul articulates believers' present glory. Though not yet glorified entirely or completely, God's adopted children nonetheless participate in the Son's glory in the present as those whose new identity is established in the Firstborn Son of God.

8.3. Summary of the Argument

In my systematic treatment of the phrase συμμόρφους τῆς εἰκόνος τοῦ υἱοῦ αὐτου, I have argued that Romans 8:29b refers to believers' participation in the Firstborn Son's rule over creation as God's eschatological family and as renewed humanity. This rule is the reinstitution of humanity's dominion over creation as God's vicegerents, as is narrated in Genesis 1:26-28 and picked up in Psalm 8:5-8. Believers are "conformed to the image of [God's] Son" on the basis of their adoption into God's family (Rom 8:14-16) and thus their participation in the Messiah's Sonship (Rom 8:29c). Adopted children of God share in the Firstborn Son's inheritance (Rom 8:17), his possession of and rule over the earth, which is to say that they share in the Son's glory (Rom 8:17). Conformity to the Son is glorification, the fulfillment of God's purposes for calling his children (Rom 8:28-30). Believers are glorified in part in the present (Rom 8:30c) through their participation with God in bringing redemption to creation (Rom 8:18-28); they will be glorified in full at the resurrection, when they too will experience the resurrection of the body (Rom 8:23) and, with the Firstborn Son, will be at the right hand of the Father (Rom 8:34), crowned with glory and honor, and with all things under their feet.

I return my reader to one of the key questions of this book: What is the goal of salvation? For too long, scholars and laymen alike have myopically viewed justification and salvation as ends in themselves, whether for the benefit of the individual or of the incorporative body of Christ. The goal of salvation is believers' conformity to the Son of God—their participation in his rule over creation as God's eschatological family and as renewed humanity—but only and always with the purpose of extending God's hand of mercy, love, and care to his wider creation. This was humanity's job in the beginning; it will be believers' responsibility and honor in the future; it is God's purpose in calling his people in the present.

BIBLIOGRAPHY

Aalen, S. 1976. "Glory, Honour." Pages 44-52 in vol. 2 of *The New International Dictionary of New Testament Theology*. Edited by Colin Brown. Exeter, UK: Paternoster.

Achtemeier, Paul J., ed. 1985. *Harper's Bible Dictionary*. San Francisco: Harper & Row.

Adams, E. 2002. "Paul's Story of God and Creation: The Story of How God Fulfills His Purposes in Creation." Pages 19-43 in *Narrative Dynamics in Paul: A Critical Assessment*. Edited by Bruce Longenecker. Louisville: Westminster John Knox.

Aichele, George. 1997. *Sign, Text, Scripture: Semiotics and the Bible*. Sheffield: Sheffield Academic.

Albl, Martin C. 1999. *"And Scripture Cannot Be Broken": The Form and Function of the Early Christian Testimonia Collections*. Supplements to Novum Testamentum 96. Leiden: Brill.

Baird, William. 2007. *History of New Testament Research*. Vol. 2, *From Jonathan Edwards to Rudolf Bultmann*. Minneapolis: Fortress.

Balz, Horst R. 1971. *Heilsvertrauen und Welterfahrung: Strukturen der paulinischen Eschatologie nach Römer 8,18-39*. Beiträge zur evangelischen Theologie 59. München: Christian Kaiser.

Barclay, John M. G. 1995. "Review of Stowers." *Journal of Theological Studies* 46 (2): 646-51.

Barnett, Paul. 1997. *The Second Epistle to the Corinthians*. New International Commentary on the New Testament. Grand Rapids: Eerdmans.

Barr, James. 1961. *The Semantics of Biblical Language*. London: Oxford University Press.

Barrett, C. K. 1962. *From First Adam to Last: A Study in Pauline Theology*. New York: Charles Scribner's Sons.

———. 1971. *A Commentary on the Epistle to the Romans*. Black's New Testament Commentaries. London: Black.

———. 1973. *The Second Epistle to the Corinthians*. Black's New Testament Commentaries. London: Black.

———. 1991. *A Commentary on the Epistle to the Romans*. 2nd ed. Black's New Testament Commentaries. London: Black.

Barth, Karl. 1933. *The Epistle to the Romans*. Translated from the 6th ed. by Edwyn C. Hoskyns. Oxford: Oxford University Press.

———. 1956. *Christ and Adam: Man and Humanity in Romans 5*. Translated by T. A. Smail. Edinburgh: Oliver and Boyd.

———. 1959. *A Shorter Commentary on Romans*. Translated by D. H. Van Daalen. London: SCM Press.

———. 1962. *Church Dogmatics IV/3.2: The Doctrine of Reconciliation*. Edited by G. W. Bromiley and T. F. Torrance. Translated by G. W. Bromiley. Edinburgh: T&T Clark.

Bassler, Jouette M. 1996. "*A Rereading of Romans: Justice, Jews, and Gentiles*, by Stanley K. Stowers." *Journal of Biblical Literature* 115 (2): 365-68.

Bauckham, Richard. 2008. *Jesus and the God of Israel: God Crucified and Other Studies on the New Testament's Christology of Divine Identity*. Grand Rapids: Eerdmans.

———. 2010. *Bible and Ecology: Rediscovering the Community of Creation*. London: Darton, Longman & Todd.

Bauer, Walter, F. W. Danker, W. F. Arndt, and F. W. Gingrich (BDAG). 2000. *A Greek-English Lexicon of the New Testament and Other Early Christian Literature*. 3rd ed. Revised and edited by Frederick William Danker. Chicago: University of Chicago Press.

Beale, G. K. 1999. *The Book of Revelation: A Commentary on the Greek Text*. New International Greek Testament Commentary. Grand Rapids: Eerdmans.

———. 2004. *The Temple and the Church's Mission: A Biblical Theology of the Dwelling Place of God*. New Studies in Biblical Theology. Downers Grove, IL: InterVarsity Press.

———. 2008. *We Become What We Worship: A Biblical Theology of Idolatry*. Downers Grove, IL: InterVarsity Press.

Beasley-Murray, P. 1980. "Romans 1:3f: An Early Confession of Faith in the Lordship of Jesus." *Tyndale Bulletin* 31: 147-54.

Behm, J. 1975. "*morphe ktl.*" Pages 742-59 in vol. 4 of *Theological Dictionary of the New Testament*. Edited by G. Kittel and G. Friedrich. Translated by G. Bromiley. Grand Rapids: Eerdmans.

Beker, J. C. 1980. *Paul the Apostle: The Triumph of God in Life and Thought.* Edinburgh: T&T Clark.

Berquist, Millard J. 1941. "The Meaning of Δόξα in the Epistles of Paul." PhD diss., Southern Baptist Theological Seminary.

Bertram, Georg. 1971. "συνεργός, συνεργέω." Pages 871-76 in vol. 7 of *Theological Dictionary of the New Testament.* Edited by Gerhard Friedrich. Translated by Geoffrey Bromiley. Grand Rapids: Eerdmans.

Best, Ernest. 1955. *One Body in Christ: A Study in the Relationship of the Church to Christ in the Epistles of the Apostle Paul.* London: SPCK.

———. 1987. *Second Corinthians.* Interpretation: A Bible Commentary for Teaching and Preaching. Edited by James Luther Mays. Atlanta: John Knox.

Billings, J. Todd. 2007. *Calvin, Participation, and the Gift.* Oxford: Oxford University Press.

———. 2011. *Union with Christ: Reframing Theology and Ministry for the Church.* Grand Rapids: Baker Academic.

Bingham, D. J. 2005. "Irenaeus's Reading of Romans 8: Resurrection and Renovation." Pages 114-32 in *Early Patristic Readings of Romans.* Edited by L. L. Welborn and K. Gaca. New York: T&T Clark.

Bird, Michael F., and Preston M. Sprinkle. 2008. "Jewish Interpretation of Paul in the Last Thirty Years." *Currents in Biblical Research* 6 (3): 355-76.

Bird, Phyllis A. 1981. "'Male and Female He Created Them': Gen 1:27b in the Context of the Priestly Account of Creation." *Harvard Theological Review* 74: 129-59.

Black, Matthew. 1962. "The Interpretation of Romans viii 28." Pages 166-72 in *Neotestamentica et Patristica: Festschrift fur Oscar Cullmann.* Novum Testamentum Supplements 6. Leiden: Brill.

———. (1973) 1981. *Romans.* New Century Bible Commentary. Grand Rapids: Eerdmans.

Blackwell, Ben C. 2010. "Immortal Glory and the Problem of Death in Romans 3.23." *Journal for the Study of the New Testament* 32 (3): 285-308.

———. 2014. "You Are Filled in Him: *Theosis* and Colossians 2–3." *Journal of Theological Interpretation* 8 (1): 103-23.

Boa, Kenneth. 2001. *Conformed to His Image: Biblical and Practical Approaches to Spiritual Formation.* Grand Rapids: Zondervan.

Bockmuehl, Markus. 1997. "The Form of God (Phil. 2:6): Variations on a Theme of Jewish Mysticism." *Journal of Theological Studies* 48 (1): 1-23.

Bousset, Wilhelm. (1913) 1970. *Kyrios Christos: A History of the Belief in Christ from the Beginnings of Christianity to Irenaeus.* Translated by J. E. Steely. Nashville: Abingdon.

Bouttier, Michael. 1966. *Christianity According to Paul*. Translated by F. Clarke. London: SCM Press.

Brandenburger, E. 1962. *Adam und Christus: Exegetisch-religionsgeschichtliche Untersuchung zu Röm. 5 12-21 (1. Kor. 15)*. Wissenschaftliche Monographien zum Alten und Neuen Testament 7. Neukirchen: Neukirchener Verlag.

Braumann, G. 1975. "*Morphe*." Pages 705-8 in vol. 1 of *The New International Dictionary of New Testament Theology*. Edited by Colin Brown and David Townsley. Grand Rapids: Eerdmans.

Bray, Gerald, ed. 1998. *Romans*. Ancient Christian Commentary on Scripture: New Testament VI. Downers Grove, IL: InterVarsity Press.

Brockington, L. H. 1950. "Presence." Pages 172-76 in *A Theological Word Book of the Bible*. Edited by Alan Richardson, DD. London: SCM Press.

——. 1951. "The Greek Translator of Isaiah and His Interest in ΔΟΞΑ." *Vetus Testamentum* 1 (1): 23-32.

——. 1955. "The Septuagintal Background to the New Testament Use of δόξα." Pages 1-8 in *Studies in the Gospels: Essays in Memory of R. H. Lightfoot*. Edited by D. E. Nineham. Oxford: Blackwell.

Brown, Francis, S. R. Driver, and Charles A. Briggs, eds. 1972. *A Hebrew and English Lexicon of the Old Testament*. Translated by Edward Robinson. Oxford: Clarendon.

Bruce, F. F. 1971. *1 and 2 Corinthians*. New Cambridge Bible Commentary. London: Oliphants.

——. 1984. *The Epistles to the Colossians, to Philemon, and to the Ephesians*. New International Commentary on the New Testament. Grand Rapids: Eerdmans.

——. (1985) 2003. *Romans*. Tyndale New Testament Commentaries 6. Edited by Leon Morris. Grand Rapids: Eerdmans.

Bultmann, Rudolf. 1952. *Theology of the New Testament*. Vol. 1. Translated by Kendrick Grobel. London: SCM Press.

Burke, Trevor J. 2006. *Adopted into God's Family: Exploring a Pauline Metaphor*. New Studies in Biblical Theology. Edited by D. A. Carson. Downers Grove, IL: InterVarsity Press.

——. 2008. "Adopted as Sons (υἱοθεσία): The Missing Piece in Pauline Soteriology." Pages 259-88 in *Paul: Jew, Greek, and Roman*. Edited by Stanley E. Porter. Leiden: Brill.

Burrowes, B. 2007. "The Origin of Paul's Image and Adam Christologies." Page 53 in *Annual Meetings American Academy of Religion, Society of Biblical Literature: Abstracts 2007, San Diego, CA, November 17-20*, no. S17-71.

Byrne, Brendan, SJ. 1979. "Sons of God—Seed of Abraham." Analecta Biblica 83. Rome: Biblical Institute Press.

———. 1983. "Paul's Understanding of the Sexual Relationship in 1 Corinthians 6:18." *Catholic Biblical Quarterly* 45 (4): 608-16.

———. (1996) 2007. *Romans*. Sacra Pagina Series 6. Edited by Daniel J. Harrington, SJ. Collegeville, MN: Liturgical Press.

———. 2010. "An Ecological Reading of Rom. 8.19-22: Possibilities and Hesitations." Pages 83-93 in *Ecological Hermeneutics: Biblical, Historical and Theological Perspectives*. Edited by David Horrell, Christopher Southgate, and Francesca Stavrakopoulou. Edinburgh: T&T Clark.

Byrskog, Samuel. 2008. "Christology and Identity in an Intertextual Perspective: The Glory of Adam in the Narrative Substructure of Paul's Letter to the Romans." Pages 141-62 in *Identity Formation in the New Testament*. Edited by Bengt Holmberg and Mikael Winninge. Wissenschaftliche Untersuchungen zum Neuen Testament 227. Tübingen: Mohr Siebeck.

Caird, George B. 1944. "The New Testament Conception of Doxa." DPhil diss., Oxford University.

———. 1969. "The Glory of God in the Fourth Gospel: An Exercise in Biblical Semantics." *New Testament Studies* 15 (3): 265-77.

———. 1980. *The Language and Imagery of the Bible*. London: Duckworth.

Calvin, John. 1960. *The Epistles of Paul the Apostle to the Romans and to the Thessalonians*. Translated by R. MacKenzie. Edited by D. W. Torrance and T. F. Torrance. Calvin's Commentaries. Grand Rapids: Eerdmans.

Campbell, Constantine. 2012. *Paul and Union with Christ: An Exegetical and Theological Study*. Grand Rapids: Zondervan.

Campbell, Douglas A. 2009. *The Deliverance of God: A Reappraisal of Justification in Paul*. Grand Rapids: Eerdmans.

Carey, Greg. 2005. *Ultimate Things: An Introduction to Jewish and Christian Apocalyptic Literature*. St. Louis: Chalice.

Carrez, Maurice. 1964. *De la souffrance a la gloire: De la doxa dans la pensee paulinienne*. Neuchatel: Delachaux et Niestle.

Carson, Herbert M. 1960. *The Epistles of Paul to the Colossians and Philemon: An Introduction and Commentary*. Grand Rapids: Eerdmans.

Chambers, Oswald. 1985. *Conformed to His Image*. Perrysburg, OH: Welch.

Chandler, Daniel. 2007. *Semiotics: The Basics*. London: Taylor & Francis.

Charlesworth, James H., ed. 1983a. *Apocalyptic Literature and Testaments*. Vol. 1 of *The Old Testament Pseudepigrapha*. Edited by James H. Charlesworth. Peabody, MA: Hendrickson.

———, ed. 1983b. *Expansions of the "Old Testament" and Legends, Wisdom and Philosophical Literature, Prayers, Psalms and Odes, Fragments of Lost Judeo-Hellenistic Works.* Vol. 2 of *The Old Testament Pseudepigrapha.* Edited by James H. Charlesworth. Peabody, MA: Hendrickson.

Chester, Andrew. 2007. *Messiah and Exaltation: Jewish Messianic and Visionary Traditions and New Testament Christology.* Wissenschaftliche Untersuchungen zum Neuen Testament 207. Edited by Jörg Frey. Tübingen: Mohr Siebeck.

Chilton, Bruce D. 1983. *The Glory of Israel: The Theology and Provenience of the Isaiah Targum.* Journal for the Study of the Old Testament Supplement Series 23. Sheffield: JSOT Press.

Christoffersson, O. 1990. *The Earnest Expectation of the Creature.* Coniectanea biblica: New Testament Series 23. Stockholm: Almqvist.

Church of England: Mission and Public Affairs Council Report. 2005. "Sharing God's Planet: A Christian Vision for a Sustainable Future." London: Church House Publishing.

Ciampa, Roy. 2013. "Genesis 1–3 and Paul's Theology of Adam's Dominion in Romans 5–6." Pages 103-22 in *From Creation to New Creation: Essays on Biblical Theology and Exegesis.* Edited by Daniel M. Gurtner and Benjamin L. Gladd. Peabody, MA: Hendrickson.

Ciampa, Roy, and Brian Rosner. 2007. "1 Corinthians." Pages 695-752 in *Commentary on the New Testament Use of the Old Testament.* Edited by G. K. Beale and D. A. Carson. Grand Rapids: Baker Academic.

———. 2010. *The First Letter to the Corinthians.* Pillar New Testament Commentary. Edited by D. A. Carson. Grand Rapids: Eerdmans.

Clifford, Richard J. 2002. *Psalms 1–72.* Abingdon Old Testament Commentaries. Edited by Patrick D. Miller. Nashville: Abingdon.

Clines, D. J. A. 1968. "The Image of God in Man." *Tyndale Bulletin* 19: 53-103.

Cobley, Paul, and Litza Jansz. 2010. *Introducing Semiotics: A Graphic Guide.* London: Icon Books.

Cohick, Lynn H. 2013. *Philippians.* Story of God Bible Commentary. Edited by Tremper Longman III and Scot McKnight. Grand Rapids: Zondervan.

Collins, John J., ed. 1979. *Apocalypse: The Morphology of a Genre. Semeia* 14.

———. 1995. "A Throne in the Heavens: Apotheosis in Pre-Christian Judaism." Pages 41-56 in *Death, Ecstasy, and Other Worldly Journeys.* Edited by John J. Collins and Michael Fishbane. New York: State University of New York Press.

———. (1984) 1998. *The Apocalyptic Imagination: An Introduction to Jewish Apocalyptic Literature.* 2nd ed. Grand Rapids: Eerdmans.

———. 2000. "From Prophecy to Apocalypticism: The Expectation of the End." Pages 129-61 in *The Encyclopedia of Apocalypticism*. Volume 1 in *The Origins of Apocalypticism in Judaism and Christianity*. Edited by John J. Collins. New York: Continuum.

———. 2007. "Pre-Christian Jewish Messianism: An Overview." Pages 1-20 in *The Messiah in Early Judaism and Christianity*. Edited by Magnus Zetterholm. Minneapolis: Fortress.

———. 2009. "The Interpretation of Psalm 2." Pages 49-66 in *Echoes from the Caves: Qumran and the New Testament*. Studies on the Texts of the Desert of Judah 85. Edited by Florentino García Martínez. Leiden: Brill.

———. (1995) 2010. *The Scepter and the Star: Messianism in Light of the Dead Sea Scrolls*. 2nd ed. Grand Rapids: Eerdmans.

———. 2013. "The Royal Psalms and Eschatological Messianism." Pages 73-89 in *Aux Origines Des Messianismes Juifs: Actes du colloque international tenu en Sorbonne, à Paris, les 8 et 9 juin 2010*. Edited by David Hamidović. Leiden: Brill.

Collins, Raymond F. 1999. *First Corinthians*. Sacra Pagina Series 7. Edited by Daniel J. Harrington, SJ. Collegeville, MN: Liturgical Press.

Conzelmann, Hans. 1975. *1 Corinthians: A Commentary on the First Epistle to the Corinthians*. Hermeneia—A Critical and Historical Commentary on the Bible. Edited by George W. MacRae, SJ. Translated by James W. Leitch. Philadelphia: Fortress.

Cousar, Charles B. 2009. *Philippians and Philemon*. The New Testament Library. Edited by C. Clifton Black, M. Eugene Boring, and John T. Carroll. Louisville: Westminster John Knox.

Craig, Edward. 1998. "Ontology." Pages 117-18 in vol. 7 of *Routledge Encyclopedia of Philosophy*. Edited by Edward Craig. New York: Routledge.

Craigie, Peter C. 1983. *Psalms 1–50*. Word Biblical Commentary 19. Edited by Bruce M. Metzger. Waco, TX: Word Books.

Cranfield, C. E. B. 1975. *A Critical and Exegetical Commentary on the Epistle to the Romans: Introduction and Commentary on Romans I—VIII*. International Critical Commentary. Edinburgh: T&T Clark.

———. 1985. *Romans: A Shorter Commentary*. Grand Rapids: Eerdmans.

Cullmann, Oscar. 1959. *The Christology of the New Testament*. Translated by Shirley C. Guthrie and Charles A. M. Hall. London: SCM Press.

Dahl, N. A. 1952. "Two Notes on Romans 5." *Studia Theologica* 5: 37-48.

———. 1974. *The Crucified Messiah and Other Essays*. Minneapolis: Augsburg.

Davies, G. Henton. 1962. "Glory." Pages 401-3 in *The Interpreter's Dictionary of the Bible*. New York: Abingdon.

Davies, W. D. (1948) 1980. *Paul and Rabbinic Judaism: Some Rabbinic Elements in Pauline Theology*. 4th ed. Philadelphia: Fortress.

Davila, James R. 1999. "Of Methodology, Monotheism and Metatron: Introductory Reflections on Divine Mediators and the Origins of the Worship of Jesus." Pages 3-20 in *The Jewish Roots of Christological Monotheism: Papers from the St. Andrews Conference on the Historical Origins of the Worship of Jesus*. Edited by Carey C. Newman, James R. Davila, and Gladys S. Lewis. Supplements to the Journal for the Study of Judaism 63. Leiden: Brill.

——. 2000. "The Dead Sea Scrolls and Merkavah Mysticism." Pages 249-64 in *The Dead Sea Scrolls in Their Historical Context*. Edited by Timothy H. Lim. Edinburgh: T&T Clark.

de Boer, M. C. 1988. *The Defeat of Death: Apocalyptic Eschatology in 1 Corinthians 15 and Romans 5*. Journal for the Study of the New Testament Supplement Series 22. Sheffield: JSOT Press.

——. 2000. "Paul and Apocalyptic Eschatology." Pages 345-83 in *The Encyclopedia of Apocalypticism*. Vol. 1 in *The Origins of Apocalypticism in Judaism and Christianity*. Edited by John J. Collins. New York: Continuum.

Deissmann, Gustav A. 1912. *St. Paul: A Study in Social and Religious History*. Translated by Lionel R. M. Strachan. New York: Hodder & Stoughton.

Dodd, C. H. 1932. *The Epistle of Paul to the Romans*. London: Hodder & Stoughton.

——. 1954. *The Bible and the Greeks*. London: Hodder & Stoughton.

Dunn, James D. G. 1973. "Jesus—Flesh and Spirit: An Exposition of Romans 1:3-4." *Journal of Theological Studies* 24: 40-68.

——. 1988a. *Romans 1–8*. Word Biblical Commentary 38A. Dallas: Word Books.

——. 1988b. *Romans 9–16*. Word Biblical Commentary 38B. Dallas: Word Books.

——. 1989. *Christology in the Making: A New Testament Inquiry into the Origins of the Doctrine of the Incarnation*. 2nd ed. London: SCM Press.

——. 1996. *The Epistles to the Colossians and to Philemon*. New International Greek Testament Commentary. Grand Rapids: Eerdmans.

——. 1998a. *The Christ and the Spirit: Collected Essays of James D. G. Dunn*. Vol. 1, *Christology*. Edinburgh: T&T Clark.

——. 1998b. *The Theology of Paul the Apostle*. Grand Rapids: Eerdmans.

——. 2004. "Was Jesus a Monotheist?" Pages 104-19 in *Early Jewish and Christian Monotheism*. Edited by Loren T. Stuckenbruck and Wendy E. S. North. Journal for the Study of the New Testament Supplement Series 263. New York: T&T Clark.

——, ed. 2005. *The New Perspective on Paul: Collected Essays*. Tübingen: Mohr Siebeck.

————. 2009. *"If Sons, Then Heirs: A Study of Kinship and Ethnicity in the Letters of Paul*, by Caroline Johnson Hodge." *Journal of Theological Studies* 60 (2): 643-45.

Dunne, John A. 2011. "The Regal Status of Christ in the Colossian 'Christ Hymn': A Re-evaluation of the Influence of Wisdom Traditions." *Trinity Journal* 32: 3-18.

Eastman, Susan. 2002. "Whose Apocalypse? The Identity of the Sons of God in Romans 8:19." *Journal of Biblical Literature* 121 (2): 263-77.

Edwards, James R. 1992. *Romans*. New International Biblical Commentary: New Testament Series 6. Edited by W. Ward Gasque. Peabody, MA: Hendrickson.

Eisenbaum, Pamela. 2009. *Paul Was Not A Christian: The Original Message of a Misunderstood Apostle*. New York: HarperCollins.

Eltester, Friedrich-Wilhelm. 1958. *Eikon im Neuen Testament*. Berlin: Verlag Alfred Topelmann.

Esler, Philip. 2003. *Conflict and Identity in Romans: The Social Setting of Paul's Letter*. Minneapolis: Fortress.

Evans, Craig A., and James A. Sanders. 1993. *Paul and the Scriptures of Israel*. Journal for the Study of the New Testament Supplement Series 83. Studies in Scripture in Early Judaism and Christianity 1. Sheffield: JSOT Press.

Fahlbusch, Erwin. 2003. "Order of Salvation." Pages 836-38 in vol. 3 of *The Encyclopedia of Christianity*. Edited by Erwin Fahlbusch, Jan Milič Lochman, John Mbiti, Jaroslav Pelikan, and Lukas Vischer. Leiden: Brill.

Fahy, T. 1956. "Romans 8:29." *Irish Theological Quarterly* 23: 410-12.

Fee, Gordon. 1987. *The First Epistle to the Corinthians*. New International Commentary on the New Testament. Rev. ed. Grand Rapids: Eerdmans.

————. 1994. *God's Empowering Presence: The Holy Spirit in the Letters of Paul*. Peabody, MA: Hendrickson.

————. 1995. *Paul's Letter to the Philippians*. New International Commentary on the New Testament. Grand Rapids: Eerdmans.

————. 2004. "Paul and the Metaphors of Salvation." Pages 43-67 in *The Redemption: An Interdisciplinary Symposium on Christ as Redeemer*. Edited by Stephen T. Davis, Daniel Kendall, and Gerald O'Collins. Oxford: Oxford University Press.

————. 2007. *Pauline Christology: An Exegetical-Theological Study*. Peabody, MA: Hendrickson.

Fewster, Gregory P. 2013. *Creation Language in Romans 8: A Study in Monosemy*. Linguistic Biblical Studies 8. Edited by Stanley E. Porter. Leiden: Brill.

Fishbane, Michael. 1985. *Biblical Interpretation in Ancient Israel*. New York: Oxford University Press.

Fitzmyer, Joseph A. 1993. *Romans*. Anchor Bible 33. New York: Doubleday.

Fletcher-Louis, Crispin H. T. 2002. *All the Glory of Adam: Liturgical Anthropology in the Dead Sea Scrolls*. Studies on the Texts of the Desert of Judah. Edited by F. Garcia Martínez. Boston: Brill.

Flynn, Shawn W. 2014. *YHWH Is King: The Development of Divine Kingship in Ancient Israel*. Supplements to Vetus Testamentum 159. Leiden: Brill.

Forster, Arthur Haire. 1930. "The Meaning of Doxa in the Greek Bible." *Anglican Theological Review* 12 (4): 311-16.

Fossum, Jarl. 1992. "Son of God." Pages 128-37 in vol. 6 of *Anchor Bible Dictionary*. Edited by David Noel Freedman. 6 vols. New York: Doubleday.

Fowl, Stephen E. 2005. *Philippians*. Two Horizons New Testament Commentary. Grand Rapids: Eerdmans.

Fowler, James A. 2005. *Union with Christ*. Fallbrook, CA: C.I.Y. Publishing.

Freedman, David Noel, Gary Herion, David Graf, and John Pleins, eds. 1992. *The Anchor Bible Dictionary*. New York: Doubleday.

Fretheim, Terence E. 2005. *God and World in the Old Testament: A Relational Theology of Creation*. Nashville: Abingdon.

Gaffin, Richard B. 1978. *The Centrality of the Resurrection: A Study in Paul's Soteriology*. Grand Rapids: Baker.

———. 1987. *Resurrection and Redemption: A Study in Paul's Soteriology*. Phillipsburg, NJ: Presbyterian and Reformed.

———. 1993. "Glory, Glorification." Pages 348-50 in *Dictionary of Paul and His Letters*. Edited by Gerald F. Hawthorne, Ralph P. Martin, and Daniel G. Reid. Downers Grove, IL: InterVarsity Press.

Garland, David E. 1998. *Colossians and Philemon*. NIV Application Commentary. Grand Rapids: Zondervan.

———. 1999. *2 Corinthians*. New American Commentary 29. Nashville: Broadman & Holman.

Garner, D. B. 2002. "Adoption in Christ." PhD diss., Westminster Theological Seminary.

Gibbs, John G. 1971. *Creation and Redemption*. Leiden: Brill.

Giblin, Charles. 1970. *In Hope of God's Glory: Pauline Theological Perspectives*. New York: Herder and Herder.

Gibson, J. C. L. 1998. *Language and Imagery in the Old Testament*. Peabody, MA: Hendrickson.

Goff, Matthew. 2003. "*All the Glory of Adam: Liturgical Anthropology in the Dead Sea Scrolls*, by Crispin Fletcher-Louis." *Journal of Biblical Literature* 122 (1): 165-75.

Goldingay, John. 2006. *Psalms*. Vol. 1, *Psalms 1–41*. Baker Commentary on the Old Testament Wisdom and Psalms. Edited by Tremper Longman III. Grand Rapids: Baker Academic.

Gorman, Michael. 2001. *Cruciformity: Paul's Narrative Spirituality of the Cross*. Grand Rapids: Eerdmans.

———. 2009. *Inhabiting the Cruciform God: Kenosis, Justification and Theosis in Paul's Narrative Soteriology*. Grand Rapids: Eerdmans.

Gow, A. S. F., and A. F. Schofield, eds. and trans. (1953) 1997. *Nicander: The Poems and Poetical Fragments*. Bristol: Bristol Classical Press.

Gray, John. 1979. *The Biblical Doctrine of the Reign of God*. Edinburgh: T&T Clark.

Grelot, Pierre. 2006. *The Language of Symbolism: Biblical Theology, Semantics, and Exegesis*. Translated by Christopher R. Smith. Peabody, MA: Hendrickson.

Grieb, Katherine A. 2002. *The Story of Romans: A Narrative Defense of God's Righteousness*. Louisville: Westminster John Knox.

Gunkel, H. (1933) 1998. *Introduction to the Psalms*. Completed by J. Begrich. Translated by J. D. Nogalski. Macon, GA: Mercer University Press.

Hafemann, S. J. 1993. "Suffering." Pages 919-21 in *Dictionary of Paul and His Letters*. Edited by Gerald F. Hawthorne, Ralph P. Martin, and Daniel G. Reid. Downers Grove, IL: InterVarsity Press.

———. 2005. *Paul, Moses, and the History of Israel*. Exeter, UK: Paternoster.

Hahn, F. 1969. *The Titles of Jesus in Christology: Their History in Early Christianity*. Translated by H. Knight and G. Ogg. New York: World.

Hahne, Harry A. 2006. *The Corruption and Redemption of Creation: Nature in Romans 8.19-22 and Jewish Apocalyptic Literature*. Library of New Testament Studies 336. Edited by Mark Goodacre. London: T&T Clark.

Hall, Douglas J. 1986. *Imaging God: Dominion as Stewardship*. Grand Rapids: Eerdmans.

Hancher, Michael. 1981. "Humpty Dumpty and Verbal Meaning." *The Journal of Aesthetics and Art Criticism* 40: 49-58.

Hansen, G. Walter. 2009. *The Letter to the Philippians*. Pillar New Testament Commentary. Edited by D. A. Carson. Grand Rapids: Eerdmans.

Harris, Murray J. 2005. *The Second Epistle to the Corinthians*. New International Greek Testament Commentary. Grand Rapids: Eerdmans.

Harrison, E. F. 1982. "Glory." Pages 477-83 in vol. 2 of *The International Standard Bible Encyclopedia*. Edited by Geoffrey W. Bromiley. Grand Rapids: Eerdmans.

Harrison, James. 2011. *Paul and the Imperial Authorities at Thessalonica and Rome: A Study in the Conflict of Ideology*. Tübingen: Mohr Siebeck.

Harvey, John D. 1992. "The 'With Christ' Motif in Paul's Thought." *Journal of the Evangelical Theological Society* 35 (3): 329-40.

Hasitschka, Martin. 2010. "Dem 'Bild' Des Sohnes Gottes 'Gleichgestaltet' Werden (Rom 8, 29)." Pages 347-56 in *Perché stessero con Lui: Scritti in onore di Klemens Stock SJ, nel suo 75° compleanno.* Edited by Lorenzo De Santos and Santi Grasso. Rome: Gregorian & Biblical Press.

Hawthorne, Gerald F. 1983. *Philippians.* Word Biblical Commentary 43. Waco, TX: Word Books.

———. 1998. "In the Form of God and Equal with God (Philippians 2:6)." Pages 96-110 in *Where Christology Began.* Edited by Ralph P. Martin and Brian J. Dodd. Louisville: Westminster John Knox.

Hay, David H. 1973. *Glory at the Right Hand: Psalm 110 in Early Christianity.* Society of Biblical Literature Monograph Series 18. Nashville: Abingdon.

———. 2000. *Colossians.* Abingdon New Testament Commentaries. Edited by Victor Paul Furnish. Nashville: Abingdon.

Hays, Richard B. 1989. *Echoes of Scripture in the Letters of Paul.* New Haven, CT: Yale University Press.

———. 1996. "'The Gospel Is the Power of God for Salvation to Gentiles Only'? A Critique of Stanley Stowers' *A Rereading of Romans.*" *Critical Review of Books in Religion* 9: 27-44.

———. 1997. *First Corinthians.* Interpretation: A Bible Commentary for Teaching and Preaching. Louisville: John Knox.

———. 2000. "The Letter to the Galatians: Introduction, Commentary, and Reflections." Pages 181-348 in vol. 11 of the *New Interpreter's Bible.* Nashville: Abingdon.

———. (1983) 2002. *The Faith of Jesus Christ: The Narrative Sub-Structure of Galatians 3:1–4:11.* 2nd ed. Grand Rapids: Eerdmans.

———. 2005. *Conversion of the Imagination: Paul as Interpreter of Israel's Scripture.* Grand Rapids: Eerdmans.

———. 2008. "What Is 'Real Participation in Christ'?: A Dialogue with E. P. Sanders on Pauline Soteriology." Pages 336-51 in *Redefining First-Century Jewish and Christian Identities: Essays in Honor of Ed Parish Sanders.* Edited by Fabian E. Udoh. Notre Dame, IN: University of Notre Dame Press.

Hegermann, H. 1990. "δόξα, δοξάζω." Pages 344-49 in vol. 1 of *Exegetical Dictionary of the New Testament.* Edited by Horst Balz and Gerhard Schneider. Grand Rapids: Eerdmans.

Heil, John Paul. 2005. *The Rhetorical Role of Scripture in 1 Corinthians.* Studies in Biblical Literature 15. Edited by Sharon H. Ringe. Atlanta: Society of Biblical Literature.

———. 2010. *Philippians: Let Us Rejoice in Being Conformed to Christ.* Society of Biblical Literature, Early Christianity and Its Literature 3. Edited by Gail R. O'Day. Atlanta: Society of Biblical Literature.

Hellerman, Joseph H. 2015. *Philippians.* Exegetical Guide to the Greek New Testament. Edited by Andreas J. Köstenberger and Robert W. Yarbrough. Nashville: Broadman & Holman.

Hellholm, David. 1986. "The Problem of Apocalyptic Genre and the Apocalypse of John." Pages 13-64 in *Early Christian Apocalypticism: Genre and Social Setting.* Semeia 36. Decatur, GA: Scholars Press.

Hendriksen, William. 1980. *Romans: 1–8.* Vol. 1. New Testament Commentary. Edinburgh: Banner of Truth Trust.

Hengel, Martin. (1975) 1976. *The Son of God: The Origin of Christology and the History of Jewish-Hellenistic Religion.* Translated by John Bowden. London: SCM Press.

———. 1983. *Between Jesus and Paul: Studies in the Earliest History of Christianity.* London: SCM Press.

———. 1995. *Studies in Early Christology.* Edinburgh: T&T Clark.

Hermann, Johannes, and Werner Foerster. 1965. "κληρονόμος." Pages 776-85 in vol. 3 of *Theological Dictionary of the New Testament.* Edited by G. Kittel and G. Friedrich. Translated by G. Bromiley. Grand Rapids: Eerdmans.

Hodge, C. 1972. *A Commentary on Romans.* Geneva Series of Commentaries. London: Banner of Truth Trust.

Holladay, William L. 1971. *A Concise Hebrew and Aramaic Lexicon of the Old Testament.* Leiden: Brill.

———. 1986. *Jeremiah 1: A Commentary on the Book of the Prophet Jeremiah; Chapters 1–25.* Hermeneia—A Critical and Historical Commentary on the Bible. Edited by Paul. D. Hanson. Philadelphia: Fortress.

Hooker, Morna D. 1959–1960. "Adam in Romans 1." *New Testament Studies* 6: 297-306.

———. 1971. "Interchange in Christ." *Journal of Theological Studies* 22: 349-61.

———. 1975. "Philippians 2:6-11." Pages 151-64 in *Jesus und Paulus.* Edited by E. Earle Ellis and Erich Grässer. Göttingen: Vandenhoeck & Ruprecht.

———. 1990. *From Adam to Christ.* Cambridge: Cambridge University Press.

Horrell, David G. 2010. *The Bible and the Environment: Towards a Critical Ecological Biblical Theology.* London: Equinox.

Horsley, Richard A. 2000. "The Kingdom of God and the Renewal of Israel: Synoptic Gospels, Jesus Movements, and Apocalypticism." Pages 303-43 in *The*

Encyclopedia of Apocalypticism. Vol. 1 of *The Origins of Apocalypticism in Judaism and Christianity*. Edited by John J. Collins. New York: Continuum.

Horton, Michael S. 2007. *Covenant and Salvation: Union with Christ*. Louisville: Westminster John Knox.

Hughes, Philip Edgcumbe. 2001. *The True Image: The Origin and Destiny of Man in Christ*. Eugene, OR: Wipf and Stock.

Hultgren, Arland J. 2011. *Paul's Letter to the Romans: A Commentary*. Grand Rapids: Eerdmans.

Hunsinger, George. 2008. "Election and the Trinity: Twenty-Five Theses on the Theology of Karl Barth." *Modern Theology* 24 (2): 179-98.

Hunter, A. M. 1955. *The Epistle to the Romans: Introduction and Commentary*. London: SCM Press.

Hurtado, Larry. 1993. "Son of God." Pages 900-906 in *Dictionary of Paul and His Letters*. Edited by G. F. Hawthorne, R. P. Martin, and D. G. Reid. Downers Grove, IL: InterVarsity Press.

———. 1999. *One God, One Lord: Early Christian Devotion and Ancient Jewish Monotheism*. 2nd ed. London: T&T Clark.

———. 2003. *Lord Jesus Christ: Devotion to Jesus in Earliest Christianity*. Grand Rapids: Eerdmans.

Hyldahl, N. 1956. "A Reminiscence of the Old Testament in Romans i. 23." *New Testament Studies* 2: 285-88.

Jenni, Ernst, and Claus Westermann. 1997. *Theological Lexicon of the Old Testament*. 3 vols. Translated by Mark E. Biddle. Peabody, MA: Hendrickson.

Jervell, J. 1960. *Imago Dei: Gen 1,26f. im Spätjudentum, in der Gnosis und in den paulinischen Briefen*. Forschungen zur Religion und Literatur des Alten und Neuen Testaments 58. Göttingen: Vandenhoeck & Ruprecht.

Jewett, Robert. 1971. *Paul's Anthropological Terms: A Study of Their Use in Conflict Settings*. Arbeiten zur Geschichte des antiken Judentums und des Urchristentums 10. Edited by Otto Michel and Martin Hengel. Leiden: Brill.

Jewett, Robert, and Roy D. Kotansky. 2007. *Romans*. Hermeneia—A Critical and Historical Commentary on the Bible. Edited by Eldon Jay Epp. Minneapolis: Fortress.

Johnson, David H. 1992. "The Image of God in Colossians." *Didaskalia* 3 (2): 9-15.

Johnson Hodge, Caroline. 2007. *If Sons, Then Heirs: A Study of Kinship and Ethnicity in the Letters of Paul*. Oxford: Oxford University Press.

Jónsson, Gunnlaugur A. 1988. *The Image of God: Genesis 1:26-28 in a Century of Old Testament Research*. Translated by Lorraine Svendsen. Coniectanea Biblica. Old Testament Series 26. Stockholm: Almqvist & Wiksell.

Jowers, Dennis W. 2006. "The Meaning of *Morphe* in Philippians 2:6-7." *Journal of the Evangelical Theological Society* 49 (4): 739-66.

Juel, Donald. 1988. *Messianic Exegesis: Christological Interpretation of the Old Testament in Early Christianity*. Philadelphia: Fortress.

Kaminsky, Joel. 1995. *Corporate Responsibility in the Hebrew Bible*. Library of Hebrew Bible/Old Testament Studies 196. Sheffield: Sheffield Academic.

Käsemann, Ernst. 1964. *Essays on New Testament Themes*. Translated by W. J. Montague. London: SCM Press.

———. 1968. "Critical Analysis of Philippians 2:5-11." *Journal for Theology and the Church* 5: 45-88.

———. 1971. *Perspectives on Paul*. Translated by M. Kohl. Philadelphia: Fortress.

———. 1980. *Commentary on Romans*. Translated and edited by G. W. Bromiley. Grand Rapids: Eerdmans.

Keck, Leander E. 1988. *Paul and His Letters*. Rev. and enl. ed. Philadelphia: Fortress.

Keener, Craig S. 2005. *1–2 Corinthians*. New Cambridge Bible Commentary. Edited by Ben Witherington III. Cambridge: Cambridge University Press.

Keesmaat, Sylvia C. 1999. *Paul and His Story: (Re)interpreting the Exodus Tradition*. Journal for the Study of the New Testament Supplement Series 181. Sheffield: Sheffield Academic.

Kim, Jung Hoon. 2004. *The Significance of Clothing Imagery in the Pauline Corpus*. London: T&T Clark.

Kim, Seyoon. 1981. *The Origin of Paul's Gospel*. Wissenschaftliche Untersuchungen zum Neuen Testament 2/4. Tübingen: Mohr.

———. 2002. *Paul and the New Perspective: Second Thoughts on the Origin of Paul's Gospel*. Grand Rapids: Eerdmans.

Kim, Tae Hun. 1998. "The Anarthrous *huios theou* in Mark 15:39 and the Roman Imperial Cult." *Biblica* 79: 221-41.

Kinzer, Mark S. 1995. "'All Things Under His Feet': Psalm 8 in the New Testament and in Other Jewish Literature of Late Antiquity." PhD diss., University of Michigan.

Kittel, Gerhard. 1964. "δοκέω, δόξα, δοξάζω, συνδοξάζω, ἔνδοξος, ἐνδοξάζω, παραάδοξος." Pages 232-55 in vol. 2 of *Theological Dictionary of the New Testament*. Edited by Gerhard Kittel. Translated by Geoffrey Bromiley. Grand Rapids: Eerdmans.

Kittel, Helmuth. 1934. *Die Herrlichkeit Gottes: Studien zu Geschichte und Wesen eines neutestamentlichen Begriffs*. Berlin: Walter de Gruyter.

Koehler, Ludwig, and Walter Baumgartner. 2001. "כבד." Pages 455-58 in vol. 2 of *The Hebrew and Aramaic Lexicon of the Old Testament.* Edited by Ludwig Koehler and Walter Baumgartner. Translated by M. E. J. Richardson. Leiden: Brill.

Koehler, Ludwig, and Walter Baumgartner. 1994–2000. *The Hebrew and Aramaic Lexicon of the Old Testament.* 5 vols. Translated and edited by M. E. J. Richardson. Leiden: Brill.

Koen, W. Irvin. 2010. *Conformed to His Image.* Bloomington, IN: Xlibris.

Kramer, Werner R. 1966. *"Christ, Lord, Son of God."* Studies in Biblical Theology 50. Translated by Brian Hardy. London: SCM Press.

Kreitzer, L. J. 1993. "Adam and Christ." Pages 9-15 in *Dictionary of Paul and His Letters.* Edited by G. F. Hawthorne, R. P. Martin, and D. G. Reid. Downers Grove, IL: InterVarsity Press.

Kruse, Colin G. 2012. *Paul's Letter to the Romans.* Pillar New Testament Commentary. Grand Rapids: Eerdmans.

Kürzinger, Josef. 1958. "σύμμόρφους τῆς εἰκόνος τοῦ υἱοῦ αὐτου (Röm 8,29)." *Biblische Zeitschrift* 2: 294-99.

Lambrecht, Jan. 1999. *Second Corinthians.* Edited by Daniel J. Harrington. Collegeville, MN: Liturgical Press.

Law, Jeremy. 2010. "Jürgen Moltmann's Ecological Hermeneutics." Pages 223-39 in *Ecological Hermeneutics: Biblical, Historical and Theological Perspectives.* Edited by David Horrell, Christopher Southgate, and Francesca Stavrakopoulou. Edinburgh: T&T Clark.

Leaney, A. R. C. 1964. "Conformed to the Image of His Son (Rom 8:29)." *New Testament Studies* 10: 470-79.

Lee, Aquila H. I. 2005. *From Messiah to Preexistent Son: Jesus' Self-Consciousness and Early Christian Exegesis of Messianic Psalms.* Wissenschaftliche Untersuchungen zum Neuen Testament 2. Edited by Jörg Frey. Tübingen: Mohr Siebeck.

Lee, Yongborn. 2012. *The Son of Man as the Last Adam.* Eugene, OR: Pickwick.

Leenhardt, Franz J. 1961. *The Epistle to the Romans: A Commentary.* Translated by Harold Knight. London: Lutterworth.

Letham, Robert. 2011. *Union with Christ in Scripture, History, and Theology.* Phillipsburg, NJ: P&R.

Levison, John R. 1988. *Portraits of Adam in Early Judaism: From Sirach to 2 Baruch.* Journal for the Study of the Pseudepigrapha Supplement Series 1. Edited by James H. Charlesworth. Sheffield: JSOT Press.

———. 2004. "Adam and Eve in Romans 1.18-25 and the Greek Life of Adam and Eve." *New Testament Studies* 50 (4): 519-34.

Liefeld, Walter L. 1997. *Ephesians*. IVP New Testament Commentary Series. Downers Grove, IL: IVP Academic.

Limburg, James. 2000. *Psalms*. Westminster Bible Companion. Edited by Patrick D. Miller and David L. Bartlett. Louisville, KY: Westminster John Knox.

Lindsay, Hugh. 2009. *Adoption in the Roman World*. Cambridge: Cambridge University Press.

Litwa, M. D. 2008. "2 Corinthians 3:18 and Its Implications for *Theosis.*" *Journal of Theological Interpretation* 2: 117-33.

———. 2012. "Transformation Through a Mirror: Moses in 2 Cor. 3:18." *Journal for the Study of the New Testament* 34 (3): 286-97.

Loane, Marcus L. 1968. *The Hope of Glory: An Exposition of the Eighth Chapter in the Epistle to the Romans*. London: Hodder & Stoughton.

Lohse, Eduard. 1971. *Colossians and Philemon: A Commentary on the Epistles to the Colossians and to Philemon*. Translated by James W. Leitch. Hermeneia—A Critical and Historical Commentary on the Bible. Edited by George W. MacRae, SJ. Philadelphia: Fortress.

Longenecker, Bruce W. 1991. *Eschatology and the Covenant: A Comparison of 4 Ezra and Romans 1–11*. Journal for the New Testament Supplement Series 57. Sheffield: JSOT Press.

Longenecker, Richard N. 1990. *Galatians*. Word Biblical Commentary 41. Edited by Bruce M. Metzger, David A. Hubbard, and Glenn W. Barker. Waco, TX: Word Books.

———. 1999. *Biblical Exegesis in the Apostolic Period*. 2nd ed. Grand Rapids: Eerdmans.

———, ed. 2005. *Contours of Christology in the New Testament*. Grand Rapids: Eerdmans.

———. 2011. *Introducing Romans: Critical Issues in Paul's Most Famous Letter*. Grand Rapids: Eerdmans.

Louw, Johannes P., and Eugene A. Nida. 1989. *Greek-English Lexicon of the New Testament Based on Semantic Domains*. 2 vols. New York: United Bible Societies.

Luther, Martin. 1954. *Commentary on the Epistle to the Romans*. Translated by J. Theodore Mueller. Grand Rapids: Zondervan.

———. 1972. *Lectures on Romans: Glosses and Scholia*. Vol. 25 of *Luther's Works*. Edited by H. C. Oswald. Philadelphia: Muhlenberg.

Macaskill, Grant. 2011. "Review Article: The Deliverance of God." *Journal for the Study of the New Testament* 34 (2): 150-61.

———. 2013. *Union with Christ in The New Testament*. Oxford: Oxford University Press.

MacDonald, Margaret Y. 2000. *Colossians and Ephesians*. Sacra Pagina Series 17. Edited by Daniel J. Harrington, SJ. Collegeville, MN: Liturgical Press.

Marcovich, M. 2001. *Origenes: Contra Celsum, Libri VII*. Supplements to Vigiliae Christianae 54. Leiden: Brill.

Marshall, I. H. 1969. *Kept by the Power of God: A Study of Perseverance and Falling Away*. London: Epworth.

Martin, Ralph P. 1967. *Carmen Christi: Philippians 2:5-11 in Recent Interpretation and in the Setting of Early Christian Worship*. London: Cambridge University Press.

———. 1974. *Colossians and Philemon*. New Century Bible Commentary. New York: HarperCollins.

———. (1986) 2014. *2 Corinthians*. 2nd ed. Word Biblical Commentary 40. Grand Rapids: Zondervan.

Martínez, Florentino García, ed. 1996. *The Dead Sea Scrolls Translated: The Qumran Texts in English*. 2nd ed. Translated by Wilfred G. E. Watson. Grand Rapids: Eerdmans.

Mason, Eric F. 2009. "Interpretation of Psalm 2 in *4QFlorilegium* and in the New Testament." Pages 67-82 in *Echoes from the Caves: Qumran and the New Testament*. Studies on the Texts of the Desert of Judah 85. Edited by Florentino García Martínez. Leiden: Brill.

Matera, Frank. 2003. *II Corinthians: A Commentary*. Louisville: Westminster John Knox.

———. 2012. *God's Saving Grace: A Pauline Theology*. Grand Rapids: Eerdmans.

McCormack, Bruce. 2010. "Election and the Trinity: Theses in Response to George Hunsinger." *Scottish Journal of Theology* 63 (2): 203-24.

McDowell, Catherine. 2015. "The Image of God in the Garden of Eden: The Creation of Humankind in Genesis 2:5–3:24 in Light of mīs pî pīt pî and wpt-r Rituals of Mesopotamia and Ancient Egypt." In *Mesopotamia and Ancient Egypt*. Siphrut: Literature and Theology of the Hebrew Scriptures 15. Winona Lake, IN: Eisenbrauns.

McGrath, Brendan. 1952. "'*Syn*' Words in Saint Paul." *Catholic Biblical Quarterly* 14 (3): 219-26.

McKim, Donald K. 1996. *Westminster Dictionary of Theological Terms*. Louisville: Westminster John Knox.

Michaels, J. R. 1999. "The Redemption of Our Body: The Riddle of Romans 8.19-22." Pages 92-114 in *Romans and the People of God*. Edited by S. K. Soderlund and N. T. Wright. Grand Rapids: Eerdmans.

Michel, Otto. 1966. *Der Brief an die Römer*. 4th ed. H. A. W. Meyer Kritisch-exegetischer Kommentar über das Neue Testament. Göttingen: Vandenhoeck & Ruprecht.

Middleton, J. Richard. 2005. *The Liberating Image: The Imago Dei in Genesis 1.* Grand Rapids: Brazos.

Moltmann, Jürgen. 1985. *God in Creation: An Ecological Doctrine of Creation.* The Gifford Lectures 1984–1985. London: SCM Press.

Montague, George T., SM. 2011. *First Corinthians.* Catholic Commentary on Sacred Scripture. Edited by Peter S. Williamson and Mary Healy. Grand Rapids: Baker Academic.

Moo, Douglas. 1996. *The Epistle to the Romans.* New International Commentary on the New Testament. Grand Rapids: Eerdmans.

———. 1998. *The Letters to the Colossians and to Philemon.* Pillar New Testament Commentary. Grand Rapids: Eerdmans.

———. 2013. *Galatians.* Baker Exegetical Commentary on the New Testament. Grand Rapids: Baker Academic.

Moo, Jonathan. 2008. "Romans 8.19-22 and Isaiah's Cosmic Covenant." *New Testament Studies* 54: 74-89.

Moo, Jonathan A., and Robert S. White. 2014. *Let Creation Rejoice: Biblical Hope and Ecological Crisis.* Downers Grove, IL: InterVarsity Press.

Morris, Leon. 1988. *The Epistle to the Romans.* Pillar New Testament Commentary. Grand Rapids: Eerdmans.

Morris, Paul. 1992. "Exiled from Eden: Jewish Interpretation of Genesis." Pages 117-66 in *A Walk in the Garden: Biblical, Iconographical and Literary Images of Eden.* Journal for the Study of the Old Testament Supplement Series 136. Edited by Paul Morris and Deborah Sawyer. Sheffield: JSOT Press.

Moule, C. F. D. 1958. *The Epistles of Paul the Apostle to the Colossians and to Philemon: An Introduction and Commentary.* Cambridge: Cambridge University Press.

———. 1977. *The Origin of Christology.* Cambridge: Cambridge University Press.

Mounce, R. H. 1995. *Romans.* New American Commentary 27. Nashville: Broadman & Holman.

———. 1997. *The Book of Revelation.* Rev. ed. New International Commentary on the New Testament. Grand Rapids: Eerdmans.

Mowery, Robert. 2002. "Son of God in Roman Imperial Titles and Matthew." *Biblica* 83: 100-110.

Muller, Richard A. 1985. *Dictionary of Latin and Greek Theological Terms: Drawn Principally from Protestant Scholastic Theology.* Grand Rapids: Baker Academic.

Muraoka, T. 2009. *A Greek-English Lexicon of the Septuagint.* Leuven: Peeters.

Murray, John. 1959. *The Epistle to the Romans: The English Text with Introduction, Exposition, and Notes: Chapters 1–8.* New International Commentary on the New Testament. Grand Rapids: Eerdmans.

————. 1961. *Redemption Accomplished and Applied*. Edinburgh: Banner of Truth.

Nanos, Mark D. 1996. *The Mystery of Romans: The Jewish Context of Paul's Letter.* Minneapolis: Fortress.

Neder, Adam. 2009. *Participation in Christ: An Entry into Karl Barth's Church Dogmatics.* Columbia Series in Reformed Theology. Louisville: Westminster John Knox.

Neugebauer, Fritz. 1961. *In Christus = En Xristoi: eine Untersuchung zum paulinischen Glaubensverständnis.* Göttingen: Vandenhoeck & Ruprecht.

Newman, Carey C. 1992. *Paul's Glory-Christology: Tradition and Rhetoric.* Supplements to Novum Testamentum 69. Leiden: Brill.

Nickelsburg, George W. E. 2001. *1 Enoch 1: A Commentary on the Book of 1 Enoch, Chapters 1–36; 81–108.* Hermeneia—A Critical and Historical Commentary on the Bible. Edited by Klaus Baltzer. Minneapolis: Fortress.

Nickelsburg, George W. E., and James C. VanderKam. 2012. *1 Enoch 2: A Commentary on the Book of 1 Enoch, Chapters 37–82.* Hermeneia—A Critical and Historical Commentary on the Bible. Edited by Klaus Baltzer. Minneapolis: Fortress.

Niebuhr, Ursula M. 1984. "Glory." *Biblical Theology Bulletin* 14: 49-53.

Novenson, Matthew V. 2012. *Christ Among the Messiahs: Christ Language in Paul and Messiah Language in Ancient Judaism.* Oxford: Oxford University Press.

Oakes, Peter. 2004. "Conflict and Identity in Romans: The Social Setting of Paul's Letter." *Journal for the Study of the New Testament* 26 (4): 512-14.

O'Brien, Peter T. 1982. *Colossians, Philemon.* Word Biblical Commentary 44. Dallas: Word.

————. 1991. *The Epistle to the Philippians: A Commentary on the Greek Text.* New International Greek Testament Commentary. Grand Rapids: Eerdmans.

————. 1993. "Firstborn." Pages 301-3 in *Dictionary of Paul and His Letters.* Edited by Gerald F. Hawthorne, Ralph P. Martin, and Daniel G. Reid. Downers Grove, IL: InterVarsity Press.

————. 2001. *The Epistle to the Philippians: A Commentary on the Greek Text.* Grand Rapids: Eerdmans.

Ogden, C. K., and I. A. Richards. 1945. *The Meaning of Meaning.* New York: Harcourt, Brace.

Ortlund, Dane. 2014. "Inaugurated Glorification: Revisiting Romans 8:30." *Journal of the Evangelical Theological Society* 57: 111-33.

Osiek, Carolyn. 2000. *Philippians, Philemon.* Abingdon New Testament Commentaries. Edited by Victor Paul Furnish. Nashville: Abingdon.

Owen, E. C. E. 1932. "Δόξα and Cognate Words." *Journal of Theological Studies* 33 (131): 265-79.

Patella, Michael. 2005. *Word and Image: The Hermeneutics of the Saint John's Bible.* Collegeville, MN: Liturgical Press.

Pauli, C. W. H., trans. 1871. *The Chaldee Paraphrase on the Prophet Isaiah.* London: London Society's House.

Payne, Philip B. 2009. *Man and Woman, One in Christ: An Exegetical and Theological Study of Paul's Letters.* Grand Rapids: Zondervan.

Peppard, Michael. 2011. *The Son of God in the Roman World: Divine Sonship in Its Social and Political Context.* Oxford: Oxford University Press.

Peterson, Jeffrey. 1997. "A Rereading of Romans: Justice, Jews, and Gentiles." *Restoration Quarterly* 39 (1): 50-53.

Peterson, David. 2001. *Possessed by God: A New Testament Theology of Sanctification and Holiness.* New Studies in Biblical Theology. Downers Grove, IL: InterVarsity Press.

Peterson, Robert. 2010. "To Reconcile to Himself All Things: Colossians 1:20." *Presbyterion* 36 (1): 37-46.

Porter, J. R. 1965. "Legal Aspects of the Concept of 'Corporate Personality' in the Old Testament." *Vetus Testamentum* 15: 361-80.

Porter, Stanley E. 1993. *Verbal Aspect in the Greek of the New Testament, with Reference to Tense and Mood.* Studies in Biblical Greek 1. Edited by D. A. Carson. New York: Peter Lang.

Porter, Stanley E., and Christopher D. Stanley, eds. 2008. *As It Is Written: Studying Paul's Use of Scripture.* Atlanta: Society of Biblical Literature.

Portier-Young, Anathea E. 2011. *Apocalypse Against Empire: Theologies of Resistance in Early Judaism.* Grand Rapids: Eerdmans.

Powers, Daniel G. 2001. *Salvation Through Participation: An Examination of the Notion of the Believers' Corporate Unity with Christ in Early Christian Soteriology.* Sterling, VA: Peeters.

Prickett, Stephen. 1986. *Words and the Word: Language, Poetics and Biblical Interpretation.* Cambridge: Cambridge University Press.

Ramsey, Arthur M. 1949. *The Glory of God and the Transfiguration of Christ.* London: Longmans, Green.

Raurell, F. 1979. "The Religious Meaning of 'Doxa' in the Book of Wisdom." Pages 370-83 in *La Sagesse de l'Ancien Testament.* Bibliotheca Ephemeridum Theologicarum Lovaniensium 51. Edited by M. Gilbert. Leuven: Leuven University Press.

Reid, Marty L. 1996. *Augustinian and Pauline Rhetoric in Romans Five: A Study of Early Christian Rhetoric.* Mellen Biblical Press Series 30. Lewiston, NY: Mellen.

Reumann, John. 2008. *Philippians: A New Translation with Introduction and Commentary.* Anchor Yale Bible 33B. Edited by John J. Collins. New Haven, CT: Yale University Press.

Ricoeur, Paul. 1977. *The Rule of Metaphor: Multi-Disciplinary Studies on the Creation of Meaning in Language*. Translated by Robert Czerny. Toronto: University of Toronto Press.

Ridderbos, Herman. 1975. *Paul: An Outline of His Theology*. Translated by John Richard de Witt. Grand Rapids: Eerdmans.

Robinson, H. Wheeler. 1981. "The Hebrew Conception of Corporate Personality." Pages 25-44 in *Corporate Personality in Ancient Israel*. Rev. ed. Edinburgh: T&T Clark.

Robinson, John A. T. 1952. *The Body: A Study in Pauline Theology*. Studies in Biblical Theology 5. London: SCM Press.

Rogerson, J. W. 1970. "The Hebrew Conception of Corporate Personality: A Re-examination." *Journal of Theological Studies* 21: 1-16.

Rosner, Brian. 2013. *Paul and the Law: Keeping the Commandments of God*. New Studies in Biblical Theology. Edited by D. A. Carson. Downers Grove, IL: InterVarsity Press.

Rowe, C. Kavin. 2005. "New Testament Iconography? Situating Paul in the Absence of Material Evidence." Pages 289-312 in *Picturing the New Testament: Studies in Ancient Visual Images*. Wissenschaftliche Untersuchungen Zum Neuen Testament 2:193. Tübingen: Mohr Siebeck.

Sampley, J. Paul. 2000. "The Second Letter to the Corinthians." Pages 1-180 in vol. 11 of *The New Interpreter's Bible*. Nashville: Abingdon.

Sanday, W., and A. C. Headlam. 1902. *A Critical and Exegetical Commentary on the Epistle to the Romans*. International Critical Commentary. Edinburgh: T&T Clark.

Sanders, E. P. 1977. *Paul and Palestinian Judaism: A Comparison of Patterns of Religion*. Philadelphia: Fortress.

Sandmel, Samuel. 1962. "Parallelomania." *Journal of Biblical Literature* 81: 1-13.

Schaefer, Konrad. 2001. *Psalms*. Berit Olam. Edited by David W. Cotter. Collegeville, MN: Liturgical Press.

Schlatter, A. 1995. *Romans: The Righteousness of God*. Translated by S. S. Schatzmann. Peabody, MA: Hendrickson.

Schmidt, Werner H. 1969. "Gott und Mensch in Ps. 8: Form und uberlieferungsge-schictliche." *Theologische Zeitschrift* 25: 1-15.

Schmisek, Brian. 2013. "The Body of His Glory: Resurrection Imagery in Philippians 3:20-21." *Biblical Theology Bulletin* 43 (1): 23-28.

Schreiner, Thomas R. 1998. *Romans*. Baker Exegetical Commentary on the New Testament. Grand Rapids: Baker Academic.

———. 2001. *Paul, Apostle of God's Glory in Christ: A Pauline Theology*. Downers Grove, IL: IVP Academic.

————. 2010. *Galatians*. Zondervan Exegetical Commentary on the New Testament 9. Grand Rapids: Zondervan.

Schweitzer, Albert. 1931. *The Mysticism of Paul the Apostle*. Translated by William Montgomery. London: A&C Black.

Scott, James M. 1992. *Adoption as Sons of God: An Exegetical Investigation into the Background of [huiothesia] in the Pauline Corpus*. Tübingen: J. C. B. Mohr.

————. 1993. "Adoption, Sonship." Pages 15-18 in *Dictionary of Paul and His Letters*. Edited by G. F. Hawthorne, R. P. Martin, and D. G. Reid. Downers Grove, IL: InterVarsity Press.

Scroggs, Robin. 1966. *The Last Adam: A Study in Pauline Anthropology*. Philadelphia: Fortress.

Segal, Alan F. 1990. *Paul the Convert: The Apostolate and Apostasy of Saul the Pharisee*. New Haven, CT: Yale University Press.

Seifrid, Mark A. 1993. "In Christ." Pages 433-36 in *Dictionary of Paul and His Letters*. Edited by Gerald F. Hawthorne, Ralph P. Martin, and Daniel G. Reid. Downers Grove: IL: InterVarsity Press.

————. 2001. "Unrighteous by Faith: Apostolic Proclamation in Romans 1:18–3:20." Pages 105-46 in *Justification and Variegated Nomism: The Paradoxes of Paul*. Edited by D. A. Carson and Peter T. O'Brien. Grand Rapids: Baker Academic.

————. 2007. "Romans." Pages 607-94 in *Commentary on the New Testament Use of the Old Testament*. Edited by G. K. Beale and D. A. Carson. Grand Rapids: Baker Academic.

————. 2014. *The Second Letter to the Corinthians*. Pillar New Testament Commentary. Grand Rapids: Eerdmans.

Seitz, Christopher. 2014. *Colossians*. Brazos Theological Commentary on the Bible. Grand Rapids: Brazos.

Shauf, Scott. 2006. "Galatians 2:20 in Context." *New Testament Studies* 52: 86-101.

Siber, Peter. 1971. *Mit Christus leben: eine Studie zur paulinischen Auferstehungshoffnung*. Abhandlungen zur Theologie des Alten und Neuen Testaments 61. Zürich: Theologischer Verlag.

Silva, Moisés. 1994. *Biblical Words and Their Meaning: An Introduction to Lexical Semantics*. Rev. and exp. ed. Grand Rapids: Zondervan.

————. 2005. *Philippians*. Baker Exegetical Commentary on the New Testament. 2nd ed. Grand Rapids: Baker Academic.

Soards, Marion L. 1999. *1 Corinthians*. New International Biblical Commentary: New Testament Series. Edited by W. Ward Gasque. Peabody, MA: Hendrickson.

Societatis Philologae Bonnensis, ed. 1910. *Heraclitus: Quaestiones Homericae*. Lipsiae: In Aedibus B. G. Teubneri.

Stowers, Stanley K. 1994. *A Rereading of Romans: Justice, Jews, and Gentiles*. New Haven, CT: Yale University Press.

Stuhlmacher, P. 1994. *Paul's Letter to the Romans: A Commentary*. Translated by S. J. Hafemann. Louisville: Westminster John Knox.

Tannehill, Robert C. 1967. *Dying and Rising with Christ: A Study in Pauline Theology*. Berlin: Verlag Alfred Töpelmann.

———. 2007. "Participation in Christ." Pages 223-37 in *The Shape of the Gospel: New Testament Essays*. Eugene, OR: Cascade.

Taylor, Vincent. 1955. *The Epistle to the Romans*. Epworth Preacher's Commentaries. London: Epworth.

Theron, Daniel J. 1956. "'Adoption' in the Pauline Corpus." *Evangelical Quarterly* 28: 7-14.

Thielman, Frank. 1995. "The Story of Israel and the Theology of Romans 5–8." Pages 169-95 in *Romans*. Vol. 3 of *Pauline Theology*. Minneapolis: Fortress.

Thiselton, Anthony C. 2000. *The First Epistle to the Corinthians: A Commentary on the Greek Text*. New International Greek Testament Commentary. Grand Rapids: Eerdmans.

Thompson, Marianne Meye. 2005. *Colossians and Philemon*. Two Horizons New Testament Commentary. Grand Rapids: Eerdmans.

Thrall, Margaret E. 1994. *Introduction and Commentary on II Corinthians I—VII*. Vol. 1 of *The Second Epistle to the Corinthians: A Critical and Exegetical Commentary*. International Critical Commentary. Edinburgh: T&T Clark.

Thurston, Bonnie B., and Judith Ryan. 2009. *Philippians and Philemon*. Sacra Pagina Series 10. Edited by Daniel J. Harrington, SJ. Collegeville, MN: Liturgical Press.

Tooman, William A. 2011. *Gog of Magog: Reuse of Scripture and Compositional Technique in Ezekiel 38–39*. Forschungen zum Alten Testament 2. Tübingen: Mohr Siebeck.

Urassa, Wenceslaus Mkeni. 1998. *Psalm 8 and Its Christological Re-Interpretations in the New Testament Context: An Inter-Contextual Study in Biblical Hermeneutics*. European University Studies, Series 23, Vol. 577. Frankfurt: Peter Lang.

Van Kooten, George H. 2008a. *Paul's Anthropology in Context: The Image of God, Assimilation to God, and Tripartite Man in Ancient Judaism, Ancient Philosophy and Early Christianity*. Wissenschaftliche Untersuchungen zum Neuen Testament 232. Tübingen: Mohr Siebeck.

———. 2008b. "Why Did Paul Include An Exegesis of Moses' Shining Face (Exod 34) in 2 Cor 3? Moses' Strength, Well-Being and (Transitory) Glory, According to Philo, Josephus, Paul, and the Corinthian Sophists." Pages 149-82 in *The Significance of Sinai: Traditions About Divine Revelation in Judaism and Christianity*.

Edited by George J. Brooke, Hindy Najman, and Loren T. Stuckenbruck. Themes in Biblical Narrative: Jewish and Christian Traditions 12. Leiden: Brill.

Vanhoozer, Kevin J., ed. 2005. *Dictionary for Theological Interpretation of the Bible.* London: SPCK.

Vermes, Geza, ed. 1987. *The Dead Sea Scrolls in English.* 3rd ed. Harmondsworth: Penguin Books.

von Gall, Freiherrn. 1900. *Die Herrlichkeit Gottes: Eine Biblisch-Theologische Untersuchung.* Giessen: J. Ricker'sche Töpelmann.

Wagner, J. Ross. 1997. "The Christ, Servant of Jew and Gentile: A Fresh Approach to Romans 15:8-9." *Journal of Biblical Literature* 116 (3): 473-85.

Wagner, Thomas. 2012. *Gottes Herrlichkeit: Bedeutung und Verwendung des Begriffs kābōd im Alten Testament.* Vetus Testamentum Supplements 151. Leiden: Brill.

Wallace, Daniel B. 1996. *Greek Grammar Beyond the Basics: An Exegetical Syntax of the New Testament.* Grand Rapids: Zondervan.

Wanamaker, Charles A. 1980. "The Son and the Sons of God: A Study in Elements of Paul's Christological and Soteriological Thought." PhD diss., University of Durham.

———. 1987. "Philippians 2.6-11: Son of God or Adamic Christology?" *New Testament Studies* 33: 179-93.

Warfield, B. B. 1950. *The Person and Work of Christ.* Edited by S. G. Craig. Grand Rapids: Baker.

Wedderburn, A. J. M., and Andrew T. Lincoln. 1993. *The Theology of the Later Pauline Letters.* Cambridge: Cambridge University Press.

Wenham, Gordon J. 1987. *Genesis 1–15.* Word Biblical Commentary 1. Waco, TX: Word Books.

White, A. Blake. 2012. *Union with Christ: Last Adam and Seed of Abraham.* Frederick, MD: New Covenant Media.

Wikenhauser, Alfred. 1960. *Pauline Mysticism: Christ in the Mystical Teaching of St. Paul.* Translated by Joseph Cunningham. Freiburg: Herder and Herder.

Wilckens, Ulrich. 1978. *Röm 1–5.* Vol. 1 of *Der Brief an die Römer.* Evangelisch-Katholischer Kommentar zum Neuen Testament. Zurich: Benziger Verlag.

———. 1980. *Röm 6–11.* Vol. 2 of *Der Brief an die Römer.* Evangelisch-Katholischer Kommentar zum Neuen Testament. Zurich: Benziger Verlag.

Wilden, Anthony. 1987. *The Rules Are No Game: The Strategy of Communication.* London: Routledge & Kegan Paul.

Wilson, Gerald H. 2002. *Psalms Volume I.* NIV Application Commentary. Grand Rapids: Zondervan.

Wilson, R. M. 2005. *A Critical and Exegetical Commentary on Colossians and Philemon*. International Critical Commentary. London: T&T Clark.

Wilson, Walter T. 1997. *The Hope of Glory: Education and Exhortation in the Epistle to the Colossians*. Novum Testamentum Supplements. Leiden: Brill.

Witherington, Ben, III. 1994. *Paul's Narrative Thought World: The Tapestry of Tragedy and Triumph*. Louisville: Westminster John Knox.

Witherington, Ben, III, with Darlene Hyatt. 2004. *Paul's Letter to the Romans: A Socio-Rhetorical Commentary*. Grand Rapids: Eerdmans.

Wolter, Michael. 2015. *Paul: An Outline of His Theology*. Translated by Robert L. Brawley. Waco, TX: Baylor University Press.

Worthington, J. D. 2011. *Creation in Paul and Philo: The Beginning and Before*. Tübingen: Mohr Siebeck.

Wright, N. T. 1983. "Adam in Pauline Christology." Pages 359-90 in *Society of Biblical Literature 1983 Seminar Papers*. Edited by Kent Harold Richards. Chico, CA: Scholars Press.

———. 1986. *The Epistles of Paul to the Colossians and to Philemon: An Introduction and Commentary*. Downers Grove, IL: InterVarsity Press.

———. 1987. "Reflected Glory: 2 Corinthians 3:18." Pages 139-50 in *The Glory of Christ in the New Testament: Studies in Christology*. Edited by L. D. Hurst and N. T. Wright. Oxford: Oxford University Press.

———. 1991. *The Climax of the Covenant: Christ and the Law in Pauline Theology*. Edinburgh: T&T Clark.

———. 1992. *The New Testament and the People of God*. Vol. 1 of *Christian Origins and the Question of God*. Minneapolis: Fortress.

———. 1999. "New Exodus, New Inheritance: The Narrative Sub-Structure of Romans 3–8." Pages 160-68 in *Pauline Perspectives: Essays on Paul, 1978–2013*. Minneapolis: Fortress.

———. 2002. "The Letter to the Romans: Introduction, Commentary, and Reflections." Pages 363-770 in vol. 10 of *The New Interpreter's Bible* 10. Nashville: Abingdon.

———. 2003. *The Resurrection of the Son of God*. Vol. 3 of *Christian Origins and the Question of God*. Minneapolis: Fortress.

———. 2004a. "Redemption from the New Perspective?" Pages 69-100 in *The Redemption: An Interdisciplinary Symposium on Christ as Redeemer*. Edited by Stephen T. Davis, Daniel Kendall, and Gerald O'Collins. Oxford: Oxford University Press.

———. 2004b. *Romans, Part 1: Chapters 1–8*. Vol. 1 of *Paul for Everyone*. London: SPCK.

———. 2009a. *Justification: God's Plan & Paul's Vision*. Downers Grove, IL: InterVarsity Press.

———. 2009b. *Paul in Fresh Perspective*. Minneapolis: Fortress.

———. 2010. "Whence and Whither Pauline Studies in the Life of the Church." Pages 407-21 in *Pauline Perspectives: Essays on Paul, 1978–2013*. Minneapolis: Fortress.

———. 2012. "Messiahship in Galatians." Pages 510-46 in *Pauline Perspectives: Essays on Paul, 1978–2013*. Minneapolis: Fortress.

———. 2013a. *Paul and the Faithfulness of God*. Vol. 4 of *Christian Origins and the Question of God*. Minneapolis: Fortress.

———. 2013b. "Paul and the Patriarch." Pages 554-92 in *Pauline Perspectives: Essays on Paul, 1978–2013*. Minneapolis: Fortress Press.

———. 2014a. "Justification by (Covenantal) Faith to the (Covenantal) Doers: Romans 2 Within the Argument of the Letter." Pages 95-108 in *Doing Theology for the Church: Essays in Honor of Klyne Snodgrass*. Edited by Rebekah A. Eklund and John E. Phelan Jr. Eugene, OR: Wipf and Stock.

———. 2014b. "Messiahship in Galatians?" Pages 3-23 in *Galatians and Christian Theology: Justification, the Gospel, and Ethics in Paul's Letter*. Edited by Mark E. Elliott, Scott J. Hafemann, N. T. Wright, and John Frederick. Grand Rapids: Baker Academic.

———. 2015. *Paul and His Recent Interpreters*. Minneapolis: Fortress.

Yarbro Collins, Adela. 1986. "Introduction: Early Christian Apocalypticism." Pages 1-12 in *Early Christian Apocalypticism: Genre and Social Setting. Semeia* 36. Decatur, GA: Scholars Press.

———. 2000. "Mark and His Readers: The Son of God Among Greeks and Romans." *Harvard Theological Review* 93: 85-100.

———. 2007. "The Messiah as Son of God in the Synoptic Gospels." Pages 21-32 in *The Messiah in Early Judaism and Christianity*. Edited by Magnus Zetterholm. Minneapolis: Fortress.

Yarbro Collins, Adela, and John J. Collins. 2008. *King and Messiah as Son of God: Divine, Human, and Angelic Messianic Figures in Biblical and Related Literature*. Grand Rapids: Eerdmans.

Yarbrough, L. O. 1995. "Parents and Children in the Letters of Paul." Pages 126-41 in *The Social World of the First Christians: Essays in Honor of Wayne A. Meeks*. Edited by L. M. White and O. L. Yarbrough. Minneapolis: Fortress.

Zetterholm, Magnus. 2007. "Paul and the Missing Messiah." Pages 33-56 in *The Messiah in Early Judaism and Christianity*. Edited by Magnus Zetterholm. Minneapolis: Fortress.

Ziesler, John. 1989. *Paul's Letter to the Romans*. New Testament Commentaries. Valley Forge, PA: Trinity Press International.

AUTHOR INDEX

SUBJECT INDEX

Finding the Textbook You Need

The IVP Academic Textbook Selector
is an online tool for instantly finding the IVP books
suitable for over 250 courses across 24 disciplines.

ivpacademic.com